A Saint for East and West

A Saint for East and West

Maximus the Confessor's Contribution to Eastern and Western Christian Theology

Edited by

DANIEL HAYNES

Contributors:

David Bradshaw   Nikolaos Loudovikos

Adam Cooper   Andrew Louth

Vladimir Cvetković   John Milbank

Christophe Erismann   Edward Siecienski

Luis Granados   Torstein T. Tollefsen

Adrian Guiu   Melchisedec Törönen

Metropolitan Kallistos Ware   Baron Rowan Williams

Joshua Lollar

CASCADE *Books* · Eugene, Oregon

A SAINT FOR EAST AND WEST
Maximus the Confessor's Contribution to Eastern and Western Christian Theology

Cascade Books
An Imprint of Wipf and Stock Publishers
199 W. 8th Ave., Suite 3
Eugene, OR 97401

www.wipfandstock.com

PAPERBACK ISBN: 978-1-62032-200-0
HARDCOVER ISBN: 978-1-4982-8657-2
EBOOK ISBN: 978-1-5326-6600-1

Cataloguing-in-Publication data:

Names: Haynes, Daniel, editor. | Louth, Andrew, introduction writer

Title: A saint for East and West : Maximus the Confessor's contribution to Eastern and Western Christian theology / edited by Daniel Haynes.

Description: Eugene, OR: Cascade Books, 2019 | Includes bibliographical references and index.

Identifiers: ISBN 978-1-62032-200-0 (paperback) | ISBN 978-1-4982-8657-2 (hardcover) | ISBN 978-1-5326-6600-1 (ebook)

Subjects: LCSH: Maximus, Confessor, Saint, approximately 580–662 | Theology, Doctrinal | Philosophical theology

Classification: BR65.M416 H195 2019 (paperback) | BR65.M416 (ebook)

Manufactured in the U.S.A.   01/09/19

To see a world in a Grain of Sand,
And a Heaven in a Wild Flower,
Hold Infinity in the palm of your hand,
And eternity in an hour.

—William Blake

Contents

Preface | ix

Acknowledgements | xi

Contributors | xiii

Abbreviations | xvii

Introduction | xix
  —ANDREW LOUTH

Part One: Reception and Influence

1   Eriugena's Appropriation of Maximus Confessor's Anthropology | 3
  —ADRIAN GUIU

2   Saint Maximus the Confessor, the Filioque, and the Papacy:
  From Proof Text to Mediator | 31
  —EDWARD SIECIENSKI

3   A Logician for East and West: Maximus the Confessor
  on Universals | 50
  —CHRISTOPHE ERISMANN

Part Two: Anthropology, Christology, and Spirituality

4   The Imitation of Christ according to Saint Maximus the
  Confessor | 69
  —KALLISTOS WARE

5   Freedom and Heteronomy: Maximus and the Question
  of Moral Creativity | 85
  —ADAM COOPER

6   Maximus the Confessor on the Will | 102
  —DAVID BRADSHAW

7   The Action of the Holy Spirit in Christ, according to Saint Maximus the Confessor | 115
       —LUIS GRANADOS

Part Three: Ontology and Metaphysics

8   Remarks on the Metaphysics of Saint Maximus the Confessor | 137
       —MELCHISEDEC TÖRÖNEN

9   Nature, Passion, and Desire: Saint Maximus' Ontology of Excess | 142
       —ROWAN WILLIAMS

10   Christianity and Platonism in East and West | 149
       —JOHN MILBANK

11   Theurgic Attunement as Eucharistic Gnosiology: Divine *Logoi* and Energies in Maximus the Confessor and Thomas Aquinas | 204
       —NIKOLAOS LOUDOVIKOS

12   The Metaphysics of Maximus: Becoming One with God | 223
       —TORSTEIN T. TOLLEFSEN

13   Maximus the Confessor's View on Participation Reconsidered | 231
       —VLADIMIR CVETKOVIĆ

14   Christ and the Contemplation of Nature in Maximus the Confessor's *Ambigua to John* | 245
       —JOSHUA LOLLAR

Bibliography | 261
Index | 273

Preface

In many areas of contemporary culture, it seems incongruous to consider that a figure from the past could inform present-day life. However, there are those luminous saints of old who challenge us to think things anew. St. Maximus the Confessor is one such saint. Despite the fact that Maximus is a deeply cherished saint of both Eastern and Western Christian traditions, his theology is still not very well known or understood.

Over the last couple of decades, there has been a renaissance of interest in the thought of the Confessor in both traditions. Numerous monographs and articles have been published attesting to his brilliance and importance for understanding central dogmas of both East and West. There is even an interest in aligning Maximus' metaphysics with modern developments in science. The noted Maximus scholar Paul Blowers has recently explored the compatibility of Maximus' doctrine of the *logos* and *logoi* with the scientific theory of evolution.[1] I believe Maximus' theology has the greatest potential to open up ecumenical dialogue and understanding between the major branches of Christianity. And it is this prospect which sparked not only my Ph.D. dissertation on Maximus' doctrine of grace at the University of Nottingham, but principally the multi-day workshop on his theology at the sixteenth International Conference on Patristic Studies at Oxford University in 2011, out of which the present volume emerged.

In this book, leading scholars, spiritual masters, and theologians engage with Maximus' thought in creative ways. They examine the historical influences and intellectual trajectories of Maximus' theological synthesis in depth, and new theological vistas open up to create possible paths forward in ecumenical understanding.

For practical purposes the book is broken up into three key parts: (1) reception and influence; (2) anthropology, Christology, and spirituality; and

1. Blowers, "Unfinished Creative Business: Maximus the Confessor, Evolutionary Theodicy, and Human Stewardship in Creation."

ix

(3) ontology and metaphysics. Maximus' vision of the cosmos and the Christian life would not make such distinctions, but this approach was chosen in order to make his theology more esculent for the reader. Andrew Louth provides an erudite introduction to the importance of Maximus' theology for today and how the authors in this volume contribute towards it. Then in part one, Adrian Guiu, Edward Siecienski, and Christophe Erismann trace the historical and intellectual pathways of Maximus' theological influence. Part two unpacks Maximus' moral and spiritual theology in relation to his Christology and cosmic vision. Metropolitan Kallistos (Timothy Ware), Adam Cooper, David Bradshaw, and Luis Granados offer fresh perspectives on these classical Maximian subjects. Finally, in part three hieromonk Törönen, Baron Rowan Williams, John Milbank, Nikolaos Loudovikos, Torstein Tollefsen, Vladimir Cvetković, and Joshua Lollar venture deep into Maximus' ontology and metaphysics of creation. Through their analyses, each contributor shows how Maximus' thought took shape in Eastern and Western Christian theology. The Confessor's theological genius creates a vision of the world that makes him truly a saint for East and West.

Daniel Haynes
Feast of William Laud, 2017

Acknowledgements

I would first like to thank my family for their support of the many hours of labor on this project. Without their grace and patience, this book would not have been possible. The international team of scholars in this volume is world class, and the generosity of their agreement to contribute towards its creation is beyond measure. Of course, the gathering together of such diverse perspectives on Maximus' theology could not have occurred without the support of the organizers of the quadrennial International Conference on Patristic Studies at Oxford University, where the multi-day workshop on the Confessor's thought was held in August 2011. Exceeding thanks goes to my Ph.D. supervisor, Dr. Mary Cunningham, for her advice and support in organizing the Maximus workshop. Finally, I would like to thank our publisher, Wipf and Stock, for their immense patience with the torpid pace of manuscript preparation. All of these elements came together to share this book with the world.

Contributors

David Bradshaw is a professor of philosophy at the University of Kentucky in Lexington. His research focuses on the ways that ancient Greek philosophy shaped medieval philosophy and religious thought, and how these, in turn, contributed to the formation of modernity. He is most celebrated for his book *Aristotle East and West: Metaphysics and the Division of Christendom* (2007) with Cambridge University Press. Professor Bradshaw also serves in an editorial capacity on many projects with the Council for Research in Values and Philosophy.

Adam G. Cooper is a senior lecturer at the John Paul II Institute for Marriage and Family in Melbourne Australia. His research interests focus on incarnational and historical theology, as well as the interface between theology and philosophy. He has published scholarly and popular articles on theology and the church fathers, with a focus on the moral theology and theology of the body. His STL thesis was entitled "Performative Nuptiality: A Liturgical Theology of the Body." His books are *The Body in Saint Maximus the Confessor: Holy Flesh, Wholly Deified* (2005) and *Life in the Flesh: An Anti-Gnostic Spiritual Philosophy* (2008), both with Oxford University Press. He is currently preparing a third book on deification in contemporary Catholic theology.

Vladimir Cvetković is an independent researcher in Göttingen, Niedersachsen, Germany. His previous appointments include an external lectureship at the University of Aarhus in Denmark and a visiting researcher at the University of St. Andrews and the University of Oslo. His research is primarily centered in ecumenical theology and how confessional beliefs took shape in Eastern and Western theology, but his work also explores theological metaphysics in Eastern Orthodoxy. He recently published *God and Time: St. Gregory of Nyssa's Teaching on Time* (in Serbian), and has a forthcoming volume on the newly canonized archimandrite Justin Popovic entitled *Heiliger Justin (Popović) von Ćelije, Über den Ökumenismus.*

Christophe Erismann is a professor in the Byzantine and Modern Greek Studies Department at the University of Vienna. He has held positions at the Universities of Cambridge, Helsinki, and Lausanne, where he taught medieval philosophy for several years as Swiss National Science Foundation Professor. Since autumn 2015, he leads the European Research Council project (CoG 648298) "Reassessing Ninth Century Philosophy. A Syncronic Approach to the Logical Tradition" at the Institute for Byzantine Studies, University of Vienna. His research focuses on the reception of Greek logic (mainly Aristotle's Categories and Porphyry's *Isagoge*) in late ancient, patristic, and early medieval philosophy. He is the author of *L'homme commun: la genèse du réalisme ontologique durant le haut Moyen Âge* (2011).

Rev. Professor Luis Granados Garcia, D.C.J.M., is a priest of the Disciples of the Hearts of Jesus and Mary and teaches at the Pontifical John Paul II Institute for Studies on Marriage and Family and at the Universidad Eclesiástica San Dámaso in Madrid, Spain. He has published numerous articles and church publications, such as "The End of History: The Parousia of Christ as Cosmic Liturgy" (2012); *El misterio de la fecundidad: La comunicación de su Gloria* (2013); *From Ash to Water: Meditations on Lent* (2014); and *Water from the Rock: Meditations from Palm Sunday to Divine Mercy Sunday* (2014).

Adrian Guiu is Assistant Professor of Humanities at Wilbur Wright College in Chicago. He received his Ph.D. from the University of Chicago's School of Divinity with his dissertation on Johannes Scotus Eriugena. Dr. Guiu teaches ethics, introduction to religion, and comparative religion.

Fr. Joshua Lollar received his Ph.D. from Notre Dame University and an MDiv. from St. Vladimir's Seminary. His research is focused on Maximus Confessor. He is an adjunct professor in the Religion Department at Kansas University and is the full time priest of St. Nicholas mission in Lawrence, KS.

The Very Reverend Nikolaos Loudovikos is Professor of Dogmatics and President of the University Ecclesiastical Academy of Thessaloniki, Greece, Honourary Research Fellow at the University of Winchester, and Visiting Professor at the Institute for Orthodox Christian Studies, Cambridge. His recent books include: *A Eucharistic Gnosiology,* forthcoming; *Striving for Participation: Being and Methexis in Gregory Palamas and Thomas Aquinas*

(2010); *The Terrors of the Person and the Ordeals of Love: Critical Meditations for a Postmodern Theological Ontology* (2009); and *A Eucharistic Ontology: Maximus the Confessor's Eschatological Ontology of Being as Dialogical Reciprocity* (2010) with Holy Cross Press.

Andrew Louth is a priest of the Russian Orthodox Church and Professor Emeritus in the Department of Theology and Religion at the University of Durham. His interests in research lie mostly in the history of theology in the Greek tradition after the fifth century during the period of the Byzantine Empire to 1453. His voluminous body of publications include *Maximus the Confessor* (1996) with Routledge; *St. John Damascene: Tradition and Originality in Byzantine Theology* (2002) with Oxford University Press; and *Greek East and Latin West: The Church AD 681–1071* (2007) with St. Vladimir's Seminary Press.

John Milbank is Professor Emeritus in Religion, Politics and Ethics in the Department of Theology and Religious Studies at the University of Nottingham. He has previously taught at the Universities of Lancaster, Cambridge, and Virginia. He is the author of several well-known books with Willey-Blackwell *Theology and Social Theory* (1990), *Being Reconciled: Ontology and Pardon* (2003), and *Beyond Secular Order: The Representation of Being and the Representation of the People* (2013). He is one of the editors of the Radical Orthodoxy series. He has endeavored in his work to resist the idea that secular norms of understanding should set the agenda for theology and has tried to promote the sense that Christianity offers a rich and viable account of the whole of reality. He has sustained interests in developing a political and social theology and is currently pursuing a long-term project to develop a fully-fledged "Trinitarian ontology."

Edward Siecienski is Associate Professor of Philosophy, Clement and Helen Pappas Professor of Byzantine Civilization and Religion at Stockton University. His areas of research interest include historical theology, patristic and Byzantine studies, and Christian thought. One of his most influential works is *The Filioque: History of a Doctrinal Controversy* (2010) with Oxford University Press. His most recent book is *The Papacy and the Orthodox: A History* (2017) with Oxford University Press.

Torstein T. Tollefsen is Professor of Philosophy at the University of Oslo, where he received his Ph.D. His dissertation was on the cosmology of St. Maximus Confessor, which he published with Oxford University Press in the Oxford Early Christian Studies series (2008). Tollefsen's research centers on ancient philosophy and the philosophy of Late Antiquity. His main interest is in the philosophy of the Greek church fathers within the period of 300–900. In particular, he examines metaphysics and cosmology, spirituality and philosophy, and the theology of the icon. He also works on the Cappadocian fathers, Dionysius the Areopagite, Maximus the Confessor, John Damascene, and Theodore the Studite.

Melchisedec Törönen is a monk in the Community of St. John the Baptist, Tolleshunt Knights, Essex. He received his Ph.D. from the University of Oslo, and is the author of *Union and Distinction in the Thought of St. Maximus the Confessor* (2007) with Oxford University Press.

The Most Reverend Metropolitan Kallistos Ware of Diokleia is a titular metropolitan of the Ecumenical Patriarchate in Great Britain. He was Spalding Lecturer of Eastern Orthodox Studies at Oxford University for many years and has authored numerous books and articles pertaining to the Orthodox Christian faith and Orthodoxy's relationship to broader culture. He is most known for his books *The Orthodox Church* (1963) and *The Orthodox Way* (1995), but his most extensive publications stem from his translation work. Together with G. E. Palmer and Philip Sherrard, he has translated four volumes of the *Philokalia*.

Rowan Williams was the 104th Archbishop of Canterbury and is currently the Baron of Oystermouth and Master of Magdalene College, Cambridge University. He is acknowledged internationally as an outstanding theological writer, scholar, and teacher. He has been involved in many theological, ecumenical, and educational commissions. He has written extensively across a very wide range of related fields of professional study—philosophy, theology (especially early and patristic Christianity), spirituality, and religious aesthetics. His long list of celebrated works includes *Eucharistic Sacrifice: The Roots of a Metaphor* (1982); *On Christian Theology* (2000); *Arius: Heresy and Tradition* (2001); *Wrestling with Angels: Conversations in Modern Theology* (2007); *Dostoevsky: Language, Faith and Fiction* (2008); *Being Christian: Baptism, Bible, Eucharist, Prayer* (2014).

Abbreviations

ACW	Ancient Christian Writers
Cap.	Saint Gregory of Palamas: *The One Hundred and Fifty Chapters*
CCCM	*Corpus Christianorum Continuatio Mediaevalis*
CCSG	*Corpus Christianorum, Series Graeca*
CH	Pseudo-Dionysius: *De Coelesti Hierarchia*
CHLGEMP	*Cambridge History of Later Greek and Early Medieval Philosophy*
CWS	Classics of Western Spirituality
DN	Pseudo-Dionysius the Areopagite: *De Divinis Nominibus*
EH	Pseudo-Dionysius: *De Ecclesiastica Hierarchia*
ET	Proclus: *Elements of Theology*
Eth. Nic.	Aristotle: *Nicomachean Ethics*
Enn.	Plotinus: *Enneads*
KL	Hans Ur Von Balthasar (trans. Brian Daley): *Kosmic Liturgy*
MCF	*Maximus Confessor: Actes du Symposium sur Maxime le Confesseur, Fribourg, 2–5 septembre 1980*
MT	Pseudo-Dionysius: *De Mystica Theologia*
NPNF	*Select Library of the Nicene and Post-Nicene Fathers of the Christian Church*
Periph.	John Scotus Eriugena: *Periphyseon*
PG	*Patrologiae Cursus Completus, Series Graeca*
PL	*Patrologiae Cursus Completus, Series Latina*

PT	Proclus: *Platonic Theology*
SC.	*Sources Chrétiennes*
SCG	Thomas Aquinas: *Summa Contra Gentiles*
ST	Thomas Aquinas: *Summa Theologiae*

The Works of St. Maximus Confessor

Ad Thal.	*Quastiones ad Thalassium.*
Amb.	*Ambigua*
Cap. Gnost.	*Capita Theologica et Oeconomica*
De Char.	*Centuriae de Charitate*
Ep.	*Epistle*
LA	*Liber Asceticus*
Myst.	*Mystagogia*
Or. Dom.	*Orationis Dominicae Expositio*
Pyrrh.	*Disputatio cum Pyrrho*
Qu. Dub.	*Quastiones et Dubia*
Th. Pol.	*Opuscula Theologica et Polemica*

Introduction

ANDREW LOUTH

In his lifetime, Maximus belonged to both sides of the Mediterranean Christian world, on the point of fracturing as a result of the rise of Islam and its military success; so much so that his fellow Greeks regarded him as a traitor. At one point in the trial of the Saint, the exasperated high court official, the Sakellarios, asked Maximus, "Why do you love the Romans, and hate the Greeks?" To which he replied, "We have a commandment not to hate anyone. I love the Romans because we share the same faith, whereas I love the Greeks because we share the same language."[2] A couple of centuries later, Anastasius the Librarian found texts of Maximus, which he translated into Latin as evidence of Byzantine support for the two key issues beginning to divide East and West: the *Filioque* and papal primacy.[3] Maximus continued to be read in the Byzantine tradition and was the center of much discussion in the hesychast controversy;[4] in the West, he remained virtually unknown until his rediscovery by modern scholarship.

Much of this modern scholarly interest in Maximus approaches him as a giant who spans East and West. In the two editions of Hans Urs von Balthasar's seminal *Cosmic Liturgy*, this theme develops from seeing Maximus as standing between Eastern and Western Christendom, to seeing him as one who unites in himself East and West in a global sense.[5] Maximus is still seen as crucial in the ostensible issues that divide Eastern and Western

2. *Relatio motionis* 11, in Allen and Neil (eds.), *Maximus the Confessor and His Companions*, 70–71.

3. Ably discussed by Siecienski in this volume.

4. See an article by Fr. Maximus of Simonopetra, due to be published in the proceedings of the Maximus Conference held in Belgrade 2009.

5. See my "St Maximus the Confessor between East and West."

Christians;[6] but among modern scholars, there has been a tendency to move from the obvious issues to broader issues of what one might call *mentalité*: something more indefinable that separates Eastern and Western Christians, concerned less with specific doctrinal matters (or even practical, liturgical issues: for example, leavened *vs.* unleavened bread), than with a different cast of mind, a different way of approaching theology and even the Christian life. Mostly this means philosophy, and Catholic scholar's attempts to align Maximus—certainly one of the most interesting Greek fathers from a philosophical point of view—with Aquinas, manifest in a body of works published in the 1970s and early 1980s by (mostly Dominican) patristic scholars, such as Riou, Garrigues, Léthel, and Piret,[7] and a more recent culmination in the brilliant work by Antoine Lévy (also a Dominican).[8] From another perspective, this is a refinement of a tendency to contrast East and West by offering a contrast between St. Gregory Palamas and St. Thomas Aquinas, that maybe emerged in Paris in the period *entre-deux-guerres*: it is not difficult to see that Maximus provides more for philosophers to chew over than Palamas, though the shadow of the earlier contrast stretches darkly over consideration of the different philosophical approaches of Maximus and Aquinas.[9]

Most of these papers, given at a workshop at the Oxford Patristics Conference in 2011 on Maximus the Confessor, are concerned with philosophical issues in Maximus: questions of moral philosophy and the notion of the will, questions of logic, or philosophical questions involved in his understanding of the relationship of God and the cosmos. The presence of Aquinas is sometimes explicitly in the background, sometimes a more shadowy presence. That, however, raises a question about the nature of the implied contrast. Aquinas was a product of the medieval schools; though primarily a theologian, a master of the sacred page, he was also a trained philosopher. The question of Maximus' philosophical training is more obscure. In the preface to his *Mystagogia*, he remarks that he was "privately educated, and not initiated at all in matter of rhetoric" (ἰδιωτείᾳ συντεθραμμένος καὶ λόγων

---

6. For an analysis of Maximus' relevance to the doctrinal issues dividing East and West, see Larchet, *Maxime le Confesseur, médiateur entre L'Orient et l'Occident*; to the traditional issues of the *Filioque* and papal primacy, Larchet adds the question of original sin.

7. These works were published in the 1970s in the series *Théologie Historique* (Paris: Beauchesne): no. 22 (1973), no. 38 (1976), no. 52 (1979), no. 69 (1983), all with prefaces by M. J. Le Guillou.

8. Lévy, *Le Créé et l'incréé: Maxime le Confesseur and Thomas d'Aquin*.

9. As is very evident in the contribution to this volume by John Milbank.

τεχνικῶν παντελῶς ἀμύητος).[10] This is a modesty *topos*, but that does not mean that it is not true: that Maximus did not even benefit from a proper rhetorical training (something born out, I think, by his Greek style, which is either simple or tortuous). Training in philosophy was yet a further stage beyond an education in rhetoric. It is indeed difficult to detect Maximus' philosophical pedigree; it is arguable that he owes it all to his reading of Christian authors—Origen, Evagrios, the Cappadocian Fathers, Nemesios of Emesa (whom he may have discovered himself: there is little trace of the influence of Nemesios before Maximus), and for more developed Neoplatonic ideas, the author of the Dionysian corpus. Attempts have been to link Maximus with Stephanos the Philosopher, who it is thought came to teach in Constantinople in Herakleios' reign; however, the most recent research suggests that this leads nowhere, for lack of evidence.[11]

If we take this seriously, then it follows that Maximus' philosophical speculation is subordinate to theological—and perhaps even more, ascetical/pastoral, and also liturgical—concerns. This need not be regarded as any kind of limitation; it simply means that we need to be alert to Maximus' mode of discourse, which is never purely philosophical (the nearest, I think, we come to a predominantly philosophical discourse is in the two *Centuries on Theology and the Incarnate Dispensation of the Son of God*, but the suggestion that these centuries are to be regarded as a response to Origenism places it back in the theological sphere, though one where philosophical issues are paramount). This awareness lies behind several of the contributions to this symposium: those, for instance, by Adam Cooper, Joshua Lollar, Torstein Tollefsen, Fr. Melchisedec, Vladimir Cvetković, and Rowan Williams. Cvetković, for example, pursues Maximus' understanding of participation through the pages of his liturgical treatise, the *Mystagogia*, where he finds much reflection on the nature of participation in the context of participation in the Body and Blood of Christ in Holy Communion. This readiness to pass through different genres of theological/philosophical reflection and not to keep them separate certainly seems to be a key to understanding Maximus.

Similarly, the question of the relation of the creature to the uncreated God is not for Maximus a purely philosophical matter; it has implications for the nature of our communion with God. Maximus himself can move from one genre of reflection to another in a disconcerting way: *Amb.* 41, for instance, suddenly changes from a theological/cosmological discourse to a discourse that seems primarily logical, shading into the ascetic, in section 1312B–1313B, before ending with "another contemplation of this

---

10. *Myst.* 31–2, ed. C. Boudignon, CCSG 69 (Tounhout: Brepols, 2011).

11. Roueché, "Stephanus the Philosopher and Ps. Elias."

difficulty." The way in which, very often, Maximus presents several different reflections in response to a problem, ἀπορία, that has been put to him is not something to be passed over: it suggests a tentativeness about his reflections, a willingness to consider several different approaches without deciding between them, without feeling the need to provide a definitive solution, which reminds one of what John Keats called "negative capability:" "That is, when a man is capable of being in uncertainties, mysteries, doubts, without any irritable reaching after fact and reason."[12] What we find in Maximus is, I would suggest, not some sharply defined philosophical or theological doctrine, but rather a capacity for seeing connections, for relating one notion to another, and at the center of all these links and connections lies the mystery of Christ, in which everything coheres—and coheres not just in some intellectual way, but begins to make sense as we enter more deeply into the mystery of Christ. Rowan Williams provides a striking example of this capacity for making connections, when he notices the way in which the dialectic between *logos* and *tropos*, between the *logos* or principle of being or nature, and the *tropos* or mode of existence is taken by Maximus from its use in Trinitarian theology, where it had been used since the Cappadocians, and applied to an ascetic analysis of human existence. The *logos* of being defines the nature of God's creation, which is inviolable; the *tropos* of existence in rational beings is up to us, it is what we have made of our *logos* of being, and enables Maximus to develop an understanding of virtue as natural.

This comes out very clearly in a brief exchange in the *Dialogue with Pyrrhus*. At one point, the deposed patriarch remarks with amazement: "What then? Are the virtues natural?" (Aristotle had denied that the moral virtues are natural: *Eth. Nic.* II. 1103A.18–20). Maximus replies that they are natural. Pyrrhus comes back with the objection that "if the virtues are natural, why do they not exist equally in those of the same nature?" "But they do," Maximus replies to the baffled patriarch (at least according to most MSS). "How do you account for such inequality amongst ourselves?" Pyrrhus retorts. Maximus responds: "Because we do not equally act out what is natural. If everyone acted out what was natural in accordance with their origin, then just as there is one nature manifest in all, so it would be with virtue, and there would be no better or worse." Pyrrhus objects that, "if what is natural to us proceeds not from disciplined training [the Greek is ἄσκησις], but from creation, and virtue is natural, why do we acquire the virtues, which are natural, through toil and disciplined struggle?" Maximus responds thus:

---

12. Letter to George and Thomas Keats, Sunday 21 Dec. 1817, in *Letters of John Keats*, 72.

Disciplined training and the toils that go with it were devised
simply for the purpose of separating from the soul in those who
love virtue the deceit that infects it through the senses. It is not
as if the virtues have been lately introduced from outside. For
they were inserted in us from creation, as has been already said.
Once therefore deceit has been completely expelled from us, at
that moment, too, the soul manifests the radiance of its natural
virtue. He therefore who is not foolish is sensible; and he who is
not cowardly or foolhardy is courageous; and he who is not undisciplined is chaste; and he who is not unjust is just. By nature
reason is wisdom, discernment is justice, the incensive faculty
is courage, and the desiring faculty chastity. Therefore with the
removal of what is contrary to nature [παρὰ φύσιν] only what
is natural [κατὰ φύσιν] is accustomed to be manifest. Just as, if
rust is removed, there is manifest the natural gleam and luster
of iron.[13]

Virtue is natural; the cardinal virtues describe the lineaments of that
nature. It is only because of a deceit lodged in the soul that disciplined training and toil is necessary. I have avoided translating ἄσκησις as asceticism, for
that seems to me to prejudge immediately issues that need consideration.
The word ἄσκησις generally means training or exercise, so I have translated
it to mean "disciplined training;" but the verb from which it is derived,
ἀσκέω, originally meant to work with raw materials, and I am attracted by
the idea that the root meaning of ἄσκησις, too, is to work with raw materials,
the raw materials of our humanity, and out of it to make something fine. It
seems to me to accord with what Maximus meant by ἄσκησις, for he saw human kind as created in the image of God with the purpose of attaining the
divine likeness. That working with the raw materials of our humanity—even
in paradise—would entail uniting our being and our eternal being, both
gifts of God, by means of well-being, and so bringing into being an eternal
well-being in which the divine image attains the divine likeness. This triad
(being, well-being, eternal being) is a fundamental aspect of Maximus' ontology of the created rational being, and expresses Maximus' idea that virtue
(well-being) unites God's gifts of being and eternal being, leading to eternal
well-being, the eternal life with God for which created rational beings are
intended.

This capacity to relate seems to me to be fundamental to Maximus'
approach to theology. The emphasis on the inviolability of the natural derives from his doctrine of creation *ex nihilo*, from which it follows that there

---

13. Maximus, *Pyrrh.* (PG 91: 309B–312A), text in Prp. Maksim Ispovednik, *Disput
s Pirrom* (Moscow, 2004), 174–76.

is nothing in creation that does not come from God the good Creator. It re-emerges in his conviction of the naturalness of virtue: virtue restores nature to itself. Furthermore, it is central to his opposition to monotheletism. "Nothing natural is opposed to God:"[14] from this premise it follows that Christ's human nature cannot be lacking, one cannot deny a natural human will in Christ on the grounds that it would potentially oppose his divine will. Indeed, to suggest that Christ's human nature was defective in this way runs counter to the whole principle of the divine *oikonomia*.

One could illustrate this feature of Maximus' reflection in various ways. One might be to look at the manifold ways in which the notion of *logos* functions in his thought. Theodor Haecker once suggested that each language has a "heart-word" (*Herzwort*), "words which sounds from the heart, which betray to us where this individual heart is most inclined, what is its greatest care, what its grief, its longing, its passion, its joy and its pleasure is," and that in the Greek language *logos* is such a *Herzwort*, difficult to translate, as it embraces a variety of connotations: word, principle, definition, meaning, reason. Maximus, perhaps, betrays sensitivity to this *Herzwort*, remarkable even among the Greeks. There is the *logos* of being, which we have already noticed; the *logoi* of judgment and providence, deriving immediately, it would seem, from Evagrios; and the *logos* of being extends into the *logoi* of well-being and eternal being. *Logos* forms one partner in a dialectic play with *tropos*. It forms part of another triad, *nous–logos–pneuma*, the form the divine image takes in the human.[15] Finally, centrally, there is the one *Logos* and the many *logoi*: the one *Logos*, who is the Son of the Father, and the many *logoi* that form the deep structures of the created order, and are in some way identical with the one *Logos*. For "the one *Logos* is the many *logoi*, and the many are one," as he affirms repeatedly in *Amb.* 7.[16] It is not surprising that Maximus was drawn to comment on a couple of lines from St. Gregory the Theologian's poem, "Counsels to Virgins": "The high *Logos* of God plays in every kind of form, mixing, as he wills, with his world here and there." He links this with the mysterious verse of Psalm 41—"Abyss calls to abyss in the noise of your cataracts"—and comments that "every contemplative and mind, because of its invisible nature and the depth and multitude of its thoughts, is to be compared to an abyss, since it passes beyond the ordered array of the phenomena and comes to the place

---

14. *Opusc.* 7 (PG 91: 80A).

15. *Amb.* 10 (PG 91: 1196A).

16. E.g., PG 91: 1081B.

of intelligible reality."[17] The whole of this *Ambiguum*, on the play of the *Logos*, consists of a series of suggestions: maybe this, maybe that.

I mentioned at the beginning that, behind seeing Maximus as belonging to the East and the West, there lurks the question of his relationship to Aquinas, an issue addressed directly by Loudovikos (in relation to Lévy's work) and haunting Milbank's reflections. As I've already remarked, any comparison at the level of philosophy has to reckon with the very different idioms of Maximus and Aquinas. I've tried to sketch something of what Maximus' theological/philosophical idiom seems to me to entail. It is very different from Aquinas' idiom. Aquinas' theological idiom is that of the medieval schools, which was based on the use of *quaestiones* in disputations (in principle, public). As Fergus Kerr has put it, the method employed here, "was not intended to reach a compromise or supposed consensus, by splitting the difference between conflicting interpretations. It allowed the disputants to discover the strengths and weaknesses of opposing views; but the aim was to work out the truth by considering and eliminating error, however common or plausible or seemingly supported by authority."[18] Maximus is certainly concerned with eliminating error, mostly, it would seem, errors associated with Origenism that had a tenacious hold on many of his contemporaries, Byzantine ascetics, but "working out the truth:" it seems to me that Maximus was more concerned with *working towards* the truth, a truth ultimately beyond human grasp, something discerned apophatically. The question of Maximus and Aquinas, which captures in some kind of microcosm the question of Eastern *vs.* Western theology, seems to me more a question of how very different idioms in theology can be allowed to coexist, which will certainly involve finding fundamental points of agreement, or mutual alignment, but goes beyond this into much less tractable territory.

17. *Amb.* 71 (PG 91: 1408D).
18. Kerr, *After Aquinas*, 8.

PART ONE

Reception and Influence

1

Eriugena's Appropriation of Maximus Confessor's Anthropology

Adrian Guiu

This essay looks at the way John Scottus Eriugena appropriates and constructively employs Maximus Confessor's anthropology. It claims that the fivefold division of being, appropriated from Maximus Confessor's *Ambiguum* 41, constitutes the framework of the *Periphyseon*. In my understanding, Maximus Confessor's vision of the human being as the "workshop of creation," as the synthesis of all aspects of creation, as the agent of unification, provides the anthropological premise for Eriugena's own dialectical division of the genus of nature. It is within the framework of Maximus' ontology centered on "man as the workshop of creation," that Eriugena has recourse to the tradition of the liberal arts. Therefore, the division of the genus of nature, as an exercise of dialectic, has to be understood within the framework of Eriugena's appropriation of Maximus Confessor's fivefold division of being and its corollary, the anthropology of the *officina omnium*. The project of the *Periphyseon* is driven by the possibility that through the application of the arts man could become the *officina omnium* in spite of the Fall; if intellectual knowledge of creation can be achieved, then the return of all creation to the unity of the intelligible human being and ultimately to God will be warranted.

Introduction

Previous studies by E. Jeauneau[1] and I-P. Sheldon Williams[2] have noted the Greek influences on John the Scot. This essay builds on their insights by trying to see how Eriugena appropriates and uses the Greek fathers, and especially Maximus Confessor.

The reason for this analysis is not to try to gauge in an exact manner who has more influence or to argue that Eriugena's merit is to have managed to bring together such disparate sources, although the latter is no small merit in itself. Among the medieval thinkers, only Thomas Aquinas can match this great feat of consensus building (*consensus machinari*) displayed by the great Irishman.[3] Nevertheless, by focusing on the Greek sources I do not mean to say that these are more important than Augustine or Ambrose for the project of Eriugena.

This essay will focus on Eriugena's main discussion and exposition of Maximus Confessor's *Ambiguum* 41[4] as found in Book II of the *Periphyseon*.[5] In Book II, after reviewing the fourfold division of being offered at the beginning of Book I, the Nutritor[6] introduces another division of being by way of a complementary example. This division, and Eriugena's way of appropriating and expounding it will become the fundamental framework of the entire work and is responsible for giving the project its clear structure. My claim is that Books III through V of the *Periphyseon* are an extensive exploration and clarification of several important points made by Maximus the Confessor in *Ambiguum* 41. First, there is the fivefold division of beings. Second, Maximus' anthropology according to which the human being is

---

1. Jeauneau, "Jean l'Erigène et les *Ambigua ad Iohannem*," 343–64, reprinted in Jeauneau, *Etudes Erigéniennes*, 189–210; and "Jean Scot Erigène et le grec," 5–50, reprinted in Jeauneau, *Etudes Erigéniennes*, 85–132.

2. See Williams, "Eriugena's Greek Sources," 1–15. See also his *The Cambridge History*, 425–536.

3. According to Sheldon-Williams: "These strands are so closely interwoven that it is impossible to treat them separately" (*The Mind of Eriugena*, 7).

4. Confessor, *Amb.* 41 (PG 91: 1304D–1316A). When citing Maximus directly I will give the Latin of Eriugena's translation found in Confessor and Erigena, *Maximi Confessoris Ambigua Ad Iohannem*; for the English translations, I have used Louth, *Maximus the Confessor*. Also, I have used the Romanian translation by Stăniloae. I have checked the translations against the Greek original and, where appropriate, amended them.

5. For the *Periphyseon* I shall cite the Migne column number and the page number (PL 122) and line number of the critical edition by Jeauneau, CCSG 18, 161–65. I have also used the Sheldon-Williams and O'Meara translation.

6. Throughout this article I shall refer to the two main characters mainly through the Latin designations found in the original text: Nutritor (teacher) and Alumnus (pupil).

seen as the workshop of creation (i.e., the place where all aspects are unified and therefore responsible for the unification of the cosmos.). Thirdly, Maximus provides the Irishman with a fundamental methodological insight: both Scripture and the cosmos are places of divine manifestation. One needs to train oneself in order to gain the right vision and be able to distinguish the divine presence.

Thus, Maximus provides Eriugena with an arsenal of conceptual tools that will provide the armature for his *magnum opus*. The great insight of Eriugena is to weave these together with the liberal arts tradition in which he stands by virtue of his education. The task of this essay will be to expound the way Eriugena interprets *Ambiguum* 41 and manages to wean out an ontological framework, which allows him to expand the purview of his own division of the genus of nature—the initial project of the *Periphyseon*—to a cosmic scale.

Maximus' Anthropology

Eriugena starts Book II with a recapitulation of the fourfold division of the genus *natura*. After this, almost as an aside, he presents Maximus' division of being found in *Ambiguum* 41. Why does Eriugena introduce Maximus into the discussion? The answer provided by the texts themselves is that it is both out of a desire to confirm his position but also in order to offer a slightly different vantage point.[7] He will devote a lengthy exposition to Maximus' division, but my claim is that in the *Periphyseon*, the Maximian division will gain a greater importance than just an example or an alternative view.

The first of these fivefold divisions of universal nature (σύμπασα φύσις) is between created and uncreated. The second division is between the intelligible and the sensible. The third division is the division of the sensible between heaven and earth. In the fourth division, earth is divided between paradise and the inhabited world. In the fifth division, man, the workshop (*officina*) of creation,[8] is divided into man and woman. Eriugena describes

---

7. *Periph.* II (PL 122: 529C; CCCM 162: 9, ll. 152–55): "*Si enim multiplex rerum omnium diuisio iterumque adunatio multipliciter demonstrata fuerit, ad cognitionem principalium causarum quae principaliter a deo conditae sunt patefacta uia facilius apparebit.*" The reason, given by the Nutritor, for the recourse to Maximus is the advantage of a multifarious view. This is a stock example of Eriugena's methodology: the *multiplex theoria*. Thus, he anticipates the scholastic procedure of putting several authorities on the table and then critically engaging them. He adds: "*praesertim cum ipsius diuisio nostra praedicta diuisione in nullo discrepare uideatur except . . . location?*"

8. See *Amb.* 41 (PG 91: 1305A).

what Maximus does here as "the division of the substance of all things that have been made from the Supreme Cause."[9] In his view, Maximus' division is similar to his own; the only difference is that he splits the third element, created nature, into three and does not distinguish the fourth from the first. Moreover, the Nutritor thinks that Maximus' division complements his own.

According to Maximus' account, the human being is introduced last because it is the "natural link, everywhere mediating between the extremes through their proper parts and reducing to a unity in himself things which in nature are widely disparate."[10] Thus, the crucial element of the unification of creation is Maximus' view of the human being as the synthesis of creation. He calls the human being the laboratory of all creation because all the aspects of creation—sensible, intellectual, and vegetative—are present in it. Humans span all the ontological levels of creation. "For he is composed of the two universal parts of created nature by way of a wonderful union. For he is the conjunction of the sensible and the intelligible, that is, the extremities of all creation."[11] As the synthesis and recapitulation of creation, the true vocation of the human being is to mediate and harmonize the different levels of creation by "supply[ing] a middle term between the extreme elements of creation; for in it they are joined to one another and from being many become one. For there is no creature, from the highest to the lowest, which is not found in man, and that is why he is rightly called the workshop of all things."[12]

Thus, the most significant element of Maximus' division for Eriugena is the status of the human being. I argue that the central status of the human being, as *officina omnium*, as the hub in which all aspects of creation intersect, becomes crucial for Eriugena's own enterprise in the *Periphyseon*: the division or *exitus* of created beings followed by the return of all beings to

---

9. *Periph.* II (PL 122: 531A; CCCM 162: 11, ll. 191–92): "*Eorum quae facta sunt substantiae diuisionem a summa omnium causa.*"

10. Ibid. (PL 122: 530C; CCCM 162: 10, ll. 181–84): "*ueluti coniunctio quaedam naturalis uniuersaliter per proprias partes medietatem faciens extremitatibus, et in unum ducens in se ipso multum secundum naturam a se inuicem distantia spatio . . . .*"

11. Ibid. (PL 122: 531B; CCCM 162: 11, ll. 196–99): "*Est enim ex duabus conditae naturae uniuersalibus partibus mirabili quadam adunatione compositus, ex sensibili nanque et intelligibili, hoc est creaturae ex extremitatibus coniunctus.*"

12. Ibid. (PL 122: 530D; CCCM 162: 10, ll. 89–91: 530CD, p. 10, ll. 88–89): "*humana natura medietatem eis praestat; in ea enim sibi inuicem copulantur et de multis unum fiunt. Nulla enim creatura est a summo usque deorsum quae in homine non reperiatur, ideoque officina omnium iure nominatur. In ea siquidem omnia confluunt quae a deo condita sunt unamque armoniam ex diuersis naturis veluti quibusdam distantibus sonis componunt.*"

their divine origin. In the center of these two cosmic processes is the human being, as the mediator between the *Logos* and creation.

The task of the human person is laid out clearly by Maximus; it is created last, "so that by the unification which brings all things to God as Cause, he, starting from what before was his proper division and proceeding through the intermediaries by successively combining with them, to God, should reach the end of his ascent into the heights, which passes from all things through union [in Him] in whom there is no division."[13]

In Eriugena's reading, Maximus' account of the return constitutes an epistemological road map to God. The driving force behind Maximus' account of the return is the activity of the human being, which culminates in what Maximus calls a perfect, indivisible knowledge of the mind, resembling angelic knowledge.

Thus, the human being proceeds to unify its own division, that between man and female; this yields to what Eriugena, following Maximus, calls the unity of human nature. From here, the human being proceeds to unify paradise and the inhabited globe, which yields a spiritual earth.[14] After this, the unity of the inhabited globe and paradise, the spiritual earth, will be brought together into one with heaven "through the perfect similarity of his life in respect to virtue to that of the angels."[15] Ultimately, the last of the divisions will be resolved, that between the intelligibles and sensibles: "Then . . . by joining the intelligibles and the sensibles in addition to these—that is the unifications of natures that have been mentioned—through the equality of his knowledge with that of the angels, he will make all creatures one single creature, not separated in him in respect of knowledge and ignorance, for he will have a [g]nostic science of reasons in the things that are, equal to the angels without any difference . . . ."[16]

13. Ibid. (PL 122: 531A; CCCM 162: 10–11, ll. 184–88): ". . . *ut ad deum utpote causalem omnia unitate congregante, ex propria prius divisione inchoans, ac deinde per media conexione ordineque progrediens, in deum acciperet finem ipsius ex omnibus factae per unitatem ascensionis excelsae, in quo non est diuisio.*" For a detailed account of Maximus' anthropology see the great monograph: Thunberg, *Microcosm and Mediator.*

14. Ibid. (PL 122: 534AB; CCCM 162: 14, ll. 259–63): "*an sic orbis terrarum et paradisus in unam terram applicabuntur, ut ipsa terra . . . in simplicitatem quandam naturae reuocabitur, ut plus spiritualis quam corporealis esse credatur?*" (The inhabited globe and paradise will be brought together into that one earth . . . in such a way that even the earth will be recalled into a simplicity of nature so as to be believed to be spiritual rather than corporeal in nature).

15. Eriugena cites Maximus here: *Periph.* (PL 122: 534C): "*ipsam angelis angelis vitae omnino secundum vritutem.*"

16. Ibid. (PL 122: 535B; CCCM 162: 15, ll. 290–95): "*Intelligibilia et sensibilia cum his copulans (hoc est cum praedictis naturarum adunationibus) per ipsam ad angelos scientiae aequalitatem unificaret creaturam, simul omnem creaturam, non separatam in*

According to the Nutritor, Maximus speaks of two kinds of knowledge in describing this process of unification: the first is a discursive knowledge that apprehends beings in their diversity and materiality, according to their genus and species.[17] This is the mode of knowing specific to the first three stages of unification. After the last division (the unification of the sensible and intelligible) is resolved, the mind ascends to God unencumbered, through a kind of noetic knowledge. It knows all things through an intellectual knowledge (which forgoes any contact with sensible elements) by way of their primordial causes. At this level, no creature intervenes between the mind and God. Eriugena (like Maximus) calls this level a "gnostic knowledge."[18] This epistemological level constitutes the unification of all things because here even the material aspect is reduced and absorbed back into the spiritual. The process of the return leads to the unification of the intelligible and the sensible worlds through the attainment of a knowledge on a par with angelic knowledge: "through the equality of his knowledge with that of the angels, he will make all creatures one single creature, not separated in him in respect of knowledge."[19]

> *But now* he seems to teach that the unification of natural substances is in the *intellect alone*[20] but not in the things themselves, that is to say, that it is not those things which through generation into diverse genera and diverse forms and infinite individuals received from the Creator's providence their intelligible or sensible diversity, but their primordial causes and reasons, that

---

eo secundum scientiam et ignorantiam."

17. Ibid. (PL 122: 535B; CCCM 162: 15–16, ll. 300–305): "*In prioribus enim nil aliud uidebatur suasisse nisi omnium rerum sensibilium et intelligibilium in unitatem quandam adunationem, ita ut nil separabile nil corporeum nil uarium in eis remaneat, sed ut mirabilis quadam regressione inferiora semper in superiora transeant*" (For in what went before he seemed to teach nothing else than a certain unification into unity of all the sensibles and intelligibles so that nothing would remain in them that was separable, nothing that was corporeal, nothing that was variable, but that by a wonderful return the lower natures will always pass into the higher).

18. "And thus makes all creation one single creation, no longer divided by what it can know and what it cannot know; because it acquired a [g]nostic knowledge (*gnostike episteme*) of the reasons/*logoi* of things according to which the infinite pouring out of the gift of true wisdom inviolably and without intermediary furnishes to those who are worthy a concept of God beyond explanation and understanding?" (*Amb.* 41, PG 91: 1308A).

19. *Periph.* II (PL 122: 535A; CCCM 162: 15, ll. 292–95): "*per ipsam ad angelos scientiae aequalitatem unificaret creaturam, simul omenm creaturam, non separatam in eo secundum scientiam et ignorantiam.*"

20. My emphasis.

are gathered into a certain unification, and that by an act of the intelligence, not in the thing itself.[21]

There are several insights about the character and levels of human knowledge, which Eriugena derives from Maximus' account in *Ambiguum* 41 and correlates with elements from Boethius and Augustine. Next, the Nutritor cites Augustine's *De vera religione* in order to provide an authoritative proof for his understanding of intellectual knowledge. "Between our mind by which we have an understanding of the Father himself, and the truth through which we understand him, no creature intervenes."[22] After this, Eriugena reinforces the possibility gleaned from Augustine's text by adducing a citation from Pseudo-Dionysius' *Ecclesiastical Hierarchy*: "For the understanding is what things really are, in the words of St. Dionysius: 'The knowledge of the things that are, is the things that are.'"[23] This equivalence between intellectual knowledge and the true being of things is more than a marginal observation but constitutes the methodological premise of the *Periphyseon*.

Besides Maximus, the other ancient authority upon which Eriugena relies when forging his epistemology is Gregory of Nyssa. As a translator of Gregory of Nyssa's *De Opificio Hominis*, Eriugena was deeply acquainted with the Cappadocian father's Christian Neoplatonism. Eriugena also relies on Gregory of Nyssa's theology of two creations in forging his understanding of the human being. From Gregory, Eriugena appropriates the notion of a corporate intelligible humanity that constitutes a distinct ontological level, almost in the manner of a Neoplatonic hypostasis, which intermediates between the *Logos* and creation. At this level, humanity is unitary, fully intelligible and universal: it is an idea in the divine mind, and it has an

---

21. Ibid. (PL 122: 535B–C; CCCM 162: 16, ll. 305–12): "*Nunc uero docere uidetur adunationem naturalium substantiarum in intellectu solummodo non autem in ipsis rebus esse, hoc est non eas res quae per generationem in diuersa genera diuersasque formas infinitosque numeros iuxta creatoris prouidentiam intelligibilem sensibilemue acceperunt uarietatem, sed ipsas primordiales suas causas rationesque in adunationem quandam actione intelligentiae, non autem re ipsa colligi.*"

22. Ibid. (PL 122: 531B; CCCM 162: 11, ll. 201–3), with reference to *De vera religione*, LV, 113 (CCSL 32: 259): "*Inter mentem nostram qua ipsum intelligimus patrem et ueritatem per quam ipsum intelligimus nulla interposita creatura est.*"

23. Ibid. (PL 122: 535C–D (CCCM 162: 16, ll. 305–12): "*Intellectus enim rerum ueraciter ipsae res sunt, dicente sancto Dionysio: 'Cognitio eorum quae sunt quae ea quae sunt est.*'" Cf. Dionysius the Areopagite, *De Ecclesiastica Hierarchia*, I, 3 (PG 3: 376A). Jeauneau, whose authoritative edition of the text I follow, considers this an added comment from the so called second Irish commentator. He puts it in the main text in italics as well. Nevertheless, the correlation made by the commentator between Augustine and Dionysius is in the spirit of the author.

intelligible knowledge that knows created things according to their unity, not according to their distinction.

> For in that primordial and general creation of all human nature no one knows himself as a species nor begins to have a particular knowledge of himself, for there is one general and common knowledge possessed by all, known only to God. There all men are one, and that one is made in the image of God, in Whom all are created.[24]

Building on Gregory of Nyssa's *imago dei* theology, Eriugena establishes a fundamental similarity between the intellect and the *Logos* both contain the intellectual principles of all things. The human mind is endowed with "every species, difference and property of irrationality, and all things which are naturally learnt concerning it, since the knowledge of all these and similar things is established in it."[25] According to the Nutritor, "there is a kind of concept in man of all the sensible and intelligible things the human mind can understand."[26] The only difference is that the Son contains them as causes and the intellect as effects. The Word communicates the causes to the intellect and the latter becomes a second-degree locus of the divine ideas: as the *Logos* in whom all the causes and principles of things are pre-contained[27] precedes everything *ontologically*, so the intellect precedes all things *epistemologically*.

> Just as the understanding of all things which the Father made in his only begotten Word is their essence and is the substance of all those attributes which are understood to be attached by nature to the essence, so the knowledge of all things which the Word of the Father has created in the human soul is their essence and the subject of all those attributes which are discerned

---

24. *Periph.* IV (PL 122: 776D–777A; CCCM 164: 52, ll. 1425–30): "*Nam in illa primordiali et generali totius humanae naturae conditione nemo se ipsum specialiter cognoscit, neque propriam notitiam sui habere incipit; una enim et generalis cognitio omnium est ibi, solique deo cognita. Illic nanque omnes homines unus sunt, ille profecto ad imaginem dei factus, in quo omnes creati sunt.*"

25. Ibid. (PL 122: 769B; CCCM 164: 41, ll. 1104–7): "*omnes species, omnisque differentia, et proprietas ipsius irrationabilitatis, et omnia quae circa eam naturaliter cognuscuntur, quoniam horum omnium et similium notitia in ipso condita est.*"

26. Ibid. (PL 122: 768B; CCCM 164: 40, ll. 1077–79): "*Num tibi uidetur rerum omnium sensibilium et intelligiblium, quae potest humana mens intelligere, notionem quandam in homine esse?*"

27. *Periph.* II (PL 122: 560B (CCCM 162: 47, ll. 1079–80): "*omnium naturarum primordiales causas perfectissimas creauit*" (the perfection of the primordial causes of all natures).

to be attached by nature to the essence. . . . The intellectual knowledge of the soul is prior to all the things which she knows and is all the things which she foreknows. Therefore, all things subsist as causes in the Divine Understanding, but as effects in human knowledge.[28]

Thus, the same essence of things is seen *causaliter* in the divine *Logos* and *effectualiter* in the human intellect.[29] The *Logos* is referred to as the *sapientia creatrix*, and the human mind is called the *sapientia creata*. The primordial causes are in the, but the primordial effects are in the human intellect: God creates all things in Christ the *Logos* which contains in itself the principles of all things as effects.

The mind qua *sapientia creata* coincides with the generic, primordial humanity in which all things are created. There is a deep similarity between the mind and the *Logos*, based on the *imago dei* theology. The intellect's precedence is then one of knowledge whereas the *Logos* precedes everything ontologically. This is in consonance with Eriugena's emphasis on knowledge and reason. The *Logos* is the source of all things ontologically, but the intellect is their source epistemologically. Ideally, from the perspective of the primordial creation, the two are similar to the degree that the Nutritor affirms: "and you no longer see, I think, any difference between the image and the principal Exemplar except in respect of subject."[30]

Thus, from Gregory of Nyssa's theology of two creations, Eriugena appropriates the notion of a corporate intelligible humanity that constitutes a distinct ontological level and an intermediate between God the creator and created beings. Therefore, for Eriugena, the human being as intellect acquires the status of intermediary between the *Logos* as the unity of all causes and the manifested effects of these causes.

Thus, Eriugena's vision of the human intellect as an intermediary between the *Logos* is the result of his reworking of Gregory of Nyssa's theory of the primordial intelligible humanity and of fusing it with Maximus' ontology. This is in a way the fundamental move of his epistemology. Even for

---

28. *Periph.* IV (PL 122: 779B–C; CCCM 164: 55, ll. 1527–35): "*Quemadmodum intellectus omnium, quae pater fecit in suo uerbo unigenito, essentia eorum est et cunctorum quae circa eam naturaliter intelliguntur, ita cognitio omnium, quae patris uerbum in humana anima creauit, essentia est eorum omniumque quae circa eam naturaliter dinoscuntur . . . ita cognitio intellectualis animae praecedit omnia quae cognoscit, et omniae quae praecognoscit est, ut in diuino intellectu omnia causaliter, in humana uero cognitione effectualiter subsistant.*"

29. See McGinn, *The Growth of Mysticism*, 105.

30. *Periph.* II (PL 122: 598B; CCCM 162: 99, ll. 2388–90): "*nec iam cernis, ut opinor, ullam dissimilitudinem imaginis et principalis formae praeter rationem subiecti.*"

fallen human nature, this primordial status remains the beacon and ideal. It acts like a magnet that attracts and uplifts the fallen mind.

Overall, Eriugena follows Maximus in describing the Fall as the failure of the human being to fulfill its task of unifying creation. Because it is the synthesis and center of all creation, the actions of humans have ontological consequences. Their ignorance leads to dispersal and differentiation and their ascent in knowledge brings about the unification of creation:

> When created man was not naturally moved according to his proper principle—I mean God—but he preferred to turn towards those things that are beneath himself, of which he was the divinely appointed principle; he moved voluntarily contrary to his nature through an irrational impulse and abused the natural ability given to him by the divine act for the unification of the separated beings rather than for the separation of beings.[31]

Humans forfeit their status of mediators by not moving towards God. Instead of becoming the agent of union and harmony, ignorance brings about a skewed perspective on creation, which leads to its fragmentation and disorder. Pride and presumption bring about the ignorance of one's true nature and vocation. Ignorance amounts to a skewed perspective on creation, which leads to its fragmentation and disorder: "the unity of man was dissipated into infinite divisions and variations."[32]

The greatest consequence of the Fall is the fragmentation of creation. In order to convey this idea, Eriugena provides an inverse perspective view of the fragmented creation: if man had not sinned, none of the division would have occurred. He offers a "what if" scenario according to which all creation would still be one in human nature. The sensible would not be different from the intelligible in man, but man would be all intellect.[33]

> And if he were not in a state of sin there would not be in him the division of the sexes, but there would be only man, the inhabited globe would not in him be separated from paradise, but the whole of earthly nature would in him be paradise, that is a spiritual way of life[;] . . . the sensible nature would not in him

31. Ibid. (PL 122: 536D–537A; CCCM 162: 18, ll. 352–56): "*Quoniam itaque, inquit [Maximus], naturaliter, ut creatus est, circa immutabile proprium principium, dico autem deum, homo non est motus, circa vero ea quae sub ipso sunt, quorum ipse in divinitus principari ordinatus est, contra naturam volens insipienter est motus, ea in separatorum data sibi naturali potentia per generationem in ipsam adunandorum magis abusus est separationem . . .*"

32. Ibid. (PL 122: 536D; CCCM 162: 17, ll. 350).

33. Ibid. (PL 122: 536C; CCCM 162: 17, ll. 342–43): "*sensibilis natura ab intelligibili in eo non discreparetur, totus enim esset intellectus.*"

be distinct from the intelligible, for he would be all intellect, ever and immutably attached to his creator and in no way inferior to his primordial causes.[34]

Here, Eriugena describes the intellectual prowess of humans in their primordial creation. As *sapientia creata*, the human being shares in the intellectual knowledge of angels and most importantly it mediates between other creatures and the *Logos*. Therefore, in order to unify creation, to perform the *reditus*, which amounts to weaving back the torn-apart cosmos, the human being has to attain the "virtus gnostica;" it has to reach the level of gnostic knowledge by returning to its original status of *sapientia creata*. So, in a way, the process of self-formation and education of the human being coincides with the progressive unification of creation. Therefore, weaving the tapestry of reality back into one piece, repairing the fractured creation, as the task of the human being, is achieved by returning to the level of knowledge it had shared with the angelic beings before the Fall. This knowledge would be exempt of ignorance and would bring about the unity of all levels of the cosmos:

> For [the angels] know the reasons of all created natures in themselves by a single apprehension of the intellect as there is in the wisest human soul a single and inseparable knowledge of the various arts, so that ignorance, whether in angels or in rational souls brings about no segregation of natures, and [g]nostic science will be their unification.[35]

One issue that is not fully clarified is whether this kind of perfect intellectual knowledge could be realized even in our current condition after the Fall. This is actually one of the great dilemmas for the two discussants: to what degree is the role of the human being described by Maximus still a reality even after the Fall? Clarifying this would have tremendous consequences for the status and role of the great dialogue: can the *Periphyseon* be regarded

---

34. Ibid. (PL 122: 536C–D; CCCM 162: 17, ll. 335–44): "*Et si non peccaret, non esset in eo diuisio sexuum sed solummodo homo est; non separaretur in eo orbis terrarum a paradiso sed omnis terrena natura in eo esset paradisus, hoc est spiritualis conuersatio . . . sensibilis natura ab intelligibili in eo non discreparetur, totus enim esset intellectus creatori suo semper et immutabiliter adhaerens et nullo modo a primordialibus causis.*"

35. Ibid. (PL 122: 535C–D; CCCM 162: 16, ll. 148–54): "*Naturarum enim omnium conditarum rationes in semet ipsis sub uno quodam intelligentiae tenore cognoscunt, quaeadmodum in quadam sapientissima anima diuersarum artium una eademque et inseparabilis cognitio est, ita ut ignorantia siue in angelis . . . siue in rationabilibus animabus segregationem rerum faciat, scientia uero adunationis causa fiat.*" Bertin's translation "la science gnostique" follows manuscript P (Paris, BNF, lat. 12964), Jeauneau's version IV (CCCM 162: 176–77, ll. 790–800): "*scientia uero gnostica adunationis causa fiat.*"

as an actual attempt by Eriugena to show that a perfect intellectual knowledge is possible even in the condition of the Fall? The comment provided by the second Irish commentator[36] immediately after the Augustine citation offers an insightful, valuable and enlightening extrapolation. The ensuing remarks seem to intimate unequivocally that the human being could still perform its duty to mediate between the different aspects of creation even after the Fall: "Through these words of the most holy Father we are given to understand that even after the Fall, human nature did not totally loose its nature but still maintains it."[37]

In Book IV, the teacher will argue for the same position, this time in his own words and relying on his own authority:

> If then the perfect knowledge both of herself and her creator was present in human nature before the Fall, it would not be remarkable if in reason we found that she then possessed the fullest knowledge of natures similar to her own, like the celestial essences, and those inferior to herself such as this world with its causes, which are subject to the intellect, and that this science still abides in her, know in potency but in the highest men in act.[38]

This passage stands at a crucial juncture of the argument in Book IV. Through an exegetical *tour de force*, the teacher tries to establish that man has been created last because in the first creation, at the level of the intelligible, all creatures are created in the human intellect; this grants the human being precedence in terms of epistemology. In the teacher's (and in Eriugena's) view the epistemological precedence is equivalent to an ontological precedence. "Furthermore if the things themselves subsist truly in the their notions rather than in themselves, and the notion of them are naturally present to man, therefore in man are they universally created."[39]

36. This appears as marginalia in the Reims-R manuscript (Version I–II), but it is included in the main body in the Bamberg-B manuscript.

37. Ibid. (PL 122: 531B; CCCM 164: 11, ll. 95–100): "*Quibus verbis sanctissimi patris datur intelligi humanam naturam etiam post prevaricationem dignitatem suam non penitus perdidisse sed adhuc obtinere.*"

38 Periph. IV (PL 122: 778C; CCCM 164: 44, ll. 1485–90): "*Si ergo humanae naturae ante peccatum inerat et suimet perfecta cognition et creatoris sui. Quid mirum si rationabiliter de ea intelligitur plenissimam scientiam sui naturarum (ut sunt caelestes essentiae) et inferiorum se (ut est mundus iste cum rationibus suis intellectui succumentibus) habuisse, et adhuc sola possibilitate, et in re ipsa in summis homnibus?*"

39. Ibid. (CCCM 164: 774A: 48, ll. 1300–1305): "*Porro si res ipsae in notionibus suis uerius quam in se ipsis subsistunt, notitiae autem earum homini naturaliter insunt, in homine igitur uniuersaliter creatae sunt.*"

Thus, in Eriugena's view, even after the Fall, the return to the unity of God as the principle and source of all things created is realized by achieving the level of unencumbered intellectual knowledge that coincides with the unification of creation: intellectual knowledge yields a unified perspective in which all diversity according to genus and species and to the various categories is reduced back into unity through analysis.[40] The hope of Eriugena (and of the two discussants) is that through the correct use of the rules of reason (i.e., through the careful application of dialectic and its two main procedures of division and analysis), all plurality will ultimately be reduced back to unity. Relying on the crutches of the arts and "treading on the path of reason," the human being might still be the great unifier. Through the epistemological activity of the human being, all the substances ascend to divine unity through the same stages they have descended into the human being. His wager is that the human being could still achieve perfect knowledge and thus bring back all creatures to the unity of the *sapientia creata* level.

> For things which from the outside appear to the corporeal sense to be various and manifold in places, times, qualities, quantities, and the other differences of sensible nature, in their reasons according to which they were created by the creator of all things and eternally subsist in the immutable condition of their nature and by certain rules of the divine providence, are seen by the pure intellect which inquires into the truth of all things, which finds out all things and which considers all things to be an indivisible unity and are so.[41]

However, there are crucial differences with regard to the way Maximus and Eriugena envisage the unification of creation. For Maximus the solution to the fragmentation is Christological, whereas for Eriugena the human being plays a much more preeminent role. After pointing to the failure of humans to fulfill their role of laboratory and σύνδεσμός, Maximus says that the renewal of natures in the text of Gregory of Nazianzus (this is what he set out to clarify) refers to Christ's incarnation; he expounds how everything is reunited and rebound through the descent and ascent of the *Logos*.

---

40. Trouillard, "La *Virtus Gnostica* selon Jean Scot Érigène," 331–54; see also Stock, "The Philosphical Anthropology of Johannes Scottus Eriugena," 1–57 and his "Intelligo me esse. Eriugena's *cogito*," 328–35.

41. *Periph.* II (PL 122: 544A–B; CCCM 162: 26, ll. 538–45): "*Ea nanque quae extrinsecus corporeo sensui uaria multipliciaque locis, temporibus, qualitatibus, quantitatibus caeterisque sensibilis naturae differentiis apparent, in suis rationibus, secundum quas a creatore omnium condita sunt aeternaliterque immutabili suae naturae statu certisque diuinae prouidentiae regulis subsistent, puro intellectui rerum omnium ueritatem inquirenti, inuenienti, consideranti unum indiuiduum esse uidentur et sunt.*"

Through his descent and ascent, Christ mends all the fractures of the cosmos and unifies all five divisions. Christ repairs the division between man and woman through his birth, sanctifies every aspect of our world through his human life. He unites heaven and earth by taking the human flesh to heaven: by assuming human nature, "he encompasses the whole creation through its intermediaries and the extremities through their own parts."[42] Christ unifies human beings in himself through the hypostatic union; but uniting himself to human nature, the natural bond of all things, he recapitulates[43] all things in himself and thus unites himself to the whole creation. Through his descent into human nature and his ascent through all the levels of the cosmos, the *Logos* brings together in himself and thus harmonizes all the principles of beings and realizes the unity of the cosmos:

> With us and through us he encompasses the whole creation through its intermediaries and the extremities through their own parts. He binds about himself each with the other, . . . paradise and inhabited world, heaven and earth, things sensible and things intelligible, since he possesses like us sense and soul and mind. . . . Thus he divinely recapitulates the universe in himself, showing that the whole creation exists as one, like another human being . . . .[44]

In his exegesis of *Ambiguum* 41, Eriugena follows Maximus' account of cosmic renewal and unification through the recapitulation of the *logoi* (principles of creation achieved in the descent and ascent of Christ). Nevertheless, for him the incarnation itself is part of the epistemological scenario involving the human being. To put it briefly, one could say that the emphasis for him is not as much on the *Christological* aspect of the unification as it is for Maximus. Maximus' ontology is based on the incarnation and on his appropriation and application of the Chalcedonian two natures and hypostatic union theology.

42. Confessor, *Amb.* 41 (PG 91, 1310C).

43 Ibid. (PG 91: 1309C): "*Iuxta prius redditum modum, divinitus omnia in seipsum recapitulavit unam subsistentem simul omnem creaturam.*"

44. Ibid. (PG 91: 1312A; CCSG 18: 184–85, ll. 135–45): "*Et nobiscum et propter nos simul omnem creaturam per mediatates ueluti propriam partium extrema comprehendens, et circa seipsum insolubiter paradisum orbemque terrarium coniunxit, caelum et terram, sensibilia et intelligibilia, corpus quippe et sensum et animam secundum nos habens et intellectum, quibus quasi partibus per singula unicuique uniuersaliter cognatam associans extremum, iuxta prius redditum modum, diuinitus omnia in seipsum recapitulauit unam subsistentem simul omnem creaturam, quasi alium hominem, partium suarum ad se inuicem coitu completam ostendens.*" (θεοπρεπῶς τὰ πάντα εἰς ἑαυτὸν ἀνεκεφαλαιώσατο, μίαν ὑπάρχουσαν τὴν ἅπασαν κτίσιν δείξας, καθάπερ ἄνθρωπον ἄλλον, τῇ τῶν μερῶν ἑαυτῆς πρὸς ἄλληλα συνόδῳ συμπληρουμένην).

For Eriugena, however, the limelight falls on the epistemological abilities of reason as a mediator between the Word as the source of all the causes and creation. Although he is aware of the limitations of reason, the *Periphyseon* represents an attempt to unify the universe through dialectics and its main operations, division and analysis. Thus, he finds in Maximus' *Ambiguum* 41 a model for his own account of division and return, the great project of the dialogue. His wager is that the human being, trained by the arts and adhering to its highest faculty, the intellect, might be able to unify nature. In Eriugena's reading, Maximus offers an exemplary application of dialectic to the cosmic processes of creation and return to God. He appropriates Maximus' understanding of the human being as the workshop of creation and builds the great dialogue around it. The *Periphyseon* is thus best seen as an attempt to realize the hope of unification—that in Maximus' view was forfeited through the Fall. Thus Maximus Confessor's ontology, found in *Ambiguum* 41, provides the framework for the enterprise of the great dialogue.

The Methods of Return: Liberal Arts vs. Askesis

As I pointed out earlier, the most significant difference between Maximus and Eriugena is with regard to the way in which they envisage the realization of the return to divine unity. Maximus, the monk, remains steeped in the spiritual practice of cleansing the faculties in order to prepare them for the contemplation of creation. The first stage in the process of return is the πρακτική. The *vita practica* first deals with the passions and once these are brought under control, the positive virtues are acquired. Only after having ordered the faculties and made them subservient to reason, can one discern through natural contemplation (θεωρία φυσική) the principles of creation and of Scripture hidden underneath the sensible appearance. Finally, one reaches the third stage, θεολογία, which amounts to a unitary vision of all created beings in the one *Logos*, Christ.

For Maximus, practice (πραξις) and contemplation of nature (θεωρία φυσική) are thoroughly complementary and the balance between the two yields true philosophy. Thus, in Maximus' view, praxis and *logos*, cannot and should not be detached. They overlap and operate in tandem. In fact, he presents them as a continuum: contemplation follows upon praxis and is its ultimate goal. Praxis, however, is not discarded but remains a constant presupposition. "Almsgiving heals the irascible part of the soul; fasting

extinguishes the concupiscible part, and prayer purifies the mind and prepares for the contemplation of reality."[45]

The beginning of *Ambiguum* 10 offers another clear exposition of
Maximus' understanding of the faculties and the way they relate to the different activities. First, he explicitly disagrees with those who say that true
philosophy is achieved only through reason and contemplation without the
recourse to practical exercises (μελετάω). He insists that true philosophy
needs ascetic struggle in order to be able to achieve a true contemplation
of the meaning of things. "For the role of reason is to order the movement
of the body; by correct thinking, reason restrains, like a bridle, any turning
aside towards what is out of place; contemplation, like a most radiant light
manifesting truth itself, it orders through knowledge the rational and sensible choice of what is thought and judged."[46] Thus, for Maximus, knowledge
is necessarily rooted in bodily practice and the practice of virtues. Reason as
the highest faculty, depends on the order and control of the lower faculties.

Maximus then offers a hierarchy of the faculties involved in the process
of knowledge. "For the movement of the body is ordered by reason which
by correct thinking restrains, as by a bridle, any turning aside towards what
is out of place, and the rational and sensible choice of what is thought and
judged is reckoned to contemplation, like a most radiant light manifesting
truth itself."[47] Thus, for Maximus, knowledge is necessarily rooted in bodily
practice and the practice of virtues. Reason as the highest faculty depends
on the order and control of the lower faculties and the well functioning of
reason depends on the ordering of bodily movements. True philosophy, in
Maximus' view is the product of the right balancing of practice and reason,
of πρᾶξις and λόγος.

For Eriugena "the training" of the faculties does not necessarily entail
ascetic exercises. Rather, the means for attaining the intelligible level is going through the *enkuklios paideia* in order to become attuned to the right
"vision" of the cosmos, which for him amounts to the level of intellectual

---

45. Confessor, *De Char.* I.79 (PG 90: 977C): "μὲν ἐλεημοσύνη, τὸ θυμικὸν μέρος της
ψυχης θεραπεύει. ἡ δὲ νηστεία, τὴν μὲν ἐπιθυμίαν μαραίνει. ἡ δὲ προσευχή, τὸν νουν
καθαίρει, καὶ πρός τὴν των ὀντων θεωριαν παρασκευάζει."

46. Confessor, *Amb.* 10 (PG 91, 1108A): "τοὐναντίον δὲ διηρμένην τῇ πράξει τήν
ἀληθῆ περι τὰ ὄντα κρίσιν αὐτῶν καὶ ἐνεργειαν, ἥν δὴ φιλοσοφιαν ὀντως πληρστάτην
ἐγωγε τολμήσας μόνην ὁρίζομαι . . . λόγῳ? Καὶ θεωρίᾳ κατορθοῦσθαι αὐτὴν ἀποφνάμενον,
ὡς τῳλόγῳ συνημμένης πάντως της πράξεως, καί της ἐπ᾽ αὐτῇ κρίσεως τῇ θεωρίᾳ
περιεχομένης."

47. Ibid. (PG 91, 1108B): "εἴ περ λόγου μὲν τὸ τάσσειν τὴν τοῦ σώματος κίνησιν,
οἷον χαλινῷ τινι τῷὀρθῷλογισμῷ τῆς πρὸς ἀτοπίαν φορᾶς ἐπιστημόνως ἀναχαιτίζοντος,
θεωρίας δὲ τὸ τὰ χαλῶς νοηθέντα τε καὶ κριθέντα ἐμφρόνως αἱρεισθαι ψηίζεσθαι, οἱονεὶ
φῶς παμφαέσθαι δι᾽ ἀληθοῦς γνώσεως τὴν ἀλήθειαν αὐτὴν δεικνυούσης."

knowledge. For Eriugena, the liberal arts are the necessary correction spectacles which the soul needs in order to relearn the right view of creation and thus to be able to return to the primordial condition. "For although through the accident of its transgression of the divine command whereby it became forgetful of itself and its creator the mind is born unskilled and unwise, yet when it is reformed by the rules of doctrine (*doctrinae regulis*) it may discover again in itself its God and itself and its skill and the art."[48]

Eriugena reads Maximus' account of unification through the human being as an *epistemological* ascent through all the levels of reality until one finally reaches intellectual knowledge of beings. For him, the return to the primordial state entails an epistemological progress, a change of vision.

The *Periphyseon* itself can be regarded as a true training ground for attaining the right vision of the cosmos; it is—to use the expression of Marrou—a true *exercitatio animi*,[49] meant to help the reader regain the right perspective on the cosmos and thus bring about the return of the cosmos. The extensive interpretation of Scripture through the employment of the liberal arts is the means of realizing this vision. As I will show in the next section, Eriugena, like Maximus, regards Scripture as a cosmos in miniature, as an epitome, because it reflects the different levels of reality. The fallen human being, however, needs to relearn the appropriate "seeing" in order to attain a unified perspective of creation.

The Two Books and the Two Garments of Christ

The parallelism of Scripture and nature is another concept that constitutes one of the methodological cornerstones of the *Periphyseon*. In this respect, we see Eriugena following Maximus, who established this parallelism in *Ambiguum* 10. Given that a great part of the *Periphyseon* is an exposition of the *Hexaemeron*, the idea of a convergence between Scripture and creation allows us to explain the place of scriptural interpretation in the *Periphyseon*.

---

48. *Periph.* IV (PL 122: 767C; CCCM 164: 38, ll. 1034–39): "*Quamuis enim imperita et insipiens nasci uideatur (quod ei accidit diuini transgressione mandati, qua et suimet et creatoris sui oblita est), doctrinae tamen regulis reformata, deum suum et se ipsam suique peritiam et disciplinam . . . potest reperire.*"

49. This was the insight of Henri-Irenee Marrou about Augustine's early dialogues and the *De Trinitate*; thus the convoluted character of the dialogue is not due to a lack of rhetorical prowess but it is intentional; rather it has a pedagogical-performative rationale; the digressions are supposed to refine, train, and correct the understanding of the readers in order to prepare them for the contemplation of the divine realities. In a similar manner the digressions and sometimes convoluted character of the conversation are meant as a "training ground" for using the arts in the proper way for reading Scripture and creation. See Marrou, *Histoire De l'Éducation*.

In light of Maximus' idea of parallelism between creation and Scripture, Eriugena's own procedure gains some clarity. For Eriugena, as for Maximus, Scripture is an epitome of the cosmos and therefore, in order to interpret the cosmos one needs to interpret Scripture. This parallelism is more than a metaphor for Eriugena; because it is an ontological aspect of reality, the book of Scripture reflects the book of creation and provides a privileged conduit to it.[50]

In *Ambiguum* 10, Maximus offers a series of contemplations on a variety of biblical texts. These texts amount to exemplary reading performances meant to take one from the level of the "letter" to that of interior *logos* both with regard to creation and to Scripture. At the center of these readings is the account of the transfiguration, which for Maximus becomes the *apotheosis* of the passage through the levels of reality and the progression through the various stages of knowledge: from the garments of the visible things to their symbolic meaning, and on to their unseen meaning.

More importantly, Maximus establishes a parallelism and symmetry between the written and the natural laws. "So the two laws—both the natural and the written laws—are of equal honor and teach the same things; neither is greater or less than the other . . . ."[51] For Maximus, both laws are conduits to God because both Scripture and creation intimate the divine *Logos*, Christ, through the "letters" imprinted in them.

According to Maximus, this parallelism is grounded in Christ, who is the *Logos*, the reason both of Scripture and of creation. The best expression of this is found in the image of the two garments of Christ in the Transfiguration account. The two garments correspond to: "the forms and shapes in which those things that have come to be are put forward to be seen. . . . For the creator of the universe and the lawgiving Word is hidden as manifest, since he is invisible by nature, and is manifested as hidden, lest he is believed

---

50. Eriugena's view of the "two books" will also be put to good use by the masters of the twelfth century. See Otten, "Nature and Scripture: Demise of a Medieval Analogy," 257–84. See also her "The Parallelism of Nature and Scripture," 81–102. See further de Lubac, *Medieval Exegesis*, 76–78. See also Duclow, "Nature as Speech and Book," 131–40. On the connections between reading nature and reading Scripture, see Harrison, *The Bible, Protestantism, and the Rise of Natural Science*; I do not fully agree with Harrison's too stark contrast between allegorical and literal readings and the consequences thereof for the reading of creation. As the case of Eriugena shows, there was much more continuity between literal and allegorical readings. There is a wide spectrum between literal and allegorical interpretations in Eriugena's case. Nevertheless, the value of Harrison's insight is that reading Scripture was an exercise of reading creation and vice versa. This understanding for the status of scriptural interpretation puts Eriugena's enterprise into a clarifying light: reading Scripture and reading creation are for him two complementary and almost coinciding ideas.

51. Ibid. (PL 122: 1128D).

by the wise to be subtle in nature."[52] These forms and shapes are both the symbols of the visible creation and the syllables and letters of Scripture, based on the idea that both Scripture and creation are places of manifestation of Christ.

> The first law, in conformity to the *logos*, depicts the harmonious texture of the whole as a book which has as syllables and letters, the various bodies thickened through the coming together of different qualities which are the first and closer to us; It also has words which are more remote and finer. Through their reading the *Logos*, which is woven into them, is discerned. . . . The second [law], revealed through teaching, is depicted as another world constituted of heaven and earth and those in between: ethical philosophy, natural and theological philosophy.[53]

The Nutritor refers to this passage in the context of his own excursus into physical interpretation. He refers to Maximus' interpretation in order to warrant his own procedure to dwell on "physical" issues with regard to the interpretation of Scripture. The Nutritor claims that he is emulating Abraham in his procedure:

> And if Christ at the time of his Transfiguration wore two vestures white as snow, namely the letter of the Divine Oracles and the sensible appearance of visible things, why should we be encouraged diligently to touch the one in order to be worthy to find Him whose vesture it is, and forbidden to inquire about the other, namely the visible creature, how and by what reasons it is woven, I do not clearly see. For even Abraham knew God not through the letters of Scripture, which had not yet been composed, but by the revolutions of the stars as other animals do, without being able to understand their reasons? I should not have the temerity to say this of the great and wise theologian.[54]

---

52. Confessor, *Amb.* 10 (PG 91: 1129C).

53. Ibid. (PG 91: 1129A): "Νοῶ τὸν ὁμαλῶς ὅτι μάλιστα κατὰ λόγον διευθυνόμενον διὰ τῶν ἐν αὐτῷ συμφυῶν θεαμάτων βίβλου τρόπον τὸ ἐναρμόνιον τοῦ παντὸς ὕφασμα ἔχοντα, γράμματα μὲν καὶ σθλλαβὰς ἐχούσης, τὰ πρὸς ἡμας πρῶτα, προσεχῆ τε καὶ μερικά, καὶ πολλαῖς παχυνόμενα κατὰ σύνοδον ποιότητι σώματα, ῥήματα δὲ , τὰ τούτων καθολικώτερα, πόρρω τε ὄντα καὶ λεπτότερα, ἐξ ὧν σοφῶς ὁ διαχαράξας καὶ ἀρρήτως αὐτοῖς ἐγκεραχαραγμενος λόγος ἀναγινωσκόμενος ἀπαρτίζεται . . . τὸν δὲ μαθήσει κατορθούμενον, διὰ τῶν αὐτοικατορθούμενον, διὰ τῶν αὐτοὶ σοφῶς ὑπηγορευμένον, ὥσπερ κόσμον ἄλλον ἐξ οὐρανοῦ καὶ γῆς καὶ τῶν ἐν μέσω, τῆς ἠθικῆς φημι καὶ φυσικῆς καὶ θεολογικῆς φιλοσοφίας σθνιστάμενον, τὴν ἄφατον καταμνύειν τοῦ ὑπαγορεύσαντος δύναμιν . . . ."

54. *Periph.* III (PL 122: 723D–724A; CCCM 163: 149–50, ll. 4351–63): "*Et si duo uestimenta Christi sunt tempore transformationis ipsius candida sicut nix (diuinorum*

Following Maximus, Eriugena will also adopt the correspondence between the levels of Scripture and the hierarchy of science. The discussion about the levels of Scripture and the correlation to the levels of the cosmos is offered in the *Homily on the Prologue of John*,[55] where Eriugena explicitly establishes a parallel between the cosmos of Scripture and the cosmos of creation. According to him, Scripture is like another cosmos: *Divina siquidem scriptura mundus quidam est intelligibilis, suis quattuor partibus, veluti quattuor elementis, constitutus* (*Hom. Prol. in Ioh.* 291b). The abyss or the inferior part of the earth corresponds to ethics. Ethics and history "are surrounded by the air of natural science . . . called by the Greeks, physics.[56] Above and beyond all of this, there is a fiery and ardent sphere of the empyrean heaven; that is this high contemplation of divine nature which the Greeks call *theologia*; no intellect could penetrate beyond it."[57] The task of the interpreter then is to ascend from ethics and history to physics and ultimately to theology.[58]

Maximus himself establishes a parallel between the elements of Scripture and those of creation in *Ambiguum* 38.[59] There Maximus provides even more specificity to his view of the parallelism. "The general reason of the spiritual meaning of Scripture appears tenfold to contemplation: through place, time, genus, person, occupation, practice, natural philosophy and contemplation, presence and future, or type and truth."[60] After

---

uidelicet eloquiorum littera et uisibilium rerum species sensibilis), cur iubemur unum uestimentum diligenter tangere, ut eum cuius uestimentum est mereamur inuenire, alterum uero (id est creaturam uisibilem) prohibemur inquirere et quomodo et quibus rationibus contextum sit, non satis uideo. Nam et Abraham non per litteras scripturae, quae nondum confecta fuerat, uerum conuersione siderum deum cognouit. An forte simpliciter sicut et caetera animalia solas species siderum aspiciebat, non autem rationes eorum intelligere poterat? Non temere hoc de magno et sapienti theologo ausim dicere."

55. See Scot, *Homélie sur le prologue de Jean*, 327–28.

56. Ibid. (PL 122: 291C, 270): "*Aer ille naturalis scientiae circumvoluitur: quam . . . graeci vocant phusikh.*"

57. Ibid. (PL 122: 291C, 272): "*Extra autem omnia et ultra, aetherus ille ingeusque ardor empyrii caeli, hoc est, superae contemplationis divinae naturae, quam graeci theologiam nominant; ultra quam nullus egreditur intellectus.*"

58. Again Eriugena seems to extrapolate from a passage of Maximus in *Amb.* 10 (PG 91: 1129A): "The second [referring to Scripture], known through teaching, or through those orders found in it, is presented wisely as another world, composed of heaven, and earth and of those in the middle, of moral, natural, and theological, hymning the ineffable power of the unspoken one."

59. Blowers, "The World in the Mirror of Holy Scripture."

60. Confessor, *Amb.* 38 (PG 91: 1293A), Stăniloae, 376; see also *Amb.* 21 (PG 91: 1241D), where Maximus establishes a symmetry between the four Gospels, the four elements of the cosmos and the four virtues. According to the Confessor, the Gospels

this, Maximus offers a demonstration of passing from plurality to unity: the reader is shown how to traverse the various stages until through the threefold division of philosophy he ascends to the one *Logos* of Scripture.[61] First, one passes through the five categories of Scripture: time, place, genus, person, dignity; these are reduced to the threefold division of philosophy: ethical, natural, and theological. These are further contracted into the categories of present and future; from here, one proceeds to reduce all "reasons" and "meanings" to the one Reason/*Logos*, Christ.

The most important difference between the two is that for Maximus the parallelism of Scripture and creation is grounded in his *Logos* ontology: Christ as the *Logos* unifies all the *logoi* (reasons) of Scripture and of creation.[62] For Eriugena, the coincidence of Scripture and nature is centered on Christ, but he does not base it on the *logoi* metaphysics. Eriugena does not employ Maximus' *Logos-logoi* conceptual pair in order to explain the passage from unity to plurality.

Nevertheless, the theory of the two books becomes for Eriugena the fundamental hermeneutical principle of the *Periphyseon* because it allows him to write a physiology and to carry it out through the interpretation of Scripture; thus, the lengthy exegesis of Genesis is Eriugena's way of putting the parallelism of Scripture and creation into practice. It is through the exegesis of Scripture that he wants to read creation and to achieve a unifying perspective. Thus, from the perspective of "the two garments" theory, the purpose of the extensive interpretation of Scripture can become somewhat clearer.

---

constitute the synthesis of the various elements: thus the Gospel of Matthew links earth and justice; that of Mark is the unification of water and right balance; that of Luke, of air and goodness; that of John of ether and prudence. Maximus' symmetry could very well be the source of Eriugena's parallelism between Scripture and creation.

61. Maximus offers a demonstration of the passing through and unification of the categories of creation in *Amb.* 41. There he describes how Christ unifies creation by bringing together the particulars and universals. The *logoi* of the distinct and particular are comprehended in the rationalities of the universal and general. And the rationalities of the general and universal are comprehended by wisdom, while the *logoi* of the particular, contained in a variety of ways in the general ones, are comprehended by prudence. The *logoi* simplify and forsake the symbolic variety from within individual things in order to be unified by Christ the *Logos*. See Guiu, "Christology and Philosophical Culture," 111–16.

62. Tollefsen, *The Christocentric Cosmology,* 71–75.

The Return

Eriugena's account of the return and of its structure also confirms the crucial role of Maximus' division for the *Periphyseon*. In hindsight, from the vantage point of the return, the preeminence of Maximus' division is confirmed. Based on the Neoplatonic principle of symmetry between the *exitus* and *reditus*, Eriugena's account of the return reflects the account of creation.[63] Thus, books IV and V of the *Periphyseon* attempt to explain how the return of all creation occurs through the return of the human being because all things were created in it according to its creation *ad imaginem*. The account of the return is more extensive than that of creation itself, because it constitutes the crux of the matter of the *Periphyseon*: how can all divisions be returned and reduced to the primordial unity of the primordial causes in the Word?[64]

What especially bothers the Alumnus is the character of the return. First, there is the question of the unification of sexes achieved in Christ. Second, there is the unification of paradise with earth. Third, there is the issue of the question of the manner of the return: "how the return of all the aforementioned substances into the One and (their) unification are to come to pass, whether in the thing itself . . . or whether it is only in the concept?"[65] So the questions that trigger this great dialogue are related to the several claims made by the teacher as a direct result of his interpretation of Maximus.[66]

The tutor replies that a proper answer requires a longer detour: it is at this point that the interpretation of the creation account starts and the result

63. Eriugena recapitulates Maximus' fivefold division several times in Book V. See *Periph.* V (PL 122: 875D), and also *Periph.* V (PL 122: 893B; CCCM 165: 48, ll. 1507–12): "*Et hoc etiam naturarum omnium quae facta sunt quinquepertita divisio, quae ab apostolica auctoritate, ut Maximus in Ambiguis XXXVII capitulo scribit, tradita est, lucidissime declarat, reditusque iterum et adunatio earundem per easdem diuisiones et conuolutiones totius creaturae in unum et postremo in ipsum deum.*"

64. This is the point of contention between East and West: the Nutritor casts it as an attempt to correct the position of Augustine and Boethius, for whom the passing of one genus into another is not possible ontologically. The Nutritor adduces a multitude of witnesses (mainly Eastern) in order to defend Maximus' account, according to which it is possible for the body to be changed into soul. For this reason, the teacher will offer the opinions of Ambrose, John Chrysostom, and Gregory of Nyssa.

65. *Periph.* II (PL 122: 544A; CCCM 162: 26, ll. 532–37): "*quomodo omnium substantiarum praedictarum reditus in unum atque adunatio futura sit: utrum se ipsa . . . an solo contuitu.*"

66. Ibid. (PL 122: 545A; CCCM 162: 27, ll. 566–67): "*De his igitur obscuris quaestionibus, quae per me ipsum ad liquidum intueri nequeo, luculentius a te disserendum esse aestimarim.*"

is this meandering six-hundred-page dialogue. They both agree that "every inquiry into truth should take its beginning" from the divine oracles (i.e., Scripture).[67]

This discussion, I claim, constitutes a crucial turn in the argument of the book. The ensuing great dialogue picks up and develops the query of the pupil on the character of the return. It marks the moment in which the two conversants appropriate Maximus' framework, the fivefold division and return of the creature. From here on the main task of the teacher will be to elucidate what Maximus means by the unification of natures. Eriugena's own project, the proper division of the genus nature, will be thus subsumed to Maximus' division, which instead of being just a divagation will provide the incentive for a sometimes-convoluted reply to various pressing questions about the return of creation.

So, the two main premises of the return are the encompassing character of human nature as the locus of all creation[68] and Christ's assumption of universal human nature. As in the *exitus,* in the return the human being is the mediator between the *Logos* and creatures. This idea is fundamental to Eriugena's vision, both with regard to the *exitus* and with regard to the *reditus.* He never tires to underline it: "When the Word assumed the nature of man, did he not take upon himself every creature, visible and invisible, and was he not the savior of everything which, being in man, he took upon himself?"[69]

There are several instances in which the Nutritor gives a sequential account of the return. He differentiates between a general and a special return.[70] The general return is divided into two stages that both center on the human being as the linchpin between creation in its various divisions, and the humanity assumed by Christ.

The first stage he calls the general return of all sensible creatures, including bodies and corporal nature: "the transformation of the whole sensible creature contained within the confines of this world, of all bodies . . . into its hidden causes."[71] The return into the hidden causes however amounts

---

67. Ibid. (PL 122: 545B; CCCM 162: 27, ll. 578–79): "*Ratiocinationis exordium ex diuinis eloquiis assumendum esse aestimo.*"

68. This element is mostly derived from Gregory of Nyssa's account of double creation in *De Opificio Hominis.*

69. *Periph.* V (PL 122: 913C; CCCM 165: 76, ll. 2415–17): "*Nonne uerbum assumens hominem omnem creaturam uisibilem et inuisibilem accepit, et totum quod in homine accepit saluum fecit?*"

70. See Gersh, "The Structure of the Return," 108–25.

71. *Periph.* V (PL 122: 1020A–B; CCCM 165: 224, ll. 7277–84): "*in transmutatione totius sensibilis creaturae quae intra huius mundi ambitum continetur . . . in suas causas*

to the return into the integrity and universality of the human being as an intelligible entity, as the *sapientia creata*, created in the image of God. In light of this, the human being is the principle, the medium, through which the entire creation is redeemed. It is at this level that the human being acts as a mediator through its ability to bring the elements of creation together by applying the proper knowledge.

Thus, for Eriugena the return amounts to this unification of all divisions through the activity of human knowledge in order to achieve the universal human nature: "We do not say that the masses and forms of visible and sensible bodies will be resurrected, but that in the resurrection of man . . . they will return with man and in man into their causes and principles which were created in man."[72]

The level of the *sapientia creata,* of the universal, intelligible human being as an intermediary, is the major difference between Eriugena's and Maximus' account of the return. For Eriugena the human being at the intellectual level, comprising the various levels of creation, is the *arche* and *telos* of creation. Thus, it has a much more prominent role to play in the return in the account of the return. "Therefore in assuming human nature he [i.e., Christ] assumed every creature. If he then has saved and restored the human nature which he assumed, he also restored every creature, visible and invisible."[73] For Eriugena, the emphasis falls on the mode in which the human being as *sapientia creata* comprises all the aspects of creation and thus mediates between the *sapientia creatrix*, Christ the Word, and created beings.

Thus, when it comes to the general return, the human being still has a central role, even after the Fall: the human being has a prominent role to play because it is both the locus and the instrument of this unification. "So it is from the unification of the division of man into two sexes that the return and unification through all the other divisions will take its start."[74]

---

occultas." Gersh's analysis also bears this out: "The general return is to the integral state of human nature and to the natural good which it contains, as signified by the biblical account of life in paradise." See Gersh, *The Structure of the Return,* 120.

72. Ibid. (PL 122: 913D; CCCM 165: 76–77, ll. 2430–33): "*Visibilium et sensibilium corporum moles et species resurrecturas non dicimus sed . . . in suas causas et rationes, quae in homine factae sunt, in resurrectione hominis cum homine et in homine reuersuras.*"

73. Ibid. (PL 122: 912C; CCCM 165: 74, l. ll. 2369–71): "*Ac per hoc si humanam naturam, quam accepit, saluauit et restarauuit, omnem profecto creaturam uisibilem et inuisibilem restaurauit.*"

74. Ibid. (PL 122: 893C; CCCM 165: 49, ll. 1527–28): "*Proinde ex adunatione diuisionis hominis in duplicem sexum praedictarum diuisionum incipit ascensus et adunatio.*" This is also a point made by Otten: "It is in man's thinking that we can trace

The second aspect of the general return of human nature is focused on the incarnation of Christ: "when it was saved by Christ into the original condition in which it was created, and into the dignity of the divine image which is as it were a kind of paradise which was obtained by it by the merits of the One."[75] This return is made possible by the restoration of human nature achieved through Christ's incarnation and assumption of human nature. "The return of the whole of human nature into its first condition shall be in him who took the whole nature upon himself, namely in the incarnate word of God."[76] Thus, by assuming universal human nature, Christ assumes all creatures. "For when the word of God took upon himself our human nature he took upon himself every created substance which is contained in that nature."[77]

It is at the second stage of the return where Eriugena envisages the role of the incarnation, and where Maximus' Christology[78] gains importance for Eriugena. The teacher calls this return, the return to the divine image, as the return to the primordial human condition; he also refers to it as the return to paradise as the pristine human condition. The possibilities of perfection forfeited through the Fall are regained through the universal human nature assumed and redeemed by Christ. Christ's humanity repairs all divisions and foreshadows the destiny of all humanity in its universal instantiation. Eriugena preserves the cosmic character of the incarnation but connects it to the mediator role of human reason in its intellectual capacity. For Maximus, Christ's incarnation transforms reality by assuming the principles of all things according to the Chalcedonian model.[79] Eriugena, however, also

---

the movement of procession and reditus as the universe's line of direction and in the end it is in man's speculation on the self that we are led to find that movement's roots," see Otten, "Nature and Scripture," 208. See also her analysis of the return in Otten, "The Dialectic of the Return," 406.

75. Ibid. (PL 122: 1020B; CCCM 165: 224, ll. 7287–90): "*Secundus uero modus suae speculationis obtinet sedem in reditu generali totius humanae naturae in Christo saluatae in pristinum suae conditionis statum ac (ueluti in quendam paradisum) in diuinae imaginis dignitatem, merito unius* [i.e., *Christi*]."

76. Ibid. (PL 122: 978D; CCCM 165: 165, ll. 5393–95): "*Tota itaque humanitas in ipso, qui eam totam assumpsit, in pristinum reuersura est statum, in uerbo dei uidelicet incarnato.*"

77. Ibid. (PL 122: 912C; CCCM 165: 74, ll. 2366–68): "*Ipsum siquidem dei uerbum, quando accepit humanam naturam, nullam creatam substantiam praetermisit, quam in ea non acceperit.*"

78. Cf. Colish, "John the Scot's Christology," 138–45; cf. also Perl, "Metaphysics and Christology," 258–70. Both Perl and Colish notice that Eriugena modifies the Chalcedonian approach of Maximus.

79. The threefold account offered here is not contradictory with the twofold account offered in an earlier section; the single difference is that the "general return" in

assigns a crucial role to human knowledge, which mediates between Christ and creation.

The third aspect of the return represents the ascent beyond "the laws and limitations of nature" to the "superessential plan" of divine transformation. The third aspect of the return amounts to going beyond the natural limit: "it is concerned with those who besides ascending to the highest point of the nature which is created in them, shall, through the abundance of the grace of God . . . pass beyond all the laws and limitations of nature and on that superessential plane be transformed into God himself."[80]

In Book V, the linchpin in the account of return and unification is human knowledge. Through the epistemological ascent, humans achieve the return and the unification of the various divisions to their primordial condition of a unitary idea in the divine mind. Although he does not neglect the role of Christ's incarnation as the assumption and redemption of universal human being, the focus for Eriugena is much more on the mediator role of the human being. The possibility of intellectual unification envisaged by Maximus for the prelapsarian human being is the epistemological beacon for Eriugena.

Faithful to his own style of offering a multiplicity of vantage points, the teacher offers yet another description of the return; this time he describes a seven-stage account, which allows us to grasp the continuity between the three different stages of the return:

> The first will be the transformation of the earthly body into vital motion; the second of vital motion into sensation; the third of sensation into reason; then of reason into mind, wherein lies the end of every rational creature, then this fivefold unification of the parts of our nature (body, vital motion, sensation, reason and mind) are no longer five but one, in each case the lower nature becoming absorbed in the higher; this shall be followed by the three more stages of ascent: first the transformation of mind into the knowledge of all things with come after God; secondly, of that knowledge into wisdom, that is into the innermost

---

the second account has only two elements: *Periph.* V (PL 122: 1001B; CCCM 165: 197, ll. 6390–95): "*Est enim generalis et est specialis, generalis quidem in omnibus qui ad principium conditionis suae redituri sunt, specialis uero in his qui non solum ad primordia naturae reuocabuntur, sed etiam ultra omnem naturalem dignitatem in causam omnium (quae deus est) reditus sui finem constituent.*" (The general return is the lot of all things which shall be brought back to the principle of their creation; the special return of those which shall not only be restored to the primordial causes of their nature, but shall achieve the consummation of their return, beyond every rank in the hierarchy of nature, in the cause of all things, which is God).

80. *Periph.* V (PL 122: 1020B; CCCM 165: 224).

contemplation of the truth, thirdly and lastly, the supernatural merging of the perfectly purified souls into God himself and their entry into the darkness of the incomprehensible Light which conceals all causes of things.[81]

The intertwining between the levels of knowledge and the levels of reality, in Eriugena's understanding, appears even clearer in this passage. In Eriugena's view, the return of all creation is realized through the progression through the various levels of knowledge with each new level bringing about an increased level of unity: from the fivefold faculties to reason, from reason to mind and from there into the principal knowledge of the principles of creation ("knowledge of things that come after God") up to the ineffable merger with the divine incomprehensibility.

The upshot of Eriugena's account is that the return of creation as a whole depends on the human being and that the restoration of creation coincides with the restoration of primordial, intelligible human nature (the true meaning of paradise according to the teacher). Eriugena takes his cue from Maximus in his emphasis on the incarnation and on the fact that Christ assumed the universal human nature. However, the nuances of his understanding of the incarnation intimate quite a different perspective. It is through the intellect and its knowledge (acquired through the liberal arts) that the human being aspires to become the workshop of creation (in spite of the Fall) and thus to become the hub where all the aspects of creation are unified again. Therefore, the incarnation of the *Logos* is understood within the epistemological framework that has the human intellect (as an idea in the divine mind) at its center.

Conclusion

Maximus Confessor provides Eriugena not just with a series of ideas but also with an ontological framework, which encompasses the human being

---

81. Ibid. (PL 122: 1020 C–D; CCCM 165: 224–25, ll. 7300–10): "*Ac primus erit mutation terreni corporis in motum vitalem, secundus vitalis motus in sensum, tertio sensus in rationem, dehinc reationis in animum, in quo finis totius rationalis creaturae constituitur. Post hanc quique veluti partium nostrae naturae adunationem (corporis videlicet et vitalis motus sensusque rationisque intellectusque) ita ut non quinque sed unum sint, infrioribus semper a superioribus consummates . . . sequentur alii tres ascensionis gradus. Quorum unus transitus animi in scientiam omnium quae post deum sunt, secundus scientiae in sapeintiam, hos este contemplationem intimam veritatis quantum creaturae conceditur, tercius (qui et summus) purgatissimorum animorum in ipsum deum supernaturaliter occasus ac veluti incomprehensibilis et inaccessibilis lucis tenebras in quibus causae omnium absconditur.*"

and all other aspects of creation. It is within this framework that the project of the *Periphyseon* as a whole has to be understood: the division of the genus of nature, undertaken in Book I is subsumed under the grander purview of Maximus' division of being. Moreover, the Confessor's anthropology of the human being as a center and synthesis of creation allows him to extend the purview of dialectics to creation itself. Finally, the parallelism established by Maximus between Scripture and creation as manifestation of the divine *Logos*, is the fundamental methodological principle of the work.

Thus, the driving hope of the *Periphyseon* is that the human being, through intellectual knowledge applied in the right manner, might achieve the perfect knowledge of creation and thus become again the workshop of creation. The *Periphyseon* is, in many ways, the attempt of the two discussants to attain this intellectual level by abiding to the rules of the liberal arts. It is within the framework of Maximus' ontology centered on "man as the workshop of creation" that Eriugena's own division of the genus "natura" has to be understood.

2

Saint Maximus the Confessor, the Filioque, and the Papacy

From Proof Text to Mediator

Edward Siecienski

Introduction

For over a millennium, Eastern and Western Christians have been separated by a church-dividing schism caused by two seemingly irresolvable theological issues.[1] The first concerns the procession of the Holy Spirit and the recitation of the Nicene Creed—i.e., the *filioque*—and whether the Spirit

---

1. The other issues involved in the debate (e.g., purgatory, azymes, fasting practices, the use of silken vestments, beards), while often given more attention in East-West polemical exchanges, cannot be placed on the same level as the papacy and the Creed in terms of their significance. As for the dating of the schism, although difficult to pinpoint the beginning of the break—1054 being the most common date—it can be argued that the schism formally began in 1009. In that year, according to Chartophylax Nicetas (of Maronea), there was a "schism between the two Sergii" (Patriarch Sergius and Pope Sergius IV), leading to the removal of the pope's name from the diptychs in Constantinople. Although the pope continued to be commemorated in the other Eastern churches (e.g., Jerusalem and Antioch), this was the last time (excepting the Latin occupation and brief periods of *unia* following Lyons and Florence) that the Bishop of Rome was included in the dyptichs at the imperial capital.

proceeds "from the Father" or "from the Father and the Son."[2] The second is the role of the Bishop of Rome, and whether he enjoys "by divine ordinance . . . a pre-eminence of ordinary power over every other Church"[3] or merely a "primacy of honor" as "first among equals." For centuries theologians on both sides of the East-West divide have debated these issues in harshly polemical terms, producing numerous tracts and florilegia attacking the other for their alleged heresies. Even today, in an ecumenical atmosphere far more congenial than centuries past, the blogosphere is full of websites whose sole purpose is to demonstrate, through proof-texts, the heterodoxy of the religious other. On the papacy, Orthodox critiques have been supplemented by the writings of Protestant Christians, some of which continue to echo the claim that the pope is the very antichrist foretold in the Book of Revelation.[4]

However, there have been figures throughout the centuries that have spoken to these issues without the polemical invective so characteristic of post-schism East-West exchanges. Among the most significant of these is Maximus the Confessor, a saint revered by Christians East and West, whose writings on the *filioque* and the papacy have served at various times as both proof-text and mediator. The aim of this paper is to trace the use of the Confessor's writings on these two subjects, documenting the ways both Catholic and Orthodox Christians have utilized Maximus' corpus in the past, and then examining how his theology may help those presently engaged in ecumenical dialogue.

The *Filioque*

Let us begin with the *filioque*. Despite having written little by way of trinitarian speculation, Maximus found himself, alongside Cyril of Alexandria, Basil the Great, and Epiphanius of Salamis, among the most cited of the Greek fathers in the centuries-long debate over the procession of the Holy Spirit. Although of some of the texts allegedly authored by Maximus have

2. For a full history of the debates surrounding this issue see Siecienski, *The Filioque*.

3. *Pastor Aeternus* 3.

4. Visiting Mount Athos, author William Dalrymple made the mistake of admitting to his host that he was a Roman Catholic. "My God, I'm so sorry," said the monk. "The abbot never gives permission for non-Orthodox to look at our holy books, particularly Catholics. The abbot thinks the present pope [John Paul II] is the anti-Christ and his mother the Whore of Babylon. He says that they are now bringing about the Last Days spoken about by St. John in the Book of Revelation. . . . Please, don't tell anyone in the monastery that you're a heretic. If the abbot found out I'd be made to perform a thousand prostrations." Dalrymple, *From the Holy Mountain*, 10.

since proven to be misattributed,[5] four passages from the Confessor became staples in East-West exchanges on the procession.

The first text comes from *Quaestiones ad Thalassium* 63, where, in an exegesis of Zechariah 4:2–3, Maximus wrote:[6]

> For the Holy Spirit, just as he belongs to the nature of God the Father according to his essence so he also belongs to the nature of the Son according to his essence, since he proceeds inexpressibly from the Father through his begotten Son.[7]

The second text comes from *Quaestiones et dubia* 34, where he wrote:

> Just as the *nous* is cause of a word, so, also [the Father is the cause] of the Spirit through the mediation of the *Logos*. And just as we are not able to say that the word is of the voice, neither can we say that the Son is of the Spirit.[8]

The third, found often in anti-unionist florilegia, from the *Diversa capita ad theologiam et oeconomiam*, where Maximus affirms that:

> There is one God, because the Father is the begetter of the unique Son and the fount of the Holy Spirit: one without confusion and three without division. The Father is the unoriginate

---

5. The first was from the Dialogus cum Macedoniano, a work usually included in the Pseudo-Athanasian corpus but considered for centuries as the work of Maximus. "For indeed the Son has been born from the substance of the Father (and therefore is the only-begotten Son); the Holy Spirit proceeds from the substance of the Father" (*Dialogo cum Macedoniano*, PG 28: 1208). The second selection was from the *scholia* on De *divinis nominibus* of Dionysius. Although Maximus cannot be totally excluded as a source for some of the texts, modern scholars now believe the *scholia* was largely the work of the sixth-century writer, John of Scythopolis. "For the very reason that God and Father moved timelessly and lovingly, without division or diminution, coming forth into a distinction of persons totally above the mode of unity and above the mode of simplicity, with the Radiance (of His glory) coming forth into existence, as the living image, and the most Holy Spirit proceeding worshipfully and overabundantly from the Father as the Lord teaches" (PG 4: 221). The *Epigraphae* of John Beccus also contained several spurious quotations, including three from the *Dialogus de Sancta Trinitate in quo colloquuntur orthodoxus et anomoeus arianista*, a work, like the *Dialogus cum Macedoniano*, that is usually included in the Pseudo-Athanasian corpus although its authorship is still uncertain.

6. He said to me, "What do you see?" And I said, "I see a lampstand all of gold, with a bowl on the top of it; there are seven lamps on it, with seven lips on each of the lamps that are on the top of it. And by it there are two olive trees, one on the right of the bowl and the other on its left" (Zech 4:2–3).

7. Confessor, *Ad Thal.* 63 (CCG 22: 155).

8. Confessor, *Qu. Dub.* 34 (CCG 10: 151); Eng. trans. in Prassas, *St. Maximus the Confessor*, 147.

intellect, the unique essential Begetter of the unique *Logos*, also unoriginate, and the fount of the unique everlasting life, the Holy Spirit.[9]

The fourth, and certainly most significant text, is the *Letter to Marinus*, composed in 645 or 646, after the monothelites in Constantinople attacked the orthodoxy of Pope Theodore for his (alleged) use of the *filioque* in his synodal letter.[10] Maximus wrote to the priest Marinus in Cyprus that:

> the men of the Queen of cities [i.e., Constantinople] have attacked the synodal letter of the present most holy Pope, not in all the chapters you have written about, but only two of them. One relates to the theology and makes the statement that, "The Holy Spirit proceeds from the Son." . . . In the first place they [i.e., the Romans] produced the unanimous evidence of the Roman Fathers, and also of Cyril of Alexandria, from the study he made of the gospel of St. John. . . . From this they showed that they themselves do not make the Son the cause of the Spirit for they know that the Father is the one cause of the Son and the Spirit, the one by begetting and the other by procession, but they show the progression through him and thus the unity of the essence.[11]

Given its importance as an early and explicit reference to the *filioque* from a Greek source, it should not be surprising that this text first surfaced when the debate became contentious in the ninth century, during the so-called Photian Schism. Hoping to demonstrate the orthodoxy of the Roman position, Anastasius the Librarian of Rome first produced the *Letter to Marinus*, which (he hoped) would satisfy Greek critics by explaining the doctrine in such a way that it fully conformed with Eastern trinitarian thought.

> Moreover, we have from the letter written by the same Saint Maximus to the priest Marinus concerning the procession of the Holy Spirit, where he implies that the Greeks tried, in vain, to make a case against us, since we do not say that the Son is a cause or principle of the Holy Spirit, as they assert. But, not incognizant of the unity of substance between the Father and

9. Confessor, *Cap. Gnost.* 4 (PG 90: 1180); Eng. trans. in Palmer, Sherrard, and Ware, *The Philokalia*, 165.

10. Although the authenticity of this text has been debated for centuries, and (at times) questioned by both Latins and Greeks, I have argued elsewhere that the case for authenticity is bolstered by its conformity with Maximus' trinitarian theology. See Siecienski, "The Authenticity of Maximus," 189–227. For an opposing view see Karayiannis, "O AGIOS MAXIMOS O OMOLOGHTHS," 379–98.

11. Confessor, *Th. Pol.* 10 (PG 91: 136).

the Son, as he proceeds from the Father, we confess that he proceeds from the Son, understanding *processionem*, of course, as
"mission."[12]

Here, Anastasius emphasized Maximus' explicit denial that the Son
is a cause or principle (*non causam vel principium*) of the Spirit, thus ad-
dressing the charge of Photius had leveled against the Carolingians. He also
went out of his way to interpret *processionem* as "mission," an interpretation
that would have fully conformed to the Eastern understanding that it was
only in the economy of salvation that the Spirit came as a gift from the Son.
This irenicism was also demonstrated by another admirer and translator of
Maximus, John Scotus Eriugena. While most of the Carolingians denied the
orthodoxy of the Patriarch Tarasius' confession that the Holy Spirit proceeds
"through the Son," Erigena defended the formula based on the Confessor's
use of it in both *Quaestiones ad Thalassium* 63 and the *Letter to Marinus*.[13]
For Erigena, both East and West professed the belief that "it is from the
substance of Father that the Son is born and the Holy Spirit proceeds" (*ex
substantia Patris et Filius nascitur, et Spiritus sanctus procedit*).

By the eleventh century, the positions of East and West had hardened
and a clear dialectic was established—either the Spirit proceeded "from the
Father alone" as the Greeks maintained, or "from the Father and the Son" as
the Latins professed. Maximus was no longer used to build bridges; his work
was instead reduced to a series of proof-texts used to attack the orthodoxy
of the religious other. For the Latins, Maximus provided a Greek witness to
the orthodoxy of the *filioque*. In the *Contra Errores Graecorum*, for example,
Thomas Aquinas included a selection from *Quaestiones ad Thalassium* 63,
where he (mis)quoted the Confessor to say that "the Holy Spirit naturally
exists by God the Father according to his essence, so also he truly *exists by
the Son* according to his nature and essence, as it were, proceeding as God
from the Father through the Son."[14]

For the Greeks, Maximus played a quite different role. In the debates
following the Council of Lyons in 1274, for example, both unionist Patriarch
John Beccus and his opponent Gregory of Cyprus cited the Confessor to

12. Anastasius, *Anastasius ad Ioannem Diaconum* (PL 129: 560–61).

13. Eriugena, *De divisione naturae* 2, 34 (PL 122: 613). It should be noted that Eriugena, following Maximus and Nazianzus, assumes *substantia* to be the Latin equivalent of ὑπόστασις, which he differentiates from *essentia* or οὐσίας.

14 Aquinas, *Contra Errores Graecorum* 2, 16; Eng. trans. Likoudis, *Ending the Byzantine Greek Schism*, 175. Maximus had actually written that the Holy Spirit "belonged
to the Son," not "exists by the Son." Thomas, cannot be blamed for the misquotation.
It had been taken from the *Libellus de fide ss. Trinitatis* of Nicholas of Cotrone, which
included many spurious and erroneous selections from the fathers.

prove their respective positions. In the *Epigraphae* of Beccus, Maximus was cited as a witness to the belief that any reference in Greek patristic literature to procession ἐκ τοῦ Πατρὸς δὶ Υἱοῦ, was equivalent to the Latin belief in procession *ex Patre filioque*.[15] His opponent, Gregory of Cyprus, strongly disagreed, arguing instead that what Maximus advocated in the *Letter to Marinus* was the "eternal manifestation" of the Spirit through the Son, not his procession proper. He wrote:

> The great Maximus, the holy Tarasius, and even the saintly John knew that the Holy Spirit proceeds from the Father, from whom it subsists with respect to both its hypostasis and cause of its being. And at the same time, they acknowledge that the Spirit flows forth, is manifested, shines forth, appears, and is made known through the Son.[16]

Later it would be Gregory Palamas who would cite the Confessor as a witness against the Latin teaching, seeing in Maximus an early advocate of the essence-energy distinction. In a passage examining Maximus' *Quaestiones ad Thalassium* Palamas wrote:

> Whenever you hear him say that the Holy Spirit proceeds from both, because it comes from the Father essentially through the Son, understand reverently that he is teaching that the natural powers and energies of God are poured forth but not the Spirit's divine hypostasis.[17]

Nilus Cabasilas, Palamas' successor at Thessalonica, also used Maximus in his attack upon the theology of the Latins, citing the *Letter to Marinus* as a clear refutation of filioquism. Cabasilas conceded the fact that during the time of Maximus East and West were of one mind on the matter of the Spirit's procession, writing:

> He [i.e., Maximus] fittingly believed this explanation [by the Romans], one common both to Cyril of Alexandria and the Roman Fathers . . . that the Father is the cause of the Son and the Holy Spirit, one by generation, the other by procession, but that the Son is not the cause of the Spirit. . . . Moreover, if formerly some heard the Roman fathers say that the Spirit proceeds also from the Son, one must not believe that the Son is the cause,

---

15. Cf. Gill, "John Beccus, Patriarch of Constantinople," 253–66.

16. Cyrpus, *Apologia pro tomo suo* (PG 142: 262).

17 Palamas, *Logos Apodeiktikos* 2, 20.

but rather that they are expressing his flowing forth through the Son.[18]

The fact that the Latins now maintained that the Son *was* a cause of the Spirit demonstrated for Cabasilas how far they had strayed from the patristic teaching, and it explained why they currently denied the authenticity of the text.[19] For his part, Cabasilas had no doubts about the letter's authenticity, believing it to be the perfect "proof-text" for the position of Photius.[20]

This is why, at the Council of Florence in 1438–39, Mark of Ephesus and the Greeks came prepared to offer the *Letter to Marinus* as a means to union, believing its acceptance by the Latins would be a *de facto* admission that the Eastern position was correct. The problem, of course, was that the Latins were acutely aware of this, which is why they continued to cast doubts on the letter's authenticity. When one of the Latin delegates, Andrew of Rhodes, made the mistake of introducing the text,[21] the Greeks pounced upon the opportunity and told the Romans: "If this letter is accepted gladly on your part, the union will happily proceed."[22] The Latins, unwilling to concede the point at so early in the proceedings, "chided the Bishop of Rhodes" for his use of the *Letter to Marinus*, a document that they would not admit "because it is not found to be complete."[23]

Yet, despite the Latins' rejection, following the public debates the emperor once again attempted to introduce the *Letter to Marinus* as a means to reunion, asking the Greeks:

---

18. Calabasilas, *Five Discourses* 5, 6–7; text in Kislas, *Sur le Saint-Esprit*, 379–81.

19. "But it is completely ridiculous for the Latins to be at war against themselves, sometimes not being ashamed to bring it forth against us and declaring that this letter of the divine Maximus is genuine . . . and other times, when we defend ourselves from this letter in a way that seems best to us, they maintain the opposite, ashamed to agree with their earlier position." Cabasilas, *Five Discourses* 5, 13; Kislas, *Sur le Saint-Esprit*, 385.

20. Cabasilas examined the text and found that it "preserved the ancient constructions and same style as the other writings of the divine Maximus, his stay in Rome, and his association with Marinus, as well as his just reproof against our Church" Cabasilas, *Five Discourses* 5, 12; Kislas, *Sur le Saint-Esprit*, 385.

21. In his book, *Filioque und Verbot eines anderen Glaubens auf dem Florentium*, Hans-Jürgen Marx claims that Andrew had three good reasons for risking the introduction of Maximus' Letter. "First, [to prove] that the addition (i.e., the *filioque*) was already in the Latin version of the Constantinopolitan Creed by the time of the sixth ecumenical council. Second, the Greeks had known about it. And third, that Maximus had used the Latin addition in his vehement defense against the monothelite polemicists." Marx, *Filioque und Verbot*, 223.

22. Syropoulos, *Memoirs* 6.36, 336.

23. Ibid.

If we should discover that the Latins gladly accept whatever Holy Maximus relates in his *Letter to Marinus* on the subject of the Holy Spirit, does it not seem good to you that we should unite through it?[24]

The sources differ on the reception given to this proposal. The Greek *Acta* claims that the Byzantines more than happily agreed:

> And everyone together said, "If the Latins are persuaded by this epistle, then nothing else is required for us to unite with them." . . . Therefore the synod designated the emperor to go to the pope and ask if he received the epistle and confession of Saint Maximus.[25]

The *Memoirs* of Syropolouos record that while the unionists (e.g., Bessarion and Isidore of Kiev) voted in favor of the emperor's proposal, they were opposed by Mark of Ephesus and Anthony of Heraclea, who asked:

> How can we unite with them when they accept, in word alone, the statement of Holy Maximus while among themselves they opine the opposite, even proclaiming it openly in their churches! No, they must first confess our teaching—clearly and without ambiguity.[26]

Pope Eugene IV, however, refused and insisted that the debates continue. Meanwhile, Bessarion and the unionists continued to argue their case, using (among other tools) the writings of the Confessor as support. Bessarion produced *Quaestiones ad Thalassium* 63 as proof that Maximus did not intend to deny all causality to the Son, since he clearly taught that the Spirit's eternal procession (ἐκπορεύεσθαι) took place through him.

> For, as he says, the Spirit is substantially of the Son, not newly acquired and from without, nor has the Son received it temporally, but rather he possesses it eternally and substantially just like the Father. And thus he is the cause, because the Spirit proceeds substantially from the Father through him.[27]

Like his Latin hosts, Bessarion was not convinced of the authenticity of Maximus' *Letter to Marinus*, "since it was not found in the ancient codices nor discovered among his works."[28] Yet, even if one conceded its authentic-

---

24. Ibid., 8.12, 400.

25 Gill, *Actorum Graecorum*, 392–93.

26. Syropoulos, *Memoirs* 8.12, 400.

27. Candal, *Bessarion Nicaenus*, 29–30.

28. Ibid., 43.

ity (as he did here for the sake of argument), Bessarion believed that the *Letter to Marinus* was not the clear condemnation of the Latin position that Mark and the anti-unionists had supposed. He argued that by speaking of the Spirit's procession διὰ τοῦ Υἱοῦ, Maximus allowed the Son to be *a* cause of the Spirit, although not *the* primordial or principle cause, since this role was reserved to the Father alone. This is why Bessariaon could affirm:

> That the Son is not the cause of the Spirit we can also say, for we understand the meaning of cause in the strictest sense, as used in the Greek idiom, whereby cause always is understood as the primordial first cause.[29]

Armed with this understanding of the Letter, Bessarion again put it forward as a formula for reunion, but the Latins again refused.[30] Mark of Ephesus knew why—the Romans no longer accepted the true doctrine that Maximus had once outlined (i.e., that the Son is not a cause), and now they were using corrupted texts to set the other fathers against him. Which writings did Mark accept? "I receive as authentic only those texts that are in accord with the Letter of the divine Maximus and the writings of St. Cyril. All those that are contrary I reject as false."[31] According to Mark's account, the other members of the delegation:

> answered that they did not doubt the authenticity of these passages [from the fathers], relying on the Epistle of the divine Maximus; but most of the members refused to admit the Son as a cause of the Spirit according to these passages because the wise Maximus also gives the same opinion of these passages.[32]

However, increasingly the Greek delegates came to accept the arguments of Bessarion and the Latins and moved ever closer to union. When

---

29. Bessarion of Nicea, *Refutatio Capitum Syllogisticorum* (PG 161: 240).

30. While the *Memoirs* simply say that the Latins rejected this offer, the *Acta* detail the Latin response: "For even we ourselves would say that the Son is not the primary cause of the Spirit: we assert one cause of the Son and the Spirit, the Father, the one according to generation and the other according to procession; but in order to signify the communion and the equality of the essence we also assert the procession through the Son and clearly confess the inseparability of the substance. For the Son is substantially the Son of the Father and the Holy Spirit substantially is of the Father and the Son. Since he is substantially of the Father and the Son, and the substance of the hypostasis in inseparable, therefore the Holy Spirit is also from the hypostasis of the Son. Maximus states that the pronouncements of the holy Roman fathers do not say otherwise, not only Augustine, Jerome, and Ambrose but the rest whose books manifestly assert the Holy Spirit is from the Father and the Son" (Gill, *Acta Graecorum*, 412).

31 Syropoulos, *Memoirs* 9.7, 440–42.

32. Mark of Ephesus, *Relatio de rebus a se*, 140.

finally the union decree was promulgated (which explicitly affirmed that "the Son should be signified, according to the Greeks indeed as cause, and according to the Latins as principle of the subsistence of the holy Spirit, just like the Father"),[33] Mark was alone in his refusal to sign, believing as he did "that the words of the Eastern and Western fathers can only be reconciled to each other by means of the explanation given them in the Epistle of Maximus, that is, that the Son must not be thought to be the cause of the Spirit."[34] In an interview with Pope Eugene he defended his decision:

> I express not my own opinions, I introduce nothing new into the Church, neither do I defend any errors. But I steadfastly preserve the doctrine which the Church, having received from Christ the Savior, has ever kept and keeps. This doctrine was also adhered to by the Church of Rome unanimously with that of the East until the beginning of the division.[35]

This reference to the earlier Roman teaching is a clear allusion to the position of Maximus in the *Letter to Marinus*, whose testimony Mark regarded as his defense for his refusal to bow to the "novelties" of the Latins and the teachings of this so-called ecumenical council. For the next several centuries, the *Letter to Marinus* would remain little but a proof-text for this position, cited often by the East and largely ignored by the West.

The Papacy

As with his writings on the *filioque*, Maximus' references to the papacy quickly found themselves included in the patristic florilegia assembled in the post-Photian period.[36] This time it would be the Latins who employed Maximus for their own purposes, finding in his work some of the strongest statements on the privileged place of the Church of Rome. Although there are important unresolved questions about the authorship of the texts, the weight of scholarly opinion seems to favor authenticity, albeit with some reservations.[37] The first selection, from *Opusculum* 11, was written shortly after the anti-monothelite Lateran Synod in 649. It reads:

33. Tanner, *Decrees of the Ecumenical Councils*, 526.

34. Mark of Ephesus, *Relatio de rebus*, 140.

35. Syropoulos, *Memoirs* 10.23, 159–60.

36. For the relations between Byzantium and the papacy see Dvornik, *Byzantium and the Roman Primacy*; Meyendorff, *The Primacy of Peter*; Clement, *You Are Peter*; DeVille, *Orthodoxy and the Roman Papacy*.

37. For a detailed discussion of the issues involved see Larchet, *Maxime le Confesseur*, 125–201.

For the very ends of the earth and those in every part of the world who purely and rightly confess the Lord, look directly to the most holy Church of the Romans and its confession and faith as though it were a sun of unfailing light, expecting from it the illuminating splendor of the Fathers and sacred dogmas. . . . For ever since the Incarnate Word of God came down to us, all the churches of Christians everywhere have held the greatest Church there to be their sole base and foundation, since, on the one hand, it is in no way overcome by the gates of Hades according to the very promise of the Savior, but holds the keys of the orthodox confession and faith in Him and opens the only true and real religion to those who approach with godliness, and, on the other hand, it shuts up and locks every heretical mouth that speaks unrighteousness against the Most High.[38]

The second text comes from *Opusculum* 12, and concerns the conditions under which the monothelite Patriarch of Constantinople Pyrrhus can return to the church.

If the Roman See recognizes Pyrrhus to be not only a reprobate but a heretic, it is certainly plain that everyone who anathematizes those who have rejected Pyrrhus also anathematizes the See of Rome, that is, he anathematizes the Catholic Church. I need hardly add that he excommunicates himself also, if indeed he is in communion with the Roman See and the Catholic Church of God. . . . It is not right that one who has been condemned and cast out by the Apostolic see of the city of Rome for his wrong opinions should be named with any kind of honor, until he be received by her, having returned to her, and to our Lord, by a pious confession and orthodox faith, by which he can receive holiness and the title of holy. . . . Let him [i.e., Pyrrhus] hasten before all things to satisfy the Roman See, for if it is satisfied, all will agree in calling him pious and orthodox. [For] [h]e is only wasting words who thinks he must convince or lure such people as myself, instead of satisfying or entreating the blessed pope of the most holy catholic Church of Rome, i.e., the Apostolic Throne, which is from the incarnate [S]on himself and which, in accordance with the holy canons and the definitions of faith, received from all the holy councils universal and supreme dominion, authority, and the power over all God's churches throughout the world to bind and loose.[39]

38. Confessor, *Th. Pol.* 11 (PG 91: 137–40); Eng. trans. Cooper, *The Body in St. Maximus*, 181.

39. Confessor, *Th. Pol.* 12 (PG 91: 141–46); Eng. trans. in Alfeyev, *Orthodox Christianity*, 110.

The third text, *Ex epistola sancti Maximi scripta ad abbatem Thalas-sium*, is preserved only in a Latin fragment and was probably written in 640 after the emperor offered to ratify the election of Pope Severinus in exchange for Rome's acceptance of the monothelite *Ekthesis*.[40] In the letter Rome is addressed as the "first of the churches" (*princeps ecclesiarum*), the "greatest and apostolic Church" (*maximae et apostolicae ecclesiae*) and the "firm and immovable rock" (*firmae revera et immobilis petrae*).[41] If even the weak defend the faith when attacked:

> how much more in the case of the clergy and Church of the Romans, which from old until now presides over all the churches which are under the sun? Having surely received this canonically, as well as from councils and the apostles, as from the princes of the latter [i.e., Peter & Paul], and being numbered in their company, she is subject to no writings or issues in synodal documents, on account of the eminence of her pontificate even as in all these things all are equally subject to her according to sacerdotal law.[42]

Given this exalted language, it is not surprising that following the events of 1054, as Orthodox writers began to challenge the power of the pope in the Eastern Church, Latin authors employed these texts to support the unique authority of the Bishop of Rome. The *Contra Errores Graecorum* of Thomas Aquinas quoted from *Opusculum* 11 as proof that the pope had the right to decide matters of the faith, and that communion with the Roman pontiff was necessary for salvation.[43] Once again using the *Libellus* as his basis, Thomas paraphrased *Opusculum* 12 to stress the fact that "the Church united and established upon the Rock of Peter's confession we call according to the decree of the Savior the universal church wherein we must remain for the salvation of our souls and wherein loyal to his faith and confession we must obey him."[44] This proof-texting continued through the medieval period, and even during the Council of Florence the Latins' chief spokesman, John of Montenero, quoted from *Opusculum* 11 ("All Christian churches consider this Church of Rome to be the one base and

---

40. Cf. Sherwood, *An Annotated Date List*, 43.

41. Confessor, *Ex epistola sancti Maximi* (PL 129: 583–86). See also Mansi, *Sacrorum conciliorum nova* 10, 677–78.

42. Ibid.

43. Aquinas, *Contra Errores Graecorum* 36; Eng. trans. in Likoudis, *Ending the Byzantine Greek Schism*, 184.

44. Ibid., 185.

foundation") as patristic proof that the faith of Rome was the faith of the church universal.[45]

Following the promulgation of *Pastor Aeternus* in 1870, Catholic authors increasingly used Maximus' writings to support the claim that the pope's universal jurisdiction was recognized in the East during the first millennium.[46] When Protestant and Orthodox critics of papal infallibility brought forth the condemnation of Pope Honorius in order to disprove Rome's allegedly spotless record for doctrinal orthodoxy, Catholic polemicists found Maximus' defense of Honorious in *Opusculum* 20 particularly helpful.[47] They argued that Maximus witnessed to Honorius' essential orthodoxy, arguing that the pope's *Letter to Sergius* (which was not, after all, an *ex cathedra* statement of faith) could not be read as an endorsement of monothelitism. Rome's perfect record for orthodoxy, thanks to Maximus, remained intact.

A New Understanding

Beginning with the Bonn Conferences (1874–76), ecumenically minded theologians on both sides of the East-West divide began to re-examine the work of Maximus and see in his work, especially concerning the *filioque*, a road to rapprochement. A key insight was the difference Maximus drew in the *Letter to Marinus* between ἐκπορεύεσθαι of the Spirit from the Father, and his προϊέναι through the Son. Theologians increasingly realized that the Latin formula *ex Patre Filioque procedit* was a better expression of the latter idea, not the former, and spoke to the temporal/eternal "shining forth" (ἔκλαμψις or ἔκφανσις) of the Spirit through the Son without necessarily making the Son responsible for his hypostatic existence. Interpreted along these lines, there could be (from the Eastern perspective) an orthodox reading of the *filioque* because, as Maximus had been quick to point out, there still remains in the Godhead only one beginning (ἀρχή), cause (ἀιτία), and source (πηγή)—the Father.

It was for this reason that by the twentieth century several Catholic and Orthodox theologians came to see in the *Letter to Marinus* a means to reconciliation on the issue of the *filioque*. What occurred was essentially a "hermeneutical 180"—both parties no longer interpreting Maximus according

---

45. Gill, *Acta Graecorum*, 390.

46. Cf. Allnatt, *Cathedra Petri*.

47. Honorius had written about the "one sole will" of Christ, which later led to his condemnation as a monothelite at the sixth ecumenical council. Cf. Confessor, *Th. Pol.* 20 (PG 91: 228–45).

to their respective positions (i.e., using him as a proof-text), but instead allowing Maximus to become the hermeneutical lens through which their own teaching could be better understood. For the East, it meant recognizing that in the teaching of the fathers, Maximus included, one could not relegate "all references to procession διὰ Υἱοῦ "solely to the temporal mission of the Holy Spirit."[48] Orthodox theology needed to recover the patristic teaching that the Spirit comes forth as "incomprehensible Life . . . springing up wholly from . . . the beginning of all, the Father," but that it moves "towards the Son" and comes to abide in him as his goal.[49] This resting or abiding in the Son is answered by the eternal "shining forth" of the Spirit from the Son, which is what the Eastern fathers (e.g., Maximus) intended to convey when they differentiated between the Spirit's unique procession (ἐκπόρευσις) from the Father and his eternal "progression" or "shining forth" from the Son (i.e., his προϊέναι or ἔκλαμψις).[50]

Among Catholics there were those like Yves Cardinal Congar and Andres Halleaux, who explicitly endorsed this hermeneutical reversal, asking whether the West "after having affirmed for such a long time that the διὰ τοῦ Υἱοῦ was the equivalent of the *filioque* . . . [could agree] in return that the *filioque* goes back to the διὰ τοῦ Υἱοῦ . . . [and thus] recognize the fundamental authenticity of monopatrism?"[51] In 1995 the Catholic Church appeared to heed this suggestion, as it confessed that "the Father alone is the principle without principle (ἀρχὴ ἄναρχος) of the two other persons of the Trinity, the sole source (πηγή) of the Son and of the Holy Spirit . . . (who) takes his origin from the Father alone in a principal, proper, and immediate manner."[52] The Roman Catholic Church affirmed that the doctrine of the *filioque* could never contradict this truth, "nor the fact that he [i.e., the

---

48. Lossky, "The Procession of the Holy Spirit," 94. Oliver Clément echoed this belief, arguing that the Orthodox needed to recognize that "the double affirmation that the Spirit proceeds from the Father alone and that his sending by the Son concerns only his temporal mission, cannot account, it seems, for either the richness of the Revelation or for all the expressions of the Fathers." Clément, *Essor du christianisme oriental*, 18.

49. Stăniloae, *Theology and the Church*, 96.

50. On the basis of this understanding Stăniloae recognized the "orthodoxy" of certain reunion formulas then being proposed in the West, including the idea that "the Spirit proceeds from the Father who begets the Son" and "In taking his origin (ἐκπορευόμενον) from the one Father who begets the one Son, the Spirit proceeds (πρόνευση) out of the Father as origin, by his Son." However, he "judged it preferable not to use the word 'proceed' for the relation of the Spirit to the Son, since it can give the impression of a confusion of this relation with the procession of the Spirit from the Father." Instead he suggested "terms which have been used by the Eastern fathers" such as "'shines out from' or 'is manifested by'" *Spirit of God*, 177.

51. Congar, *I Believe in the Holy Spirit*, 187.

52. "The Greek and Latin Traditions," 39.

Father] is the sole origin (μία αἰτία) of the ἐκπόρευσις of the Spirit."[53] Echoing Maximus, the Vatican recognized that there was an important difference between ἐκπορεύεσθαι ("which can only characterize a relationship of origin to the principle without principle of the Trinity: the Father") and προϊέναι/ *procedere*. According to the Clarificaton, it was Maximus (whose *Letter to Marinus* was quoted at length) who best expressed the Roman teaching that "the *filioque* does not concern the ἐκπόρευσις of the Spirit issued from the Father as source of the Trinity, but manifests his προϊέναι (*processio*) in the consubstantial communion of the Father and the Son."[54]

Orthodox reaction to the Roman document was, with few exceptions, very positive.[55] Metropolitan John Zizioulas urged Rome to move even closer to Maximus' position as outlined in the *Letter to Marinus* and claimed that the "single cause" (μία αἰτία) principle should be the basis for further discussion on the *filioque*:

> for as St. Maximus the Confessor insisted . . . the decisive thing . . . lies precisely in the point that in using the *filioque* the Romans do not imply a "cause" other than the Father. . . . If Roman Catholic theology would be ready to admit that the Son in no way constitutes a "cause" (αἰτία) in the procession of the Spirit, this would bring the two traditions much closer to each other with regard to the *filioque*.[56]

Maximus had, once again, become a bridge-builder. Concerning the papacy, study of Maximus' writings continues to play an important role as Christians—Catholic, Protestant, and Orthodox—discuss and debate the issue of primacy, and in particular the role of the Bishop of Rome in the universal church.[57] While certainly there are still Catholic apologists who employ Maximus as a patristic proof-text for *Pastor Aeternus*, modern scholarship, Catholic and Orthodox, has attempted to move beyond polemics and tried to study these texts in context in order to develop a better understanding of the papal office as it was exercised in the patristic era.[58]

53. Ibid.

54. Ibid., 40.

55. A more critical assessment was offered by Larchet, "À Propos de la Récente," 3–58.

56. Zizioulas, "One Single Source."

57. Both the Anglican and Orthodox Churches are currently engaged in international dialogues on the issues of primacy, conciliarity, and the role of the Bishop of Rome. Among the more significant statements have been the 1999 ARCIC document "The Gift of Authority," and the 2007 "Ravenna Statement" issued by the Catholic-Orthodox Joint International Commission.

58. Among recent studies on Maximus' ecclesiology and the role of the papacy are

Perhaps the most detailed study of Maximus' views on the papacy comes from Jean-Claude Larchet, who examined all the texts in question in his book *Maxime le Confesseur, mediateur entre l'Orient et l'Occident*. Larchet tried to contextualize Maximus' "enthusiasm" for the papacy in light of the monothelite debates, when Rome was his sole ally against the heretical hierarchs of the East. For Larchet and others, including Andrew Louth, Maximus' exalted language about the See of Rome manifests "the glow of gratitude he [i.e., Maximus] must have felt following the Lateran synod, for the support he had found in Rome" and besides, it was "written about the *Church* of Rome, not the papacy as such."[59] This does not mean that Maximus was being disingenuous, but instead simply recognizes that these texts were written at a time when Rome alone held the line against heresy, and thus had earned the kind of praise Maximus heaped upon her.

Was the See of Rome, as Maximus seemed to say in *Opusculum* 12, equivalent to the "Catholic Church" with whom all should be in communion? When asked at his trial to which church he belonged—i.e., with which patriarchate did he have communion—Maximus replied: "'The God of all pronounced that the Catholic Church was the correct and saving confession of the faith in him when he called Peter blessed because of the terms in which he had made proper confession of him."[60] For Maximus, the true foundation of the church is Peter's faith, and in so much as Rome had consistently confessed that faith, she was the true church.[61] This was why

---

Larchet, *Maxime le Confesseur*, 125–201; Larchet, "The Question of the Roman Primacy," 188–209; Garrigues, "Le sens primaute romaine," 6–24; Louth, "The Ecclesiology of Saint Maximos," 109–20.

59. Louth, "The Ecclesiology of Saint Maximos," 117.

60. *Letter of Maximus to Anastasius*; Eng. trans. Allen and Neil, *Maximus the Confessor*, 121.

61. The interpretation of Matthew 16:18 in the East tended to emphasize Peter's confession of faith as the "rock" upon which the church is built, rather than the person of Peter himself. This is most evident in Origen's *Commentary on Matthew* 12.11, where he writes: "But if you suppose that upon the one Peter only the whole church is built by God, what would you say about John the son of thunder or each one of the Apostles? Shall we otherwise dare to say, that against Peter in particular the gates of Hades shall not prevail, but that they shall prevail against the other Apostles and the perfect? Does not the saying previously made, 'The gates of Hades shall not prevail against it,' hold in regard to all and in the case of each of them? And also the saying, 'Upon this rock I will build My Church?' Are the keys of the kingdom of heaven given by the Lord to Peter only, and will no other of the blessed receive them? . . . 'Thou art the Christ, the Son of the living God.' If anyone says this to Him . . . he will obtain the things that were spoken according to the letter of the Gospel to that Peter, but, as the spirit of the Gospel teaches to everyone who becomes such as that Peter was. For all bear the surname 'rock' who are the imitators of Christ, that is, of the spiritual rock which followed those who are being saved, that they may drink from it the spiritual draught. But these

Maximus himself preferred communion with the Romans rather than his native people (i.e., the Byzantines), because concerning the wills of Christ Rome alone had spoken correctly. He said: "I love the Romans because we share the same faith, whereas I love the Greeks because we share the same language."[62] This is why scholars like Adam Cooper rightly claim that for Maximus in the seventh century communion with the Bishop of Rome remained a "critical factor, properly inseparable from the right confession of the faith in the realization of the unity of the Church."[63] However, Cooper, Larchet, and others are also correct in recognizing that if communion with the See of Rome was normative, this state of affairs was entirely contingent on Rome's continued orthodoxy, which remained a necessary precondition for all the praise and powers she had received.[64]

However, despite his belief that Rome had thus far preserved the true faith and "shut every heretical mouth," it would be wrong to employ Maximus as a patristic witness to the idea of an infallible teaching office. In fact, during his trial Maximus accepted at least the theoretical possibility that he might be forced to break communion with Rome should it too fall victim to the monothelite madness. When told that the *apocrisarii* had arrived from Rome and were prepared to commune with the monothelite hierarchy in Constantinople Maximus would not believe it. His accusers asked him, "But what if the Romans should come to terms with the Byzantines? What will you do?" Maximus' reply was: "The Holy Spirit, through the apostle, condemns even angels who innovate in some way contrary to what is preached."[65] Maximus, it seems, had not made the logical leap from "Rome has not erred" to Rome "could not err," although the popes themselves had already begun to think along these lines.[66]

If it is inappropriate to cite Maximus as an early witness to an emerging universal jurisdictional authority or infallible teaching office, it must also be admitted that in Maximus there is far more than the "primacy of

---

bear the surname of rock just as Christ does. But also as members of Christ deriving their surname from Him they are called Christians, and from the rock, Peters" (English translation: ANF 9.456).

62. *Relatio Motionis* 11; 71.

63. Cooper, *The Body in St. Maximus*, 184.

64. Larchet, *Maxime le Confesseur*, 187–201.

65. *Relatio Motionis* 7; 63.

66. Pope Gelasius (492–96) seems to have been the first pope to assert that not only had Rome never erred with regards to doctrinal decisions, but that the Apostolic See *could not err*. For recent histories of the development of the papal teaching office see Schimmelpfennig, *The Papacy*; La Due, *The Chair of St. Peter*; Schatz, *Papal Primacy*; Eno, *The Rise of the Papacy*; Tierny, *The Origins of Papal Infallibility*.

honor" usually accorded Rome in post-schism Orthodox literature. For Maximus, Rome was indeed the *princeps ecclesiarum*, acting as a "reference and norm in terms of faith for the other churches" with the authority to bind and loose, "that is, to adjudicate exclusion from the Church and reintegration into it, not only with regards to bishops in his Church, but patriarchs who erred in heterodoxy."[67] This was why, according to Louth, it was necessary for the contrite Pyrrhus make his way to Rome; since it was the pope alone who had the authority to accept the Constantinopolitan patriarch's confession of faith.

The foundation for Rome's authority within the church is certainly linked to her record for doctrinal orthodoxy, which remains a necessary precondition for her primacy. However, Maximus also cited Rome's unique apostolic foundation as a chief reason for her place within the church, and not solely her political importance as first capital of the Empire.[68] Maximus often refers to Rome as the "Apostolic See" where the "princes" or "chiefs" (κορυφάιων) of the apostles taught and died, their tombs forever standing as a reminder of their ministry and martyrdom. In *Opusculum* 11 Maximus seemingly links Rome's record for orthodoxy with the "very promise of the Savior" in Matthew 16:18–19, perhaps indicating an exclusively Petrine grounding for Roman authority.[69] While this is still open for debate, many scholars defining Rome's apostolicity in terms of its foundation by both Peter and Paul, one certainly finds in Maximus more than an honorary primacy based on accommodation to political realities. For the Confessor, Rome's privileged place "is from the incarnate Son himself . . . and in accordance

---

67. Larchet, "The Question of the Roman Primacy," 190.

68. Orthodox theologians (e.g., John Meyendorff) have typically argued that canon 3 of Constantinople and canon 28 of Chalcedon simply "admitted the principle that ecclesiastical administration coincided with the secular structure of the Empire," grounding Rome's primacy in her political importance rather than her apostolic origin. See Meyendorff, *Byzantine Theology*, 100. Catholic theologians have tended instead to emphasize apostolic, and in particular Petrine, foundation as the true ground for Roman authority.

69. Adam Cooper is among those who accept this argument, claiming that in Maximus "Rome's pre-eminence is not seen exclusively to be conditional upon the orthodoxy of its confession, but is also bound up with the promise of Christ, his bestowal of the keys to the Church in the person of Peter, and the succession of Peter's episcopacy located in Rome." Cooper, *The Body in St. Maximus the Confessor*, 183. John Meyendorff expressed the more common Orthodox position when he wrote that the East never denied that the pope was Peter's successor, but believed that it was not "decisive" for their recognition of Rome's privileged status. For the Byzantines, Rome's "precedence over all other apostolic churches was that its Petrine and Pauline apostolicity was in fact added to the city's position as the capital city." Meyendorff, "St. Peter in Byzantine Theology," 68.

with the holy canons and the definitions of faith;" her apostolic foundation among the reasons that she will "prevail against the gates of Hades" and continue to act as the immovable rock against the raging waters of heresy.

As with the *filioque*, in the matter of the papacy Maximus challenges both East and West to re-examine the dialectic established centuries ago between a "universal ordinary jurisdiction" and a "primacy of honor." Neither position was held by Maximus in the seventh century, and it is intellectually dishonest to pretend that they were. In fact, the weight of historical evidence points instead to the far more problematic truth that in the church of the first millennium a monolithic view of the papacy's role and powers simply did not exist. A study of Maximus testifies to the complexity of the problem, in so much as he defies attempts by both sides to frame the debate in simple terms. But as was the case for modern study of the *filioque*, perhaps it is possible to perform a hermeneutical 180—i.e., interpreting the primacy according to the witness of the fathers rather than trying to fit the patristic witness into post-schism categories. Admittedly, this would not be simple; but as Protestant, Catholic, and Orthodox scholars discuss and debate the role of the Bishop of Rome in the undivided church, it seems that this approach is far more honest, and more promising.

3

A Logician for East and West
Maximus the Confessor on Universals

CHRISTOPHE ERISMANN

The philosopher and theologian of the seventh century Maximus the Confessor provides an excellent example of the development of logic in Christian context during late Antiquity and the early Byzantine period.[1] His reflections are the result of an insightful reading of earlier patristic thought—in particular of the original and powerful ontology developed by Gregory of Nyssa[2] and the revised version of Aristotelianism upheld by Leontius of Byzantium[3]—and of good knowledge of the works of the Neoplatonic school of Alexandria, which was probably acquired thanks to Stephen of Constantinople and his teaching at the Imperial Academy.

1. From an historical point of view, the attitude of late ancient Christian authors slowly evolved with regard to Aristotelian logic, beginning with direct opposition and condemnation of logic as exogenous to Christian thought, and concluding with adoption and wide use, in particular for defining terms and for clarifying reasoning. For a general sketch of this movement, see de Ghellinck, "Quelques appréciations de la dialectique," 5–42; and Frede, "Les Catégories d'Aristote," 135–73. Maximus belongs to an era which was favorable to logic.

2. On Gregory's ontology, see Cross, "Gregory of Nyssa on Universals," 372–410 and the chapter on Gregory of Nyssa in Erismann, *L'Homme commun*, 149–86.

3. See Reindl, *Der Aristotelismus bei Leontius von Byzanz* and Moutafakis, "Christology and Its Philosophical Complexities," 99–119.

Maximus is an important milestone in the history of logic in early Byzantine philosophy, both because of his own work and because many collections of definitions and compendia of logic came to circulate under his name and authority.[4] The fact that it was transmitted under Maximus' name probably gave this logical matter enhanced legitimacy and helped its acceptance. His contribution to this area, in particular insofar as the theory of universals is concerned, was to be influential not only in the Greek-speaking East, but also in the Latin West.

I will proceed in three steps in this contribution: first, I will place Maximus' logical thought in the context of the study of logic in Christian milieu and present the terms of the discussion about universals as it was held in the philosophical circle of his time; I will then analyze Maximus' theory of universals—one of the logical-ontological problems of his time (and of ours); and I will conclude with some brief remarks on the posterity of his solution, both in the Greek-speaking East and the Latin-speaking West.

Maximus' Contribution in Context

Considering Maximus' logical-ontological thought makes necessary a sketch of the intellectual movement in which it takes place, the slow appropriation of Aristotelian logic by Christian authors of late Antiquity. I shall make some remarks about what must be understood by logic in this context and who are the relevant authors.

What is meant by logic? Obviously not a formal language but a set of philosophical terms of direct or mediate Aristotelian origin, reflections about their reference in reality, and finally some powerful explanatory conceptual schemes—first and foremost the content of Aristotle's *Categories* and of the text which was supposed to introduce them, the Neoplatonist Porphyry's *Isagoge*.[5] Just like Aristotle's *Categories*, Christian logic is a reflection on predication and on its grounding in things, on the types of beings there are, and on the relation of language to reality; it also involves a clearly ontological dimension. In the *Categories*, Aristotle provides the means of classifying both predicates and beings. This classification of beings and predicates was to be a seminal conceptual scheme for later philosophical thought, both in pagan and Christian contexts, (Greek, Syriac, and Latin thought). The Aristotelian theory of categories was the foundation of logical and ontological

---

4. A good example is provided by Rouéché, "A Middle Byzantine Handbook," 71–98.

5. Let us add the theoretical elements drawn from the *De interpretatione* and syllogistics, however these elements only play a minor role in the argument of this article.

thought in late Antiquity and the first centuries of the Middle Ages. The *Categories* provided the theoretical tools which later reflection developed and structured. Among the tools are: the division of substance and accident (a property that is either essential or accidental); the criteria of inherence and predication (*esse in* and *dici de*); the ontological square consisting of the exhaustive classification of beings into particular or primary substances (e.g., Peter or Paul); universal or secondary substances (e.g., the species cat, tortoise, etc); particular accidents (this white) and universal accidents (e.g., the color red); and the classification in ten categories (substance, quantity, quality, relation, etc.). In the *Isagoge*, Porphyry provided a complement to these instruments by adding remarks on individuality, genera and species, and the relation between an individual and the universals that are predicated of it.

When speaking of the history of logic in Christian context, it is important to distinguish two groups of authors. First, there were the Christian Neoplatonic philosophers who were generally members of the School of Alexandria and did not write theological works but authored commentaries on Aristotle.[6] Second, there were theologians who, in their theological work, appeal to Aristotelian logic in order to clarify their terminology and strengthen their reasoning. There are more examples of this methodology from the middle of the sixth century onwards, such as Theodore of Raithu in his *Proparaskeue* and Leontius of Byzantium. Their interest in logic stems first and foremost from the fact that it is understood as permitting—maybe even as consisting in—an adequate definition of terms. A correct definition of fundamental terms (*ousia, physis, hypostasis*, etc.) was taken to be a good way of avoiding heresy, according to a conception which became widespread from the sixth century onwards in Christological debates related to Chalcedon (in particular in the opposition to Miaphysites). Only two authors worked both as theologians and as exegetes of Aristotle: Boethius and John Philoponus.

Maximus belongs to the second group. We must not expect from authors of this group, and therefore from Maximus, an explicit and detailed theory of universals or a proper theory about logic and its ontological implications. Such authors tend to state only what they need in order to develop the metaphysics and the theology they wish to put forth. In the case of Maximus, the textual materials present in the *Ambigua*, in the *Opuscula theologica et polemica* 14, 23, 26 (hereafter *OThP*),[7] and in *Letters* 12 and 15

---

6. Elias and David are typically Christian names, but their texts do not betray any Christian commitment whatsoever; on this point see Wildberg, "Three Neoplatonic Introductions to Philosophy," 33–51.

7. Doubts have been formulated as to the authenticity of some of the *Opuscula* (*Th.*

are sufficiently rich to allow a reconstruction of his position and to situate him on the map of the various possible types of ontologies.

Maximus provides a good example of the Christian trend of rethinking Aristotelian logic, which reached its climax with John of Damascus' *Dialectica*.[8] Maximus' motivation is essentially theological in nature—he wishes, among other things, to defend the conclusions of the Council of Chalcedon. He nevertheless demonstrates a philosophical background[9] and training, which was remarkable for the time period. Maximus was very much involved in Christological discussions—which included (in philosophical terms) the problem of the relation between an individual and its nature, that is, its species. It is therefore not surprising to find him discussing universals and their mode of being. He develops a realist theory of universals, which is of Aristotelian inspiration. Maximus' thought about universals takes place against a twofold background: the Aristotelian and Porphyrian logical tradition[10] and its exegesis by Neoplatonic philosophers from the School of Alexandria on the one hand, and Christian logic on the other—mainly the new understanding of *ousia* as common and synonymous with *physis*—which had been developed by the Cappadocian fathers and by Leontius of Byzantium.

The Late Ancient Problem of Universals

Among the philosophers of the Neoplatonic School of Alexandria—the main institutional framework for the practice of philosophy in the time of Maximus—the problem of universals was a codified question, which was supposed to be discussed at a given step of the curriculum of studies and in a precise exegetical context. The debate was determined by the three questions Porphyry asks in his introduction to Aristotle's *Categories* called the *Isagoge* (note that the two fundamental texts for the contribution of the

---

Pol.); useful remarks, especially as to the case of *Th. Pol.* 23, are to be found in Roosen, "Epifanovich Revisited." I will not enter this discussion here. While Maximus may well not have been the author of this or that Opuscule, it nonetheless seems correct to consider that they reflect his position and state his understanding of the matter, as confirmed by the presence of similar elements in works whose authenticity is not doubted, some of the *Letters* for example.

8. On John Damascus' reading of the *Categories*, see Erismann, "A World of Hypostases," 251–69.

9. On this, see remarks in Mueller-Jourdan, *Typologie spatio-temporelle de l'ecclesia Byzantine* and Lackner, "Studien zur philosophischen Schultradition."

10. A good overview of Maximus' knowledge of logical tools is given by. Törönen, *Union and Distinction*, 13–34.

"philosophers" are the same as those which provide the basis of Maximus' logical knowledge). The *Isagoge* was studied at the beginning of the Neoplatonic course of studies, after the Prolegomena to philosophy, and before Aristotle's *Organon*, which began with the *Categories*.

At the beginning of his *Isagoge*, Porphyry asks three questions the answer to which lies, according to him, in more advanced studies than the logic he proposes to introduce. His exegetes do not follow this methodological recommendation and make the *Isagoge* the place where they discuss this issue. Porphyry asks about natural genera and species, "whether they subsist, whether they actually depend on bare thoughts alone, whether if they actually subsist they are bodies or incorporeal, whether if they actually subsist they are bodies or incorporeal, and whether they are separable or are imperceptible items and subsist about them."[11]

The Neoplatonic exegesis of the *Isagoge* and the attempts to answer Porphyry's questions allowed an interesting doctrinal construction to emerge, which provides a synthesis of Platonic and Aristotelian elements. This doctrine defines three states of universals:[12]

1. The universals *before* the many (πρὸ τῶν πολλῶν): these are a revised version of Platonic ideas, interpreted as the models, the creative *logoi* or ideal paradigms, which subsist in the Demiurge's intellect (or in the mind of God in a Christianized version of the doctrine)

2. The universals *in* the many (ἐν τοῖς πολλοῖς): the forms that are immanent to individuals;

3. The universals *after* the many (ἐπὶ τοῖς πολλοῖς): the abstract concepts of immanent forms. This threefold division is sometimes associated with three points of view: the "theological," the "physical," and the "logical."

Alexandrian Neoplatonic thought took place after strong criticisms of Platonism, first by Aristotle in the *Categories*, then by the Stoics, and finally by Alexander of Aphrodisias. This deflationist move had as a result

---

11. Porphyry, *Isagoge* 1: 9–14 (in Busse, *Porphyrii Isagoge*): αὐτίκα περὶ τῶν γενῶν τε καὶ εἰδῶν τὸ μὲν εἴτε ὑφέστηκεν εἴτε καὶ ἐν μόναις ψιλαῖς ἐπινοίαις κεῖται εἴτε καὶ ὑφεστηκότα σώματά ἐστιν ἢ ἀσώματα καὶ πότερον χωριστὰ ἢ ἐν τοῖς αἰσθητοῖς καὶ περὶ ταῦτα ὑφεστῶτα, παραιτήσομαι λέγειν βαθυτάτης οὔσης τῆς τοιαύτης πραγματείας καὶ ἄλλης μείζονος δεομένης ἐξετάσεως. As noted by Chiaradonna, "What is Porphyry's *Isagoge?*" 21, this list of questions provides a list of four modes of being: pure concepts, bodies, separable incorporeals, and immanent incorporeals: "the list provides a preliminary . . . map of Porphyry's ontology which includes transcendent incorporeals, immanent incorporeals . . . and bodies."

12. For a formulation of this doctrine, see, among others, Proclus, *In primum Euclidis elementorum,* 50:16—51:6.

the abandonment of a strong theory of separate Platonic universals. There was a general agreement at the time not to recognize existence to universals separate from individuals, with the exception of divine ideas.

A good example of the state of reflection on these issues a few decades before Maximus' contribution is provided by Ammonius (ca. 435/445–517/526), who held a chair of philosophy at Alexandria. In his commentary on Porphyry, he introduces the Neoplatonic theory of the three states of universals as follows:

> In order to explain what [Porphyry's] text means, let us present it with an example, for it is not true that [philosophers] refer simply and by chance to some things as bodies, to others as incorporeals, but they do it after reasoning, and they do not either contradict each other, for each of them says reasonable things. Imagine a ring with a seal [representing] for example Achilles, and a number of pieces of wax; suppose that the ring imprints its seal into all the pieces of wax; suppose now that someone comes later and looks at the pieces of wax and notices that all [the imprints] come from the same seal; he will have in himself the mark, that is, the imprint, in his discursive faculty; so we can say that the seal on the ring is "before the multiple," the imprint in the wax is "in the multiple," and the one which is in the discursive faculty of the one who imprints it is "after the multiple" and "posterior in the order of being;" this is what must be understood in the case of genera and species.[13]

In the following part of the text (41:20—42:26), Ammonius applies the distinction of the three modes of being of universals to the case of the universal man. The Demiurge has, in his mind, the idea of the universal man, which is the archetypal paradigm for the creation of particular men. The universals before the multiple are intelligible substances, which precede sensible individuals. The universal man is also understood as the form of man, which is, according to Ammonius, the same for all the individuals of the species (πάντες τὸ αὐτὸ εἶδος τοῦ ἀνθρώπου ἔχουσιν). This form is

---

13. Ammonius, *In Porphyrii Isagogen*, 41:10-20: "Ἵνα δὲ σαφὲς ᾖ τὸ λεγόμενον, δι' ὑποδείγματος διεξέλθωμεν τῷ λόγῳ. οὐδὲ γὰρ ἁπλῶς οὕτως καὶ ὡς ἔτυχεν οἱ μὲν σώματα αὐτὰ λέγουσιν οἱ δὲ ἀσώματα, ἀλλὰ μετὰ λογισμοῦ τινος, οὐδὲ ἐναντιοῦνται ἀλλήλοις· εἰκότα γὰρ ἕκαστοι λέγουσιν. ἐννοείσθω τοίνυν δακτύλιός τις ἐκτύπωμα ἔχων, εἰ τύχοι, Ἀχιλλέως καὶ κηρία πολλὰ παρακείμενα, ὁ δὲ δακτύλιος σφραγιζέτω τοὺς κηροὺς πάντας. ὕστερον δέ τις εἰσελθὼν καὶ θεασάμενος τὰ κηρία, ἐπιστήσας ὅτι πάντα ἐξ ἑνός εἰσιν ἐκτυπώματος, ἐχέτω παρ' αὐτῷ τὸν τύπον ὅ ἐστι τὸ ἐκτύπωμα ἐν τῇ διανοίᾳ. ἡ τοίνυν σφραγὶς ἡ ἐν τῷ δακτυλιδίῳ λέγεται πρὸ τῶν πολλῶν εἶναι, ἡ δὲ ἐν τοῖς κηρίοις ἐν τοῖς πολλοῖς, ἡ δὲ ἐν τῇ διανοίᾳ τοῦ ἀπομαξαμένου ἐπὶ τοῖς πολλοῖς καὶ ὑστερογενής. τοῦτο οὖν ἐννοείσθω καὶ ἐπὶ τῶν γενῶν καὶ εἰδῶν.

inseparable from sensible individuals. Finally, after having observed several men, we form by abstraction in our mind the concept of man on the basis of the common characteristics that are shared by all men. This concept is posterior (ὑστερογενής)[14] to individuals. This general orientation can be recognized in Maximus' thought; the main lines of his ontology are compatible with those of Neoplatonic Alexandrinian scholasticism.

Maximus on Universals

Maximus develops two theories[15] in relation to the problem of universals: his theory of *logoi* and his theory of universals properly speaking. This means that he states an exemplarist theory and an ontological theory—in Neoplatonic terms, a theory of universals before the many (*ante rem*) and a theory of universals in the many (*in re*). The first of these theories has been well studied, in particular by Torstein Tollefsen.[16] Since the present article concentrates on the second theory, a brief summary of the first is sufficient. *Logoi* are divine thoughts that pre-exist creation and to the entities themselves. There are *logoi* both of universal entities and of individuals. God has a *logos* of the human species and also a *logos* of Socrates. To each created thing corresponds a *logos*. Divine knowledge or wisdom is identified with the sum of all the *logoi*.

Beside this doctrine, Maximus develops a theory of universals, which cannot be identified with that of *logoi*. Maximus' position on universals was influenced by a number of authors who preceded him. In particular, his theory is strongly determined by the thought of the Cappadocian fathers—Basil of Caesarea and Gregory of Nyssa—in the fourth century. The main doctrinal result of Cappadocian thought on these matters is a reformulation of the distinction that Aristotle makes in the *Categories* between primary substances (individual entities) and secondary substances (genera and species). The Cappadocians reverse Aristotle's pattern, in which both types of entities are given the name *ousia* and in which primacy is attributed to individuals. They keep the distinction between particular and universal entities, but reformulate it in terms of a distinction between *ousia* and hypostasis. They state that the distinction between *ousia* and hypostasis must

---

14. The term obviously originates in Aristotle's *De anima*; see Aristotle, *De anima*, I, 1 (402 b7): "the universal animal either is nothing or is posterior," (τὸ δὲ ζῷον τὸ καθόλου ἤτοι οὐθέν ἐστιν ἢ ὕστερον).

15. I keep for a later study the issue of concept formation according to Maximus.

16. See Tollefsen, *The Christocentric Cosmology*, 64–137 (chapter 3); Tollefsen, "Unity in Plurality," 115–22. See also Dalmais, "La théorie des '*logoi*,'" 244–49.

be understood as analogous to the distinction between that which is common (*koinon*) and that which is proper or particular (*idion*), that is, as the distinction between species and individual.[17] Therefore there exist common entities (*ousiai*) and particular entities (*hypostases*). The distinction between primary and secondary substances is reformulated with the help of a non-Aristotelian concept, that of hypostasis. The Aristotelian couple primary/secondary substance is replaced by the couple hypostasis/essence (*ousia*). This thesis postulates that an *ousia* is necessarily common. It involves a restriction in the definition of the word *ousia* and a drastic reduction of the number of entities that can be counted as *ousiai*. If an *ousia* is, by definition, a common (and in this sense, universal) entity, this means that individuals cannot be *ousiai*. Individuals are instances of common *ousiai*—their species or nature—but cannot themselves be considered as *ousiai*; they are hypostases. "*Ousia*" then refers only to the specific (and occasionally generic) essence, and not to the individual entity, which is referred to by "*hypostasis*." In consequence, in philosophical language, what Gregory means by *ousia* is only Aristotle's secondary substance. The term *ousia* is used only to refer to essence, understood as an Aristotelian secondary substance, which is common to all the members of the same species.

Maximus endorses this understanding of *ousia* as being necessarily common. He knows Aristotle's terminology of primary substances, but does not retain it in his own thought: he prefers to give the name "hypostasis" to the individual considered as a particular instance of a common substance. An *ousia* in Maximus' ontology is a universal entity.[18] Consider the following statement:

> Essence and nature are the same thing. Both belong to what is common and universal, insofar as they are predicated of many things which differ in number and insofar as they are never circumscribed in one person.[19]

17. According to Basil of Caesarea, *Lettres* I, 53:1–3 (*Letter* 236): "There is the same difference between essence and hypostasis as between what is common and what is particular, for example, between animal and a certain man" (Οὐσία δὲ καὶ ὑπόστασις ταύτην ἔχει τὴν διαφορὰν ἣν ἔχει τὸ κοινὸν πρὸς τὸ καθ᾽ ἕκαστον, οἷον ὡς ἔχει τὸ ζῷον πρὸς τὸν δεῖνα ἄνθρωπον).

18. I agree completely with Thunberg, *Microcosm and Mediator*, 84: "for both Leontius and Maximus, Aristotle's *substantia prima* has more or less disappeared . . . and thus the element of individuality is no longer safe-guarded by the term [οὐσία] in any of its senses."

19. Confessor, *Th. Pol.* 14 (PG 91: 149B): ἄμφω γάρ κοινόν καί καθόλου, ὡς κατά πολλῶν καί διαφερόντων τῷ ἀριθμῷ κατηγορούμενα, καί μήποτε καθοτιοῦν ἑνί προσώπῳ περιοριζόμενα. In the absence of a critical edition, texts are quoted from Migne's *PG*, which uses for Maximus' text the edition by Combefis, *S. Maximi Confessoris*

It is possible to understand more precisely what Maximus means by *ousia*. He presents "species" (εἶδος), "nature" (φύσις), and "*ousia*" as synonymous (PG 91, 260D–261A). By these terms, he refers to a universal entity of which the members are individuals and not other universals, that is, most special species in Porphyry's terminology.

This has an important doctrinal consequence: admitting the real existence of universal entities. If essences are necessarily common, this means that either they really exist according to a mode of being which remains to be outlined, or they do not exist. The second alternative would be equivalent to saying that the sensible world completely lacks substance and is just a heap of accidents. As this is unacceptable from the traditional Aristotelian point of view, the first alternative is the one to be retained, as confirmed in the following passage, in which Maximus endorses a definition, and which refers to the Cappadocian fathers:

> an essence is . . . according to the Fathers, a natural entity (ὀντότης φυσική) which is [predicated] of several which differ by hypostases.[20]

An *ousia* is a natural kind—a ὀντότης φυσική as Maximus calls it. *Ousiai*, that is specific universals, are naturally existing realities. For Maximus, as for the earlier philosophical tradition, the problem of universals is that of the status of natural genera and species; artifacts are not taken into account and not much interest is dedicated to species and genera of categories other than that of substance.

Maximus merges two aspects of the problem of universals: that of predicability and that of multiple realizabilities. This can be seen in the two ways in which *ousia* is described: *koinon* ("common," an ontological description) and *katholon* ("universal"), a description related to predication. An *ousia* is universal in that it can be predicated of many, and it is common in that it is an entity which can be multiplied realized and, in consequence, shared by individuals, which are spatially and temporally different. Multiple realizability grounds predication. Because the universal is completely realized in the individual, it is correct to predicate the universal name of the individual. The proposition "Socrates is a man" is correct because Socrates fully instantiates the specific universal man.

The way in which Maximus uses expressions like "difference by hypostases" or "by number" highlights the community of essence. Individuals

---

Graecorum.

20. Ibid., *Th. Pol.* 26 (PG 91: 276A): Οὐσία ἐστί . . . κατά δέ τούς Πατέρας, ἡ κατά πολλῶν καί διαφερόντων ταῖς ὑποστάσεσιν ὀντότης φυσική. I understand this sentence with the κατηγορούμενον from two lines above.

of the same species do not differ essentially from one another; they are, in Maximus' words, consubstantial (ὁμοουσίοι),[21] a concept that originates in Trinitarian theology. *Homoousios* is that which has the same essence as another, like Peter and Paul, but differs by the characteristics of its hypostasis (i.e., by its accidental properties). Particulars are not individuated by their essence, but only by their accidents.

The mode of being of *ousiai* is clearly set forth. These entities only exist in particular individuals. Maximus' ontology contains particular individuals and universal entities. These universal entities are fully realized in individuals and have no separate existence. Maximus proves this with the help of the classical argument of deletion:

> If universals consist of particulars, then if the particular examples of any *logos* in accordance with which things exist and consist should perish, then it is quite clear that the corresponding universals will not continue to be.[22]

Maximus' theory is straightforward: take the example of the species cat. If all particular cats ceased to exist, the universal cat, which only exists

21. The use of this term to speak about the human species is traditional in patristic thought from the fourth century onwards. We find it in the writings of Athanasius of Alexandria, who applies the term ὁμοούσιος to the human species in his second Letter to Serapio, where he states that, as men, "we are consubstantial to one another" (*Ad Serapionem*, II, 3 [PG 66: 612B; SC XV, 150]: ὁμοούσιοί ἐσμεν ἀλλήλων). The same use may be found in Gregory of Nyssa, one of the most important sources of Maximus. In his treatise *On the Distinction of Ousia and Hypostasis* (formerly known as Basil of Caesarea's *Letter* 38), Gregory states the following: "When several are taken together, as for example, Paul, Silvanus, and Timothy, and one seeks a definition of the substance of these human beings, no one will give one definition of substance for Paul, another for Silvanus, and yet another for Timothy. No, whatever the terms used to indicate the substance of Paul, they will also apply these to the others, and they are consubstantial with one another who are designated by the same definition of substance" (250–51), *Letter* 38, in Basil, *Lettres* I, 19–26: Ὅταν οὖν δύο ἢ καὶ πλειόνων κατὰ τὸ αὐτὸ ὄντων, οἷον Παύλου καὶ Σιλουανοῦ καὶ Τιμοθέου, περὶ τῆς οὐσίας τῶν ἀνθρώπων ζητεῖται λόγος, οὐκ ἄλλον τις ἀποδώσει τῆς οὐσίας ἐπὶ τοῦ Παύλου λόγον, ἕτερον δὲ ἐπὶ τοῦ Σιλουανοῦ καὶ ἄλλον ἐπὶ τοῦ Τιμοθέου, ἀλλὰ δι' ὧν ἂν λόγων ἡ οὐσία τοῦ Παύλου δειχθῇ οὗτοι καὶ τοῖς ἄλλοις ἐφαρμόσουσι, καί εἰσιν ἀλλήλοις ὁμοούσιοι οἱ τῷ αὐτῷ λόγῳ τῆς οὐσίας ὑπογραφόμενοι. The application of the vocabulary of consubstantiality to the human species came to be approved, much later, by the Council of Chalcedon, as this text speaks of the twofold consubstantiality of Christ, with the Father in divinity on the one hand, and with all men in humanity on the other hand (ὁμοούσιον τῷ Πατρὶ κατὰ τὴν θεότητα καὶ ὁμοούσιον ἡμῖν τὸν αὐτὸν κατὰ τὴν ἀνθρωπότητα).

22. Confessor, *Amb.* (PG 91: 1189CD): Εἰ γάρ τά καθόλου ἐν τοῖς κατὰ μέρος ὑφέστηκεν, οὐδαμῶς τό παράπαν τόν τοῦ καθ' αὐτά εἶναί τε καὶ ὑφεστάναι λόγον ἐπιδεχόμενα τῶν κατὰ μέρος διαφθειρομένων παντί που δῆλόν ἐστιν ὡς οὐδέ τά καθόλου στήσεται.

in particular cats, would also cease to exist. Universals are therefore ontologically dependent on particulars. Even if his terminology differs from that
of Aristotle, Maximus agrees with the position stated in *Categories* 2b6–7,
where Aristotle notes that without primary substances, the other entities
could not subsist. Maximus bases his thought on the same principle as Aristotle in the *Categories*: substantial individuals (*hypostases* in the case of
Maximus) are the foundation of all reality. The only entities endowed with
independent existence are the *hypostases*. The other entities—such as specific and generic universals—only exist in the hypostases. The particulars
provide the ontological basis on which universals exist. Maximus adapts to
the notion of *hypostasis* the Aristotelian thesis in the *Categories* according
to which the primary substance allows the existence of the other entities.

According to Maximus, it is thus possible to conceive the suppression
of a universal. This sets a contrast between *ousia* and *logos*: a *logos* pre-exists
individuals and is not affected by their cessation. By contrast, a universal
ousia begins to exist with the first individual and ceases to exist when the
last one disappears. Its existence is simultaneous to that of the individuals.

Universals subsist in the individuals that instantiate them. This instantiation is a complete realization: the universal is fully present in each
individual. Maximus states that the particular has in itself the entire (ὅλον)
universal.[23] This position allows Maximus not only to follow the teaching
of the *Categories* in which it is said that substance does not admit more or
less,[24] it also allows him to avoid postulating degrees of being or of substance; indeed both his Aristotelian readings and the anti-Arian polemics
had encouraged him to become very wary of degrees of being.

Universals exist in *hypostases* fully and as universals. *OThP* 23—a text,
which is not by Maximus, but reflects his beliefs—states that a *hypostasis*
is composed of a specific common essence (which is in this sense universal) and of a bundle of properties, which makes the *hypostasis* particular.[25]
This allows Maximus to state that a *hypostasis* is "that which possesses, in
addition to the universal (μετὰ τοῦ καθόλου), particularity (ἰδικόν)."[26] The
hypostasis does not have its own essence, but shares a common essence
with all the other members of the species. That which makes it particular

---

23. Confessor, *Letter* 12 (PG 91: 489D): ὡς τοῦ μερικοῦ, ἤτουν ἰδικοῦ ὅλον ἔχοντος ἐν
ἑαυτῷ τό καθόλου, ἤτοι τό κοινόν καί γενικόν, πληρέστατον.

24. Aristotle, *Categories,* 2B22–28 and 3B33–4A9.

25. Confessor, *Th. Pol.* 23 (PG 91: 265D): Ὑπόστασίς ἐστιν, ἡ τό κοινόν τε καί
ἀπερίγραπτον ἐν τῷ τινι ἰδίως παριστῶσα καί περιγράφουσα, οἷον ὁ δεῖνα.

26. Confessor, Ὑπόστασίς ἐστι, τό μετά τοῦ καθόλου, ἔχον τι καί ἰδικόν.

is, following the explanation of individuality given by Porphyry,[27] a unique bundle of non-essential properties.

The interesting element that Maximus brings to the problem of universals, and which justifies the interest a historian of philosophy may take in his position, is the attempt he makes to conceive the immanence of the universal in the individual. He uses the term *enhypostaton*—which originates in Christological debates[28]—in order to qualify the mode of being of the specific universal, that is the realization of the species in the individuals. As Maximus himself says (*OThP* 14): *enhypostaton* is that which exists naturally (φυσικῶς) in individuals.[29] Here, the idea of existence is expressed by καθ' ὕπαρξιν.

The interesting point in Maximus' texts is that he applies explicitly the concept of *enhypostaton* to specific universals. He takes up, and adds emphasis to, the formulation of the concept of *enhypostaton* provided by Leontius of Byzantium;[30] but Leontius' text does not mention species. In

27. In the *Isagoge*, Porphyry states that its unique bundle of properties (ἄθροισμα ἰδιοτήτων) makes one individual distinct from other individuals of the same species (*Isagoge*, 7: 19–27). Porphyry's explanation was quickly taken up, and elaborated upon, by Christian authors as early as the fourth century (see Basil, *Contra Eunomium*, II, 4, 21 and II, 28, 31).

28. For a history of the term *enhypostaton*, see Gleede, *The Development of the Term* ἐνυπόστατος, 139–55.

29. Confessor, *Th. Pol.* 14 (PG 91: 152D–153A): Ἐνυποστάτου ἴδιόν ἐστι, ἢ τό μετ' ἄλλου διαφόρου κατά τήν οὐσίαν ἐν ὑποστάσει γνωρίζεσθαι καθ' ἕνωσιν ἄλυτον· ἢ τό ἐν ἀτόμοις φυσικῶς τυγχάνειν καθ' ὕπαρξιν.

30. In his *Contra Nestorianos et Eutychianos*, Leontius of Byzantium provides a clear formulation of what must be understood about *enhypostaton* as a description of the mode of being of *ousia*: the fact of having being in another without being an accident. The idea is to conceive non-separate existence (as opposed to a separate Platonic existence, in which case the substance would be seen in itself) for universal substances: "hypostasis and *enhypostaton* are not the same thing, just as substance and *enousion* are different. For hypostasis indicates the individual and *enhypostaton* indicates the substance. And hypostasis marks off the person through characteristic properties, whereas *enhypostaton* indicates that something which has its being in another and is not seen in itself is not an accident. Such are all qualities, those that are called essential and those that are called added to the essence, neither of which is substance, that is, an subsistent thing, but is always seen around substance, like color in a body and knowledge in a soul" (οὐ ταὐτὸν ᾧ οὗτοι ὑπόστασις καὶ ἐνυπόστατον ὥσπερ ἕτερον οὐσία καὶ ἐνούσιον· ἡ μὲν γὰρ ὑπόστασις τὸν τινὰ δηλοῖ τὸ δὲ ἐνυπόστατον τὴν οὐσίαν· καὶ ἡ μὲν ὑπόστασις πρόσωπον ἀφορίζει τοῖς χαρακτηριστικοῖς ἰδιώμασι· τὸ δὲ ἐνυπόστατον τὸ μὴ εἶναι συμβεβηκὸς δηλοῖ ὃ ἐν ἑτέρῳ ἔχει τὸ εἶναι καὶ οὐκ ἐν ἑαυτῷ θεωρεῖται· τοιαῦται δὲ πᾶσαι αἱ ποιότητες αἵ τε οὐσιώδεις καὶ ἐπουσιώδεις καλούμεναι ὧν οὐδέτερα ἐστιν οὐσία τουτέστι πρᾶγμα ὑφεστὼς ἀλλὰ ὃ ἀεὶ περὶ τὴν οὐσίαν θεωρεῖται ὡς χρῶμα ἐν σώματι καὶ ὡς ἐπιστήμη ἐν ψυχῇ.)(PG 86: 1277C). The issue of *enhypostaton* in Leontius has been the subject of several studies, among others: Krausmüller, "Making Sense of the Formula of Chalcedon," 484–513; Lang, "*Anhypostatos-Enhypostatos*," 630–57; Gockel,

contrast, Maximus links the term with the problem of universals, in particular when he states that *enhypostaton* means that "which by no means
subsists by itself, but is considered in others, as a species in the individuals
subordinate to it."[31] A universal is *enhypostaton* in that it is not a *hypostasis*,
but subsists in the individual *hypostases*, which are under it in the structure
of Porphyry's Tree. The universal man does not have its own hypostasis, but
subsists in the hypostasis of Peter, in that of Paul, etc.

In the *OThP* 14, Maximus adds, in relation to the *enhypostaton*, "that
which is common according to the essence, i.e., the species, is that which
subsists really (πραγματικῶς) in the individuals which are subordinate to it,
and it is not considered in a pure concept."[32]

This last definition is interesting on several accounts: it highlights community as being a characteristic of the specific universal, and it states the immanence of universals, which exist in the individuals that are placed under
them. But most importantly, it rejects a conceptual reading of the position
of Maximus. The universal *really* subsists in the individuals (πραγματικῶς is
the word used by Maximus), and it is not a conceptual construct. Maximus
rejects both a Platonic conception of universals in which they exist separately (and therefore in which universals would be their own *hypostases*) and a
nominalist theory in which universals only have conceptual existence. In its
ontological sense, the word *enhypostaton* expresses the ontological status of
that which does not exist independently like a *hypostasis*, but which subsists
as realized in a *hypostasis*, e.g., a species or a nature. An entity that is *enhypostaton* does not subsist independently but is realized in all the *hypostases*
under it, and, in consequence, it is considered to be in them. *Enhypostaton*
is the mode of being of universals. They do not exist, following Plato, in a
separate or independent way, but only, following Aristotle, in the individuals—the *hypostases*. That which is *enhypostaton* only exists in *hypostases*,
without itself being a *hypostasis*. Therefore, human nature is not considered
in a *hypostasis* of its own, but in each individual human being.

Note that when Maximus, in our passage, states that a universal essence is not just a mere concept (οὐκ ἐπινοίᾳ ψιλῇ); he deliberately uses the

---

"A Dubious Christological Formula?" 515–32.

31. Confessor, *Letter* 15 (PG 91: 557D–560A): ἐνυπόστατον δέ, τό καθ' αὐτό μέν
οὐδαμῶς ὑφιστάμενον, ἐν ἄλλοις δέ θεωρούμενον, ὡς εἶδος ἐν τοῖς ὑπ' αὐτό ἀτόμοις.

32. Ibid., *Th. Pol.* 14 (PG 91: 149BC): Ἐνυπόστατόν ἐστι, τό κατά τήν οὐσίαν κοινόν,
ἤγουν τό εἶδος, τό ἐν τοῖς ὑπ' αὐτό ἀτόμοις πραγματικῶς ὑφιστάμενον, καί οὐκ ἐπινοίᾳ
ψιλῇ θεωρούμενον. The wording which is chosen here to characterize *ousia* ontologically—πραγματικῶς ὑφιστάμενον—is strongly influenced by Leontius of Byzantium's
vocabulary, from which Maximus borrows in particular the concept πρᾶγμα ὑφεστώς
(*Contra Nestorianos et Eutychianos*, PG 86: 1277C).

vocabulary of Porphyry's first question about the status of universal entities in the *Isagoge*, which also indicates that Maximus' theory of universals is a philosophical answer to this problem. In the *Isagoge*, Porphyry states the question of whether universals exist or whether they are pure concepts (ἐν μόναις ψιλαῖς ἐπινοίαις).[33] This is also proof of the extent of Maximus' philosophical culture.

So Maximus distinguishes two modes of being. The first is that of the *hypostasis* (a concrete existence as an entity which allows all other entities to subsist), and the second is that of the *ousia*, understood as a secondary substance or a nature, common to all the individuals of a species, which exists in a number of *hypostases* as *enhypostaton*, that is, as having reality thanks to, and in, *hypostases*. To be *enhypostaton* is a necessity for the universal. Non-instantiated universals do not exist.

Enhypostaton is the concept used to express the fact that an entity is immanent in a *hypostasis*. The idea is to elucidate the relation of a species to its individuals not in terms of predication, but in terms of an ontological relation. In the *Categories*, the only available pattern for a relation of inherence seems to have been that of an accident in a subject. The mode of being of accidents in a substance is insufficient to conceive the immanence of universals. The concept of *enhypostaton* seems to provide Maximus with an understanding of immanence for essential entities, a way in which to think inherence in a different manner from the inherence of accidents. *Enhypostaton* expresses a mode of immanent being in the individual, which is proper to essential entities. One could even say that the notion of *enhypostaton* fills a gap in the system of the *Categories*. In Aristotle's work, secondary substances are said not to be in a subject (3A8) contrary to accidents. However, they depend on primary substances and only exist in them. Their mode of being is not named in the *Categories*.

Maximus gives to material reality and particularity an attention that is unusual in the Christian Alexandrian and Platonic traditions. He upholds the reformulation of Aristotelian logic given by his predecessors, but is, more than them, open to the anti-Platonism of the *Categories*. His way of making individuals the ontological support of universals, thereby stating their ontological priority, and of developing the notion of *enhypostaton* in order to express the immanent mode of being of universal entities indicate

---

33. Porphyry, *Isagoge*, 1:9–14: αὐτίκα περὶ τῶν γενῶν τε καὶ εἰδῶν τὸ μὲν εἴτε ὑφέστηκεν εἴτε καὶ ἐν μόναις ψιλαῖς ἐπινοίαις κεῖται εἴτε καὶ ὑφεστηκότα σώματά ἐστιν ἢ ἀσώματα καὶ πότερον χωριστὰ ἢ ἐν τοῖς αἰσθητοῖς καὶ περὶ ταῦτα ὑφεστῶτα, παραιτήσομαι λέγειν βαθυτάτης οὔσης τῆς τοιαύτης πραγματείας καὶ ἄλλης μείζονος δεομένης ἐξετάσεως. Emphasis is mine.

his return to the central theses of the *Categories*, even if he does not use Aristotle's vocabulary.

An Epilogue about Influence

Maximus' logical and ontological contribution was to have an influential posterity. In the Greek-speaking world, Maximus' thought was diffused by compendia of logic. But the text that was to contribute the most to his posterity was John of Damascus' *Dialectica*[34] or *Capita Philosophica*. This text is a reasoned exposition of the philosophical content of Porphyry's *Isagoge*, of Aristotle's *Categories*, and of elements that are proper to the patristic tradition, the majority of which come from Maximus. John of Damascus accepts the main points of Maximus' ontology. One example of Maximus' solution can be found in John of Damascus' *Dialectica* (I have insisted on the philosophical interest of the notion of *enhypostaton*, as Maximus uses it in relation to the ontological status of species):

> In its proper sense, the *enhypostaton*

>> is . . . that which does not subsist in itself but is considered in *hypostases*, just as the human species, or human nature, that is, is not considered in its own *hypostases* but in Peter and Paul and the other human hypostases.[35]

The fact that this definition is included in the *Dialectica*, that is, in a presentation of the philosophical concepts that are necessary for theological thought, in the midst of a summary of the notions that are to be found in Aristotle's *Categories*, shows well Maximus' influence. In the mind of his Greek-speaking readers for the beginning of the Byzantine era, Maximus grounded the association of this term with the ontology of the *Categories*. It shows that Maximus instated a precise ontological reading of this concept, which expresses the immanence of the species in the individuals/hypostases under it.

Note that John of Damascus' reception of Maximus was also influential in the Latin world: the *Dialectica* was translated into Latin in the twelfth century by Burgundio of Pisa and was widely read thereafter. Maximus'

---

34. On John's dialectic, see Richter, *Die Dialektik des Johannes*. See also Oehler, "Die Dialektik des Johannes," 287–99 and Siclari, *Giovanni di Damasco*.

35. Damascus, *Dialectica*, 110: 7–10: Κυρίως δὲ ἐνυπόστατόν ἐστιν ἢ τὸ καθ' ἑαυτὸ μὲν μὴ ὑφιστάμενον ἀλλ' ἐν ταῖς ὑποστάσεσι θεωρούμενον, ὥσπερ τὸ εἶδος ἤγουν ἡ φύσις τῶν ἀνθρώπων ἐν ἰδίᾳ ὑποστάσει οὐ θεωρεῖται ἀλλ' ἐν Πέτρῳ καὶ Παύλῳ καὶ ταῖς λοιπαῖς τῶν ἀνθρώπων ὑποστάσεσιν.

ideas in the text benefitted from this diffusion. A consequent part of Maximus' influence in the Latin West took place before the ninth century. The Carolingian philosopher and theologian John Scottus Eriugena translated Maximus' *Ambigua ad Iohannem* and *Quaestiones ad Thalassium.*[36] He was very receptive to his thought.[37] He translated the significant passage on the fact that the universal is deleted if all individuals placed under it are deleted.[38]

36. These translations have been edited in two works: Maximi Confessoris, *Ambigua ad Iohannem* and *Quaestiones ad Thalassium.* On Eriugena's translations, see Jeauneau, "Jean Scot traducteur de Maxime," 257–76.

37. See Kavanagh, "The Influence of Maximus," 567–96.

38. Confessor, *Ambigua ad Iohannem* (PL 101:1654–59): *Si enim uniuersalia in particularibus subsistunt, nullo modo omnino per seipsa esse et subsistere rationem accipientia, particularibus corruptis, undique clarum est quomodo neque uniuersalia stabunt: partes enim in uniuersalitatibus et uniuersalitates in partibus et sunt et substitutae sunt, et nulla contradicit ratio.*

PART TWO

Anthropology, Christology, and Spirituality

4

The Imitation of Christ according to Saint Maximus the Confessor

TIMOTHY KALLISTOS (WARE)

"What is your aim as a Christian?
To imitate Christ . . . the great and hidden mystery . . ."

ST. JOHN CHRYSOSTOM[1]

Every aspect of the teaching of St. Maximus the Confessor, and not least his interpretation of the imitation of Christ, is to be understood in the light of what was for him the heart and focal point of all theology: the incarnation of God the Word. As he affirmed in *Questions to Thalassius*, "This is the great and hidden mystery, this is the blessed end on account of which all things were created. This is the divine purpose foreknown before the creation of the world."[2] As these words indicate, Maximus did not regard the incarnation of Christ simply as a contingency plan designed to put things right after they had gone astray through the fall. The incarnation expresses,

---

1. Chrysostom, *Adversus Judaeos*, VIII, 9 (PG 48: 941).
2. Confessor, *Ad Thal.* 60 (CCSG 22: 75, 32–35).

on the contrary, God's original intention for his creation. It is not only the answer to sin but also the key to the meaning of the cosmos in its totality.

Such an approach to the incarnation immediately calls to mind the standpoint of other thinkers in both East and West: in particular, Maximus' contemporary St. Isaac of Nineveh, *alias* "Isaac the Syrian,"[3] and the thirteenth-century Schoolman Duns Scotus. It leads us to ask: Would God have become incarnate, even if there had been no fall into sin? Now this is for us a hypothetical and even an unreal question, for the only situation that we actually know by personal experience is that of a fallen world; and, as Fr. Georges Florovsky has pointed out,[4] the fathers did not concern themselves with hypothetical questions. However, if we persist in putting such a query to Maximus, then his answer must surely be in the affirmative. The incarnation is part of God's primordial purpose in creating the world. Creation and incarnation are integrally related.

Developing this view of the incarnation as the key to the meaning of the cosmos, Maximus understood it not merely as an historical event in the past that has happened once for all, but equally as a continuing and contemporary reality that is to be accomplished in the personal life of each one of us. "The divine Word of God," he wrote in the *Ambigua* or *Disputed Questions*, "wills to affect the mystery of His Incarnation always and in everyone."[5] Taking up an idea put forward by Origen and St. Gregory of Nyssa, Maximus held that Christ is to be born in the soul of each believer through the action of love: "It is always Christ's will to be born mystically, becoming incarnate through those who are saved, and making the soul that gives birth to Him a virgin mother."[6]

Maximian theology, in the words of Canon A. M. Allchin, can be described as "a great hymn to the unity of all things."[7] This is conspicuously true of his treatment of the incarnate economy of Christ. As he stated in a fundamental passage of the *Ambigua*, the purpose of the economy is

---

3. See Hausherr, "Un précurseur de la théorie," 316–20; reprinted in Hausherr, *Etudes de Spiritualité Orientale*, 1–5. Compare Alfeyev, *The Spiritual World of Isaac the Syrian*, 49–53.

4. Florovsky, "*Cur Deus Homo?*," 163–70, 310–14, especially 164.

5. Confessor, *Amb.* 7 (PG 91: 1084CD).

6. Ibid., *Expositio orationis dominicae*, 50, 397–400. Compare Origen, *Fragm.* 281, 11–15, 126; *Fragm.* 21.5, 235; Nyssa, *De Virginitate* II.2, 20–21, 268.

7. Allchin, "Foreword" to Lars Thunberg, *Man and the Cosmos*, 9. This work by Thunberg, together with his larger monograph *Microcosm and Mediator*, still provides the best overview in English of the theology of Maximus. Also to be recommended is the introduction to Maximus, with selected texts in translation and full bibliography, by Louth, *Maximus the Confessor*.

precisely to draw all things to unity. Christ overcomes the five basic dualities in the created order:

1. that between male and female, overcome through his virgin birth;

2. that between this world and paradise, overcome through his death and resurrection;

3. that between earth and heaven, overcome though his ascension;

4. that between the sensible and the intelligible, overcome through his sitting at the right hand of God;

5. that between the created and the uncreated, overcome in and through his very person, since as God incarnate he is both these things at once.

In confirmation of all this, Maximus ended this fundamental passage by appealing to Ephesians 1:10 and Colossians 1:6: "Thus, [Christ] fulfills the great purpose of God the Father, to recapitulate all things both in heaven and on earth in Himself, in whom everything has been created."[8] As he put it in the *Centuries on Love*, "The aim of divine providence is to unite by means of a right faith and spiritual love those separated in various ways by vice. Indeed, the Savior endured His sufferings for this very reason, in order to gather together into one the scattered children of God."[9]

"He who imitates the Lord . . . ."

Such is the context in which we should set Maximus' theology of the imitation (μίμησις) of Christ. The crucial importance that he attached to this notion of imitation is evident from the opening words of his dialogue *The Ascetic Life*:

> A brother asked an old man and said, "Please, father, tell me: What was the purpose of the Lord's becoming man?" The old man answered and said, "I am surprised, brother, that you ask me about this, since you hear the symbol of faith every day. Still, I will tell you: the purpose of the Lord's becoming man was our salvation." Then the brother said, "How do you mean, father?" The old man replied, ". . . Taking flesh by the Holy Spirit and the Holy Virgin, He showed us a godlike way of life, and He gave us holy commandments . . . ." Then the brother said, "And who, father, can perform all the commandments? There are so many."

---

8. Confessor, *Amb.* 41 (PG 91: 1304D).

9. Ibid., *De Char* IV.17, 200. See John 11:52.

The old man said, "He who *imitates the Lord* and follows in His footsteps."[10]

Dom Polycarp Sherwood rightly observed comments on this passage: "Imitation can be said to be one of the central themes of Maximus' spirituality."[11] Maximus regarded the impulse to imitate as an inherent characteristic of the "gnostic intellect" (γνωστικὸς νοῦς). "In its manner of life," he said, "[the intellect] imitates the natural laws of created things; it imitates the heavens, the sun, the eagle, the deer, the lion, the snake, the turtle dove, and so on, learning from each some quality that it needs to reproduce in itself."[12] Doubtless Maximus has been influenced here by the *dictum* of Aristotle: "Man differs from the other animals, in that he is greatly given to imitation."[13] Imitation is not only a human attribute, for, as Maximus pointed out, it is also characteristic of the animals in general.[14] Not surprisingly, René Girard quoted the words of Aristotle; but I do not think that Girard ever mentioned Maximus.

Although Maximus recognized that the intellect imitates all created things, for him imitation meant primarily and fundamentally the imitation of Christ. We are, he said, to take Christ as our "exemplar" (here he used the Latin word *exemplarium*), as our "pattern" (ὑπογραμμός) and "model" (ὑποτύπωσις). He continued: "Looking to Him, as the pioneer of our salvation, we attain the virtues through imitation, so far as this is possible for us."[15] Imitation makes the Christian "another Christ:" "Achieving all things through imitation of Christ, he becomes another Christ."[16] It is thus our vocation to be transformed into "living icons" of the Lord.[17]

This imitation of Christ has two aspects. It involves both death and resurrection (cf. Rom 6:3–5), both cross-bearing and glorification. We are to imitate the Savior first and foremost in his *kenosis*, in his self-emptying and humiliation; but we are to imitate him also by participating in his divine life.

10. Ibid., *LA* 1.3 (PG 90: 912AB, 913B).

11. Sherwood, *St. Maximus the Confessor*, 240. Sherwood draws attention to the valuable article of Hausherr, "L'imitation de Jésus Christ," 231–59; reprinted in Hausherr, *Etudes de Spiritualité Orientale*, 216–45, see especially 246–51 (in the reprint, 232–37).

12. Confessor, *Ad Thal.* (CCSG 7: 399–403, 82–135); Blowers, *Exegesis and Spiritual Pedagogy*, 144–45.

13. Aristotle, *Poetics* 4 (1448B).

14. Confessor, *Amb.* 10 (PG 91: 1189B).

15. Confessor, *Ad Thal.* 65 (CCSG 22: 301, 769–73); See Heb 2:10.

16. Confessor, *Ad Thal.* 29 (CCSG 7: 215, 64–65).

17. Confessor, *Amb.* 21 (PG 91: 1253D).

Imitation of the kenotic *Logos* is a recurrent theme in the Maximian *corpus*. Through imitation we are called to acquire the tender-hearted meekness that Jesus displayed throughout his incarnate life: "Just as Christ humiliated himself, taking the form of a servant" (Phil 2:7) and manifesting this humility to humankind in himself in both deed and word, so also the Christian, "imitating Him," is to "acquire gentleness and humility."[18] Faithful to this divine example, those who truly believe in Christ will, like him, refrain from any kind of retaliation. "As exact imitators of Him and as genuine keepers of His commandments," they will apply to themselves the apostle's words: "When reviled, we bless; when persecuted, we suffer it; when slandered, we try to conciliate" (1 Cor 4:12).[19] As Maximus put it, developing the point:

> He who loves Christ is bound to imitate Him to the best of his ability. Christ, for example, was always conferring benefits on people; He was longsuffering when they were ungrateful and blasphemed Him; and when they beat Him and put Him to death, He endured it, imputing no evil at all to anyone.[20]

Imitation of Christ signifies in this way that we are to reproduce in ourselves his "love for humankind" (φιλανθρωπία) by suffering with all who are in distress and by taking their burdens upon our own shoulders:

> Let us strive to make our own the afflictions of others, so that in our relations with our own kind we may imitate Him who "took upon Himself our infirmities and bore our diseases" (*Isaiah.* 53:4; *Matthew* 8:17). Let us honour through our actions the self-emptying, full of love for us (φιλάνθρωπον), which He underwent for our sake, that we too may be counted worthy to behold His glory and to participate in it.[21]

This imitation of the kenotic Christ means, among other things, that we share in his experience of temptation: "The Lord Himself set an example for us by being tried in the desert by the chief of the evil spirits; and then, after returning to civilization, He was tried also by those possessed by the demons."[22] Thus, when assailed by temptation, we are to keep our gaze "fixed on the Lord's example (τύπος):"

---

18. Confessor, *Ep.* 13 (PG 91: 509CD).
19. Confessor, *LA* 34 (PG 90: 940B).
20. Confessor, *De Char.* IV.55; Eng. trans. Ceresa-Gastaldo, 216.
21. Confessor, *Ep.* 12 (PG 91: 505A).
22. Confessor, *LA* 5 (PG 90: 916B).

The demons either tempt us directly or arm against us those who have no fear of the Lord. They tempt us directly when we withdraw from human society, as they tempted our Lord in the desert. They tempt us through other people when we spend our time in the company of others, as they tempted our Lord through the Pharisees. But, whichever line of attack they choose, let us repel them by keeping our gaze fixed on the Lord's example.[23]

The most striking occasion on which Christ set us an example of resistance to temptation was his agony in the garden of Gethsemane. This event in the Gospels led Maximus to insist—during the monothelite controversy—upon the possession by the incarnate Christ of a human will and of genuine human freedom.[24] In Maximus' words:

> When He said as man, "Not My will but Yours be done" (*Luke* 22:42), He gave Himself as a type and example of the setting aside of our own will, so as to fulfil perfectly the divine will, even though because of this we find ourselves face to face with death. . . . As man, He who is also God by nature wills in accordance with the economy that the cup may pass from Him; and in this way He typifies what is human, as the wise Cyril [of Alexandria] taught us, so that He may take away from our nature all shrinking from death, and may steel and arouse us to a brave assault against it, I mean against death.[25]

In every respect, then, we are to live "in a manner that imitates Christ" (Χριστομιμήτως).[26] Above all, such imitation means following him upon the way of the cross. If we are to show "living and active faith" in the Lord, this signifies that we are to gain "the power of His Cross and death, of His burial and resurrection." Thus we are to become "like Him in everything except for identity with Him in nature."[27] We are to obey his injunction to the one who seeks to be a disciple, "Let him deny himself and take up his cross and follow me" (Matt 16:24).[28] Just as Jesus made a "good confession" before Pontius Pilate, it is our hope "that we also may be accounted worthy through

---

23. Confessor, *De Char.* II.13, 94–96.

24. See Lethel, *Théologie de l'agonie du Christ.*

25. Confessor, *Th. Pol.* 7 (PG 91: 80D, 84BC).

26. Confessor, *Th. Pol.* 8 (PG 91: 92B).

27. Confessor, *Ep.* 25 (PG 91: 613CD). On the significance of the last clause, "except for identity with Him in nature," see below, note 43.

28. Quoted in Confessor, *Amb.* 32 (PG 91: 1284D).

His grace to imitate Him in this, if the occasion arises," even though it may lead to martyrdom.[29]

While exhorting us in these various ways to imitate Christ, Maximus also reversed this in a bold and somewhat unexpected manner, maintaining that God in his turn is also to imitate us. He derived this notion of "mimetic inversion" from Gregory of Nyssa. Expounding the clause in the Lord's Prayer, "Forgive us our trespasses, as we forgive those who trespass against us" (Matt 6:12), Gregory suggested that in saying this we are, as it were, issuing an order to God: "What I have done, do You do likewise; let the Lord imitate the servant."[30] One who says the Lord's Prayer, stated Maximus, "makes himself a pattern of virtue for God. . . . He exhorts God, who is beyond all imitation, to come and imitate him . . . and he begs God to treat him as he himself has treated his neighbour."[31] In this way, "God and man are exemplars (παραδείγματα) to each other."[32]

". . . becoming everything that God is . . . ."

Thus far, we have been examining what Maximus had to say about the imitation of Christ in his *kenosis*. It is time to consider the second and complementary aspect of *imitatio Christi*: the following of Christ in his glory. Extending the scope of such imitation to include instances from sacred history before Christ, in *Ambigua* 10 Maximus mentioned persons in the Old Covenant who made God their model and exemplar. Moses was one such instance: "Having made God Himself the type and paradigm of the virtues, he modelled himself on Him, like a picture faithfully preserving an imitation of the archetype. . . . Because of his participation in glory, his face shone with grace before all men, so that he became a figure of the Godlike figure."[33]

Alongside Moses' vision of God at Sinai, Maximus appealed also to Elijah's vision at Horeb: "Wondering at its glory and wounded by its beauty, he longs to emulate it."[34] Another notable example of one who imitated God is Melchizedek, and in his case, the imitation is to be seen as specifically Christological:

29. Confessor, *Ep.* 14 (PG 91: 544AB).

30. Nyssa, *De oratione Dominica, hom.* 5, 23–4. See Ware, "'Forgive Us. . . as We Forgive,'" 53–76, especially 68–69.

31. Confessor, *Or. Dom.* (CCSG 23: 64, 23–24).

32. Confessor, *Amb.* 10 (PG 91: 1113B).

33. Confessor, *Amb.* 10 (PG 91: 1117C). See Exod 31:29–35; 2 Cor. 3:13.

34. Confessor, *Amb.* 10 (PG 91: 1124A). See 1 Kgs 19:9–13.

He was worthy to be made like the Son of God. For, so far as is
possible, he became by grace and disposition such as the Giver
of grace is Himself believed to be by essence. . . . He was counted
worthy to be an image of Christ our God and of His ineffable
mysteries. . . . Through the unchanging inclination of his will
towards good he imitated Him who is by nature unchanging.[35]

Yet another Old Testament example of divine imitation was Abraham, who "was mystically assimilated by faith to the *logos* concerning the Monad."[36]

In these instances taken from the Old Testament, it is noteworthy that Maximus did not speak only of imitation, but used the much stronger language of participation or incorporation: Moses enjoyed "participation in glory;" Melchizedek became "by grace" what God is "by essence;" Abraham was "assimilated" to God. In the words of Maximus already quoted, it is said that, by imitating Christ in his *Kenosis*, "we too can be counted worthy to behold His glory and to participate in it."[37] As Maximus asserted in *Ambigua* 10, the soul of the saint is "ineffably assimilated to God;" "he attains true and blessed union with the Holy Trinity," and "so far as is possible he imitates through the habit of the virtues the goodness that remains ever unchanging."[38]

Now in itself the language of imitation can be understood in a moralistic and even a Pelagian sense. It might imply no more than a following of Christ (or God) from afar, a copying of him from a distance through our own ethical conduct and ascetic effort. But the passages cited above clearly indicate that Maximus had in view something far more forceful and organic. *Imitatio Christi* involves not merely an external resemblance but a direct "sharing" and "participation," a realistic "assimilation" and "union." Between Christ, our divine exemplar, and us there is contact, touching, an exchange and interpenetration by which we humans are radically transformed. Fr. Sophrony, founder of the Orthodox Monastery of St. John the Baptist in Essex, exactly sums up the Maximian understanding of imitation in the title of a book: *His Life Is Mine.*

The close connection that Maximus envisaged between imitation and participation is evident from the way in which, within a single sentence, he

---

35. Confessor, *Amb.* 10 (PG 91: 1137D, 1141C, 1145A). See Gen 14:18–20; Ps 110:4; Heb 6:20—7:22.

36. Confessor, *Amb.* 10 (PG 91: 1200B: compare 1145D).

37. Confessor, *Ep.* 12 (PG 91 : 505A); see note 21. On the concept of participation in Maximus, see Tollefsen, *The Christocentric Cosmology*, 239–78.

38. Confessor, *Amb.* 10 (PG 91: 1193D–1196AB).

juxtaposed the noun μέθεξις and the adverb εὐμιμήτως: "The one who can do good, and who actually does it, is truly God by grace and participation (κατὰ χάριν καὶ μέθεξιν), because in happy imitation (εὐμιμήτως) he has taken on the energy and characteristics of God's own beneficence."[39]

What makes possible this imitation of Christ's glory and our direct participation in it is precisely the event that, as we have already emphasized, lies at the heart of Maximus' entire theology: the incarnation of God the Word. In a striking way he expounded the meaning of the incarnation in terms of mutual exchange, using what Dr. Lars Thunberg has called "the *tantum-quantum* formula"[40] (in Greek, (τοσοῦτον . . . ὅσον). God's descent at the incarnation has made possible man's ascent to deification (θέωσις). To invert the saying of Heraclitus, the way down and the way up are one and the same.[41] Just as God's assumption of our humanness is full and complete, so to the same extent our human participation in the divine life is full and complete, apart from the proviso that Maximus was careful to specify in the passage cited earlier, "except for identity with Him in nature."[42]

As Maximus asserted in a key passage:

> Man becomes God to the same extent that (τοσοῦτον . . . ὅσον) God becomes man; for because of God man is elevated by divine ascension to the same degree that God, for man's sake, has emptied Himself and descended without change to the last extremities of our nature.[43]

God's descent to the depths, through incarnation, crucifixion, and death, renders possible man's ascent to the heights of the divine realm. God goes down to hell, and man goes up to heaven. As Maximus wrote elsewhere, concerning those who, by observing the commandments, "assiduously cultivate the beauty given to them by grace:" "By emptying themselves of the passions they lay hold of the divine to the same degree as that to which (τοσοῦτον . . . ὅσον) the *Logos* of God, deliberately emptying Himself of His own sublime glory, became truly man."[44]

There is in this manner a two-way exchange or, as Maximus expressed it, "a blessed transposition." God has assumed from us our human nature, and in return has communicated to us his divine life: "God becomes man

39. Confessor, *Myst.* 24 (CCSG 69: 68, 1122–25).

40. Thunberg, *Man and the Cosmos*, 171.

41. Heraclitus, Fragment 60, 164.

42. Confessor, *Ep.* 25 (PG 91: 613D); see note 27.

43. Confessor, *Amb.* 60 (PG 91: 1385BC).

44. Confessor, *Or. Dom.* (CCSG 23: 32–33, 102–6).

for the sake of man's deification, and man becomes God through God's Incarnation. . . . The icon ascends to the Archetype."[45] God's hominization and man's deification are correlative. "He deifies us by grace to the same extent that (τοσοῦτον . . . ὅσον) He became man by nature according to the economy."[46]

In all this Maximus was developing a theme that has deep roots in Scripture and in the earlier patristic tradition. The notion of salvation through mutual participation is found already in the Epistle to the Hebrews and the Gospel of John. A key concept in Hebrews is the solidarity and kinship between Christ the High Priest and those for whom he makes intercession: "He who sanctifies and those who are sanctified are all of one stock" (2:11; compare 2:17; 4:15). Such also is the *leitmotif* of the high-priestly prayer in John 17: "As you, Father, are in me, and I in you, so also may they be one in us. . . . The glory that you have given me I have given to them, that they may be one even as we are one: I in them and you in me, may they be perfectly one" (17:21-23). Christ is the door (John 10:7), Jacob's ladder (John 1:51), the portal and bond of union between earth and heaven. He is one with God the Father and at the same time one with us; through him and in him we are made one with God, and the Father's glory becomes our glory.

Even more explicitly, St. Paul foreshadowed Maximus' *tantum-quantum* formula: "You know the grace of our Lord Jesus Christ, that though he was rich, yet for your sake he became poor, so that through his poverty you might become rich" (2 Cor 8:9). Christ's riches are his eternal glory, while his acceptance of poverty denotes his identification with our fallen human condition. The sharing is reciprocal: Christ shares in our death, and we share in his life.

What St. Paul expressed metaphorically in terms of riches and poverty, St. Irenaeus of Lyons stated more directly: "We follow the only sure and true Master, the *Logos* of God, our Lord Jesus Christ, who in His superabundant love became that which we are, so as to make us to be that which He is."[47] In the epigrammatic phrase of St. Athanasius of Alexandria, "He became man

---

45. Confessor, *Amb.* 7 (PG 91: 1084C, 1085C).

46. Confessor, *Ad Thal.* 65 (CCSG 22: 237, 784-86).

47. Irenaeus, *Adversus Haereses* V.14. Compare *Adv. Haer.* IV.20.2, 630: the "Light of the Father" shines forth from the flesh of Christ (a reference to the Transfiguration?); we in our turn are "enfolded" in that Light, and so the glory of the Father becomes *our* glory. Compare John 17:22.

that we might become God."[48] As Gerard Manley Hopkins affirmed, "I am all at once what Christ is, since He was what I am."[49]

Because Maximus in this way based his ascetic theology of imitation and participation upon the reality of Christ's incarnation, it is abundantly evident that he was very far from being a Pelagian in his soteriology. Christ as Savior has not merely set us an example, which we have then to imitate by our own efforts. It is true that imitation of Christ demands from us, on the human side, the active involvement of our free will. But such imitation by our own free will is only possible because of what Christ has already effected through his divine initiative. *Imitatio Christi* is not just subjective, but it is made possible by the objective fact that God has become man. It therefore presupposes at every point the presence and effectual operation of God's grace. It is to be interpreted not solely in a moralistic sense but in *ontological* terms.

According to Maximus, then, imitation leads to deification.[50] That which God is by nature, we humans are called to become by grace. Linking this with the doctrine of our creation in the divine image, Maximus wrote: "What He is in His essence the creature may become by participation. That is why man is said to be created in the image and likeness of God." Making a distinction between image and likeness, he continued: "Every intelligent nature is in the image of God, but only the good and wise attain His likeness."[51] "With all the fullness of our being," stated Maximus, "we coinhere fully in the fullness of God, becoming everything that God Himself is, except for identity of essence."[52] He even went so far as to assert in the *Ambigua* 7, "God and those worthy of God have in all things one and the same energy."[53] We note here the careful distinction that Maximus made between the divine essence and the divine energies. Anticipating St. Gregory Palamas in the fourteenth century, he maintained that the saints are united to God in his energies, whereas his essence remains beyond participation.[54] We attain

48. Athanasius, *De incarnatione* 54. Compare Athanasius, *Ad Adelphium* 4 (PG 26: 1077A): "He became man that He might deify us in Himself."

49. "That Nature is a Heraclitean Fire and of the comfort of the Resurrection," in *Poems of Gerard Manley Hopkins*, 112.

50. On Maximus' understanding of *theosis*, see most recently Russell, *The Doctrine of Deification*, 262–95.

51. Confessor, *De Char.* III.25 (Ceresa-Gastaldo, 120–39).

52. Confessor, *Amb.* 41 (PG 91: 1308B). Compare *Ep.* 25 (PG 91: 613D): "except for identity with Him in nature" (see notes 27 and 43).

53. Confessor, *Amb.* 7 (PG 91: 1076C).

54. On Maximus' use of the essence-energies distinction, see Karayiannis, *Maxime le Confesseur*; Tollefsen, *The Christocentric Cosmology*, 174–238; Renczes, *Agir de Dieu*

communion with God according to his energies, but not, as already emphasized, "identity with Him in nature."[55]

As well as claiming that God and the saints have one and the same
energy, Maximus also asserted that they share a single will. As he said in his
letter to John the Cubicularius (one of his earliest surviving writings), "In
this way [i.e., through the action of love] we are all as it were one nature, so
that we are able to have one inclination (γνώμη) and one will (θέλημα) with
God and with one another."[56] At a later stage, however, through his involvement in the monothelite controversy, Maximus grew more cautious about
such language, qualifying his earlier statements to this effect. "Describing
the state of the saints that will come to pass in the future," he wrote, "I said
that God and the saints will have one energy. I was referring here to that
energy which will deify all the saints in the blessedness for which we hope,
and I meant that the energy which God has by essence will become also
that of the saints by grace." Maximus then went on to qualify this. "It should
rather be said that the energy is *that of God alone*, whereas the deification
of the saints by grace is a *consequence* of this unique divine energy."[57] The
qualification made here by Maximus, concerning God and man sharing the
same energy, presumably applies equally to what he said concerning the two
sharing a single will. The saints do not have in the literal sense one identical
will with God—just as Christ's human will was not identical with his divine
will—but through voluntary obedience they conform their will to his.

". . . possessing without diminution all that is ours . . ."

In alluding above to the monothelite controversy, we have touched upon
a matter that is directly relevant to Maximus' understanding of imitation
and participation. His primary concern in that controversy was the completeness of the human nature that Christ assumed at his incarnation. If
his humanness were incomplete, then the scheme of "exchange soteriology,"
expressed in the *tantum-quantum* formula, would be fatally undermined.

---

et liberté. In using this distinction, Maximus was doubtless influenced by the Cappadocians; for a classic statement of the distinction, see Basil, *Ep.* 234, 372. On Maximus
and Palamas, see Thunberg, *Man and the Cosmos*, 137–43; Joost van Rossum, "The
λόγοι of Creation," 212–17. Allowance must be made for the different ways in which
the essence-energies distinction was understood in the Cappadocians, Maximus, and
Palamas: see the special issue of the review *Istina* (1974), particularly the articles by
Houdret and Garrigues.

55. See note 53.

56. Confessor, *Ep.* 2 (PG 91: 396C).

57. Confessor, *Th. Pol.* 1 (PG 91: 33A).

To exclude any such eventuality, Maximus insisted: "He becomes complete man, from us, on our account, and as we are, possessing without diminution all that is ours, apart from sin."[58] This integral fullness of Christ's human nature entails his possession more particularly of a human will, alongside the divine will that he shares with the Father and the Holy Spirit.

Maximus sought at all times to safeguard the integrity of Christ's human freedom. He wished to give full meaning to Christ's temptations; and these temptations would not have been real if he did not possess genuine liberty of choice, and therefore a truly human will. That is why Maximus attached such crucial importance to the agony in the garden of Gethsemane, when Christ alluded explicitly to his human will, distinguishing it from the divine will of the Father (Luke 22:42). Our salvation, according to Maximus, is in this way *willed by a divine Person*, but it is *willed in a fully human manner*, in and through a genuinely human will. Here Maximus combined the primary insights of both Alexandrian and Antiochene Christology: ". . . by a divine Person"—here he was reproducing the standpoint of St. Cyril of Alexandria, the Neochalcedonians and the Fifth Ecumenical Council; ". . . in a fully human manner"—here he was safeguarding the heritage of Antioch, reaffirmed after his death by the Sixth Ecumenical Council.

All of this is directly relevant to Maximus' doctrine of imitation. It is precisely because there is in Christ authentic human free will that he is thereby able to serve as our model for imitation. As Maximus expressed it:

> In Himself and through Himself, as man He made that which is human subject to God the Father; and in this way He gave Himself to us as the best model for imitation, so that, looking to Him as our guide to salvation, by our own free choice we may bring what is ours into harmony with God, and may no longer will anything except what He wills.[59]

What we see in the incarnate Christ, that is to say, is a human will that is veritably free, yet voluntarily obedient to the divine will; and so, by virtue of this willing submission to God the Father on Christ's part, we humans are enabled to imitate Christ, making our own free will voluntarily obedient to the will of God. If the Savior did not possess a human will, then our endeavor to imitate him would be deprived of its objective Christological basis.

---

58. Confessor, *Amb.* 41 (PG 91: 1309A). See Heb 4:15.
59. Confessor, *Pyrrh.* (PG 91: 305CD).

"The body is deified along with the soul"

There is one further point in Maximus' teaching on imitation that remains to be emphasized. Imitation of Christ involves on our part the total human person, body as well as soul. At this point, it is necessary to proceed with caution, for there are passages in the works of Maximus that might be interpreted—or, rather, misinterpreted—in a dualistic sense, appearing as they do at first sight to denigrate the body. There is, for example, his definition of self-love (φιλαυτία) as "passionate attachment to the body,"[60] or "an impassioned and mindless friendship with the body."[61] But in such passages, correctly understood, the term "body" signifies not primarily human physicality but sinful selfishness. Likewise, there is Maximus' complex teaching concerning sexuality and marriage, where, following Gregory of Nyssa, he associated these things with the fallen condition of humankind. Nevertheless, this does not mean that they are intrinsically sinful, for they are ordained by God Himself.[62]

Counterbalancing, however, the statements of Maximus concerning *philautia* and sexuality, there are other places where he endorses a holistic, unitive approach to human personhood. In the *Centuries on Theology*, for example, he declared: "The body is deified along with the soul."[63] He even adopted a positive attitude towards passion (πάθος), dissenting here from Clement of Alexandria and Evagrius, and agreeing with Pseudo-Dionysius the Areopagite.[64] According to the Areopagitic writings, anger, desire, and the other passions are "not simply evil by nature," but can be put to good use; our ascetic struggle has as its aim not to suppress these impulses but to redirect them.[65] He is therefore willing to use the term *eros* to denote not only sexual appetite, but longing for God.

Following the Areopagite, Maximus maintained that *pathos* is not to be negated but to be transformed: desire can become divine longing (*eros*),

---

60. Confessor, *De Char.* II.8 (Ceresa-Gastaldo, 92).

61. Confessor, III.8, 146. On φιλαυτία, see Hausherr, *Philautie: de la tendresse,* citing in detail the extensive use of this term in ancient philosophy and in Christian writers prior to Maximus. See also Thunberg, *Microcosm and Mediator,* 244–62.

62. See Balthasar, *Cosmic Liturgy,* 196–205. He concludes that, for Maximus, "the sexual synthesis" remains "too overloaded by the tragedy and the despairing dialectic of original sin to find a positive place among the syntheses achieved by Christ" (203–4). But this does not signify that Maximus regarded sexuality as in itself sinful.

63. Confessor, *Cap. Gnost.* II.88 (PG 90: 1168A).

64. See Ware, "The Meaning of 'Pathos,'" 315–22.

65. Dionysius, *DN* IV.25 (PG 4: 728B), 173.

anger can become divine love (*agapi*).[66] The passions, that is to say, can be "praiseworthy" as well as "reprehensible;"[67] it is even possible to speak of "the blessed passion of divine love."[68] He deliberately applied to the experience of union with God language that has strongly sexual undertones: "erotic conjunction" (ἐρωτικὴ συνάφεια),[69] "erotic fusion" (ἐρωτικὴ σύγκρασις),[70] "erotic ecstasy" (ἐρωτικὴ ἔκστασις).[71] The passible, passionate aspect of the soul, and its incensive power, are not to be repressed and repudiated but employed to positive effect in our mystical ascent.

Indeed, Maximus was positive in his estimate, not only of the human body, but also equally of the material creation as a whole. Expounding the threefold way pursued by the spiritual aspirant—*praxis, physiki,* and *theoria*—he gave a clear Christological foundation to the second stage, "natural contemplation:" contemplating the realm of nature, we apprehend the inner principles or *logoi* implanted within creation by the divine *Logos* himself.

Such is the broader context, holistic and cosmic, in which we should place Maximus' understanding of the imitation of Christ.

"The greatest is love"

Underlying the whole of Maximus the Confessor's spirituality, and not least his notion of imitation and participation, there is one dominant mastertheme: the primacy of love. It is love that provides the motive for imitation. Love is the golden key that unlocks all the doors in the Maximian castle. "Faith and hope," he wrote, "will last up to a certain point; but love, united beyond union with Him who is more than infinite, will remain to all eternity, always increasing beyond all measure. That is why 'the greatest of them is love' (1 Corinthians 13:13)."[72] In stating with regard to love, "always increasing beyond all measure," Maximus was adopting Gregory of Nyssa's belief in infinite progress or *epektasis*. What he said about love may be applied to the imitation of Christ. If love always increases and has no end, so also do imitation and participation. Even in heaven throughout the age to come, the righteous will continue to imitate Christ and to participate in

---

66. Confessor, *De Char.* II.48 (Ceresa-Gastaldo, 116).

67. Confessor, III.71 (Ceresa-Gastaldo, 176).

68. Confessor, III.67 (Ceresa-Gastaldo, 176).

69. Confessor (?), *Scholia* (PG 4: 265D).

70. Confessor, *Ad Thal.* 54 (CCSG 22: 451, 146–47).

71. Confessor, *Cap. Gnost.* I.39 (PG 90: 1097C).

72. Confessor, *De Char.* III.100 (Ceresa-Gastaldo, 192).

him always more and more, with what Maximus termed "an ever-moving stability" (ἀεικίνητος στάσις).[73]

73. Confessor, *Ad Thal.* 59 (CCSG 22: 53, 131).

5

Freedom and Heteronomy
Maximus and the Question of Moral Creativity

Of the many circles within which Maximus the Confessor is invoked as an authority, one that merits particular attention in recent studies lies in the field of moral theology. While criticisms emerging from the disciplines of historical and systematic theology have sometimes held up Maximus' staunch defense of the doctrine of two wills in Christ as an embarrassing but typically Byzantine example of theological hair-splitting, not a few scholars have lauded the way the Confessor's expositions on the topic, particular in his reflections on Jesus' prayer in the Garden of Gethsemane, may contribute towards a clearer understanding of the nature of human volition and its moral actualization. One example of this positive appropriation may be seen in an article by New Zealand theologian Ivor Davidson subtitled "The Ontological Dynamics of Incarnational Intention."[1] Davidson takes issue with criticisms that allege that, by ascribing two wills to Christ, Maximus and the traditional proponents of dyothelete Christology end up with an implausible account of Jesus' conscious subjectivity. Besides asking too much of a Christological method whose interests and anxieties were more metaphysical and theological than they were physiological or psychological, the error in such allegations, argues Davidson, lies in regarding

1. Davidson, "Not My Will," 178–204.

our own fallen experience of volition as humanly normal and therefore as the adequate criterion of what Christ's experience of volition ought to be like. Drawing on Maximus' evolving concept of gnomic will (γνώμη), and the rationale behind his eventual denial of its presence in Christ, Davidson exposes the superficial and illusory character of freedom as it is commonly conceived in many contemporary moral theories. If Maximus' idea of freedom includes "the kind of self-determination appropriate to our real status as God's creatures," then, according to Davidson:

> [t]he diverse factors that complicate and impede such authentic direction—the kinds of factors, we might say, that have been highlighted in later modernity's demise of confidence in the stability of a choosing self—are testimony to the reality that humans are not in practice half so free as might be supposed.[2]

Another example of Maximus' dyothelete Christology being enlisted in the service of moral theology is found in a still more recent essay, written in 2007, by American Ian A. McFarland, entitled "Willing is Not Choosing: Some Anthropological Implications of Dyothelite Christology."[3] McFarland similarly argues that Maximus' assignment of will to the category of nature rather than to *hypostasis* "challenges the idea that willing is the source or ground of individual identity (*hypostasis*)." And, he continues, "if identity is not reducible to the will, then the will's lack of freedom with respect to sin either now or in glory may not constitute the kind of threat to human integrity that modern Westerners are inclined to fear."[4] The mode of willing that characterizes the gnomic will, as McFarland interprets Maximus, is incapable of securing human fulfillment on its own because it is "in itself empty, directionless and (therefore) mutable."[5] True human freedom is realized not in an unlimited range of possible choices, or even in the ability to make such choices, but in "a direct and undeviating orientation to God."[6]

A third example of this recent appropriation of Maximus' dyothelete Christology in the field of moral theology appears in the action theory of Italian theologian Livio Melina.[7] According to Melina, behind Thomas Aquinas' recognition that Christ's humanity was not simply the passive instrument utilized by the divine *Logos*, but was the principle of actions that

---

2. Ibid., 194.

3. McFarland, "Willing is Not Choosing," 3–23.

4. Ibid., 4.

5. Ibid., 20.

6. Ibid., 17.

7. Melina, *The Epiphany of Love*, 90–91.

were fully human, free, and salvifically meritorious, lies the wealth of the Eastern fathers' Christological reflections, not least the distinction made by Maximus between θέλησις, understood as the natural capacity to will, and βούλησις, understood as the subjective actuation of that capacity in this or that particular way.[8] For Melina, this means that "[e]ven if the will's natural dimension is the indispensable foundation of the freedom of action, it is not yet enough to explain it: spiritual nature founds but does not determine freedom. Action that is truly free not only implies the determination of the spiritual faculties . . . [such as reason or will] but also involves the personal subject taking a stance."[9] This notion of "taking a stance," in Melina's action theory, cannot be thought of outside an interpersonal relational structure. A human being "takes a stance" not simply with respect to certain things, but above all with respect to certain persons. According to Melina, human action always bears this interpersonal character: "the human act demands to be a personal act . . ."[10] The descriptor "human" here refers to its being purposeful and voluntary action, that is, it's emerging from the common human faculties of reason and will. The descriptor "personal" refers to the specific mode in which such purposeful and voluntary action takes place, a mode whose character always includes "an interpersonal dimension," and whose defining and ultimate goal is a *communio personarum*, a communion of persons.[11] This is what Melina means when he asserts that "only with the appearance of the beloved" is the human act "complete in its final [i.e. personal] determination."[12]

On the face of things, the invocation of Maximus as a supporting authority seems to be more justifiable in the first two examples with Davidson and McFarland, but less so in the third example with Melina. Unlike Davidson and McFarland, Melina does not engage in a direct exegesis of Maximian texts, but relies on several secondary studies, freely synthesizing their results with his Thomistic and Blondelian inspired version of Christian personalism.[13] Moreover, rigorous historical research has made us more wary about readings of Maximus and other ancient thinkers that—utilizing such terms as "nature," "person," "intellect," or "will"—unwittingly import into

8. On Aquinas' appropriation of the patristic legacy on this topic, see Gondreau, "St. Thomas Aquinas," 214–45.

9. Melina, *The Epiphany of Love*, 91.

10. Ibid.

11. Ibid.

12. Ibid.

13. In this context Melina cites the work of Gauthier, "Saint Maxime le Confesseur," 51–100. Elsewhere Melina has also collaborated with Rome-based Maximian scholar P.-G. Renczes, publishing the latter's essay "La gloria del Padre," 147–57.

the language of the fathers a conceptual content derived from much later developments in theological history and indicative of interests sometimes far removed from the fathers' actual thought.[14]

But having said that, my sense is that Melina's appropriation of Maximus' insights on the nature of human volition and freedom has more going for it than at first may seem to be the case. For Melina, human freedom consists in "the power to introduce novelty into the cyclical time of history, breaking the pre-established schemes of physical laws and natural inclinations."[15] His instinct in interpreting Maximus is to avoid any reduction of morality and freedom to the practical calculation of moral values from cognitively accessible universal principles, and instead to presuppose that the specifically Christological aspect in the Confessor's analysis of human action says something crucial about the realization of all human freedom, namely, that it "only occurs in reference to the will of a person: the beloved, the Father."[16] In other words, human action is free not just when it conforms to the general *logos* of human nature, but when it arises in the mode of radical love for another person, a mode whose concrete embodiment, being personal and unique and exposed to all the variables of interpersonal freedom, will always be creative and new.

What I want to do in this study therefore is to revisit Maximus' theological exegesis of the scriptural accounts Christ's prayer in Gethsemane with a view to judging whether the creative appropriation of his anthropology along the lines outlined by Melina is justified. I shall begin by turning to a number of familiar and well-studied passages, to see whether they might yield any fresh insights when approached with three particular questions in mind. The first concerns the extent to which Maximus maintains the integrity of Christ's singular subjectivity, representing all of Jesus' speaking, acting, and suffering in such a way that in them we encounter one and the same personal "I." The second concerns the creative and novel character of Christ's speaking, acting, and suffering, the extent to which we encounter in them a completely new actuality that reveals what it means to be God, and what it means to be human, in a surprising and hitherto unexpected way. The third concerns the integration of instinct and intention, the extent to which Christ's conscious acts of will incorporate, and do not oppose, even

---

14. See the recent summary of this issue by Torrance, "Personhood and Patristics in Orthodox Theology," 700–707. On this question it may be apt to mention Vladimir Lossky's remark, reported by Torrance (ibid., 705), that "the quest for a Christian personalist anthropology in the Fathers is certainly worthwhile," even if it must be "pursued with care."

15. Melina, *The Epiphany of Love*, 4.

16. Ibid., 91.

the most instinctive human impulses and natural inclinations. With the discussion generated by these three questions, I shall proceed to offer an assessment of the possible merits in Melina's line of interpretation.

Singularity of Subject

We begin by asking to what extent Maximus maintains the integrity of one and the same personal "I" to which is properly predicated all of Jesus' speaking, acting, and suffering, particularly when it comes to that speaking, acting, and suffering manifested in his Gethsemane prayer. Exegesis of this narrative event appears in a number of places in Maximus' writings, but most of the focus in secondary studies centres on its appearance in three *Opuscula* (3, 6, and 7) and the famous *Disputation with Pyrrhus*, texts that date from a brief period in the Confessor's African sojourn between 642 and 645, subsequent to the publication of the Imperial *Ekthesis* (638) and prior to the Imperial *Typos* (647/8).[17] Maximus' chief concern in these texts is not to answer the kinds of questions we moderns might typically raise of this narrative event, but to respond to the assertion made by the *Ekthesis* that any attribution of two activities to Christ would imply two wills, and that to attribute two wills to Christ would be to envision a virtual two-personed Christ in which the divine and human elements were at best juxtaposed. The wording of the *Ekthesis* indicates an implicit intention to exclude any interpretation of the Gethsemane event that would find in it an internal struggle in Christ between "God the Word" who "wished to fulfil the salutary suffering" on the one hand, and "his humanity" which "resisted his will and was opposed to it" on the other.[18] In putting it this way, the *Ekthesis* brought to the surface a hermeneutical question of abiding importance for both Christology and theological anthropology. How can we reconcile what appears to be two conflicting desires in Jesus? "Father, if it be possible, let this cup pass from me." Here, the object of desire is avoidance of impending suffering and death. "Yet not my will, but yours be done." Here, the object of desire is the accomplishment of the Father's will, which in this case seems to necessitate existential crisis.[19] The idea that Jesus experienced an internal affective conflict seems to be at odds with an understanding of virtue

17. On dating and context see Sherwood, "An Annotated Date-List;" Allen and Neil, *Maximus the Confessor and His Companions*, 14–18; Allen, *Sophronius of Jerusalem*.

18. *Ekthesis* 10–19, 160.

19. The Gospel of Luke repeatedly expresses this sense of "divine necessity" behind Jesus' mission with the impersonal verb δεῖ. See Fitzmyer, *The Gospel according to Luke*, 179–80.

as an excellence arising from the harmonious, rational integration of our various inclinations and desires. Any such conflict would seem to be more a symptom of the kind of volitional uncertainty and unruly appetitive disintegration that characterize humanity's fallen and wounded state, and which Maximus sums up in the word γνώμη. As is well known, Maximus, while insisting on a duality of wills in Christ, rejected any notion of a natural opposition between them. There is nothing inherent in human nature that opposes its Creator. But that left him with the challenge of making sense of what has been called the "graphic realism of Jesus' initial resistance and his *coming to* a final resolve in the Gethsemane prayer . . ."[20]

Studies of Maximus' attempts in these texts to interpret Jesus' Gethsemane prayer have clarified the prominence he gives to the active role of Christ's humanity in the resolution of this resistance. Ever since Marcel Doucet's criticism of von Balthasar's over-dramatization of the duality between the *Logos* and his assumed humanity, interpreters have rightly located the drama of resolution and obedience *within* Christ's human volitional complex.[21] In his studious monograph on the topic, Demetrios Bathrellos fairly sums up scholarly consensus by asserting that in *Opusculum* 6 Maximus in particular offers "a piece of meticulous and insightful exegesis" in which he points out "in an unambiguous way that it is the *Logos as man* who addresses the Father in Gethsemane."[22]

But is this an adequate explanation? True enough, Maximus does use the "as man" formula, once, right near the end of *Opusculum* 6. The passage reads:

> Having become like us for our sake, he who is God by nature
> said to God the Father in a human manner [ἀνθρωποπρεπῶς],
> "Let not my will but yours prevail," since possessing the fullness
> of the Father's will he also has a human will as man.[23]

But it seems to me that we do not have here a simple ascription of Jesus' prayer to the *Logos* "as man." At stake here is not just a moot point in Maximian interpretation, but also a much wider issue in Christology. While a survey of texts from the history of patristic Christology attests to the ubiquity of the formulations "as God" or "as man," used to qualify Christ's various activities for the sake of a certain dogmatic precision, this way of speaking arguably falls short of accounting for the full depth and drama of

20. Blowers, "The Passion of Jesus Christ," 361–77, particularly at 367.

21. See Doucet, "La Volonté Humaine du Christ," 123–59, esp. 135–36.

22. Bathrellos, *The Byzantine Christ*, 147.

23. Confessor, *Th. Pol.* 6 (PG 91: 68C). Notice here how Maximus embellishes the words of Jesus with this verb ἰσχυσάτω, which does not appear in the Synoptics.

Christ's passion, whether in Gethsemane or elsewhere. It was against such a mathematical divvying up of Christ's various actions into those which he performed "as God" and those which he performed "as man" that Cyril's *Third Letter to Nestorius*, endorsed by the Council of Ephesus (431), required that all of Christ's actions and passions be attributed to the one subject, "the one enfleshed hypostasis of the *Logos*."[24] Elsewhere, in commenting on the Gethsemane event in *Opusculum 7*, Maximus does indeed use the "as God" and "as man" formulations a number of times. But it is not clear to me that he means them to be regarded as virtual subjects of predication, nor even as simple qualifiers. His intention can be better understood, I think, by turning to study their appearance in *Ambiguum 5*, a text dating from before the full-blown outbreak of the monothelete controversy. It is here, while defending the coherence and applicability of the Christology of Dionysius the Areopagite that Maximus proposes what I regard as his profoundest insights into the mystery of Christ's person and action.

The central thesis of *Ambiguum 5* is that while Christ is essentially divine and essentially human, the circumstances of the hypostatic union have impacted his existence and activity in such a way that his divine nature can no longer be accounted for in purely divine terms, nor his human nature in purely human terms. "He exists neither as a mere human being, nor as bare God."[25] Thus, when Maximus uses the "as God" and "as man" formulas, they must be interpreted with this thesis in clear view. So when he says, "As God, he [Christ] was the moving principle of his own humanity, while as man, he was revelatory principle of his own divinity,"[26] the point he wants to make is that one and the same subject, the incarnate *Logos*, is involved in each and every one of his actions, both "as God" and "as man" simultaneously. The characteristic properties of both natures are manifest at the existential level, in one way or another, in each particular act of the one person. Maximus' preferred way of expressing this exchange of properties in Christ is to say that he did human things in a divine way and divine things in a human way.[27]

Something similar, I believe, is going on in the formulations of *Opuscula 6* and 7. In these Maximus is at pains to bring out the dual or theandric character of all of Christ's actions, even those that seem most markedly human. In *Opusculum 7*, for example, while discerning in the two parts of the Gethsemane prayer a reference to two distinct wills, he nevertheless

---

24. Tanner, *Decrees of the Ecumenical Councils*, 56.

25. Confessor, *Amb*. 5, 20–21.

26. Confessor, *Amb*. 5, 28.

27. See further Cooper, *The Body in Saint Maximus*, 127–56.

builds into his "as man" and "as God" formulations this cross-over reciprocal qualification:

> For it appears that the same as man, who is also God by nature,
> wills in accordance with the economy that the cup pass, and in
> this he typifies what is human. . . . And again it appears that as
> God, being also a human being in essence, he wills to fulfil the
> economy of the Father and work the salvation of all.[28]

And again:

> It is made clear then that as man, being God by nature and act-
> ing humanly, he willingly accepts the experience of sufferings
> for our sake. And it is again made clear that as God, being by
> nature a human being and acting divinely, he naturally exhibits
> the signs of his divinity.[29]

It is from both these sufferings and these signs, Maximus concludes,
that "the same one is recognised as being at the same time [ὁμοῦ] both God
and man . . . ."[30] The Confessor's emphasis here and throughout the treatise
seems to be on avoiding reducing this or that action of Christ to one enacted
by him *either* "as God" *or* "as man," but on predicating actions to Christ
both "as God" *and* "as man." He champions this double predication over
against the pious but misguided monothelete tendency to credit certain actions to Christ only "as God." "For if," Maximus argues, "it is only as God
that he willed these things [hunger, thirst, weariness, and so on], and not the
same as man [καὶ οὐχ ὡς ἄνθρωπος ὁ αὐτὸς ἤθελεν], then either the body has
become divine by nature, or the *Logos* has changed his nature and become
flesh by loss of his own divinity . . . ."[31]

The same train of thought seems to be operative in *Opusculum* 6. There,
Maximus considers three ways of reading the first part of the Gethsemane
prayer, the petition, "Let this cup pass from me." The first is to understand
it as a prayer arising "from the man who is like us" (ἀπο τοῦ ἀνθρώπου . . .
τοῦ καθ᾽ ἡμᾶς), a characterization Maximus explains in terms of a will that
"often resists and contends with God."[32] But such an interpretation would
not fit the second half of the prayer in which the same subject does not
oppose but acquiesces to God's will. A second possible interpretation is to
attribute the petition to "the eternal divinity of the Only-Begotten Son," but

---

28. Confessor, *Th. Pol.* 7 (PG 91: 84C).
29. Confessor, *Th. Pol.* 7 (PG 91: 84C).
30. Confessor, *Th. Pol.* 7 (PG 91: 84C).
31. Confessor, *Th. Pol.* 7 (PG 91: 77B).
32. Confessor, *Th. Pol.* 6 (PG 91: 65BC).

this would introduce a division of will between the Father and the Son, or else it would ascribe the wish to avoid the cup also to the Father, which would negate the intelligibility of the prayer altogether. The third way of understanding the petition, a way which Maximus commends, is as belonging to "the man we know as Savior" (τοῦ κατὰ τὸν Σωτῆρα νοουμένου ἀνθρώπου). Quite possibly, it is this phrase, with its mention of *anthropos*, which would lead interpreters to say that Maximus here ascribes the prayer to Christ "as man." But, the crucial "Savior" part of this phrase for Maximus necessarily includes what is proper to Christ's divinity for, as he says a little further on, it is God's very nature to will our salvation.[33] To ascribe the petition to "the man who is Savior" is in effect to ascribe it to the man who is God. This is altogether different from ascribing it to Christ simply "as man."[34]

The Creative Newness of Christ's Action

The second question I want to explore concerns the creative and novel character of Christ's actions, the extent to which we encounter in them a completely new actuality that reveals what it means to be human in an entirely fresh and hitherto unexpected way. For this we may refer first of all to a typically Maximian theme brought out so well by Paul Blowers in his essay on the Confessor's "passiology."[35] Blowers suggests that a richer

---

33. "Τοῦτο γὰρ αυοτῷ φύσει καθέστηκε θελητόν" "This object of will" (τοῦτο θελητόν) is a reference back to the immediately previous clause to "our salvation." *Th. Pol.* 6 (PG 91: 68B).

34. Thomas Weinandy has argued that all of Christ's actions and passions should be predicated of him "as man" and none of them "as God." "If the Son of God is man and has identified himself as man, then, it seems to me, that he exists, as incarnate, totally within the parameters or boundaries of all that is human. Thus the Son of God not only has a human body, soul, intellect, will, and emotions, etc., but equally he also has an integral human 'I,' a psychological centre within which all of these are expressed and experienced. The human 'I' of Jesus is the human psychological self-consciousness of the divine Son. He thought, spoke, and acted as well as underwent all his experiences from within the limits of his human 'I.' When Jesus said 'I,' it was truly the Son of God saying 'I' in a fully authentic human manner." See Weinandy, *Does God Suffer?* 209–10. But if this is so, then in what sense can we say that Jesus is divine? Only nominally? If really and ontologically, this seems to challenge the exclusive integrality of the human "I." In short, Jesus must be able to say both "I am a man" and "I am God;" both the divine and the human must coincide in his "I;" or put another way, the divine "I" is concealed (and thereby revealed) in the human "I." If it is asked what it is in the first part of the Gethsemane prayer that manifests his divinity, one need only be reminded of the fact that this is a prayer addressed to God as "Father," a form of invocation proper to the divine Son.

35. Blowers, "The Passion of Jesus Christ," 361–77.

and psychologically more compelling exposition of the Gethsemane prayer can be found in the two other *Opuscula* (3 and 7) and the *Disputation with Pyrrhus*, especially when they are illuminated by passages in the earlier *Ambigua ad Ioannem* and the *Quaestiones ad Thalassium*. Above all, Blowers' reconsideration highlights the expression often employed by Maximus, which speaks of the way Christ makes "use" (χρῆσις) of typically human passions such as the fear of death, indeed even death itself, so as to transform them into redemptive and life-giving instruments.

To speak of Christ "using" his fear of death for salvific purposes should not be thought of in the sense of Christ opting on some occasions to "use" his *human* attributes and opting on other occasions to use his *divine* attributes, thereby effecting a kind of break between the person who does the "using" and his two, instrumental natures.[36] Rather it seems more akin to the way, for example, a person might harness the initial motions of anger that sometimes arise in him, allowing them to propel him towards acts of justice or courage, instead of allowing them the kind of undisciplined free reign that would more likely end up in acts of injustice or self-pity.[37] Moral failure or success arises not at the level of the initial affective motion, but in its respective appropriation, deployment, or "use" in this or that purposeful action. Similarly, there is in principle a blameless, even a positively "good" impulse embedded in our natural aversion to pain and death; indeed, its absence would normally indicate some sort of psychophysical abnormality. Moral evaluation applies not to its presence as such, but to how it is used.

Another context in Maximus' writings in which the novelty and freedom of Christ's action comes to light is again in the fifth *Ambiguum ad Thomam*. In discussing the meaning of the disputed Dionysian phrase "a certain new theandric activity," Maximus argues that Christ fully manifested what we recognize as our common human nature, but he did so "by way of new modalities which are not ours."[38] On this basis Maximus can say, "there is nothing human [in Christ] which, on account of its supernatural modality, was not also divine."[39] By renewing human nature, by pioneering it afresh and making of it a gift available to all, Christ shows how hu-

---

36. Ivor Davidson criticizes this conception in Hans Schwartz; see Davidson, "'Not My Will," 198.

37. Maximus envisions the positive use of impulses such as anger and desire in *Or. Dom.* 520–60 (CCSG 23: 113), and of course in the famous passage of *Ad Thal.* 1, 5–40 (CCSG 7: 47–49) where desire, pleasure, fear, and grief are transformed into virtuous dispositions in those "who take captive every thought in obedience to Christ" (2 Cor 10:5).

38. Confessor, *Amb.* 5 (CCSG 48: 28, 184).

39. Confessor, *Amb.* 5 (CCSG 48: 27–28, 173–74).

man action in its free and fulfilled state properly introduces into history an utterly singular and unexpected quality that transcends all "normal" and predictable schemes of natural causation.

With respect to the Gethsemane prayer, then, this means that Christ really did feel the properly human aversion to death, for there would be something wrong with a being that did not at some level resist its own destruction. Yet he experienced this aversion not in a way that might drive him to seek refuge in selfish or escapist behavior, but in a uniquely transcendent way, that is, in God's way, and therefore in a way that serves for human salvation. Through this unique mode of appropriation by Christ, the natural human fear of death, which so often takes the concrete form of a crippling power or overwhelmingly impulsive drive, was thereby granted a new, supernatural quality as "a precious resource of salvation and deification."[40] In this way, summarizes Blowers, Maximus envisions Christ in the Garden as "pioneering" for all human beings "a new and edifying mode" of the common human aversion to death, one that does not curtail or frustrate human aspirations, but enables their ultimate fulfillment.[41]

Integration of Instinct and Intention

The third question that calls for our attention concerns the integration of instinct and intention, the extent to which Christ's conscious acts of will incorporate, and do not oppose, even the most instinctive human impulses and inclinations. In two statements in *Opusculum 7*, Maximus affirms that Christ's natural human will "was not opposed to God;"[42] but then, in referring to the movement from the stance of aversion expressed in the first part of the prayer to the stance of agreement expressed in the second part of the prayer, says that he "turns against it" (ὥρμα κατ' αὐτοῦ).[43]

A solution to this problem has been helped greatly by the recognition that the terms used for will in many passages do not exclusively denote the rational appetite, but sometimes include reference to the lower appetitive and instinctive impulses. For example, in *Opusculum 3*, Maximus defines θέλημα as a natural desire for being, which he explains is not a conscious psychological longing, but a kind of constitutive, organizing energy within a being that orients it towards its own actuation and fulfillment.[44] Again

40. Blowers, "The Passion of Jesus Christ," 369.

41. Blowers and Wilken, *St. Maximus the Confessor*, 112, n.7.

42. Confessor., *Th. Pol.* 7 (PG 91: 81D).

43. Confessor, *Th. Pol.* 7 (PG 91: 81B).

44. Confessor, *Th. Pol.* 3 (PG 91: 45C).

in *Opusculum* 1 Maximus defines "natural will" (ψυχικόν θέλημα) as a power that "holds together in being" the various properties of a nature.[45] As Bathrellos summarizes the wider textual evidence, "the will is a unity of instinctive and rational elements."[46] This assertion is set over against the thesis of both von Balthasar and Marcel Doucet, who hold that Christ's repulsion in the face of death was "not simply a blind, vital drive to stay alive, but intelligent willing."[47]

Of course, Doucet was himself critical of von Balthasar on this issue. Already back in 1985 Doucet rejected von Balthasar's dramatic rendition of the duality of wills in Christ in terms of a symmetrical, face-to-face struggle and its resolution in advance, as it were, by the overarching will exercised by the *Logos* in becoming human to begin with. Von Balthasar's approach is well illustrated by his translation of the phrase ὥρμα κατ' αὐτοῦ with "he does violence to his own will" (*Er «stürmt gegen seinen eigenen Willen an»*).[48] Such an approach, Doucet argued, leaves no room for the possibility of speaking of a real submission and obedience on the part of Christ's human will. In Christ there can be no radical contrariety. If there is an internal tension, it is played out not between the *Logos* and his humanity, but within the dynamisms of Christ's human will itself, between the natural "velleity" or instinctive tendency to conserve one's own being, and the concrete act of will that brings such velleity into submissive obedience to God.[49] The "fighting against" that Maximus speaks of, takes place, says Doucet, "in his humanity, or more precisely, in his human will."[50]

Yet to my mind the two claims need not be so keenly opposed. It is not legitimate, without imposing a neo-Kantian interpretation on Maximus, to discount the non-rational or instinctive element of will as irrelevant to Christ's self-determination, as Bathrellos seems to do.[51] Here von Balthasar's proposed solution to the problem of opposition seems to me to make certain sense not only of Maximus' thought but also of the exigencies of the human reality. In an intellectual being, argues von Balthasar, natural desire is always, "at its root, an intellectual desire . . . ."[52] The implications are

45. Confessor, *Th. Pol.* 1 (PG 91: 12C–13A).

46. Bathrellos, *The Byzantine* Christ, 145, n.273.

47. Balthasar, *Cosmic Liturgy*, 264. Cf. Doucet, "La Volonté humaine du Christ," 135; quoted by Bathrellos, *The Byzantine Christ*, 145, n.273.

48. Balthasar, *Kosmische Liturgie*, 266 (*Cosmic Liturgy*, 268).

49. Doucet, "La Volonté humaine du Christ," 136.

50. Ibid.

51. See Bathrellos, *The Byzantine Christ*, 123.

52. Balthasar, *Cosmic Liturgy*, 264.

twofold. First, spirit or intelligence is operative in a human being not only at the level of conscious acts of choice, but penetrates all the way down to qualify in some way even the deepest instinctive drives. Second, concrete determinations of will always arise out of the intelligent but as yet unfulfilled complex of affects and desires that mark our psychophysical constitution. Of course, precisely therein lie both our unity and our vulnerability. In Christ, however, this same complex of natural drives, says Maximus, "does not precede and lead the will, as happens with us,"[53] but is itself the result of a higher act of will, namely, the will of the *Logos* who in becoming incarnate gives his humanity existence and, within the limits of a purposeful salvific project, freely makes his own the full range of its natural motions. In this way, says von Balthasar, Christ's natural fear of death was itself supported by his underlying hypostatic freedom, which supported his whole nature. His hypostatic identity, therefore, bears and results in the natural opposition of the two natures, and in its supreme personal disponibility [to the Father's will] it dissolves the opposition between them to the same degree that it brings them into being.[54]

In embracing and making his own the nature he assumed, the *Logos* personally willed and affirmed all its finite proclivities and vulnerabilities, including those which "naturally" move it in a certain healthy and blameless direction, but which in the circumstances of the saving economy would require modal re-configuration. In essence, these inclinations are human. In their modal actualization and determination by Christ, they are rendered divine.[55] Maximus can thus speak of Christ, in the very moment in which the instinctive human aversion to death arises in him and comes to expression in prayer, "turning against" the inclination manifest in this aversion. The intensity implied by this verb "turning against" is softened if we compare it to parallel expressions in the immediate context which speak of "setting aside" (ἀθέτησις), "surrendering" (ὑποκλίνω), or "constraining" (συνελαύνω) this inclination in order to bring it into union with the saving plan of the Father.[56] For von Balthasar, all of this can only make sense in as much as this natural inclination is, "from the start, already in submission . . . ."[57] In submission to what? Only to the will of the *Logos*? This is how von Balthasar has it. Must we not also add: "and also to the will of his

---

53. *Pyrrh.* (PG 91: 297D): Οὐ γὰρ προηγεῖται ἐν τῷ Κυρίῳ καθάπερ ἐν ἡμῖν, τῆς θελήσεως τὰ φυσικα.

54. Balthasar, *Cosmic Liturgy*, 266.

55 Confessor, *Th. Pol.* 7 (PG 91: 81D).

56. Confessor, *Th. Pol.* 7 (PG 91: 80D–81A).

57. Balthasar, *Cosmic Liturgy*, 269.

human nature?" But this would be to fall into the trap again of ascribing actions or events to this or that nature in a way Maximus never quite permits. While he affirms the presence of a human will, its decisive determination, its concrete actualization is never an act of a nature, nor even of a mere man, but of a singular subject who is the humanized God.[58] As Maximus asserts in *Opusculum* 3, it is the overarching salvific *skopos* of the incarnation that functions as the decisive personal orientation within which Christ's shrinking from death is integrated. Since the Son of God became a human being not primarily to suffer but to save, his natural aversion to suffering does not stand intrinsically opposed to the saving divine will, nor is it simply reigned in by a higher act of bare human volition, but arises as a normal motion of natural inclination that, in Maximus' words, is "shaped and brought into concordance with the interweaving of the natural *logos* with the mode of the economy."[59]

Concluding Application

What I have been doing in the discussion up until this point is trying to visit a number of well worked-over Maximian problems in order to generate some thoughts that will better allow us to judge the validity of one particular appropriation of Maximus' dyothelete Christology in the field of moral theology. It is my sense that all three areas of discussion open up insights that lend themselves to an interpretation of morality and human action along the lines indicated by Melina. My purpose in this concluding section is to recall briefly two aspects of Melina's thought outlined in the introduction, and see how they may dovetail with what we have gleaned from Maximus. The first was Melina's notion that human freedom consists in "the power to introduce novelty into the cyclical time of history, breaking the pre-established schemes of physical laws and natural inclinations."[60] The second was Melina's sense that the specifically Christological aspect in the Confessor's analysis of human action says something crucial about the realization of all human freedom, namely, that it "only occurs in reference to the will of a person: the beloved, the Father."[61]

It seems to me that the first of these two points fits well with what we have said about the Maximian notion of Christ as pioneer of a new and

---

58. See Confessor, *Th. Pol.* 4 (PG 91: 60A): ὡς ἄνθρωπος οὐ ψιλός, ἀλλ᾽ ἐνανθρωπήσας Θεός.

59. Confessor, *Th. Pol.* 3 (PG 91: 48C).

60. Melina, *Epiphany of Love*, 4.

61. Ibid., 91.

saving modality of human action. Christ performs human activities "in a way beyond the human."[62] He thereby inaugurates a new level of human freedom, actualizing everything that is proper to human nature but "by way of new modalities, which are not ours."[63] This is not to envisage freedom as totally autonomous and self-designing. Christ's freedom simultaneously transcends and affirms the limitations of our common human nature and bodily structure. There is much in the normal course of human experience that unfolds unavoidably as a matter of natural necessity. In Christ, however, these dynamisms provide the crucial ground and trajectory for creative and renovative action. Herein lies an obvious difference between Christ's affectivity and our own fallen proclivities. A stable disposition to perform good acts relies upon the impetus provided by the affections and desires. In the unvirtuous person, however, such affections and desires lack the appropriate order and temper, and thus, instead of impelling him towards the good, they tend to dissipate his energies and impede the singleness of heart, the clarity of purpose, and the connatural instinct for good called for by the moral situation. When faced with impending pain or evil, our natural fears and desires often tend to exercise a compelling and sometimes turbulent influence on our intentional choices. In Christ, by contrast, all these affections and desires are actively harnessed and spontaneously integrated into the free and creative actualization of a purposeful salvific project. As Maximus puts it:

> By freedom of will [ἐξουσία γνώμης], he turned the passions of nature into active deeds, though not as consequences of natural necessity, as they are in our case. Moreover, possessing what belongs to us, he passed through the possibility of our nature and, by his freedom, proved that there was moving in him that which in our case tends to bring about a seditious turbulence of will. That which with us is naturally present as a mover of will [γνώμης κινητικὸν: something which puts *gnome* into motion] is rendered by Christ's freedom something movable by will [γνώμη κινητικὸν].[64]

In Maximus' mind, this lack of necessity in Jesus is a consequence of his virgin birth, by which his human nature comes into being, not by a law of natural necessity, but by the free and supernatural act of the Word.

---

62. Confessor, *Amb.* 5 (CCSG 48: 23, 73).

63. Ibid., (CCSG 48: 28, 184).

64. Ibid., (CCSG 48: 27, 163–67). In this earlier work Maximus clearly still attributes *gnome* to Christ. Yet the point made here remains essentially applicable even when one denies *gnome*-deliberation to Christ.

The validity of the second point becomes clearer when we supplement our findings with an observation whose importance is only hinted at by Maximus, but which seems to me to be of peculiar relevance to the integration of Christ's natural human desires and their actualization within an interpersonal, filial modality. It has to do with the role of prayer as the concrete means by which this integration and actualization take place. On several occasions in the passages under discussion Maximus alludes to Jesus' act of prayer in Gethsemane as the means by which he manifests his humanity in all its weakness and constrains it to union with the Father's will.[65] But what Maximus does not seem to reflect on is the filial mode in which this prayer is expressed as personal address to God as "Father." The concrete content and intention of the prayer corresponds exactly both to Christ's filial identity and the motion of his normal human desires. Thus, Christ in Gethsemane is what a human being looks like when all his natural capacities and propensities are actuated in a divine way, or more specifically, in the way proper to the relation that pertains between the Son and the Father.[66] Those capacities and propensities, which might lead to action that undermines this relation, are in Jesus drawn, through the medium of intimate though agonising prayer, into the ambit of filial communion with the Father and, precisely through prayer, effectively made to actualize his universal saving purpose in history.

In a similar way, Melina proposes that human action is essentially filial and interpersonal. The knowledge that guides particular moral actions is discovered not in an objective cognitive recognition of a universal norm and subsequent conformity to it, but relies on a "creative moral insight" born from within the subjective and particular conditions of a concrete "I-Thou" relationship.[67] To say that human moral action is filial is to say that it has its origin and end in the reciprocal love of God the Father and his Son in the freedom of the Spirit. The proper horizon against which human action must be compared or measured is not human nature, in the first instance, nor even the divine will, but filial communion with the Father. Only by insertion into this filial relation does human action come to full flower.

---

65. See, e.g., Confessor, *Th. Pol.* 7 (PG 91: 80CD; PG 91: 81A) and *Th. Pol.* 6 (PG 91: 68C).

66. "Jesus exhibits the nature and character of God in the only way in which they can be absolutely and perfectly exhibited in the context of human behavior, namely in such a relationship as properly belongs to man over against God, the relationship of glad and willing filial obedience." Moule, "The Manhood of Jesus," 95–110, at 101.

67. On this notion of "creative moral insight," see Dinan, "The Particularity of Moral Knowledge," 66–84. Referred to by Melina, *Epiphany of Love*, 59.

Whether or not these reflections satisfy a strict exegesis of Maximus' writings, they encourage us to penetrate the letter of his texts in order to get nearer the mystery they try to express. Maximus' account of Gethsemane teaches us that human beings actualize their freedom not in the mode of decisions whose rightness is deduced from a detached and rational grasp of the truth in all its blazing objectivity, but in the mode of an interpersonal communion within which desire, born of love, is wholly captivated by the Father's redemptive vision for broken humanity. This in turn leads us to think again about the meaning of Christ's obedience, which the Confessor, in connection with the Christ hymn of Philippians 2:5–11, links especially to the Gethsemane event.[68] It consists not simply in external conformity to a heteronomous divine command, nor in a heavy-handed and forceful coercion of unwilling impulses in a direction, which they are bound to resist, but in an active interpersonal union of two desires, two freedoms. In short, Christ's obedience in the Garden is essentially an embodied form of love, the love between the Son and the Father. This obedience opens the way for our historically acquired alterity to God to be healed of its divisive and alienating quality and, through its inclusion in the loving and fruitful alterity of the divine persons, to attain the communion with God that from the beginning has defined the human vocation.

68. Confessor, *Th. Pol.* 6 (PG 91: 68C).

6

Maximus the Confessor on the Will

David Bradshaw

Historians of philosophy have, for some years, been engaged in contro-versy over the question of precisely when and how the concept of the will originated. Credit for this achievement has been variously assigned to Plato, Aristotle, the early Stoics, Seneca, Epictetus, and Augustine, although the last two—Epictetus and Augustine—are probably the leading contend-ers.[1] It is not surprising that Maximus the Confessor has played little role in this debate, for Maximus is generally not regarded as part of the canon of Western philosophy, save perhaps in a minor way because of his *scholia* on the Areopagitic corpus. Nonetheless, in 1970 the learned Dominican R. A. Gauthier devoted several pages of his commentary on the *Nicomachean Ethics* to arguing that the true originator of the concept of the will was Maximus.[2] A partial reply to Gauthier has been offered by Richard Sorabji, but otherwise his argument has largely been ignored.[3] My aim in this paper is to revisit this issue with the hope of clarifying precisely what Maximus

---

1. The pivotal role of Augustine has been argued most forcefully by Dihle, *The Theory of Will*. It is defended with some qualifications by Kahn, "Discovering the Will," 234–59, and Sorabji, *Emotion and Peace of Mind*, 319–40, although both also recognize a perhaps equally important role for Epictetus. A more emphatic case for Epictetus has been made recently by Frede, *A Free Will*, 44–48.

2. Gauthier and Jolif, *Aristote: l'Éthique à Nicomaque*, 255–66.

3. See Sorabji, *Emotion and Peace of Mind*, 337–39.

contributed to later concepts of the will. I deliberately use the plural, "concepts," for I agree with Sorabji that there is not a single concept of the will and so the question of when and by whom it was "discovered" does not admit of a determinate answer. Even so, the contribution of Maximus deserves more attention than it has received, and much can be gained by situating his thought within the context of this debate.

Maximus' teaching about the will was of course not undertaken for its own sake, but in response to monothelitism. The latter was in turn a refinement of monoenergism, the doctrine that Christ possessed a single divine-human "energy" or ἐνέργειά. Although the issue soon shifted from energy to that of whether Christ possessed one or two wills (θελήματα), it is important to bear this earlier stage of the debate in mind, for Maximus seems to have developed his thought about the two natural wills in Christ largely in isomorphism with his conviction regarding the two natural energies. This fact may help explain the direction ultimately taken by his thought about the will, as I shall suggest below.

First, let us review the main points of Maximus' teaching.[4] The central terms at issue in the debate were θέλημα and θέλησις, both nouns deriving from θέλω, to wish or be willing. Θέλημα is rare in classical Greek but appears frequently in the Septuagint and New Testament. There it has two meanings: will in the sense of determinate purpose or counsel (as in the phrase "thy will be done" in the Lord's Prayer), and will in the sense of an act of willing (as in the statement that God created the world by his will, Rev 4:11).[5] Θέλησις does not appear at all in classical Greek and remains rare through late antiquity, although it does appear eight to ten times (depending on the manuscripts) in the Septuagint and once in the New Testament. Properly speaking it ought to designate an act of willing, in keeping with the general meaning of the "σις" suffix, but in practice its meaning tended to overlap that of θέλημα. Neither was a technical philosophical term, and neither designated will in a third possible sense, that of a faculty of will. Indeed, ancient Greek had no term for a faculty of will understood as a capacity that operates independently of reason. It is true that Aristotle speaks of a deliberative faculty (τὸ βουλευτικον) and a desiring faculty (τὸ ορεκτικον), but deliberation is a function of reason, as is desire insofar as it includes rational wish (τὸ βουλησις).[6]

4. The next several paragraphs draw partly on my "Maximus the Confessor," 813–28, at 825–27.

5. For details see "*thelō, thelēma*, θέλησις" in *Theological Dictionary of the New Testament*, 44–62; Madden, "The Authenticity of Early Definitions of Will (Θέλησις)," 61–79.

6. See Aristotle, *De Anima* III.9 432B3–7, III.10 433A31–B4.

The monothelite assertion of one θέλημα and θέλησις in Christ was intended to safeguard his unity as an acting agent. Although it is not always clear whether the monothelites had in mind Christ's faculty of will, act of willing, or determinate will, they probably meant to include all three.[7] The objection raised by Maximus centered on the difficulty such a view creates for attributing any active role to the humanity of Christ. Maximus pointed repeatedly to the prayer of Christ in Gethsemane—"Father, if you will, remove this cup from me; nevertheless not my will (θέλημα) but thine be done" (Luke 22:42)—as indicating that Christ had a distinctly human θέλημα, and that this θέλημα was capable of standing in tension (although not outright contradiction) to the divine will. In this verse, θέλημα no doubt refers to what I have labeled determinate will. Nonetheless, for such a difference to be possible, Christ must also have possessed a distinctly human capacity for willing, and that is the point on which Maximus focused. (He preferred for the sake of precision to refer to the determinate will as that which is willed, τὸ θεληθέν or θελητόν.[8]) As he saw it, the recognition of two distinct faculties of will is a necessary corollary to the Chalcedonian affirmation of Christ's two distinct natures, divine and human, for without it such an affirmation would be empty.

Maximus defines this natural faculty of will as "a faculty desirous (ορεκτικεν) of what is in accordance with nature, which holds together all the attributes that belong essentially to a being's nature," or more briefly as "the essential striving (εφεσις) for things constitutive in accordance with nature."[9] Although natural will, so defined, would seem to belong to all living things, Maximus plainly is interested primarily in the form that it takes in rational beings. Hence he goes on to define it further as "a simple rational (λογική) and vital desire," and in the *Disputation with Pyrrhus* he offers a number of descriptions that presuppose reason, including that it is rational desire (λογική ορέξις), self-determination (τὸ αυτεξούσιον), and desiderative mind (νους ορεκτικός).[10] Will qua rational desire is the master faculty governing the entire process that leads to intentional action: "willingly (θέλοντες) we think (λογιζόμεθα), and wish (βουλόμεθα), and search (ζητούμεν), and consider (σκεπτόμεθα), and deliberate (βουλεύωμεθα),

---

7. See discussion in Bathrellos, *The Byzantine Christ*, 80–82 (Pyrrhus).

8. See Confessor, *Th. Pol.* 1 (PG 91: 25A–B, 16 185D–188D), *Pyrrh.* (= *Opusc.* 28, PG 91: 292C–D).

9. Confessor, *Th. Pol.* 1 (PG 91: 12C) and 14 (PG 91: 153B); cf. 3 (PG 91: 45D–48A) and 16 (PG 91: 185D) for repetitions of the first definition, and 26 (PG 91: 276C) for a repetition of the second (where it is ascribed, along with several similar definitions, to Clement of Alexandria), as well as 280A for a minor variant.

10. Confessor, *Th. Pol.* 1 (PG 91: 13C), *Pyrrh.* (PG 91: 293B, 301C, 317C).

and judge (κρινόμεθα), and are inclined towards (διατιθέμεθα), and choose (προηρουμεθα), and move towards (ορμῶμεν), and use (κεχρημεθα)."[11] Elsewhere Maximus calls it "the primary innate power among physical characteristics and movements," holding that by it alone we seek being, life, movement, thought, speech, perception, nourishment, sleep, rest, and all else that sustains nature.[12]

Maximus understands rational wish (βουλησις) and choice (προαίρεσις), which in classical thought are the primary acts of a volitional nature, as modes of θέλησις. The former is "imaginative desire both of things that are and are not up to us," or equivalently, an act of will (θέλησις) directed towards a particular object, which may or may not be in our power.[13] The latter is desire, following upon deliberation and judgment, specifically for an object within our power; it constitutes, as Maximus puts it, a combination of desire, deliberation, and judgment.[14] This way of distinguishing βουλησις and προαίρεσις is largely Aristotelian and probably reached Maximus through Nemesius of Emesa.[15] Maximus thus incorporates a great deal of the classical (and especially Aristotelian) analysis of volition under his own overarching category of θέλησις.

Another of Maximus' innovations was to distinguish from the natural will what he calls the "gnomic will" (γνωμικόν θέλημα). Maximus explains the distinction between natural and gnomic will on analogy with that between the capacity to speak, which belongs to nature, and how one speaks (το πωσ λαλειν), which belongs to hypostasis.[16] He defines the gnomic will as "the self-chosen impulse and movement of reasoning (λογισμού) towards one thing or another," or equivalently, "the self-chosen impulse causing inclination toward one thing or another."[17] As these definitions indicate,

11. Confessor, *Pyrrh.* (PG 91: 293B–C, where I take it *horōmen* is a typo for *hormōmen*); see also the similar passage at *Th. Pol.* 1 (PG 91: 21D–24A), which makes it clear that these are meant as sequential stages.

12. Confessor, *Th. Pol.* 16 (PG 91: 196A).

13. Confessor, *Th. Pol.* 1 (PG 91: 13B, 21D); cf. *Pyrrh.* (PG 91: 317C).

14. Confessor, *Th. Pol.* 1 (PG 91: 13A–B, 16B–C).

15. See Aristotle, *Nicomachean Ethics* III.2 1111B19–26 and Nemesius of Emesa, *On the Nature of Man* XXXIII.49. For further discussion of Maximus' use of Nemesius see Gauthier, "Saint Maxime le Confesseur et la psychologie," 51–100, at 71–72.

16. Confessor, *Th. Pol.* 3 (PG 91: 48A). See also *Opusc.* 3 (PG 91: 53C) and 16 (PG 91: 192B–C), where the gnomic is definitive (*aphoristikon*) of person and hypostasis.

17. Confessor, *Th. Pol.* 14 (PG 91: 153A–B), 16 (PG 91: 192B). See also the definition at *Th. Pol.* 26 (PG 91: 280A): "a sort of distinguishing movement and desire for things gathered together in respect to pleasure." However, as Madden points out ("The Authenticity of Early Definitions," 63) this opusculum is of doubtful authenticity, for it contains many definitions of which Maximus elsewhere shows no knowledge.

the gnomic will is not a faculty—which would be redundant, given the role already assigned to the natural will—but instead an act made possible by the natural will. The particular direction of the gnomic will is shaped (τυπουμενον) by a person's γνώμη—a fluid term, which in this context would seem to mean character or inclination.[18] In his most careful and systematic work on the will, *Opuscula* 1, Maximus defines the γνώμη as "a dispositional desire (ἐνδιάθετον ορεξιν) for things up to us, from which there issues προαίρεσις; that is, a disposition for things up to us that have been deliberated upon with desire."[19] Γνώμη arises when desire is oriented and established by judgment and deliberation, and it stands towards choice (προαίρεσις) as a dispositional state (ἑξις) towards the corresponding act.[20] In fact, there would seem to be little difference between the gnomic will and προαίρεσις, both being names for the choice that issues from, and is shaped by, γνώμη.

Such, at least, is what I take to be the main line of Maximus' thought on this subject. Under the pressure of his debate with the monothelites, Maximus also offers a different and more restrictive understanding of these three terms—gnomic will, γνώμη, and προαίρεσις—that should also be noted. In the *Disputation with Pyrrhus* he defines γνώμη as "a sort of act of will (ποια θέλησις) relative to some real or perceived good," one that "judges between opposites, inquires about things unknown, and deliberates about that which is unclear."[21] Γνώμη here is not a disposition, but instead acts much like βούλησις and προαίρεσις. To attribute γνώμη in this sense to Christ would render him, according to Maximus, "a mere man, deliberating as we do, being ignorant and doubting, and possessing opposite tendencies," and indeed would imply that he is sinful insofar as he lacks a clear knowledge of the good.[22] Γνώμη and, a fortiori, gnomic will must therefore on no account be attributed to Christ. Elsewhere—including, confusingly enough, in *Opuscula* 1—Maximus amplifies and extends this position, arguing that προαίρεσις too is, of necessity, a choice between good and evil, and so must be denied of Christ.[23]

It is important to note that these statements rest upon a different understanding of γνώμη and προαίρεσις than that which Maximus offers when he is defining these terms in a non-polemical way. Γνώμη as it is defined in *Opuscula* 1 is, as I have mentioned, a standing inclination or state of

---

18. Ibid., *Th. Pol.* 3 (PG 91: 48A).

19. Ibid., *Th. Pol.* 1 (PG 91: 17C).

20. Ibid. *Th. Pol.* 1 (PG 91: 17C).

21. Ibid., *Pyrrh.* (PG 91: 308C, 329D).

22. Ibid., (PG 91: 308D, 329D).

23. Ibid., *Th. Pol.* 1 (PG 91: 28D–32B), 3 (PG 91: 53C, 7 81D).

character that has been formed through judgment and deliberation. Deliberation is, in turn, merely "desire that is inquisitive (ζητικὴν) regarding some act that is up to us."[24] Granted that deliberation implies a state of uncertainty about what to do, it does not imply ignorance of the good, for the issue deliberated may be a choice among different paths all of which are good. Likewise προαίρεσις, understood simply as desire following upon deliberation and judgment, need not be a choice between good and evil, but may instead be a choice among different goods. As Demetrios Bathrellos has noted, Maximus does not in fact seem to wish to deny προαίρεσις in this broader sense to Christ, as would indeed be highly implausible given the exigencies of human existence.[25] In fact, that Christ's human will exercises προαίρεσις understood as a choice among goods would seem to be implied by Maximus' exegesis of the prayer at Gethsemane: for Maximus this prayer exhibits a movement within Christ's human will, one in which the human will, being "moved and shaped" by the divine will, comes to accept the good of the cup offered by the Father rather than the good of continuing earthly life.[26]

I would also add that, within a broader perspective, the attempt to limit προαίρεσις to choice between good and evil seems rather eccentric. Earlier fathers as authoritative as Athanasius, Basil the Great, and Gregory of Nyssa had found no difficulty in attributing προαίρεσις to God himself acting in his divine nature. Thus, Basil rejects the idea that God created the world "without choice (απροαιρετως), as the body is the cause of shadow and light the cause of brightness," and Gregory attributes creation to "the impulse of divine choice" (ἡ ὁρμὴ τῆς θείας προαιρέσεως).[27] In discussing the Trinity in his *Great Catechism*, Gregory observes that both the divine *Logos* and the Holy Spirit possess a faculty of choice (προαιρετικην δύναμιν) since no living thing is without choice (απροαιρετον).[28] Plainly these fathers do not mean to indicate that God chooses between good and evil, but only that he chooses among goods. For all of these reasons, then, it seems to me

24. Confessor, *Th. Pol.* 1 (PG 91: 16B).

25. Bathrellos, *Byzantine Christ*, 151 n.302, 191.

26. Confessor, *Th. Pol.* 3 (PG 91: 48C–49A), 6 (PG 91: 65A–68D), *Pyrrh.* (PG 91: 297A–300A); cf. the helpful discussion in McFarland, "'Naturally and by Grace,'" 410–33, at 424–26.

27. Basil, *Hexaemeron* I.7 (PG 29: 17C); Nyssa, *On the Soul and Resurrection* (PG 46: 124B).

28. Nyssa, *Great Catechism* 1 (PG 45: 13D), 2 (PG 45: 17B). "Living thing" here is *zōion*, a term that excludes plants. For further discussion of these and related passages, see my "Divine Freedom in the Greek Patristic Tradition," *Quaestiones Disputatae*, special issue on Neoplatonism, http://www.franciscan.edu/QuaestionesDisputatae/NeoplatonismPapers.

that Maximus' denial of γνώμη, gnomic will, and προαίρεσις to Christ must be understood strictly within its polemical context. For our purpose here, that of understanding Maximus' theory of the will as a contribution to the history of philosophy, it will be best to ignore such complications and to focus on those aspects of the theory that are not aimed solely at denying that Christ possesses a gnomic will.

Returning to the main lines of the theory, then, Maximus' understanding of προαίρεσις as issuing from and being "shaped" by γνώμη (in the sense of disposition or character) raises an important question: is choice determined by character, or is character merely a precondition that (as Leibniz puts it) "inclines without necessitating"? In order to give point to this question it may help to notice a couple of historical precedents. Aristotle, in a famous passage of the *Nicomachean Ethics*, likens the formation of character to throwing a stone:

Once you have thrown a stone and let it go, you can no longer recall it, even though the power to throw it was yours, for the initiative was within you. Similarly, since an unjust or a self-indulgent man initially had the possibility not to become unjust or self-indulgent, he has acquired these traits voluntarily; but once he has acquired them it is no longer possible for him not to be what he is.[29]

In other words, although character may initially be formed through some sort of indeterministic process, once formed, choices follow from it of necessity. Such a view is a version of what I will call character-based determinism, the view that choices are determined by character. A subtler form of such a view can be found in Augustine. (Whether Augustine held this view consistently I will not attempt to say, although a number of scholars have argued that he did.[30]) On this view, it is not character as a whole that determines choice, but the strengths of one's loves and desires. Thus, in *The City of God*, Augustine describes the soul as borne about by the preponderance of its loves much as a material body is borne about by its weight.[31] Elsewhere he states even more directly, "it is necessary that we do whatever attracts us more."[32] As T. Kermit Scott comments, Augustine "seems to take it as obvious that to choose is to elect what one most wants and that it makes no sense to say that I choose an action that I believe will lead to a certain

---

29. Aristotle, *Nicomachean Ethics* III.5 1114A17–21, trans. Martin Ostwald (Library of Liberal Arts).

30. For example, Scott, *Augustine*, 415–35, partly incorporated in her *Anselm on Freedom*, 31–43.

31. Augustine, *City of God* XI.28.

32. Augustine, *Exposition of the Epistle to the Galatians* 49.

end even though I really wanted another end more."[33] This too is a form of character-based determinism, although it focuses on love and desire rather than character per se.

There are a number of signs that Maximus does not hold such a view. One is the definition of gnomic will cited earlier, "the self-chosen impulse and movement of reasoning toward one thing or another." That the impulse is self-chosen (αυθαιρετος) seems to indicate a certain spontaneity that cannot be understood simply as a result of pre-existing factors.[34] This impression is confirmed by an interesting analogy Maximus offers in the course of explicating the difference between choice that is in accordance with nature and that contrary to nature: choice, he says, is like a vote in relation to the preceding judgment, regardless of whether that judgment is correct.[35] Here too there would seem to be a certain spontaneity in the act of choice that cannot be explained by preceding factors, just as a vote is not wholly explicable (although it is partially so) by the deliberation that precedes it. Finally, and from a broader standpoint, there is the role Maximus gives to individual γνώμη in the progress of a rational creature towards deification. He writes in *Ambigua 7* that "rational beings are in motion from the beginning naturally by reason of being (διά τό εἶναι), and toward the goal in accordance with γνώμη by reason of well-being (διά τό εὖ εἶναι)."[36] Likewise, in *Ambigua 10*, we read that, of the three *logoi* by which God has made all creatures—those of being, well-being, and eternal being—"the two on the extremes [i.e., being and eternal being] have God alone as cause, but the other is intermediate and depends on our own movement and γνώμη, and through itself makes the extremes what they are."[37] In these passages γνώμη seems more likely to mean an act of choice rather than a disposition, but either way, it is plain that Maximus envisages a distinctive human contribution to the achievement of well-being, one that cannot be understood solely in terms

---

33. Scott, *Augustine*, 188–89.

34. The use of the term *authairetos* in this context is unusual, although not unprecedented. Athenagoras says that men and angels are self-choosing with respect to virtue and vice, *authaireton kai tēn aretēn kai tēn kakian echontōn* (*Legatio* 24.3), and Dionysius the Areopagite attributes to rational beings "self-directed self-determination," *hē authairetos autexousiotēs* (*EH* II.3.3 400A). Among the definitions collected in *Th. Pol.* 26 is one attributed to Clement of Alexandria defining θέλησις as *nous peri ti authairetōs kinoumenos* (276C).

35. Confessor, *Th. Pol.* 1 (PG 91: 29A).

36. Confessor, *Amb.* 7 (PG 91: 1073C).

37. Confessor, *Amb.* 10 (PG 91: 1116B).

of divine agency.[38] Here too, it would seem that human γνώμη includes a crucial element of spontaneity.

This means, in contemporary terms, Maximus is closer to being a libertarian than to being a compatibilist (including a theological compatibilist). However, it would not be right to identify his view simply as libertarian, for it includes an element that contemporary libertarianism normally does not—namely, the fundamental structure contained in the three *logoi* of being, well-being, and eternal being. Because human choice always takes place within this structure it is never wholly *de novo*; but it is always a response to the invitation to deification present within God's creative intent. This is an important point about which I will have more to say in a moment.

First, however, I would like to return to the question raised at the outset, that of the place of Maximus within the history of the development of the concept of the will. Gauthier rests his case for the importance of Maximus in this regard primarily on Maximus' identification of the natural will as a faculty that is (a) innate to human nature, (b) must be distinguished sharply from the manner of use of that faculty, i.e., the gnomic will, and (c) is intrinsically directed towards things that are "in accordance with nature." Here points (a) and (b) are, as Gauthier sees it, perhaps the inevitable result of Maximus' two-fold aim of establishing that Christ possessed a human will, but not a will subject to sin.[39] But nothing constrained Maximus to add point (c), the intrinsic directedness of the natural will towards natural goods. In doing so Maximus opened up, as it were, a kind of rationality that is independent of reasoning or conscious knowledge, one that the scholastics—who were greatly influenced by Maximus via the mediation of John of Damascus—rightly recognized as integral to human nature. As Gauthier puts it:

> Natural will is without a doubt the wish [βούλησις] of Aristotle. But instead of making this wish arise, as does Aristotle, upon the indifferent foundation of desire, St. Maximus . . . makes it arise in the θέλησις, a word that Aristotle did not know just as he did not know the reality that it designates. Θέλησις is no longer a desire that is rational by accident, but a desire rational by nature, a faculty (δύναμις) moved by its own proper vitality, prior to any intervention of knowledge, toward the same universal natural good that it is the function of reason to know. This faculty belongs to human nature, and it is natural too that there arises in it, whenever a simple representation occurs, independently of

---

38. See further on this point Meyendorff, "Free Will (γνώμη) in Saint Maximus," 71–75, although Meyendorff overstates his case by translating γνώμη as 'free will.'

39. Gauthier and Jolif, *Aristote: l'Éthique à Nicomaque*, 263.

any deliberation, the act of wish [βούλησις], thus elevated for the first time to the dignity of the will.[40]

Gauthier adds that there is a direct correlation between the natural will of Maximus and the *voluntas* of the scholastics, understood as a faculty of rational appetite that is distinct from reason, on the one hand, and sensible appetite, on the other.[41]

These very interesting remarks by Gauthier have unfortunately not received the attention that they deserve. I am aware of only two published responses. Thomas Madden, in a well-known article of 1982, cites Gauthier with agreement and offers on his own account a rather similar view, although he sees Aristotelian προαίρεσις, rather than βούλησις, as the closest analogue to θέλησις. As Madden sees it,

> [Maximus'] master-stroke was to seize upon the verb root θέλω as the basis for his concept. In doing so he leapt back over all classical philosophy to a root whose spontaneous, immediate, para-rational efficacity was well known to Homer as well as to the translators of the LXX, the writers of the New Testament, and the early Fathers of the Church. This root provided solid ground—perhaps the only possible ground in the Greek vocabulary—for a faculty which would stand co-equal to intellect, yet independent of it.[42]

The other response is that of Richard Sorabji, who takes a more critical view. Sorabji summarizes the claims made by Gauthier and Madden under two points:

1. Maximus rightly defined the natural will as "a faculty directed of its essence to the good, rather than as something one calls 'will' when it happens to be so directed;"

2. "[T]he will aims at this good quite independently of reason, although reason recognizes the same good."[43]

Neither point justifies attributing any significant role in the development of the concept of the will to Maximus, according to Sorabji. The first is not particularly original, for the belief that there is a "naturally directed desire for the good" was common in ancient thought and can be found,

---

40. Ibid., 263–64 (words in brackets are my addition; "souhait" is Gauthier's normal translation for βούλησις).

41. Ibid., 262.

42. Madden, "The Authenticity of Early Definitions," 78–79.

43. Sorabji, *Emotion and Peace of Mind*, 337–38.

for example, in Aristotle's view that everyone naturally desires a happy life. In fact, Sorabji argues, Maximus' definition of natural will would seem to be an adaptation of the Stoic notion of οἰκείωσις, "that attachment that is felt by newborn infants and animals to their own physical constitution (σύστασις), and which the adult human can later extend to his entire rational constitution."[44] In support, Sorabji points to a number of verbal parallels between Maximus' definition and Stoic descriptions of οἰκείωσις, including that what is said to be preserved is one's σύστασις or constitution, that the will is συνεκτική of that constitution, and that what it holds together are the ἰδιώματα, "the attributes which the Stoics postulated as lasting through an individual's life and distinguishing it from all other individuals."[45] The second point can be dismissed even more briefly, for to be independent of reason "is not a universally agreed feature of the will" and so is irrelevant to Sorabji's ostensible topic, that of the "discovery" of the will.[46]

It seems to me that Sorabji runs roughshod over what are in fact some valuable insights. At the risk of quibbling, I would first point out that the connection of Maximus' natural will to Stoic οἰκείωσις is by no means as clear as Sorabji suggests. The verbal evidence is not particularly impressive, for σύστασις, συνεκτική, and ἰδιώματα were by the time of Maximus common terms with no particular Stoic associations, and furthermore Maximus' use of ἰδιώματα is different from that of the Stoics, for he refers to the characteristic properties of a given nature rather than an individual.[47] More importantly, for Maximus it is crucial that the natural will is a faculty (δύναμις), and this is what distinguishes his view from that of others; such as Aristotle and the Stoics, who recognize some sort of naturally directed desire for the good. As Gauthier emphasizes, it is crucial that the natural will be a faculty in order for it to be capable of motivating action in a way that is rational but not determined by reasoning—a point that Sorabji simply ignores.

Although I find the reference to οἰκείωσις unhelpful, I do think that something more can be said about what motivated Maximus to identify the natural will as a faculty, and that doing so may help to bring this idea into focus. As I mentioned earlier, the monothelite debate was a continuation of the monoenergist debate, and in fact Maximus often addresses the two issues in tandem. Now, it had long been traditional to see ἐνέργεια as the expression of δύναμις, an Aristotelian idea that had been codified into the

---

44. Ibid., 338.

45. Ibid.

46. Ibid.

47. For the commonness of these terms see the entries in Lampe's *Patristic Greek Lexicon*: almost three columns for the first, more than half for the second, and more than two for the third!

tripartite scheme of οὐσία-δύναμις-ἐνέργεια by Galen, Iamblichus, and others, and would have been known to Maximus through Nemesius of Emessa (although the latter, because he is discussing intentional action, speaks of praxis rather than ἐνέργεια).[48] In light of this correlation, the debate over whether Christ possessed a natural human ἐνέργεια was also, by implication, a debate over whether he possessed a natural human δύναμις. But, as Pyrrhus remarks in the *Disputation*—and Maximus accepts—to will (θέλειν) is a kind of "synecdoche" for to act (ενεργειν), since willing itself is a kind of activity.[49] It was therefore natural for Maximus, approaching the issue of whether Christ possessed a natural human will, to identify that will as a δύναμις that is correlative to the human ἐνέργεια. I admit that this hypothesis is speculative, as Maximus himself does not explicitly draw these connections, but it seems to me the most likely explanation of how he came to identify the natural will as a kind of δύναμις, whereas no one in the long history of discussion of will prior to him had done so.

So, there is rather more to be said for the first point of Gauthier and Madden than Sorabji allows. The second point was, as we recall, that will aims at the good in a way that is independent of reason, a point that Sorabji dismisses by observing that it is not part of the concept of the will as such. On this narrow issue Sorabji is correct. However, Gauthier and Madden plainly did not mean to claim that all subsequent thought on the will has followed Maximus' lead; their claim is rather that Maximus' concept of the will is correct, or, at least, an advance upon its major predecessors.

This is a philosophical issue that it is hardly possible to settle here. Nonetheless, I would like to point out how the element of spontaneity in Maximus' understanding of choice, to which I drew attention earlier, strengthens Gauthier's and Madden's point. One of the difficulties facing medieval discussions of the will was that of how reason can be operative in choice without determining choice. Thomas Aquinas, for example, famously suggested that reason moves the will by presenting to it its final cause, "because the understood good is the object of the will, and moves it as an end."[50] It is natural to wonder, if this is so, whether the will is determined by the conclusions of reason; and, if it is so determined, whether it is truly free. It was presumably such worries that prompted the bishop of Paris to include, among the propositions condemned in 1277, the following: "That the will necessarily pursues what is firmly held by reason, and that it cannot

48. See Nemesius of Emesa, *On the Nature of Man* XXXIV.50, terminology echoed by Maximus at *Th. Pol.* 1 (PG 91: 33A–B); and for the earlier history of the triad see my *Aristotle East and West*, 7–59, 63–64, 136.

49. Confessor, *Pyrrh.* (PG 91: 333C).

50. Aquinas, *ST* I, Q. 82, art. 4.

abstain from that which reason dictates" (no. 163), as well as another closely related proposition, "That if reason is rectified, the will is also rectified" (no. 166). The condemnation of these two propositions, as is well known, did much to contribute to the rise of medieval voluntarism.

Yet if the will is not determined by reason, then how can we avoid positing it simply as a capacity for deciding arbitrarily among alternatives? And if it is thus arbitrary, are its operations truly intelligible? It is not intelligibility alone that is the worry here—although that is important enough—but also freedom, for we normally think of someone as acting freely precisely when his reasons can be understood. If it turns out that free choice is instead like a kind of random number generator operating in the mind, then it would seem that we are at the mercy of that random process rather than free agents. This was in essence the reply of the medieval intellectualists to the voluntarists, as it is the reply today of compatibilists to libertarians.

It is in light of this debate that I find Maximus' treatment of free choice particularly intriguing. Maximus places choice in the sequence of mental operations after deliberation and judgment, so that it is informed by the operations of reason. Yet it is not determined by them, for, as I mentioned earlier, it operates like a "vote" in relation to the results of judgment; that is, the will takes these results into account while also deciding from within, through its own spontaneous movement, whether to accept them. This movement is not arbitrary, for it is an expression of the will's intrinsic orientation towards goods that are in accordance with nature. The choice itself is not, therefore, in accordance with nature—far from it!—but it is at least intelligible as an expression of this innate desire.

Granted, any form of spontaneity always leaves a further question of "why?"—in this case, why does the will express its innate desire in one way rather than another? I suspect that Maximus, if faced with this question, might refer us to his teaching regarding the divine *logoi* and the ultimate human destiny of deification. As destined for deification, human beings must be spontaneous originators of their own character, because otherwise they would not share in that aspect of the divine nature that the Greek fathers called το αυτεξούσιον, self-determination. This does not render each choice in isolation fully intelligible, but it does render intelligible why our acts of understanding reach a limit. We find in ourselves an image of the same mystery that we find in God; and this is, if not understanding, then something far better.

7

The Action of the Holy Spirit in Christ, according to Saint Maximus the Confessor

LUIS GRANADOS

Due to the focus of the studies on his Christology, Maximus'
Pneumatology has been to some extent overlooked. A good number
of studies on the Confessor have dealt with his reflections on the two wills of
Christ and his obedience to the Father at the Garden of the Olives. Maximus
is in fact decisive in the controversy against monothelism and, at the same
time, against new versions of Nestorianism.

During the seventh century, where already the divinity of Christ
(ὁμοούσιος with the Father) was accepted, Maximus had to fight for the development of the understanding of his full humanity (the full meaning of
the ὁμοούσιος). His position shows the mystery of Christ in its wholeness,
rejecting any reduction of his humanity and also any division in him. In a
sense, he represents the last consequence of the Christological Councils and
the preparation of the Third Council of Constantinople.

The thought of St. Maximus the Confessor has already shown its richness in several areas of research, especially in Christology, but what about
his understanding of the identity, presence, and action of the Holy Spirit?

The main work on Maximus' Pneumatology can be considered the research of Loosen, *Pneuma und Logos*, published in 1941.[1] We can find some articles on this issue and parts of other studies, but no further monographs.[2] Usually, the interest of Maximus' Pneumatology has been reduced to the very important problem of the "filioque."

What is the role of the Spirit in the economy of salvation according to saint Maximus the Confessor? Does his theology, centered in Christ, forget the relevance of the Holy Spirit? What are the connections between his reflections on Christ's human will and the action of the Holy Spirit?

To answer these and other questions we can follow different paths. We will try to understand the role of the Spirit in Christ and follow the path chosen by the Confessor according to his unitarian cosmological vision. For St. Maximus, the whole history of the world is divided into two by the great mystery of the incarnation. The first age is that of the descent, of the preparation of the mystery of the incarnation, the Word made flesh.[3] In the center and hinge of the door of history we find the coming of Jesus Christ. The second age belongs to the ascension, to the mystery of divinization of man. According to this division of time, we will begin showing the role of the Spirit before Christ, that is, in creation and in the preparation for his incarnation. The unity and harmony of the divine project will help us to understand the role of the Spirit in Jesus Christ and how, through the mysteries of his life, it becomes progressively *his* Spirit, the Spirit of Christ. This will help us, finally, to see the new and definitive mission of the Holy Spirit. Coming from the Father, given through Christ, the Spirit works in Christians, giving them the shape of Christ, carrying them towards the unity of all creation.

The Presence of the Spirit in Creation

"In the beginning God created heaven and earth." For Maximus, creation is a Trinitarian work. Taking into account the priority of the Father, the Confessor insists on the unity of the divine communion in the origin of the world. The Father is Creator as cause of all being, but the *Logos* and the Spirit are also present and active in this moment.

In great measure, Maximus' Trinitarian theology depends on the Cappadocian fathers. Basil and the two Gregory's, who for Maximus were great

1. Loosen, *Logos und Pneuma*.

2. Cf. Kattan, *Verleiblichung und Synergie*; Piret, "Christologie et théologie trinitaire, 215–22; Piret, *Le Christ et la Trinité*.

3. Cf. Confessor, *Ad Thal.* 22 (CCSG 7: 137, 4–139, 56).

masters, had already struggled with the Eunomium crisis to defend the divinity of the Holy Spirit. In the seventh century, this was something more or less passively accepted, and it was no longer the main focus of discussion.

In order to show the divinity of the Holy Spirit against Eunomius, the Cappadocian fathers emphasized the unique character of the divine essence and operations. Defending the divine transcendence, they tended to consider the divine actions as belonging to the divine essence, without any other distinction. In this way, the personal differences were not specially considered. Having already established the divinity of the Son and of the Spirit, Maximus argues that in the moment of creation the Father and Son were in collaboration with one another. He envisages no danger of subordinationism in his explanation.

At the same time, Maximus received from the Cappadocians, and developed further, the distinction between *logos* (λόγος) and *tropos* (τρόπος), which is decisive in his Trinitarian theology. The one divine essence (λόγος) is shown in three ways (τρόποι). In this way, he could show the articulation of the essential unity and personal difference in God more clearly than his masters. The source of creation is the whole Trinity, but each divine person offers its own way of acting, its own τρόπος.

The Confessor addresses the problem of creation and Trinity in *Quaestiones et dubia*, 136, asking about the possibility of finding a "natural proof" (φυσικὴν ἀπόδειξιν) of the Holy Trinity. He answers by showing the three modes (τρόποι) in which every being exists: in the modes of essence, difference, and life (ἐν οὐσίᾳ, ἐν διαφορᾷ, ἐν ζωῇ). The first one, the essence of everything, belongs to the Father; the second, the difference between creatures, to Wisdom, that is, to the Son; the third, the life, to the Holy Spirit. God the Father creates through his *Logos* and his *Pneuma*. The Father gives the origin, the essence; the Son the difference; and the Spirit, life.[4]

For Maximus, God the Father creates through his *Logos* and his *Pneuma*. The presence of them as the source of difference and life shows the historical dynamism of creation. In this way, the difference and dependence of the creatures are seen as a part of the gift of the Trinitarian God and not just as a limit, a decline, or decadence.

Difference and life, the roles assigned to the *Logos* and *Pneuma*, open the mystery of creation to the growth in time. The goal of the cosmos goes beyond itself. Creation is good, and there is no lack in it, but it needs time to grow and develop all the richness sown by the Creator, to reach its *telos*.

---

4. Cf. Wendebourg, *Geist oder Energie*, 219–23. See the qualifications of Berthold "The Cappadocian Roots," 51–60. For this argument see also Heinzer, "L'explication trinitaire chez l'économie," 159–72.

What is this goal of creation, and how can be discovered and described this "growth" towards it? We find a hint of Maximus' answer to these questions in *Quaestiones ad Thalassium* 15. Maximus offers a connection of the dynamism of creation with the presence of the Holy Spirit.

Three kinds of presence of the Spirit

The Confessor discusses here the witness of the Holy Scripture in the book of Wisdom (12:1): "Your incorruptible Spirit is in all" (τὸ γὰρ ἄφθαρτόν σου Πνεῦμά ἐστιν ἐν πᾶσι). How can the Holy Spirit dwell in everything, even, for example, in the sinner? Is that possible?

The Confessor develops three different degrees of the presence of the Spirit in creatures. The Spirit is "in all *simpliciter* (ἁπλῶς), insofar as it contains, provides, and moves upwards all the natural seeds."[5] Dwelling in every being for the very fact of being, his presence is higher in those living according to the law, showing the promise of Christ. But the main principle of this problem has been established by Maximus from the beginning of the *Quaestio*: he begins his answer with a decisive statement. "The Holy Spirit is not absent from any being, and with more reason, (is not absent) from those who share in some way with the *Logos*" (Τὸ Πνεῦμα τὸ ἅγιον οὐδενὸς ἄπεστι τῶν ὄντων, καὶ μάλιστα τῶν λόγου καθοτιοῦν μετειληφότων). The growing presence of the *Logos* is accompanied by a growing action of the Spirit. *Ubi Logos, ibi Pneuma*.

For that reason, the third and highest presence of the Spirit is given to those who are according to Christ (κατὰ Χριστόν) and receive the gift of filiation. In "all those who through their faith have inherited the divine and divine-maker name of Christ" (ἐν πᾶσι τοῖς τὸ θεῖον καὶ θεοποιὸν ὄντως ὄνομα τοῦ Χριστοῦ κληρωσαμένοις διὰ τῆς πίστεως) the Spirit is present "as maker of filiation, according to grace and faith" (ὡς δημιουργικὸν τῆς κατὰ χάριν διὰ τῆς πίστεως δοθείσης υἱοθεσίας). In this way, the author of the book of Wisdom "through the divine citizenship, makes the human being apt to his divine indwelling" (διὰ τῆς ἐνθέου πολιτείας ἀξίους ποιησαμένων τῆς αὐτοῦ θεωτικῆς ἐνοικήσεως).

---

5. Confessor, *Ad Thal.* 15 (CCSG 7: 103, 41–42): Ἔστιν οὖν ἐν πᾶσι μὲν ἁπλῶς, καθ᾽ ὃ πάντων ἐστὶ συνεκτικὸν καὶ προνοητικὸν καὶ τῶν φυσικῶν σπερμάτων ἀνακινητικόν.

The condensation of the *Logos*

This basic and progressive presence of the Holy Spirit in creation corresponds to a growing presence of the *Logos* of God, which is described by Maximus—following an idea by Origen—as a triple incarnation in creation, in the Holy Scripture, and in the faithful.[6] Our author develops this idea commenting on three words of a famous prayer of St. Gregory the Theologian: Παχύνεσθαι ὁ Λόγος. "The *Logos* thickens," i.e., the Word condenses himself, becomes dense.[7] The whole time of the cosmos before Christ is described with this expression.

> If the *Logos* condenses himself (Παχύνεσθαι ὁ Λόγος), as the Master (who has God in himself) says, this is because, I think, being simple and bodiless, and nourishing spiritually all the divine potencies of heaven, he decided to condense himself through his coming in the flesh (διὰ τῆς ἐνσάρκου αὐτοῦ παρουσίας) which comes from us, by us and according to us, except in sin.[8]

This progressive condensation implies different degrees of presence (παρουσία) of the *Logos*.[9] The first and broadest one corresponds to his hiding in the *logoi* of every creature, as if they were the letters of an alphabet (διά τινων γραμμάτων). A second presence of the *Logos* is given in the Holy Scripture. Now the *Logos* is not just letters but also words and sounds unified by the Spirit.[10]

6. About this triple incarnation, see Origen, *Commentaria in Evangelium Joannis* 13, 42 (PG 14: 472 D–476 A). Maximus overcomes the several difficulties of the idea of a triple incarnation of the *Logos*. Emphasizing the importance of the living and rational flesh of Christ, he rejects any relativization of the definitive and absolute incarnation of the *Logos* in Jesus.

7. Nazianzus, *Oration* 38, 7 (PG 36: 313 B): (Ο Λόγος παχύνεται) "The One without flesh is made flesh, the *Logos* condenses himself, the Invisible is seen, the Intangible is touched, the Timeless has a beginning, the Son of God becomes son of man." For a brief explanation of this words, see Balthasar, "La parola si condensa," 31–35.

8. Confessor, *Amb.* 33 (PG 91: 1285C–1288): Α Παχύνεσθαι ὁ Λόγος εἴρηται τῷ θεοφόρῳ διδασκάλῳ κατὰ τήνδε, ὡς οἶμαι, τὴν ἔννοιαν, ἢ ὅτι Λόγος ὢν ἀπλοῦς τε καί ἀσώματος, καί πάσας καθεξῆς πνευματικῶς τρέφων τάς ἐν οὐρανῷ θείας δυνάμεις, κατηξίωσε καί διὰ τῆς ἐνσάρκου αὐτοῦ παρουσίας ἐξ ἡμῶν δι' ἡμᾶς καθ' ἡμᾶς ἁμαρτίας χωρίς παχυνθῆναι.

9. Cf. Liddell-Scott, *A Greek-English Lexicon*, 1343.

10. This is the interpretation of Balthasar (*Liturgia cosmica*, 252). This idea has been developed by Kattan in *Verleiblichung und Synergie*. This idea, received from Origen, appears usually in Maximus' works. "The *Logos* of God has become body (σεσωματωμένον) in the letters of the Holy Scriptures in different ways and through enigmata" (σεσωματωμένον), *Cap. Gnost.* 2, 73. See also *Amb.* 10 (PG 91: 1128C).

Creation and Scripture are the two places where the *Logos* takes gradually consistence and, therefore, are places of a special knowledge of God. This gradualness shows the unity of the divine project and the delicacy of his condescension towards us.

For Maximus, there is no confusion between this growing presence of the *Logos* in nature and Scripture and his unique coming in the flesh (παρουσία ἔνσαρκος). The presence of the *Logos* in Christ, prepared from the very beginning of history, is, at the same time, the greatest novelty.[11] The coming of the *Logos* in nature and Scripture prepares the world for his definitive coming in the soil of the Virgin Mary. "The mystery of the Incarnation of the *Logos*," says Maximus, "possesses in itself the power (τὴν δύναμιν) of all the secrets and images of the Scripture, as well as the knowledge of visible and intelligible creatures."[12]

Thus, the path of both, *Logos* and *Pneuma*, is fulfilled in Christ, the goal of creation. They are not just two parallel ways, but also one and the same. Ubi *Logos* ibi *Pneuma*. The progressive "incarnation" of the *Logos* is performed by the Spirit and establishes the rhythm of the three laws: the law of nature, the written law, and the law of grace. From the beginning, the coming of the *Logos* in the flesh, his "condensation," is the work of the Spirit.

Image and likeness

Before we go ahead, we need to consider another distinction of the Confessor, which shows again the dynamism of growth and development introduced by God in the cosmos. The first book of the Scriptures presents God's project when he created man: "Let us make man in our image, after our likeness" (Gen 1:26). But then immediately we find that "God created man in his image; in the divine image he created him." What about divine likeness?

Following a long tradition, Maximus sees this difference between the project (image and likeness) and the result (just the image) as the indication of a path to be followed.[13] For Adam, the gift of creation implies a task:

11. This idea is developed by Balthasar (*Liturgia cosmica*, 252) beginning from *Amb.* 33. See also Blowers, *Exegesis and Spiritual Pedagogy*, 119, 168 n.114; Thunberg, *Microcosm and Mediator*, 77, 394. Another explanation of this text is offered by Sherwood, *The Earlier Ambigua*, 52.

12. Confessor, *Cap. Gnost.* I.66 (PG 90: 1108B): Τό τῆς ἐνσωματώσεως τοῦ Λόγου μυστήριον, πάντων ἔχει τῶν τε κατά τήν Γραφήν αἰνιγμάτων καί τύπων τήν δύναμιν, καί τῶν φαινομένων καί νοουμένων κτισμάτων τήν ἐπιστήμην.

13. Cf. Confessor, *Qu. Dub.* 3, 1 (CCSG 10: 170, 2–4): Τί ἐστι τό «ποιήσωμεν ἄνθρωπον. κατ᾽ εἰκόνα Θεοῦ καί ὁμοίωσιν», καί ὑποκαταβάς λέγει «καί ἐποίησεν ὁ Θεός τόν ἄνθρωπον, κατ᾽ εἰκόνα Θεοῦ ἐποίησεν αὐτόν» καί παρέλειπεν τό καθ᾽ ὁμοίωσιν.

created in God's image, he is called to walk through virtues and knowledge towards likeness. This distinction is a key element of Maximus' thought. As Lars Thunberg puts it, "the energy and conscience with which [Maximus] emphasizes the difference between image and likeness" is one of the "striking features of [his] anthropology,"[14] and, we can add, of his Christology.

Distinguishing between image and likeness, Maximus receives the influence of Origen and accepts an idea with a long and not so peaceful story.[15] Maximus is aware of the dangers this distinction had assumed in its Origenistic version. On the one hand, the necessity of a path from image to likeness could be read as a sign of imperfection in creation, and on the other hand it could be interpreted as an excessive emphasis on human effort. For Maximus, the path of creation from image to likeness implies no poverty in God's work, no lack of perfection, but the possibility of development and the promise of a new fulfillment. Difference and life, the sign of the presence of the *Logos* and *Pneuma* in every creature, come from a prior fullness, not from necessity or lack.

The distinction between image and likeness is also expressed by the Confessor with the image of the clay, from which Adam was created in the beginning. The process of this modulation was to continue through human action, progressing towards divine likeness. Like Adam, every human being is "divine clay" ($\pi\lambda\acute{\alpha}\sigma\mu\alpha$ $\Theta\epsilon o\tilde{u}$)[16] who has received the divine sign in order to obtain the definitive form through action.[17] With the coming of Christ be-

14. Thunberg, *Microcosm and Mediator*, 120. The place given by an author to the *imago Dei* can be seen as representative of his global theological position. For Saint Ireneus, for example, and for Saint Ciprianus and Lactancius, the body belongs to some extent, to the *imago Dei*. Later on, especially in the Alexandrian tradition, the image of God will be placed in the human soul. The body will be considered, in the best of cases, as the recipient of the divine image. Cf. Thunberg, *Microcosm and Mediator*, 114–119.

15. Saint Ireneus of Lyon explains paradigmatically this distinction as a necessity of growth in time: *homo nuper factus est*. Adam was created a child and was called to receive the likeness through the work of the Spirit. Cf. *Adversus Haereses* 5, 6, 1 (SC 153: 72–80). For Clement of Alexandria, this likeness, the perfection of the image, is something beyond nature and will be given in the future state (cf. *Stromata* 2, 22, SC 38: 133). Likeness is also connected to eschatology in Origen, who insists in the imitation of Christ through virtues (cf. *De Principiis* 3, 6, 1, SC 268: 234; *Homilies on Leviticus* 12, 7, GCS 6: 466). From the fourth century on, this distinction, mixed with a certain Origenist explanation, is more or less abandoned. See the explanation and bibliography offered by Thunberg, *Microcosm and Mediator*, 114, 120–24. See also Cooper, *The Body in St. Maximus the Confessor*, 95–102.

16. Confessor, *Th. Pol.* 7 (PG 91: 80B).

17. To be "divine clay" indicates the human dignity as *imago Dei* and his call to growth. "Nothing natural is contrary to God. This is evident because all these things have been created by Him, according to the generation ($\kappa\alpha\tau\acute{\alpha}$ $\gamma\acute{\epsilon}\nu\nu\eta\sigma\iota\nu$) and there is nothing reproachable in our essential constitution. . . . According to this generation

gan the mystery of the *theoplastia* (θεοπλαστία).[18] Becoming flesh, assuming the human form in the Virgin Mary, the *Logos* of God also became clay.[19] In this way both the "image-likeness" distinction and the growing presence of the Spirit in creation guide us towards the mystery of Christ.

The Role of the Spirit in Christ

What is the role of the Holy Spirit in Christ, the *Logos* made flesh? Let us begin with the mystery of incarnation, which will guide us to the following mysteries of the life of Christ.

The presence of the Trinity in the incarnation

In very different ways and occasions, St. Maximus expressed his love and devotion to the mystery of the mysteries, the incarnation of the *Logos*, in which heaven and earth are joined together. As with creation, also the incarnation is a Trinitarian work. The whole mystery of God is present in it, according to the different modes of each person. Based on several expressions by St. Ireneus of Lyon and St. Gregory of Nazianzus, Maximus creates a very interesting trilogy, which reveals this participation.[20] Let us examine

---

we are divine clay and we are the most valuable creature in nature." ('Ότι γάρ οὐδέν ἀντίκειται Θεῷ φυσικόν, δῆλον ἐκ τοῦ ταῦτα κατά γέννησιν ὑπ' αὐτοῦ δημιουργηθῆναι, καί μηδεμίαν ὑπέρ τῆς οὐσιώδους ἐν ἡμῖν τούτων συστάσεως αἰτίασιν ἔχειν· . . . κατ' ἐκείνην δέ, πλάσμα Θεοῦ καί τίμιον κτίσμα κατά φύσιν ὑπάρχομεν), *Th. Pol.* 7 (PG 91: 80B).

18. Confessor, *Th. Pol.* 4 (PG 91: 57). The term θεοπλαστία is very rare in the patristic ages. We find it in Maximus referred to the incarnation. The Confessor seems to receive it from Denys, the first one who applied it to the mystery of Jesus ("assumption of form by God," cf. Lampe, *A Patristic Greek Lexicon*, 629–30. For Denys, the *theoplastia* of Jesus for our sake, is the most evident and the most ununderstandable principle of the theology (cf. *DN* 2, 9, PG 3: 648 A). This is the mission of the angels: their gift to man consists in the communication of the mystery of the love of God, and what Gabriel revealed to Mary was the mystery of the *theoplastia* (cf. *EH* 4, 4, PG 3: 181B). The term θεοπλαστία is hardly used before Denys. In these few cases, it is used in a negative sense, to indicate pagan idolatry. Cf. Athanasius, *Contra Gentes* 19 (PG 25: 40B).

19. This is the reading of Denys, made by Maximus: "And again, look how he says that in Saint Mary, the Mother of God, it is performed the divine mystery of the ineffable *theoplastia*. He calls it *theoplastia* because God became clay (ἐπλάσθη), insofar as he became man, as the Scripture says: The Logos was made flesh (John 1:1)." *EH* 4, 4 (PG 3): ἐν τῇ ἁγίᾳ Θεοτόκῳ Μαρίᾳ γενέσθαι τῆς ἀρρήτου θεοπλαστίας τό θεαρχικόν μυστήριον. Θεοπλαστίαν δέ λέγει, δηλῶν ὅτι Θεός ἐπλάσθη, καθ' ὅ γέγονεν ἄνθρωπος, ὡς τό εἰρημένον, «ὁ Λόγος σάρξ ἐγένετο.»

20. See Ireneus, *Adversus Haereses* IV, 20, 6 (SC 100: 645); IV 38, 3 (SC 100: 955) and

one of the most evident descriptions of this Trinitarian work found in *Ad Thalassium* 60.

> This Mystery was foreknown, before all ages, only by the Father and the Son and the Holy Spirit: by the Father as his loving plan (τῷ μὲν κατ᾽ εὐδοκίαν); by the Son as his own work (τῷ δὲ κατ᾽ αὐτουργίαν); by the Spirit as his cooperation (τῷ δὲ κατὰ συνεργίαν). For Father, Son, and Holy Spirit share one knowledge, because they have one essence and power. The Father is not ignorant of the Incarnation of the Son, nor is the Holy Spirit. For the Mystery, present wholly in the Son as he worked out (αὐτουργοῦντι) our salvation by becoming flesh, is, in the order of essence, wholly the Father: not that *he* became flesh, but that he assented (οὐ σαρκούμενος ἀλλ᾽ εὐδοκῶν) to the Son's incarnation. And the Holy Spirit is present totally, in the order of essence, in the totality of the Son: not that he became flesh, but that he worked along with the Son (οὐ σαρκούμενον ἀλλὰ συνεργοῦν τῷ Υἱῷ), (the Son's) ineffable incarnation for our sake.[21]

In the mystery of Nazareth, the whole Trinity is active: the Father through the εὐδοκία, his loving plan, his benevolence; the Son through the αὐτουργία, his own work; and the Spirit through the συνεργία, his cooperation.

The contribution of the Father is described as εὐδοκία or benevolence[22] towards the Son, that is, as his gaze of satisfaction and recognition. As to Abram, the Father says to the *Logos*: "Go forth from the land of your kins-

---

the beginning of the second theological discourse of Nazianzus, *Oration* 29, 1 (SC 250: 100). Dealing with the divine revelation in the ancient covenant and to the creation of man after God's image, Saint Ireneus speaks of the benevolence of the Father (εὐδοκία), the action of the Spirit (ὑπουργία), and the service of the Son (διακονία). In his prayer to the Holy Trinity, Saint Gregory speaks of the benevolence of the Father (εὐδοκία), the *synergy* of the Son, and the mission of the Spirit. Cf. F. Heinzer, "L'explication trinitaire," 162; Riou, *Le monde et l'Église*, 218, n.5.

21. Confessor, *Ad Thal.* 60 (PG 90: 624B–C): Τοῦτο τὸ μυστήριον προεγνώσθη πρὸ πάντων τῶν αἰώνων μόνῳ τῷ Πατρὶ καὶ τῷ Υἱῷ καὶ τῷ ἁγίῳ Πνεύματι, τῷ μὲν κατ᾽ εὐδοκίαν, τῷ δὲ κατ᾽ αὐτουργίαν, τῷ δὲ κατὰ συνεργίαν· μία γὰρ ἡ Πατρὸς καὶ Υἱοῦ καὶ ἁγίου Πνεύματος γνῶσις, ὅτι καὶ μία οὐσία καὶ δύναμις. Οὐ γὰρ ἠγνόει τοῦ Υἱοῦ τὴν σάρκωσιν ὁ Πατὴρ ἢ τὸ Πνεῦμα τὸ ἅγιον, ὅτι ἐν ὅλῳ τῷ Υἱῷ τὸ μυστήριον αὐτουργοῦντι τῆς ἡμῶν σωτηρίας διὰ σαρκώσεως ὅλος κατ᾽ οὐσίαν ὁ Πατήρ, οὐ σαρκούμενος ἀλλ᾽ εὐδοκῶν τοῦ Υἱοῦ τὴν σάρκωσιν, καὶ ὅλον ἐν ὅλῳ τῷ Υἱῷ τὸ Πνεῦμα τὸ ἅγιον κατ᾽ οὐσίαν ὑπῆρχεν, οὐ σαρκούμενον ἀλλὰ συνεργοῦν τῷ Υἱῷ τὴν δι᾽ ἡμᾶς ἀπόρρητον σάρκωσιν.

22. Lampe (*A Patristic Greek*, 562–63) translates this as "good will, good pleasure (towards), favor." We find it applied to the incarnation in Ireneus, *Adversus Haereses* 1, 9, 3 (PG 7: 541B) and Clement of Alexandria, *Exc. Thdot.* 23, 114.20 (PG 9: 669B).

folk and from your father's home."[23] This benevolence indicates the order (*taxis*) of the Trinity present in the incarnation: the Son is sent by the Father.

But the main action in this mystery belongs to the Son, to his αὐτουργία (i.e., the work he performed in himself),[24] fulfilling the will of the Father. This *autourgia* indicates the uniqueness of the mission of the Son in the incarnation: the Father and the Spirit are present, but only the Son assumes the flesh in himself.[25] For that reason, this term does not indicate autonomy or independence: it is the filial fulfillment of the paternal *eudokia*, the assumption of the flesh.[26] As the *eudokia* of the Father is referred to Abram's vocation, *autourgia* is related to the filial consent (συγχώρησις) "according to the things suffered by Job."[27]

Finally, the Spirit is present through his synergy (συνεργία)[28] with the Son. This term indicates a kind of collaboration, of working with another, with the Son. Other parallel expressions of Maximus show the sense of this action of the Spirit. "My Father works and so do I"[29]—one through his *eudokia*, other by his *autourgia*, and the Holy Spirit, essentially bringing into perfection (συμπληροῦντος) in everything the *eudokia* of the Father and the *autourgia* of the Son.[30]

On another occasion, speaking about the tent of the encounter (tabernacle) of Moses with God as being fulfilled in the flesh of Christ, Maximus

---

23. Cf. *Qu. Dub.* 83 (CCSG 10: 66, 3–5): κατ' εὐδοκίαν, κατ' οἰκονομίαν, κατὰ συγχώρησιν. Καὶ τὸ μὲν κατ' εὐδοκίαν δηλοῖ τὰ κατὰ τὸν Ἀβραάμ, λέγοντα πρὸς αὐτὸν ἔξελθε ἐκ τῆς γῆς σου.

24. Cf. Lampe, *A Patristic Greek*, 272.

25. "*Autourgein* heißt wörtlich selbst tun im Gegensatz zum Tun durch einen Mittler." Loosen, *Logos und Pneuma*, 124. Cf. Stephanus, *Thesaurus Linguae Graecae*, 2572–74.

26. Cf. Confessor, *Amb.* 41. In this sense, it is interesting to show that this term (*autourgia*) does not come to the Confessor from the Alexandrian tradition (as able to safeguard the divinity of Christ), but from Denys, as part of the movements of the ecclesiastic hierarchy and sign of the humility of the Son.

27. Confessor, *Qu. Dub.* 83 (CCSG 10: 66, 7): τὸ δὲ κατὰ συγχώρησιν δηλοῖ τὰ κατὰ τὸν Ἰὼβ γενόμενα. Lampe shows several uses of συγχώρησις. In the sense of "agreement, assent, permission, will of God, of such things as are allowed without being in his absolute will" is frequently applied—as in this case—to the sufferings of Christ. We find other uses of this term ("remission, forgiveness, pardon, absolution . . .") in the works of the Confessor (especially in *Or. Dom.*). Cf. Lampe, *A Patristic Greek*, 1277–78.

28. We can translate this term as "working with, cooperation," cf. Lampe, *A Patristic Greek*, 1323.

29. John 5:17.

30. Confessor, *Ad Thal.* 2 (CCSG 7: 51, 23–26): ὁ Πατήρ μου ἕως ἄρτι ἐργάζεται, κἀγὼ ἐργάζομαι, ὁ μὲν εὐδοκῶν, ὁ δὲ αὐτουργῶν, καὶ τοῦ ἁγίου Πνεύματος οὐσιωδῶς τήν τε τοῦ Πατρὸς ἐπὶ πᾶσιν εὐδοκίαν καὶ τὴν αὐτουργίαν τοῦ Υἱοῦ συμπληροῦντος.

describes the tent as that "which the Father as *nous* projected (ἐνενόησε), the Son as *Logos* created (ἐδημιούργησε), and the Holy Spirit brought to its perfection (ἐτελείωσε)."[31]

These two expressions show the *synergia* of the Spirit as a task to be developed in time, which implies a further perfection (τελείωσις, συμπλήρωσις).[32] The works of the Father and of the Son, *eudokia* and *autourgia* need fulfillment. The project of the Father, performed by the *Logos*, is brought to its goal by the Spirit.

In this sense, following the comparison of the *eudokia* as the vocation addressed to Abram and the *autourgia* as Job's patience, the *synergy* of the Spirit is compared with the administration (*oikonomia*) of "Joseph in Egypt, who guided everything towards the accomplishment of the future things."[33]

What then is the role of the Spirit in the mystery of incarnation? His *synergia*, his fulfillment of the work of the Father and the Son, is manifested first of all in the unity of the *Logos* with the flesh of Mary.[34] Through the work of the Spirit, Jesus is the child of Mary and the Son of the Father, perfect God and perfect man. The depth of this union, as Maximus understands it, implies the beginning of something new.

> The Apostle says: "I am doing everything new."[35] . . . If the new-
> ness is a quality, it does not reveal only one operation (ἐνέργεια),

31. Confessor, *Amb.* 61 (PG 91: 1388A). The tent of the encounter is an image of the creation, of the covenant of God with Moses, and of the flesh of Christ. *Amb.* 61 (PG 91: 1385C–D): Σκηνὴ τοιγαροῦν τοῦ μαρτυρίου ἡ μυστηριώδης ἐστίν οἰκονομία τῆς τοῦ Θεοῦ Λόγου σαρκώσεως, ἥν ὁ Θεός καί Πατήρ εὐδοκήσας παρέδειξε, καί τό Πνεῦμα τό ἅγιον διά τοῦ σοφοῦ Βεσελεήλ προτυπούμενον συνεργῆσαν ἐτελείωσε, καί ὁ νοητός Μωϋσῆς ὁ τοῦ Θεοῦ καί Πατρός μονογενής Υἱός αὐτούργησε, τήν ἀνθρωπίνην φύσιν ἐν ἑαυτῷ πηξάμενος ἑνώσει τῇ καθ᾽ ὑπόστασιν.

32. The term τελείωσις indicates "completion, consummation, perfection, sanctification, consecration" (Lampe, *A Patristic Greek*, 1383), and συμπλήρωσις can be translated as "filling up, repletion, fulfillment" (Lampe, *A Patristic Greek*, 1289).

33. Confessor, *Qu. Dub.* 83 (CCSG 10: 66, 5–6): τό δὲ κατ᾽ οἰκονομίαν δηλοῖ τά κατά τόν Ἰωσήφ οἰκονομηθέντα πρός τήν τῶν μελλόντων ἔκβασιν. As we will see, the work of the Spirit in Christ is called to be continued in every human being and, thus, to be spread throughout the whole creation. The Spirit, in fact, "is the one who brings into perfection every creature" (πάντων ἐστί τῶν ὄντων πληρωτικόν), *Ad Thal.* 29, scholia 1 (CCSG 7: 215, 5–6).

34. Cf. Confessor, *Amb.* 42 (PG 91: 1324C–D): "Through his Incarnation from the Holy Spirit and from the holy Mother of God, Mary, always virgin, He 'humanized' himself perfectly, that is, He became perfect man, through the assumption of the flesh, which has an inteligent and rational soul" (σαρκωθείς ἐκ Πνεύματος ἁγίου, καί τῆς ἁγίας Θεοτόκου καί ἀειπαρθένου Μαρίας, τελείως ἐνηνθρώπησεν· τουτέστι, τέλειος γέγονεν ἄνθρωπος, κατά πρόσληψιν δηλονότι σαρκός, ψυχήν ἐχούσης νοεράν τε καί λογικήν). Cf. *Ep.* 15 (PG 91: 553C).

35. 2 Cor 5:17.

but the new and ineffable way (καινὸν καὶ ἀπόρρητον τρόπον) of manifestation of the natural operations of Christ, according to the ineffable way of the reciprocal (εἰς ἀλλήλας) *perichoresis* (περιχωρήσεως) of the natures of Christ, and his whole citizenship (πολιτείαν) as man.[36]

Arguing against monothelism, Maximus shows that the newness of the coming of Christ implies a unity that safeguards the difference of natures in Jesus Christ and therefore of their activities and wills (human and divine). Human nature implies a human principle of action will, which God calls to be exercised. If the *Logos*-made-flesh is truly *homoousios* with the Father and with us, then he will be also *homoerges*, that is, he will have the same power or energy with the Father and with us.[37]

In this way, the unity performed by the *synergia* of the Spirit in Christ is the beginning of a new path. The incarnation, the greatest of all mysteries, is not the end of the long journey of the *Logos* (and *Pneuma*) in nature and Scripture. As the hinge of history, this mystery opens the path of the mysteries of Jesus' life. For the Confessor, to assume flesh means to accept the patience of time and space. In other words, as a human being, Jesus has to walk from God's image towards divine likeness. Maximus' understanding of human nature implies that this perfection and fulfillment of the Spirit, this *telos*, is obtained during the time of Jesus.

Noted Maximus scholar Jean-Claude Larchet would perhaps disagree with this reading of the Confessor. For Larchet, Maximus sees the incarnation of Christ as the moment of the total and definitive divinization of the flesh of Christ, through his union with the divinity.[38] The *synergy* of the Spirit is fulfilled in this moment. Larchet could see establishing a path of growth of the Spirit in Christ as the temptation of considering St. Maximus a Nestorian. The insistence of the Confessor of both divine and human wills in Jesus, against monothelism, is perhaps moving his position towards the opposite pole (i.e., Nestorianism)? Nestorian's dithelism, as Maximus understood it, was not able to distinguish the difference of wills from the divergence or dualism. For Nestorianism, the way of Jesus' human will towards harmony with the divine will would imply struggle and division.

---

36. Confessor, *Pyrrh.* (PG 91: 345D–348): ὅταν λέγῃ ὁ Ἀπόστολος, Ἰδοὺ γέγονε τά πάντα καινά. . . . Εἰ δὲ ποιότης ἐστὶν ἡ καινότης, οὐ μίαν δηλοῖ ἐνέργειαν, ἀλλά τόν καινὸν καὶ ἀπόρρητον τρόπον τῆς τῶν φυσικῶν τοῦ Χριστοῦ ἐνεργειῶν ἐκφάνσεως, τῷ ἀπορρήτῳ τρόπῳ τῆς εἰς ἀλλήλας τῶν Χριστοῦ φύσεων περιχωρήσεως προσφόρως, καί τήν κατά ἄνθρωπον αὐτοῦ πολιτείαν.

37. Cf. Confessor, *Th. Pol.* 9 (PG 91: 116A): ὁμοεργής, εἴτουν ὁμοούσιος, ὁ σαρκωθείς καθέστηκε Λόγος.

38. Cf. Larchet, *La divinisation de l'homme.*

But the route Maximus considers is not of this kind of difference. Jesus' human will has to be exercised and needs time to learn, but from the very beginning of its existence in event of the incarnation, this will has been "fully divinized," marked and moved by the Spirit. Its path, then, includes no possibility of sin (with no *gnome*) or struggle with his divine will. It is a way towards the virtues, but with no possibility of sin or of opposition in Jesus.

For that reason, Maximus explains that Jesus' human will after the incarnation is "fully divinized" (θεωθέν, *deificatum*) but not "transformed in God" (θεόθεν ὅλον, *a Deo totum*). Moved and marked by the Holy Spirit, Jesus' human will is anchored in the Father's will, but it conserves its own dynamism and *logos*. It is not absorbed by his divine will. This work of the Spirit in Christ's human activity and will is in perfect synergy, and it also takes place in and through time.[39]

Therefore, the mystery of Nazareth is not everything. It is the beginning of a path in which the work of the Spirit in the flesh of Christ will be decisive. This development of the Mystery of Christ in the mysteries of his life, which is expressed in another image of the Confessor: the threefold generation of our Lord.

The Mystery developed in the mysteries: a triple generation

The path followed by Christ in his life and in his deep relationship with the Spirit is described by the Confessor as a triple generation, which corresponds with the general structure of the world: to be–to be good–to be good forever.

> The Scripture (ὁ Λόγος) knows, according to our opinion, three generations (Τρισσὴν γέννησιν): one regarding the bodies, other regarding Baptism and other regarding Resurrection. . . . My Christ manifests himself honoring (τιμήσας . . . φαίνεται) by himself all these generations.[40]

---

39. Cf. Confessor, *Th. Pol.* 20 (PG 91: 233B–236 A): Περί δέ τῆς εἰς τήν χρῆσιν ἑρμηνείας τοῦ θεολόγου καί μεγάλου τῆς Ἐκκλησίας (ἀληθείας) κήρυκος Γρηγορίου, τήν «Παρά τοῦ ἀνθρώπου τυποῦσθαι τόν λόγον φάσκουσαν οὐ τοῦ κατά τόν Σωτῆρα νοουμένου. Τό γάρ ἐκείνου θέλειν, οὐδέ ὑπεναντίον Θεῷ θεωθέν ὅλον», λίαν μέν εὐσεβοῦς ἠρτημένης ὁρίζομαι διανοίας, ὑπέρ ἧς καί ἐξ ἧς ἐσπουδάσθη τῷ φιλοπόνῳ, μικρόν δέ περί τό τῆς λέξεως ἀκριβές ἐνδεοῦς. . . . Τό δέ γε παροξυτόνως ὡς ἐξ ἀντιγράφων τινῶν ἐκφωνεῖν τό θεωθέν ὅλον, καί μή μᾶλλον ὀξυτόνως, δέοι τοῦ μή τό ἕν εἰσαχθῆναι θέλημα πρός τῶν ἐναντίων. . . . Ἡ γάρ ὀξύτονος τοῦ θεωθέν φράσις, οὔτε εἰς ταυτόν οὐσιώδους καί φυσικοῦ θελήματος ἄγει τό, ὡς ἀνθρώπου κατά τόν Σωτῆρα θέλειν.

40. Nazianzus, *Oration* 40, 2, quoted by Maximus in *Amb.* 42 (PG 91: 1316A–B): Τρισσήν γέννησιν ἡμῖν οἶδεν ὁ Λόγος, τήν ἐκ σωμάτων, τήν ἐκ βαπτίσματος, τήν ἐξ

Commenting on an idea of St. Gregory Nazianzen, Maximus assumes the presence of the three generations in the life of Christ. After his first generation in the body, Jesus experienced two other generations: in his baptism at the Jordan river and in the resurrection. This triad has been called by Lars Thunberg the "three redemptive births of Christ,"[41] which are connected with: the three human births, the three days, and the three laws. This threefold generation can be described as the ontological, ethical, and eschatological births. They establish a path of growth, which begins in the incarnation and progresses forward.

The theme of the triple generation also shows some of the limits of Loosen's study *Pneuma und Logos*. His work is divided in two parts, one devoted to the presence of the *Logos* in the humanity of Jesus by grace, and the other devoted to the same issue but in regards to the *Pneuma*. This position risks explaining the action of the Son and the Spirit as a mere juxtaposition (one next to the other). Our interest consists in showing precisely how the Spirit is *working in* the flesh assumed by the *Logos* and finally becomes the Spirit *of* Christ.

Baptism and the path of the Spirit in Christ

The main texts devoted by the Confessor to baptism are related to the sacrament and its effect in the Christians.[42] In *Ambigua* 42, Maximus offers a very short explanation.

> The One who is God by nature, accepts for our sake the generation from Baptism, for the filial adoption in the Spirit (τὴν ἐκ βαπτίσματος εἰς υἱοθεσίαν πνευματικὴν ὑπὲρ ἡμῶν ὑπελθεῖν καταδέχεται γέννησιν); for that reason, I think, the Master united the generation from Baptism to the Incarnation. He substituted in himself the generation of the body, fruit of our condemnation, with the generation in the Spirit, so that he gave those who believe in His Name, the possibility of becoming children of God.[43]

ἀναστάσεως· . . . Ταύτας δέ τάς γεννήσεις ἀπάσας παρ' ἑαυτοῦ τιμήσας ὁ ἐμός Χριστός φαίνεται.

41. Thunberg, *Microcosm and Mediator*, 369. Cf. *Amb.* 65 (PG 91: 1392B–D); *Cap. Gnost.* 1, 56 (PG 90: 1104C); *Ad Thal.* 64 (CCSG 22, 237).

42. Regarding this topic, see for example Larchet, "Le baptême selon saint Maxime," 51–70.

43. Confessor, *Amb.* 42 (PG 91: 1348C–D).

Therefore, the generation of baptism implies a new filial adoption in the Spirit. What does this mean in Christ? He is from the beginning, the very Son of God made flesh. But after his incarnation (i.e., generation in being) his human nature needs to be exercised so that it can be generated in well-being. The baptism in the Jordan witnesses the necessity of this moment in the life of Christ and the work of the Spirit in his flesh.

Maximus expresses this point with the idea of the double filiation of Christ. The eternal Son of God becomes, through the Virgin and the Holy Spirit, son of man. According to the Letter to the Hebrews (reading Psalm 39:7), Maximus describes the body of Jesus, received from the Father, as a path of obedience in which he will learn the divine Name. "God" is the name proper to his human nature. Now he is called to learn to name God as "Father," as the *Logos* of God does.[44]

"Jesus advanced in wisdom and age and grace before God and man" (Luke 2:52). Considering seriously the dynamism of the flesh, as the Confessor does, we have to accept that the human energy and will of Jesus Christ need the exercise, time of learning, and work necessary to attain the different virtues. Maximus describes the path of Jesus' human will as a *configuration and a movement* (τυπούμενον καὶ κινούμενον) of the work of God in him.[45] The Holy Spirit is the one who forms in him the ἕχεις of the virtues, transforming his natural passions.

We can understand the sense of this mystery if we remember the mystery of the *theoplastia* and the path from image to likeness of God. The modeling of the flesh now implies the movements of the human nature—his operations, passions, and acts of willing. By the mysterious unity of Christ, his passions are miraculous passions, and his wonders are suffering wonders. This is the progressive work of the Spirit in the flesh: to make the flesh *theurgos*, able to work wonders, and in this way, *synergites*, cooperator with the redemption.

---

44. Cf. Confessor, *Pyrrh.* (PG 91: 324C–D): Θυσίαν καί προσφοράν, φησίν, οὐκ ἠθέλησας, σῶμα δέ κατηρτίσω μοι. Ὁλοκαυτώματα καί περί ἁμαρτίας οὐκ ἐξεζήτησας· τότε εἶπον· Ἰδοὺ ἥκω. Ἐν κεφαλίδι βιβλίου γέγραπται περί ἐμοῦ, τοῦ ποιῆσαι τό θέλημα σου· ὁ Θεός μου, ἠβουλήθην. Ὅτι μέν καθ' ὅ ἄνθρωπος ὁ Χριστός, καί οὐ καθ' ὅ Θεός, Θεός αὐτοῦ λέγεται ὁ Πατήρ, ὥσπερ καί Πατήρ, καθ' ὅ Θεός, καί οὐ καθ' ὅ ἄνθρωπος, οὐδέ τούς δι' ἐναντίας οἶμαι διαμφιβάλλειν. Εἰ δέ καθ' ὅ ἄνθρωπος, καί οὐ καθ' ὅ Θεός, Θεός αὐτοῦ ἐστιν ὁ Πατήρ, ἄρα καί καθ' ὅ ἄνθρωπος, καί οὐ καθ' ὅ Θεός, ἠβουλήθη τό θέλημα τοῦ Πατρός καί αὐτοῦ ποιῆσαι· αὐτοῦ γάρ ἐστι καί τό τοῦ Πατρός θέλημα, Θεοῦ καί αὐτοῦ κατ' οὐσίαν ὄντος.

45. Cf. Confessor, *Th. Pol.* 7 (PG 91: 81D). See also *Th. Pol.* 3 (PG 91: 45D): φυσικῶς κινουμένη τε καί τυπουμένην ὑπό τοῦ Λόγου πρός τήν τῆς οἰκονομίας ἐκπλήρωσιν. And *Th. Pol.* 4 (PG 91: 60C): τό θέλειν αὐτοῦ κυρίως μέν ὄν φυσικόν καθ' ἡμᾶς, τυπούμενον δέ θεϊκῶς ὑπέρ ἡμᾶς.

The mystery of the baptism witnesses that, after thirty years, the flesh has been prepared by the Spirit to his hour and, at the same time, the Spirit has become the "Spirit of Christ." The Spirit has to "get used to" the flesh. In this sense, in dealing with the mystery of Trinity, Maximus asks if we can speak of "the Son of the Spirit" or the "Spirit of the Son." Using the analogy, he explains that "the word does not come from the voice and, in the same way, the Son does not come from the Spirit. Instead of "the Son of the Spirit" we must consider the "Spirit of the Son," because, the voice comes from the word, as the word comes from the mind, that is, from the Father.[46] There is an absolute origin from the Father, the only cause, and a relative one: the *Logos*.

The definitive fruit of this action of the Spirit is revealed in his hour, bringing him towards obedience (concord, harmony) to the Father. In this way, the role of the Holy Spirit in Christ helps us to understand the path of Christ's freedom and human will towards the Paschal mystery. The goal of the action of the Spirit in Christ is the prayer of the Garden of Gethsemane, where Jesus (his human will) accepts the will of the Father. The work of the Spirit in the flesh is then the education of freedom towards love through obedience.

Resurrection as a new generation of the Spirit

The third birth of Christ is his resurrection, the mystery of the last and definitive work of the benevolence of the Father (*eudokia*).

> He honors the first one through the original and vital breath; other through his Incarnation and Baptism (τῇ σαρκώσει καὶ τῷ βαπτίσματι), when He himself was baptized; the other through the Resurrection, by which he returned (ἧς αὐτὸς ἀπήρξατο), because as we became the first born among all his brothers, in the same way he became the first born among the dead.[47]

Resurrection is described by the Confessor as a return of Christ, the *Logos*, as the first born among the dead. Maximus' vision of Jesus' life allows us to speak with von Balthasar of a "narrative pre-eminence" of the cross and, we may add, of the resurrection in relationship to the incarnation.[48] For

---

46. Cf. Confessor, *Qu. Dub.* 1, 34; Sherwood, *St. Maximus the Confessor*, 42.

47. Confessor, *Amb.* 42 (PG 91: 1316A–B): τὴν μὲν τῷ ἐμφυσήματι τῷ πρώτῳ καὶ ζωτικῷ, τὴν δὲ τῇ σαρκώσει καὶ τῷ βαπτίσματι ὅπερ αὐτὸς ἐβαπτίσατο, τὴν δὲ τῇ ἀναστάσει ἧς αὐτὸς ἀπήρξατο, ὡς ἐγένετο πρωτότοκος ἐν πολλοῖς ἀδελφοῖς, οὕτω καὶ πρωτότοκος ἐκ νεκρῶν γενέσθαι καταξιώσας.

48. "Primary in this cosmic theodrama, Balthasar argues for at least a *narrative*

the Confessor, the voluntary passion and the answer of the Father through the resurrection from the dead is the fulfillment of the divine project.[49]

In a very famous and decisive text, Maximus describes the resurrection as the goal, the purpose of the whole creation:

> The one who has been guided to the ineffable and hidden energy of the Resurrection knows the purpose, by which God created originally everything (τὸν ἐφ' ᾧ τὰ πάντα προηγουμένως ὁ Θεός ὑπεστήσατο σκοπόν).[50]

The goal of creation was incarnation, the presence of Jesus Christ in the world. Now we see that the goal of incarnation, and therefore of the whole creation, is the resurrection of Christ—his presence, with his human body, at the right hand of the Father. This is the moment of the generation in being-forever (i.e., a kind of transformation through grace, πρὸς τὸ ἀεὶ εἶναι διὰ χάριτος μεταποιούμεθα).[51] Maximus describes this moment as a return to the Father, and stresses its quality: Jesus will not abandon his flesh, but he will ascend with his glorified body, which begins the work of the Spirit in his body, the church.

The Role of the Spirit in the Body of Christ

Let us finish our study by giving some hints about the action of the Spirit in the Christian. As we know, according to Maximus, the mystery of Christ opens a new time for the whole cosmos. Once the incarnation of God has been accomplished, the divinization of man can be performed.

As the Confessor says, "the *Logos* of God and God wants to perform always and in all the mystery of his Incarnation."[52] Through his Spirit, he carries the faithful towards divinization and, thus, guides all creation towards unity. "Christ," we read on his *Comment on the Pater Noster*, "always wants to be mystically generated, becoming flesh through those who are saved."[53] Ubi *Logos*, ibi *Pneuma*. The new incarnation of the *Logos* in the

---

pre-eminence of the poverty and scandalousness of the Cross." Cf. Blowers, "The Passion of Jesus," 362, 364–65.

49. Cf. Confessor, *Th. Pol.* 3 (PG 91: 48C): καὶ τὴν ἀπόρρητον καὶ μεγάλην τοῦ Πατρός ὡς Θεὸς παραδείξῃ βουλήν, σωματικῶς πληρουμένην.

50. Confessor, *Cap. Gnost.* I.66 (PG 90: 1108B): ὁ δέ τῆς ἀναστάσεως μυηθεὶς τὴν ἀπόρρητον δύναμιν, ἔγνω τόν ἐφ' ᾧ τά πάντα προηγουμένως ὁ Θεὸς ὑπεστήσατο σκοπόν.

51. Confessor, *Amb.* 42 (PG 91: 1325B).

52. Confessor, *Amb.* 7 (PG 91: 1084 C–D): Βούλεται γάρ ἀεί καί ἐν πᾶσιν ὁ τοῦ Θεοῦ Λόγος καί Θεός τῆς αὐτοῦ ἐνσωματώσεως ἐνεργεῖσθαι τό μυστήριον.

53. Confessor, *Or. Dom.* (CCSG 23: 50, 397–99): ἀεί θέλων Χριστός γεννᾶται

Christian is the work of the Spirit of Jesus Christ. During the life of Jesus, the Spirit was already working in the apostles, not only in the flesh of Christ.

St. Gregory of Nazianzus distinguishes three degrees of presence of the Spirit. With the power of healing the sick, the apostles received the first presence (*obscure*, ἀμυδρῶς). After the resurrection, a new presence (*expressius*, ἐκτυπώτερον) was given to them. Finally, during the days of Pentecost, the apostles were filled with the perfect presence of the Spirit (*perfectius*, τελεώτερον).[54] Following St. Gregory, Maximus distinguishes two moments of the action of the Spirit in the apostles. During their time with Jesus, the Spirit was acting in them as fire over the wood in a pan—heating it.[55] After the day of Pentecost, the Spirit worked directly, as fire over the wood, transforming them essentially (οὐσιωδῶς).[56]

In this way, Pentecost begins the action of the Spirit through Christ in the Christian, in the body of Christ. Therefore, Jesus' humanity, considered by Maximus in all its integrity (activity, will, passions), has been the place where the Spirit learned to dwell in humankind and divinize them. Commenting on the *Pater noster*, Maximus explains that only when the Name of the Father, that is, the Son, has been sanctified, the kingdom of God, that is, the Holy Spirit, can come to us.[57]

"The One who has the Spirit by nature (ὁ κατὰ φύσιν ἔχων τὸ Πνεῦμα) as God, has given to the Church the operations (energies) of the Spirit."[58] The work of the Spirit in the Christian will be the same he has performed in Christ—a path of filiation. The Spirit who prepared the coming of the *Logos*, his condensation, works now in our flesh according to the image of Christ.

In this way, through the *synergy* of the Spirit, the mission of Christ is accomplished.[59] The difference present in the world is guided to unity. "There is no more Greek or Jew, slave or free, male or female, but all are

---

μυστικῶς, διὰ τῶν σωζομένων σαρκούμενος. Cf. *Ad Thal.* 22 (CCSG 7: 143, 103–5).

54. Cf. Confessor, *Qu. Dub.* 5 (CCSG 10: 5), and St. Nazianzen, *Oration 41, In Pent.* 11 (PG 36: 444B-C).

55. Cf. Confessor, *Qu. Dub.* 5 (CCSG 10: 5): Καθάπερ ξύλον ἐπιτιθέμενον τηγάνῳ, εἶτα, τοῦ πυρὸς ὑφαπτομένου, διὰ μέσου τοῦ τηγάνου τῆς θέρμης τοῦ πυρὸς μεταλαμβάνει τὸ ξύλον, οὕτως τὸ πρότερον ἀμυδρῶς ἐνήργει τὸ Πνεῦμα ἐν τοῖς ἁγίοις.

56. Cf. Confessor, *Qu. Dub.* 5 (CCSG 10: 5): εἰ δέ τις κατὰ τὸ αὐτὸ ὑπόδειγμα ἐπαρεῖ τὸ διὰ μέσου τήγανον καὶ τὸ πῦρ ἀμέσως τοῦ ξύλου περιδράξεται, εὐθέως πρὸς τὴν οἰκείαν φύσιν ἀφομοιοῖ τὸ ξύλον. Οὕτως ὡς ἐν αἰσθητοῖς ὑποδείγμασιν εἰκάζειν ἔστιν τὸ οὐσιωδῶς.

57. Cf. Confessor, *Or. Dom.* (CCSG 23: 40, 230–41, 245).

58. Cf. Confessor, *Ad Thal.* 63 (CCSG 22: 153, 148–55, 170).

59. Cf. Confessor, *Or. Dom.* (CCSG 23: 54, 470–56, 510). Cf. Yeago, "Jesus of Nazareth and Cosmic Redemption," 163–93.

one in Christ."[60] Through the *Logos* and *Pneuma*, the difference and life in creation obtains its goal, and every substance is guided to the giver of everything, the Father. The *synergy* of the Spirit fulfills the *eudokia* of the Father and the *autourgia* of the Son, not only in Christ but also in the whole creation.

Conclusion

According to Maximus' thought, we can discover a deep connection between his well-known and balanced dithelism and the action of the Spirit in Christ. Between monothelism and Nestorianism, the whole affirmation of Christ's humanity (human energy and will) is linked to the active presence of the Spirit in the flesh, guiding it towards its end. In a sense, Maximus' dithelism cannot be explained without this active and respectful presence of the Holy Spirit in Christ. In this way, reflecting on the mystery of Jesus' humanity, the Confessor can show the deepest dimension of the action of the Spirit in the flesh—his *synergy*.

Pneumatology is a realm in Maximian studies that call for development. At first glance, the pneumatology of the Confessor can deceive us to relegate a secondary role to the Spirit. But for Maximus the presence and work of the Spirit, the mystery of his *synergy*, is, as a mother's work, performed in silence. As we have seen, the promises of this area of study are great and offer a decisive light to his Christology and ecclesiology.

60. Gal 3:28.

PART THREE

Ontology and Metaphysics

8

Remarks on the Metaphysics of Saint Maximus the Confessor

MELCHISEDEC TÖRÖNEN

"The high Word plays in every kind of form mixing,
as he wills, with his world here and there"

The metaphysical play of being in the thought of St. Maximus the Confessor is an interplay between the uncreated being and the created being; between the infinite and the finite, the incomparable and the comparable; between the uncreated being-beyond-being (God) and the created being. Most of the questions that one might call metaphysical or philosophical questions play a role in this interplay: creation, participation, providence, the *logoi* (λόγοι), freewill, deification, time and eschatology, and so on. Even if one were to extract from Maximus' thought the logic of unity-in-diversity, it would simply evaporate in the air unless it found an embodiment in one or another of these fields. What seems to stay at the background remains as mere decoration on the branches of the so-called Porphyrian Tree.

The interplay between the uncreated and the created sets the parameters within which we can determine what kind of metaphysics St. Maximus in actual fact represents. Regrettably far too often, even today, one can read statements along the lines of "the fundamental metaphysical basis of Maximus' thought is that of Neoplatonism,"[1] and this after so much carefully studied academic writing demonstrating quite the opposite (even while acknowledging a more refined interpretation of Neoplatonism).[2] I would therefore like to make some brief remarks on this issue.

Firstly: When Maximus says, in his famous and oft-quoted *Ambiguum* 7, that "God by his gracious will created all things visible and invisible *out of non-being*,"[3] he clearly means what he says and in so doing defines one of his most fundamental metaphysical principles. It is not by chance that Maximus repeats this principle twice within the few columns in which he elaborates on his understanding of the One *Logos* and the many *logoi* (theme so strongly reminiscent of Plotinus' Universal Intellect), and where he quotes Dionysius' version of the *scala naturae*—which in its turn strikes a very high note on the scale towards a Neoplatonic doctrine of participation. Maximus once again at the conclusion of his argument highlights the matter by stating that "it is impossible for the infinite to exist on the same level of being as finite things, and no argument will ever be capable of demonstrating that being and what is beyond being are the same."[4] Clearly, Maximus, as so many other Byzantine fathers have done, is using language from his surrounding world within the parameters of his own theological environment.

Maximus' metaphysical doctrine of being is not a doctrine of causation such that we can find, for instance, in Proclus Diadochus. Indeed, it would be very difficult to justify such a reading of Maximus. If the Neoplatonist Proclus saw the contingent reality as a series of unions and distinctions, a chain of causation and participation in which the many unfold from the One as the *archē* (αρχή), Maximus in contrast sees it as a created order of being, created out of non-being. And this creation *qua* creation participates in God its creator. This is why God for Maximus is not an *archē* in the ancient sense. God is the principle and source of creation as the creator only. Creation is not God's emanation, or God unfolding into the beings. It is God's pre-eternal and benevolent will (*logoi*) realized in time through an act

1. Cf. Perl, "Metaphysics and Christology in Maximus Confessor," 253–70; and Moore, *Origen of Alexandria and St. Maximus*.

2. Cf. Tollefsen, *The Christocentric Cosmology*. Tollefsen also offers a nuanced interpretation of a number of Neoplatonists, something which this very short paper does not attempt to do. Tollefsen's discussion of Dominic O'Meara's article "The Problem of Omnipresence," 194–200, is particularly interesting, and his observations on Plotinian metaphysics (p. 62) deserve further discussion.

3. Confessor, *Amb.* 7 (PG 91: 1077C); translations of all the references to *Amb. 7* are from Blowers and Wilken, *On the Cosmic Mystery*, 45–74.

4. Confessor, *Amb.* 7 (PG 91: 1081B).

of creation. In brief, creation is not God, but it is God manifesting his will and freedom to create.

But created beings, in particular those endowed with freewill, are very closely related to their creator. For Maximus, God's intention for creation is nothing less than a real and all-embracing participation in his divine life (i.e., deification of the human person). As Maximus himself says: "God gives them life, not the life that comes from breathing air, nor that of veins coursing with blood, but the life that comes from being wholly infused with the fullness of God."[5] And again, Maximus is very careful about ontological boundaries when he says: "The whole man, as the object of divine action, is deified by being made god by the grace of God who became man. He remains wholly man in soul and body by nature, and becomes wholly god in body and soul by grace and by the unparalleled divine radiance of blessed glory appropriate to him."[6]

Secondly, creation as susceptible to change has a certain goal and direction. The metaphysical play moves on in time and beyond time. The truth of beings is found in the age to come. As Maximus says on the last page of his great *Ambigua*, interpreting the word "play," "in comparison with the archetype that is to come of the divine and true life, our present life is play."[7] From this point of view, then, Maximus' Christian metaphysics is strongly eschatological. "Eschatological" in this context is to be understood neither as denoting an apocalyptic inferno nor a futurist utopia of a man-made paradise. It suggests that creation can find its fulfillment only in God as its end and goal, and that this fulfillment is given as a gift to those who, through the good use of their freewill, have become receptive of deification. It is a kind of teleology of transfiguration. It is worthy of notice that Maximus also distinguishes natural bodily resurrection from eschatological deification. (This, it seems to me, could be seen as a stance against *apokatastasis*.) Interpreting the symbolic difference between Easter Sunday and the "New Sunday" (which in Maximus' time was the Sunday after Easter) he says that "the transformation by grace into the likeness of God, which takes place in deification, is more honorable than natural [resurrection and] incorruptibility."[8]

Thirdly, if there is one philosophical thing in Maximus' work that is shared by the mediaeval West, it clearly is the famous Porphyrian Tree and

---

5. Confessor, *Amb.* 7 (PG 91: 1088C).

6. Confessor, *Amb.* 7 (PG 91: 1088C).

7. Confessor, *Amb.* 71 (PG 91: 1416C), translation in Louth, *Maximus the Confessor*, 168.

8. Confessor, *Amb.* 63 (PG 91: 1388B–1389B). I have moved the word "resurrection" from another part of the same text for the sake of brevity and clarity.

its Aristotelian logic tool-kit. Peter Abelard's dictum that "there is no thing which is not a particular," could have been said equally well by Maximus.[9] The importance of *differentia* is paramount for both and the usage of the various Aristotelian categories is virtually common ground. Important as it may be, the Porphyrian Tree in metaphysical terms does not seem to reach very high.

However, the notion of "difference" and the integrity of the particular being are of immense value for Maximus; and that is one point that needs to be emphasized. Broadly speaking it could be said that in Neoplatonism differentiation, ultimately, is not a positive thing. Whereas for Maximus differentiation in creation is the mark of divine and pre-eternal wisdom of the *Logos* himself with implications in the present world and in the eschatological kingdom of God. The integrity of the particular being characterizes especially the future state of bodily resurrection and of deification.

Having stressed the importance of the particular being for Maximus, he could, in this sense, be hailed as a "personalist" in our contemporary terms—and in the modern world the defense of the human person is, of course, of primary importance. My only reservation here is that we should not impose on Maximus existentialist concerns, which he himself would have rejected. Maximus was a defender of the *essential*, that is, *natural* freedom of the divine and rational natures, and therefore any kind of personalism that attributes necessity to these natures is alien to his doctrine.

Fourthly, there is an intriguing inner logic in St. Maximus' entire work that forms the matrix of his metaphysics. I have elsewhere called this logic "the principle of simultaneous union and distinction," while others have given it various other names. It sweeps through Trinitarian theology and Christology; you can discover it in cosmology, with the pre-eternal *logoi*; in the church and the Scriptures; and even Maximian understanding of the human person, the soul, and the virtues are pervaded by this principle. It also plays its part in the various themes from the contributors to the metaphysics section of this volume: in the essence-activity distinction, in the contemplation of the *logoi* in creation, and most importantly in the deification of the human person, where God is entirely united without confusion to the whole man sanctifies him, body and soul.

Finally, Maximus' metaphysical play is ultimately founded on this mutual union and distinction of the uncreated and the created, their utter union without confusion. If then, as modern philosophy puts it, "metaphysics is the theory of being, that is, the most generic account of what there is,"[10]

---

9. Cf. Marenbon, *The Philosophy of Peter Abelard.*

10. Maudlin, "Distilling Metaphysics from Quantum Physics," 461.

from a Maximian point of view it would be totally inconceivable to speak of metaphysics of any kind without a serious reference to the Being *par excellence*, that is, to the *uncreated* Being. In the modern context, a metaphysics of science obviously needs to follow empirical sciences. But can metaphysics that looks to material world *only* and which wants to be altogether "naturalized" still claim to be truly metaphysical? Maybe so, if also fundamentalist atheism can be regarded as a metaphysical statement. For Maximus, this would be a pretty boring play. He would certainly prefer that metaphysical play which, in the words of his great master St. Gregory Nazianzen, "the high Word plays in every kind of form mixing, as he wills, with his world here and there."[11]

11. Nazianzen, *To the Virgins* 2 (PG 37: 624); Confessor, *Amb.* 71 (PG 91: 1408C). I have adopted the translation of Louth in his *Maximus the Confessor*, 164. A different reading might render it "dividing the world" instead of "mixing with his world."

9

Nature, Passion, and Desire

Saint Maximus' Ontology of Excess

ROWAN WILLIAMS

Recent analysis of Maximus by theologians such as Nikolaos Loudovikos[1] and Christoph Schneider[2] has mapped out pretty clearly an ontology in which the non-conditioned creation of diversity by God, realized as an immeasurable plurality of particular reflections of and participations in the single eternal *Logos*, allows a central place to *eros* as the self-relativizing energy that drives us to our proper place in relationship. As "ekstatic," it steps out of the closed definitions we instinctively work with, opening the life of any subject, any individual substance, to the life of the other, both the finite and the infinite other. The human subject, on earth the uniquely *conscious* bearer of *eros*, models what is in fact going on at every level of the universe's life: in abandoning the myth of protected self-sufficiency, the conscious and intelligent agent, the finite *nous*, moves in the mode for which it was created, moves in alignment with the purpose of God, habitually echoing in finite form the infinite desire of God for God, of love for love. And this is made possible in a world of distorted desire by the crucial coincidence in the incarnate *Logos* between a free human habit, the "gnomic will" by which we deliberately shape the *tropos* (τρόπος) of our existence, and the

1. Particularly in Loudovikos, *A Eucharistic Ontology.*

2. Schneider, "The Transformation of Eros," 271–89.

divine and unchangeable will which is the exercise in act (εν ενεργεία) of the essence of the Trinitarian Godhead. As Loudovikos[3] has spelled out with such impressive detail in his work *Eucharistic Ontology*, this coincidence of created and uncreated action is not only celebrated but communicated in the church's focal self-identifying practice, the Eucharist. And as Schneider has argued in his very rich essay on Maximus and Lacan,[4] it is clear that any foundational opposition between desire and *logos* cannot be sustained in Maximus' framework; neither, therefore, can we defend an opposition between nature (as essentially opaque to consciousness) and the constructions of culture.[5] The Lacanian paradox of the sense of boundless libidinal energy and movement both generated and checked by the authority of the symbolic order, will, on this account, come dangerously near to simply rehearsing a particular kind of sub-Platonic pathos of innocence over against history, speech, and particularity. Lacan himself quite consciously works with such a mythology of immortal oneness interrupted by speech, though he of course does not treat the state of immortal oneness as "an" actuality in the world; it is "the real," that which surrounds the "reality" we habitually utter and imagine. But the Maximian world assumes particularity at the very beginning of finitude and agency, and looks forward to an eschatological "rest," what we might call a fully harmonious "culture" in which nature has attained its purpose of universal mutuality and (to borrow John Donne's delightful coinage) "interinanimation." It assumes a language of peace, we might say.

To put this another way: a Lacanian opposition between undifferentiated libidinal desire and the realm of culture, language, and authority proposes that the central ontological difference is between the formless and the spoken (the immortal and the mortal) within the realm of speech and experience. The symbolic order (language and particularity) necessarily generates its own frustration by invoking the other of indeterminate (and thus always frustrated) desire. The Maximian ontology, in contrast, affirms that the significant difference is between what moves as an *eros*-driven mode of existence towards its proper place within a finite universe of mutuality and the infinite act of God, which generates finite *eros* as an echo of its own love for itself in the mutual inexhaustibility of Trinitarian life. What is finite is always already propelled towards its inherent destiny in language and mutuality; there is nothing that is unreasonably natural, natural in its dissonance with other subjects and substances, or indifferent to the promise of a universal eschatological "culture." In addition, what is preconscious is

---

3. Loudovikos, *Eucharistic Ontology*, ch. 1 in particular.
4. See especially Schneider, "The Transformation of Eros," 272–76, 285–86.
5. Ibid., 276.

not a privileged or uncompromised selfhood or desire but simply "human powers insofar as they are not actualized in accordance with their natural principle."[6]

This may help us to make sense of one specific set of Maximian ideas clearly of great importance in the *Centuries on Charity* and rather open to misunderstanding in the contemporary intellectual context. *Cent.* I.17 and 25 touch on a theme that will recur several times in the text, the imperative to love all human beings equally, as God does. God loves human beings because of their nature: as we read later on,[7] "Perfect love does not split up the single human nature, common to all, according to the diverse characters of individuals." At first sight, this may look like a recommendation to what we might think of as an impersonal sort of love, indifferent to the need of specific persons and reducible to benevolence towards humanity as a whole. This is in fact completely contrary to what Maximus argues: to love human beings in their nature is to be awake to the very particular things that make each of them more or less in tune with that nature and to respond accordingly. What matters is that we should not begin by assessing the claims of human beings to be loved on the basis of individual characteristics; love is not a reward if we understand it in the light of God's love. And if we put this together with the repeated emphasis in the *Centuries* on what "dispassionate" love means, the point becomes still clearer. Nothing is by nature evil or unlovable, because all things come from the loving will of God, embodying particular reflections of the one *Logos* in their diverse *logoi*, and thus have the potential for mutuality or reconciliation; but when we view them through the lens of passion, self-serving self-referential desire, we do not see things as they are, in their nature. The basic theme is familiar from Evagrius' treatise *On Thoughts* 8, with its seminal distinction between angelic, human, and diabolical awareness of things, where the angelic consciousness knows things in their essences and the initially "neutral" human consciousness has to beware of slipping into the diabolical knowledge that sees things only in terms of their use to another self.[8] Love must be grounded in the recognition that all things are what they are by nature in virtue of their participation in the *Logos*: nothing can take away their "entitlement" to love, because they are all capable of growing through the exercise of their proper *eros* towards their destiny. All are struggling towards mutuality, the fullest possible action of reciprocally sustaining each other's lives by the gift of their own. Our own

---

6. Ibid.

7. Confessor, *De Char.* I.71; translation from Palmer, Sherrard, and Ware, *The Philokalia*, 60.

8. Evagrius, *peri logismon* 8 (SC 438), 176–79, 164–65.

love for any other person or indeed any other finite substance is rooted in our own longing to become "natural," to be in perfect mutuality. My *eros* aligns itself with theirs.

Passion-free *eros* is the desire that the other be itself—but not in quite the Levinasian sense of abjection before the other, because this is rooted in ontology for which there is no being-for-the-other abstracted from the pattern of *mutual* life giving. Passion is thus what is fundamentally anti-natural, what seeks, consciously or not, to frustrate the natural desirous movement of all finite substances in concert. Maximus can put it even more vividly in the *Centuries on Theology* II.30, where he speaks of how my failure to grow as I should into my nature is a diminishing of *Christ*. And in defining passion as a moment of frustration or stasis, we are reminded of the crucial point that at no moment *in time* is any finite substance or agent yet fully natural. To love their nature is to love both what they already are as *logos*-bearing and to love the unknown future into which their *eros* is moving them—to love the "excess" of their being, what Loudovikos would see as their "eucharistic" future as perfected gift.[9] All things are en route towards this future, and thus en route towards—as we put it earlier—a universal culture; and, to go rather beyond what Maximus himself says in so many words, this is to say that all things are always already on the way to language, to being understood and spoken, being present in the "priestly" discourse of human beings who make connecting sense of the *logoi* of what they encounter.

Loving what is true or real, free from the distortions of passion, is loving what is grounded in the *Logos*; hence the paradox asserted in *Centuries on Charity* III.37—"he who loves nothing merely human loves all men."[10] To love what is "merely human" must here mean loving simply what is contingent in this or that individual, what does not belong to their nature as related to God. Universal love is love for the individual as related to the infinite act that sustains it through its particular *logos*, its specific reflection of the one divine *Logos*. Proper Christian love thus "dispossesses" itself of its object in more than one sense. Not only does it seek to see and know the object without passion (without self-referential desire), it recognizes that the true being of the object is always in relation to something other than the beholder prior to the seeing or registering of this particular other by the beholder. Thus, there is always some dimension of what is encountered that

9. Loudovikos, *A Eucharistic Ontology*, 36–41, 152–53.

10. Translation from Palmer, Sherrard, and Ware, *The Philokalia*, 89. Thunberg, *Microcosm and Mediator*, 333, seems to take "loving nothing human" as implying that we need first to devote our love entirely to God rather than creatures. This is correct in one sense, but risks missing the point that we love humanity properly by never loving humanity in its isolation from its maker.

is in no way accessible to, or at the mercy of, this particular beholder. It is in acknowledging this relatedness to a third that a relation of love involving two finite subjects becomes authentic and potentially open to the universal. What is in relation to the "third" is precisely what exists in and by the action of that "third," which is the nature of the subject in question, the project defined by infinite act which is now working through by its own particular mode of *eros* towards its ultimate purpose. If our love is conditioned by the specific point currently reached by the other subject, it will not be universalizable; it will not be love for the whole project, nature realizing itself through *eros*. It will be love for a fiction, for the unreal object that is another finite substance conceived in abstraction from God and *logos*. We cannot properly love an *unrelated* object; if we start from that particular fiction, we rapidly come to regard the other as open to our possession because it is cut off from its ground in God/*logos*/nature. Our relation to it is no longer truly *eros*, because we have isolated it in our thoughts from its own desirous movement towards its natural place in the universal network of mutual gift. It cannot be gift to us any longer, and we cannot relate to it in gift-like mode. But if the relation is one of my *eros* communing with the *eros* of what I love—desiring the desire of the other, but not in competitive and exclusive mode—the possibility of that "eucharistic" interrelation noted already is opened up to us.

Summarizing Maximus' ontology in the light of all this, we could say that his chief contribution to a strictly metaphysical discussion (bracketing the purely theological for a moment) lies in the twofold characterization of finite being as always moving "erotically" towards its optimal position of mutual relatedness and thus always manifestly related to more than now appears—to the God who has freely uttered the creative *logos* of each element in the world, and so to a future that is necessarily involved with other subjects. As I have suggested, this means that finite being tends towards being spoken, being apprehended, represented, regenerated in human response and engagement. The healed world is one in which human beings have learned to speak truly about the environment in which they live—the Eucharist being the foretaste of that speech, in that the divine *Logos* actually transforms the stuff of the world by Word and Spirit in the sacrament. Maximus' scheme lays the foundation for an aesthetic as well as an ethic, and allows us to think of human creativity itself as an attempt to align the *eros* of the artist with the *eros* of the material around: the artist is far from being a creator *ex nihilo* because s/he is always feeling for the "impulse" in this or that aspect of the world that is moving towards a new and more nourishing relatedness, to the rest of the material order as well as to the human understanding. Those artists who insist that their work is nothing to do with the will as it is normally understood are echoing in different terms the

Maximian concern for dispassionate seeing. And in epistemological terms, we should have to define comprehensive knowing as something other than grasping the internal workings of an object; knowing would have to be an awareness of the relations in which something could stand, the meanings it could bear. More than that, it would be bound up with an actual sharing in what I have been calling the "project" of nature, a mutual process of shaping towards eschatological mutuality. Here—returning again to Schenider's essay and developing its argument a little further[11]—we can see in a particularly concentrated way the tension between a Lacanian account of how "desire for the desire of the Other" works in the psyche and what a theological account informed by Maximus might say. The Lacanian subject is endlessly frustrated by the desire of the other, which cannot be formulated, thematized, or assimilated and so cannot ever be satisfied. Language is the frontier between the speaking subject and the limitless libidinal realm: it is only in language that the desire of the other is available for imagining, yet it is precisely available for imagining *as* other and thus as always escaping. The subject is confronted by the baffling *aporia* that libidinal freedom can only be thought in terms of a dissolution of language. In contrast, the Maximian subject is drawn by a no less unassimilable desire in the other, but drawn in the hope of a fulfillment that the individual subject's own account of what is desired can never produce. The other, the infinite and the finite other, is not an obstacle to the subject's desire, an alien demand to be either submitted to or resisted. Language cannot be an alienating thing, because it mediates a desire of the other that is a promise or an offer to my desire, not an empty source of frustration. As we read in *Centuries on Theology* II.60, the *Logos* is incarnate in what he *says*, as well as what he is and does: we attain to the ultimate harmony with and in him for which we are made only through language, even if we know quite well that words alone will not bring us to him (cf. *Cent. Theol.* II.73–4). If otherness is inscribed in the finite world from the beginning in the diversity of the *logoi*, there is no necessary binary rivalry between finite subjects, and the infinite other is not a competitor for what is desired. Indeed, I can say, on the basis of the doctrine of the *logoi*, that *I am* the desire of the infinite other, in the sense that my existence is a fact only because of an act of loving freedom in which God unconditionally desires the joy of a finite other (as he eternally desires the joy of an infinite other in the life of the Trinity).

Such an ontology makes sense of both art and asceticism; it suggests a high doctrine of finite creativity (and in this respect Maximus stands close to some aspects of Bulgakov's doctrine of Sophia as the *eros* of created things

---

11. Schneider, "The Transformation of Eros," 277–80, 285–89.

towards their optimal interrelatedness, in art and liturgy alike[12]), but it also prescribes a formidable exercise of "mindfulness" in respect of human perception of the world and its distortions through the working of "passion." It is why Maximus' ontology cannot be properly thought about in separation from his analyses of faulty and misdirected desire. But perhaps the most important aspect of his metaphysical vision, the aspect that has stimulated most constructive reflection amongst contemporary theologians, is his refusal to define nature as a category of static properties. The *logos* upon which each being is established is, of course, stable; but it has no reality except as the moving principle of the history of its *tropos*, the development in time of its own particular and unique journey towards itself. Not the least of the Confessor's originalities is to make the Christological distinction of *logos* and *tropos* work as a general key to ontology. But that is entirely in keeping with a theological scheme in which it is the incarnation of the *Logos* that is the gateway to understanding anything that matters about the universe.

---

12. See the discussion of some of these themes in Williams, *Sergii Bulgakov*, 127–31, 155–59, and cf. Milbank, "Sophiology and Theurgy," 45–85, and his contribution to the present volume.

10

Christianity and Platonism in East and West

John Milbank

I. Introduction

In an essay written some time ago in the last century, by a then very young Rowan Williams, it was argued that the distinction made by the fourteenth-century Byzantine theologian Gregory Palamas between the divine essence and the equally divine energies impaired both the divine simplicity and the distinction between the created and the uncreated.[1] Williams also claimed that this deleterious development was the result in large measure of an excessive influence of Neo-Platonism, and in particular of those later Neo-Platonists like Iamblichus and Proclus, often dubbed "theurgic" Neo-Platonists, besides their Christian successor, Pseudo-Dionysius the Areopagite. In doing so, he seemed to look askance on all notions of metaphysical "participation," unless they were understood in a very minimalist and "de-mythologized" sort of way. What he appeared to favor instead was

---

1. Williams, "The Philosophical Structures of Palamism," 27–44. Williams is on oral record as no longer agreeing with all of this article and now wishing to qualify his critique of Palamas. However, the article has become canonical for the Palamas debate and therefore must still be reckoned with. Many of its crucial points remain valid, and while its strictures on Neo-Platonism now appear dated, it also unerringly pinpoints just what is at stake concerning questions to do with the forms, participation, etc.

a strict notion of divine purity and self-containment only breached by acts of divine willing to create and to bestow grace, with "deification" reduced to the idea of agreement with the divine will and purged of any sense of a "quasi-material" sharing in the divine substance.[2]

2. Ibid., 41. In this article he restricts "participation" to meaning a true "intend-ing" of God. But he here, like many others, confuses "intentionality," which derives from Augustine and implies that every thought, as a thought "of something," reaches ecstatically beyond itself, with the different (though not incompatible) Aristotelian idea that to know something is to become that thing through "information" by that thing. Ironically such a notion as applied to knowledge of God would truly place God on the same plane of being as ourselves in just the way Williams wishes to avoid, *unless* qualified by Platonic notions of participation as an "internal" sharing that paradoxically coincides with an "external" imitation. (See further in the main text below.) It is clear that later Williams' views on many matters (probably including intentionality) evolved, yet at this stage it is interesting to note the degree to which he was under the influence of a Geach/Anscombe reading of Wittgenstein, Aristotle, and Aquinas, combined with a Mackinnon-derived Kantian insistence that our knowledge is confined within ascertainable finite limits. Insofar as he also exhibited an urge towards Thomism, his Aquinas was not only Aristotelian, but his Aristotle was read through the post-Fregean eyes favored by analytic philosophy. One can of course agree with Williams after Geach and Anscombe, *Three Philosophers*, 7–11, that substance is not for Aristotle some sort of Lockean vacuous punctual point to which qualities might be "attached" (Williams suggests—perhaps rather too emphatically—that Palamas is effectively thinking in such terms.). Yet that substance is always "qualified" is an ontological as well as logical truth, and so it is too bald when Williams appears to say that Aristotelian categories like substance, quality, and accident only apply to epistemological categorization ("algebra of terms") and not to the actual composition of things. For this reading is more than dubious, both philosophically and historically.

Philosophically speaking, a brown bag is indeed only a bag because we conventionally take it to be a bag in accord with our practical usage, but if we dye the bag black it will still *truly* be usable as a bag, since it will still be operatively-speaking an isolatable, unified item, and its inherent qualities of hollowness and containment will remain. Likewise a tree *really can* go through many mutations (but not all) and still remain "a tree" in its constitutive "shape" and not just for our classificatory perception. It is therefore not *obvious* that substance, quality, and accident are not indeed in some strange sense "thingy" as well as meaningful. Nor is the Aristotelian view that *ousia* is the "form" of a thing as well the real thing itself containable on the "sense" side of the Fregean sense/reference divide, which is supposed to be mutually exclusive.

Historically speaking there has always been a hesitation between Aristotle's mainly logical deployment of the categories in the specifically logical works, and his onto-logical deployment of them in the *Metaphysics*. Aquinas unquestionably favors the priority of the latter, since (contra Geach's reading) he regards the logical categories themselves ontologically as being to do with the way formal realities *exist* in a universal "intentional" mode in our understanding which truly relates us to the thing known (*In Met.* VII. 1576). And as I mention in the main text below, the granting of the opposite priority to the categories as logical commences with Porphyry—from whence it was taken up again in the Middle Ages by figures like Gilbert of Porreta, on the basis of a misreading of Boethius, which Aquinas later corrected. Yet Porphyry adopted this stance for reasons of a specific sort of Plotinian Platonism which exalted the logical over the ontological precisely because it thought that true intellection can dispense with the mediation of matter! (This logicism will therefore later evolve into subjective idealism and empiricism.)

It is therefore arguable that the choice historically has *not* been one between a pure reading of Aristotle and a Platonically contaminated one, but rather between *two alternative Neo-Platonic options in the hermeneutics of Aristotle*, given that a hesitation between the logical and the ontological is but one of many aporetic cruxes that Aristotle in his "esoteric writings bequeathed (deliberately?) to posterity. So far then from it being the case, as Williams suggests, that the Neo-Platonists (whether Plotinian or theurgic) mistook logical for real entities, in seeking to "derive" species from genus, quality and accident from substance, and "first" concrete substance from "second" essential substance, they were rather trying to deal with a *lacuna* of generative explanation of being which Aristotle's own usage of the categories to describe the very structure of the real—either the material real (substance, accident, quality, relation, etc) or the logical real (*genus* and *species* as "universal states of substance in the mind")—manifestly left behind him. For example, it is clear that a quality (like "stickiness") *can* be transferred from one thing to another, yet Aristotle gives no full account of such a process (which would seem to involve a kind of hybrid formal-efficient causality in his own terms), so that if, indeed, as Williams says, a "quality" should not be seen as an isolatable thing in itself, one still has the question of how a certain "mode of being" is conveyed between substances. By suggesting that qualities can "proceed" or "emanate" from one thing to another and that a lesser thing "shares" in the quality of a higher thing, the Neo-Platonists do not imply, as Williams says that they do, that a quality might, as a kind of quasi-form "float virtually free" of any substance (such a suggestion awaits Avicenna).

It is, however, entirely clear that later on Williams became more sympathetic to Plato, and in *Arius*, 215–29, he provides a nuanced account of participation in the Platonic forms. He rightly insists that a form is not merely a "very perfect example" of that for which it serves as a model, but is in some crucial sense quite unlike that for which it operates as a causal paradigm. However, he goes too far in seeming to rule out all notions of "imitation" of forms by lower entities, when both Plato and Neo-Platonism are in fact replete with such language (cf. Proclus, *The Elements of Theology* 29); nor is he right to suggest, after David Burrell (in his earlier thought), that for Aquinas analogy has *nothing* to do with "resemblance," even though for Aquinas we are only "like" God in terms of God himself as the common medium (*Knowing the Unknowable God,* 343, n.76.). Neither does he ever make it clear how real the "sharing" element of participation might be—and elsewhere he exhibits an antipathy to any talk of "degrees of being," despite the fact that it is hard to eliminate this from any authentic version of Thomism, preferring to think in Scotist and Kantian terms of being as simply the zero-sum negation of a negation: "is" is "not 'is not,'" since it is not a predicate. What is also apparent is that, while his arguments against both Palamas and Arius would seem to suggest kinship with a Middle Platonic merging of the One with intellection and other qualities, he also exhibits a certain *sympathy* with Arius as conceiving God to be so transcendent that he can only mediate his nature through an act of gracious choice (227). And he notes here that the Cappadocians faced the same Plotinian dilemma as the great heresiarch: how can the absolutely ineffable God communicate himself?

This sympathy seems implausible in view of the fact that the entire bent of *Arius* would appear to be against the non-Trinitarian notion of God as a lonely and arbitrary absolute will and equally against any notion of a medium hovering "between" the uncreated and the created. And yet there is always a hesitation in Williams about embracing the full participatory metaphysics that would counter such a perspective. It is a

The same link of Palamas with the traditions of the later "theurgic" Neo-Platonists is upheld in a recent book by David Bradshaw, but in an opposite, positive spirit.[3] He wishes to praise both, and to do so because they both, on his view, allowed that the divine action really does reach out-wards and downwards to create and to deify, while at the same time the inaccessible divine mystery, which is the sole lure of sanctity, is preserved. For this view, the energies of the divine glory really are God, but they are to be distinguished in some fashion from the divine essence itself. Bradshaw hence endorses a "strong" view of participation, which also sustains a sharp triadic separation between the unparticipated, the participated, and the participating.

In the present essay, I wish to claim that both writers are making a false association. With Williams, I wish broadly to criticize Palamas (though in a slightly more muted manner with which he himself now probably agrees). But with Bradshaw, I wish to defend the theurgic tradition of both the pagans and of Pseudo-Dionysius. In order to sustain this opposite combination to either of them, I will argue that actually it is *theurgic* rather than Plotin-ian Neo-Platonism that tends to urge towards a radical divine simplicity, incompatible with Palamas' famous or infamous distinction.

Why should this matter? The real point is that, in order to grasp the coherence of my combination, one must arrive at a correct understanding of the view of participation entertained by Proclus and Pseudo-Dionysius. I

---

never-resolved (and from my perspective unnecessary) hesitation between a broadly "Catholic" (loosely "Thomistic") perspective on the one hand, and a more Protestant and "Barthian" perspective on the other, which also involves a certain reading of John of the Cross, linked to an advocacy of the spirituality of the English Benedictine tradi-tion. For this latter perspective we confront God not as participants, but in a naked stripping of all self-imaging (seen, questionably, as almost *necessarily* delusory) and self-standing (as if we could *ever be* in some sort of zero-sum rivalry with God, even from the point of view of spiritual experience) and then await the divine voice and verdict in a total solitude and darkness (which can sound very *non-ecclesial*). In line with this tendency, Williams also at times refuses Catholic notions of "created grace," which would seem indeed to confine him to the view that the divine grace, glory, or "energy" is simply God as act with respect to his eternal will, not a paradoxical "stream-ing forth" of God that participatorily remains God. But this surely risks adopting a position like that of Palamas' opponent Barlaam by affirming a "bare" divine essence, and it is notable that in the article attacking Palamas Williams scarcely at all alludes to or defends Palamas' own defence of the hesychastic experience of the uncreated light and the "theurgic" and synergistic practice of the Jesus prayer. Later and elsewhere he does indeed defend these experiences in his own voice, just as he fully grasps that God as transcendent is *non aliud* as well as *totaliter aliter*—but is all of that really compatible with Williams' more "Barthian" and "ultra-apophatic" moments, which risk hyposta-sizing the negative?

3. Bradshaw, *Aristotle East and West*.

contend that this offers an authentic reading of Platonic *methexis* (μέθεξις), which Christian theology both requires and further intensifies. This view is neither the "mythological" one of Bradshaw, which tends to suggest that some sort of literal "aspect" of the absolute can be literally "shared out," nor the demythologized view of the young Williams. Rather, it is a view that regards participation as a drastically paradoxical notion, which metaphysics and theology nonetheless cannot dispense with. A supreme aspect of this paradoxicality is the coming together of radical divine simplicity with a divine self-partition so radical that it amounts to a kind of ontological kenosis.

For this reason the rebuttal of Palamas, the endorsement of theurgy, and the explication of *methexis* all run naturally together.

2. Simplicity, Participation, and the Theurgic

How should we understand the distinction between the essence and the energies of God as articulated by Palamas? Along with many other Eastern scholars and theologians, is David Bradshaw right to say that Western Christendom has wrongly neglected this crucial distinction?

I shall argue that this claim is mistaken, and that the thought of the best theologians in the West is entirely in harmony with a proper comprehension of the relationship between the essence and the energies of God and in continuity with the thought of the Greek church fathers.

Everything with respect to such a claim depends upon how one understands the distinction between the "unparticipated One" and "participation in the One" in Neo-Platonic tradition. Within this tradition, there is much variation and quite often a lack of clarity. Is the non-participable a literally "separated" ontological realm that in no respect shares itself? As such, is it to be distinguished from another ontological aspect of the absolute principle that *is* shareable? Alternatively, should the distinction be understood in a thoroughly paradoxical fashion, such that it is the imparticipable One that is itself after all participated? This is the view eventually expressed most directly by Nicholas of Cusa, for whom in his *De Coniecturis* the "oneness-that cannot-be partaken-of" "coincides" with "the-power-to-be-partaken-of."[4]

These two different versions of participation can be read as two different comprehensions of transcendent gift—gift-terms being often used to denote "emanations" within the Neo-Platonic corpus.[5] For the first understanding, the absolute One is not itself giving, even if it is obscurely causative, because it is thoroughly impersonal. Donation is here a secondary

---

4. Cusa, *De Coniecturis* 11, 59.

5. Cf. Proclus, *ET* 7, 18, 20, 23.

ontological phenomenon, which only commences at a level below that of the absolutely unified. Everything else somehow derives from the One, yet the One gives nothing *of* itself. I think that this is essentially the model of Plotinus, as Rowan Williams in his article in fact agrees.

But in the second understanding of participation donation is primordial. For this version, that which is entirely withheld—the unparticipated— is the seemingly contradictorily reserved element that must persist within a gift in order for it to be a gift at all. For while a giver gives herself without reserve, unless within this giving she nonetheless persists in a certain reticence, she could not be distinguished as a giver from her gift, nor survive her own generosity in order to be the subject of a possible further giving in the future. Nor could the gift given be a gift, rather than a merely transferred object, if it was not a sign of the giver who remains absent from the gift itself. Finally, if the giver did not remain absent, but insisted on accompanying her own gift, the gift given would be wholly a form of pressure on the recipient, not his to freely appropriate in his own mode and at his own pleasure. It follows that, on this model, the severe restraint of the One is not the result of impersonality, but on the contrary indicates a certain transcendent eminence of personhood—even if this was never explicitly articulated by the pagan Neo-Platonists.

Such a model was nonetheless the one implicitly adopted by the theurgic Neo-Platonists, beginning with Iamblichus. To make this claim can seem curious, because often, as Rowan Williams rightly emphasizes, these thinkers seem to insist yet more than Plotinus on the ineffable transcendence of a final unity. This can be seen in relation to their conceptions of both practical and theoretical activity, where they introduce novel levels of mediation between the human soul and the One. In the former case, political reform now imitates a level within the divine realm lower than that of the One, in contrast to the position of Plotinus.[6] In the latter case, Iamblichus added a new list of higher "theurgic" virtues, to Plotinus' pupil Porphyry's list of "purificatory," "theoretical," and "paradigmatic" virtues.[7]

However, the very status of the theurgic as the "higher" virtues suggests something problematic. Theurgy is a ritual-magical practice that usually remains tied to matter, body, and the cosmos. Hence, the elevation of theurgic virtue implies a kind of height beyond normal height, which involves a strange inversion of hierarchy through recuperation of that which ascent normally abandons.

6. Cf. O'Meara, *Platonopolis*, 96.
7. Ibid., 48.

This suggests that there is also an aspect of inversion and of super-transcendence in excess of normal hierarchy in the theurgic re-conception of the One itself. And this is indeed the case. What Williams failed to acknowledge is that, in the case of Iamblichus and his intellectual successor Proclus, it is clear that when they speak of the absolute One as "imparticipable," this means that it cannot be parceled out; not just on account of its inaccessibility, but also because it is absolutely equally close to everything that proceeds from it—to all finite, restricted entities.[8] The point then is that the "participated" for these thinkers refers to elements within a hierarchy that have something that is already always specific to share, and which they can only impart in diminishing degrees. But, at the very summit of the hierarchy stands something that does so by virtue of the fact that it *exceeds* all hierarchy. What is absolute and first is really only so in terms of "aristocratic height" because it is greatest in terms of "democratic scope," as the very first proposition of Proclus' *Elements of Theology* makes clear.[9] The One is supremely intimate with everything because nothing exists except by virtue of some sort of unity. Indeed, after the energy of emanation has run out, at the bottom of the material scale, the power of unity still remains, which is why for Proclus matter regains in the very pit of being a certain simplicity characteristic of its trans-existential summit.[10]

My use here of political metaphors for theurgic ontology is justified because Iamblichus, Proclus, and later Damascius, all espoused politically a "mixed constitution" in terms of a balance of the One, the Few, and the Many, which involved a certain combining of Pythagorean tradition (as found especially in the Pseudo-Archytas) with that of Plato.[11] In the latter's *Republic,* there is famously an *aporia* whereby the city must be ruled by the philosopher who alone knows the good through contemplation, and yet civic involvement is likely to contaminate this knowledge. However, the theurgists, unlike the more separatist Plotinus, tended further to integrate the ontological and theoretical with the political, and so to seek to overcome the *aporia:* the individual good of the philosopher-ruler is inseparable from the common good of all the people. In accord with this accentuated organism, which may well be the implication of Plato's *Laws* rather than his *Republic,* Iamblichus and Proclus regarded the everyday ritual life of the city as itself the beginning of the process of deification. The philosopher ruler's monarchic supremacy was not for them therefore simply to do with his con-

---

8. Proclus, *ET* 53, 57.

9. Ibid., 1, 21.

10. Ibid., 59.

11. See again O'Meara, *Platonopolis,* 87–105.

templative "height," but also with the inclusive "scope" of his concern with justice for all, which was tantamount to a concern for the salvation of all.

In terms of theoretical ontology, the same pattern whereby, at a starry height beyond the mere summit of a pyramid, a "reach" to the entire base of the pyramid establishes a meta-primacy, is repeated when Proclus says that the first "principles" below the strictly divine realm of unity are being, life, and intellect, taken in that serial order.[12] For from a strictly hierarchical point of view, intellect is more than life, which is in turn more than being, but the greater reach of being and then life in terms of scope is taken by Proclus to reverse the normal hierarchical succession.

From this, one can conclude that "non-participability" is in fact something like a *hyperbolic* degree of self-sharing, such that unity gives everything to be, yet without dividing itself. Somehow, it gives itself absolutely and without stint; yet because it really does give, it is not identical with its diversity of gifts, which can only be gifts because they remain less than the giver. Hence, each reality is only real because it has fully received unity, yet its unity is after all but particular and incomplete: as a particular limited mode of coherence it only "shares" in the One. It must be for this reason that Proclus with seeming inconsistency does after all speak of "participation in the One," even though he often deems the One to be imparticipable.[13]

The same paradox is revealed in both Iamblichus and Proclus at every level of the scale of being before that of matter (unity, intellectuality, psychic existence), which always consists within itself in a triad of remaining, outgoing, and reversion. This triad can also be constituted as imparticipable, participated, and participating.[14] However, it is clear that the "imparticipable" element at the top of the triad itself shares in the next level above it and transmits this upper level economically within its own level via the outgoing to the lower elements within its own triadic series, which "rebound" upwards. More evidently than Plotinus, the theurgic Neo-Platonists assume that such procession involves also participation, and therefore one must conclude that by "imparticipable" they mean that which cannot be communicated within the very act of communication as the very condition for the possibility of communication. Moreover, the fact that "imparticipability" recurs at every lower level of the ontological series (or hierarchy) shows that this paradox can be inverted: what is communicated down the series is supremely that which cannot be communicated, since the "imparticipable" element always takes the lead at each stage. It is perhaps for this reason that

12. Proclus, *ET* 103, 115.

13. Ibid., 3, 5, 21.

14. Ibid., 23, 30, 35, 64.

Proclus says that the descending scale of internally triadic levels can also be considered (beginning at any point upon this scale) as *two different series* of "complete" imparticipables and "dependent" participations.[15] In strict parallel, what descends is the complete and so *indeclinable,* as it were *alongside* the declinable.

This second, paradoxical model of *methexis,* characteristic of theurgic Neo-Platonism, can be described as "participation all the way up"—or "radical participation," since it does not allow that there is any literal "reserve" in excess of communication, precisely because it is this very reserve which is "impossibly" communicated.

I would argue that it was this model that was generally adopted by Christianized Neo-Platonism, even although this was not evidently, prior to Pseudo-Dionysius the Areopagite and Boethius, under pagan theurgic influence.

This was for very good reasons. First, Christianity as monotheism insists on the absolute simplicity of God: simplicity incompatible with different "aspects" or "ontological regions" within the Godhead. Secondly, in terms of the doctrine that "God is Love," especially as spelled out in Trinitarian terms, Christianity saw "sharing" as an attribute of God's very essence, even though it also held, for monotheistic reasons, that this essence is radically incommunicable. Such an affirmation was a crucial aspect of the Christian view that God was eminently "personal" in nature. Christianity was therefore committed to both gift and paradox as fundamental dimensions of its theology. To *para-doxa*—an incomprehensibly original excess of glory, this is also to say, an incomprehensibly original excess of gift.[16]

This tradition was inherited by Gregory Palamas who—it must be stressed—was loyal to it to up to a point. For this reason, he never suggested anything like a "real distinction" in God between the reserved "essence" and the shared "energies." The question is whether he nonetheless admitted a kind of "formal distinction" between the two, if we define a formal distinction as roughly "a kind of latent division within a real unity, permitting a real if partial separation on some arising occasion." This mode of distinction is most of all associated with John Duns Scotus, Palamas' near contemporary in the West. I shall contend below that Palamas did indeed make a distinction within God along these lines and that to do so was to compromise the divine simplicity to a dangerous degree.

15. Ibid., 64.

16. This is true conceptually and probably also etymologically. Whatever may be claimed by some, nothing really forbids us from supposing that all Indo-European "do" and "da" roots are originally concerned at once with gift and outgoing manifestation or intentional action—as in "I do."

A further consideration supporting "radical participation" is that the church fathers normally spoke of *ousia* (οὐσία) in the singular, but of *energeiai* (ενεργειαι) in the plural. This implies that, since God is simple, when his energy is single it is entirely at one with uncreated *ousia*. However, when the energies are plural, then they are created energies—and this is the way that the Cappadocians generally spoke of them. A comparison can be made with Aquinas' consideration of grace: this is both uncreated and identical with God's eternal essence or created, insofar as it acts upon us.[17] For there is no realm "between" the Creator and the creation, since, for Christianity, this is an absolute ontological divide.

One can make the same point about grammatical tense with respect to the Holy Spirit, in keeping with Pauline usage. As one and uncreated, the Holy Spirit *is* eminent "gift." But insofar as the Spirit acts upon us he conveys a diversity of created "gifts." There would be no warrant for arguing that the Spirit is, in itself, according to a lesser aspect, incorrigibly plural. Indeed one point of the doctrine of the Holy Spirit, well grasped by David Bradshaw, is that it is God himself who acts energetically upon his creatures, both to create and to restore them.[18] So, while the Spirit is in a sense the point of "linkage" between the Trinity and the creation, this does not at all imply any ontological "middle realm." To the contrary, the striking Christian understanding of the Holy Spirit as the ontological connection enabling both creation and deification means that it is God himself who mediates between himself and creatures; and that the energies, which he communicates to them, simply *are* himself. And, herein lays one crucial difference between the Old Testament and the New: in the former, the divine spiritual energies were only revealed as deriving from him, not as also belonging to him—to his very being, his eternal essence.

3. Palamas, Scotus, and the Formal Distinction

The danger, then, of any even formal distinction between the essence and the energies of God is, first, that it refuses the specifically Christian view of God, which is best understood in terms of gift and paradox. Secondly, that it displaces the primacy of a Trinitarian logic whereby both the order (*logos*) and the potent vitality (*pneuma*) that we see in the world derive entirely from a God who is eminently both these things throughout his very being; "all the way up" he is utterance, and "all the way up" he is living breath.

17. Aquinas, *ST* I–II, Q. 110, A. 1 resp.
18. Bradshaw, *Aristotle East and West*, 23.

However, it is just these points, which in the main, Palamas, as Brad-shaw well argues, was trying to sustain. Against Barlaam, who (rather like Avicenna) took the view that God can only act in this world via created mediating powers, he insisted that the power by which God acts upon the creation *is* God himself and is uncreated. Thus, it is the reason for his pro-foundly mystical insistence upon uncreated *energeiai*.[19]

For Palamas the energies are *ellampsesi* (ελλάμψεσι), or "the shinings forth" of the good from the divine essence.[20] Although distinguished from the latter they are inseparable from it, just as the faculties of seeing and hearing persist in the soul even when they are not being exercised. Despite the latter circumstance, the soul remains "without composition."[21] Never-theless, one cannot for Palamas say that the soul simply "is" these faculties—within the soul they somehow introduce both a plurality and a virtuality.

Here, a certain initial resemblance to Scotus appears to view. For Scotus, the soul was as simple in nature as God was; and correspondingly, simplicity was not the key distinguishing feature of the divine as it was for Aquinas. The latter of which for whom the soul is composed of the distinc-tion between essence and being, exemplified (in the case of the human soul) as a distinction between its essence and its active powers of sensing and understanding. Scotus made "infinity" and not "simplicity" the crucial mark of the divine, and regarded all modes of activity, whether infinite or finite, as somewhat qualifying any sheer simple nature.[22]

It is for this reason that Duns Scotus takes Augustine's "psychological analogy" for the Trinity in an over-literalist fashion. The face, with which the human soul can image God with respect to simplicity, is not for Scotus compromised by the distinction of the intellectual faculties of memory, in-tellect, and will, because these are not really distinct from each other and nor are they together distinct from the substance of the soul. Thus, in his earlier Oxford version of his *Sentence Commentary*, Scotus embraces a doc-trine of the soul as radically simple, which he later qualifies in the Paris version merely in terms of a formal distinction, as opposed to a real one, between all these elements.[23] Then he is prepared to see an equally formal distinction between the divine essence and the divine persons, and between

19. Ibid., 221–62.

20. Palamas, *Triads* III, 2, 22.

21. Ibid.

22. Cf. Scotus, *Opus Oxoniense*, IV, dist 43, Q. 2, 6 for the view that "the intellective soul is the proper form of man," in contrast to Aquinas who, with greater fidelity to Aristotle, sees the power to understand as but a "proper accident" of the animal soul. See also *Op.Ox.* II, D. 16, Q. 1, 3–4, 11–12, 16.

23. Cf. Boulnois, *Être et representation*, 202.

the divine persons themselves, which he identifies more by attribute than by relation. For even though, for Scotus, God is infinitely different from us, by virtue of an infinitely high degree of intensity of being, he is still univocally "the same" as us in terms of the formal character of his essential quiddity. This is because Scotus, unlike Aquinas, chose to derive his ontology without reserve from a specific semantics, which has itself opted to regard being as logically univocal rather than equivocal. (Scotus reversed his earlier position on this score.)[24]

One thing which appears problematic about Scotus' *schema* is that (albeit partly in the name of the primacy of the will) it seems to edge back towards a Plotinian Neo-Platonism, as mediated by Avicenna, for which "essence," and especially the essence of the first principle, remains locked within itself, and any donative activity constitutes a secondary ontological moment. Thus, for Scotus, both divine intellection and the Trinitarian emanations are secondary, in formal terms, to the absolute primacy of infinity as defining the divine nature.[25]

Yet Palamas appears proximate to Scotus' onto-theological *schema*, because he compares God to the Soul and discovers in both a certain "composition" in terms of the distinction between what is always in active exercise and what remains latent. As with the great scholastic from the Borders, we do not have a "real distinction" here, but we do seem to have a "formal distinction" in terms of an irreducible difference within a simple reality that can *become* apparent.

Likewise, Palamas refuses the idea of the greatest height as democratic scope, because he seems to attribute divine omnipresence only to the divine energies and not to the divine essence. Again, in this instance, he indulges in a somewhat univocalist and onto-theological direct comparison between God and the human person. For he says that God's nature does not consist in being everywhere any more than our own nature consists in being somewhere.[26]

Once more, this suggests a kind of formal distinction between embodied human nature and spatial position, whereas for Aquinas an embodied being is necessarily individuated, and individuation occurs in part by virtue of spatially determined (or "designated") matter.[27] For Scotus, by compari-

---

24. For a correction of the crude and anachronistic "analytic" renderings of univocity by Richard Cross, see Pickstock, "Duns Scotus," 543–74.

25. Cf. again Pickstock, "Duns Scotus."

26. Palmas, *Triads* III, 2, 9.

27. Aquinas, *Quodlibetal Questions* 11, A 6. Aquinas fluctuated on the issue of whether matter of itself contributes an "extensional" component, but seems finally to have returned to the Avicennian position that it does.

son, individuation is by virtue of a property of *haecceitas* inherent to an individual thing, while matter is a quasi-form "virtually" detachable from each formed entity.[28]

In these two accounts, stability and flux are themselves positioned in very different places: for Aquinas there is an absolute unity of form that ties a creature to a specific, if mobile habitation, even though the highest part of an intellectual creature aspires beyond this. For Scotus, in contrast, the entire specificity of a creature, which in the human case is an intellectual specificity, retains its individual integrity in a more inward, ineffable manner. This means that it is more subject to exterior locational shifts and internal bodily mutation—given the Scotist acceptance of an Avicennian plurality of forms in a single substance[29]—or even to de-materialization, without losing its very identity. Aquinas favors the peasant integrity of a dweller in a specific place and heavenwards aspiration that would sustain this integrity in an eminent fashion; Scotus favors the cosmopolitan integrity of a traveller that survives essentially unaltered every horizontal movement and even every vertical one, since they have been leveled to the horizontal plane of univocity of being.

Therefore, for Palamas to say that human nature is detachable from location is perhaps surprisingly to approximate to the cosmopolitan ontological option of the Franciscan. By invoking this comparison for God, he denies, as the Dominican theologian explicitly affirms, that God is more like a super-elevated intuitive *rusticus,* than he is like a kind of map-reading cosmic voyager (*SCG* 4.1 (3)).[30] In consequence, "every place" becomes for Palamas somewhere that God might go; just as I might go to Brighton, because I heard of it. But for Aquinas, "every place" as the divine location simply *is* God, in a way remotely analogous to the way in which my bodily positioning *is* myself, with the proviso of course that in God's case "his place" (that he *is)* is in no way a limitation of his being or essence.

4. Participation in Platonic and Christian Tradition

Can Palamas' idea of an ineffable "excess" within God over his own capacities and activities be true to Christian tradition? I would suggest that it even lags behind the direction in which Plato was earlier moving. Plato increasingly

---

28. Scotus, *Ordinatio* II, D. 3, P. 1, Q. 4, N. 76; QQ. 5–6, N. 188; *Questiones in Metaphysica* 7, Q. 5.

29. Scotus, *Ordinatio* IV, D. 11, Q. 3, N. 54.

30. Cf. Milbank and Pickstock, *Truth in Aquinas,* 14, for an ironic comment on this point.

saw the *daemonic* rather than "divine" force of *eros* (ερος), belonging to the *metaxu* (μεταξύ), the "between realm," as springing directly from the divine and leading back to the divine. The latter he regarded not just as *ousia* (οὐσία), but also as *dynamis* (δύναμις), as something never without its mode of self-manifestation, of acting outwards beyond itself.[31]

Both these elements, of *eros* and *dynamis,* were taken up into Christian tradition, and Gregory of Nyssa deploys the category of *dynamis* in order to explain how the Trinitarian outgoing from the Father can be fully divine.[32] In the case of Pseudo-Dionysius the Areopagite, we get the idea of God as in himself eternally out-flowing in the double mode of the immanent *thearchia* (θεαρχία) of the Trinity and the external *hierarchia* (ἱεραρχία) of the creation—the two motions being absolutely inseparable within the divine simplicity, such that God is paradoxically "carried outside of himself."[33]

Considerably later than Pseudo-Dionysius, Maximus the Confessor operated with a distinction of *Logos* (Λόγος) and *logoi* (λόγοι), which lies profoundly close to that between the essence and the energies. However, this is by no means for Maximus a distinction *within the Godhead itself*, nor is there for him any ontological limbo between the created *logoi* and the uncreated *Logos*. Instead, the *logoi* participate in the unity of the *Logos* and convey its simplicity of order in diverse and yet harmoniously coordinated ways. Conversely, the *Logos* enfolds within its singularity the myriad diversity of the *logoi*, which are the "ideas" in God of every living creature.[34]

Jumping to the most authentic development of Eastern theology in the twentieth century, the mature thought of Sergei Bulgakov remained in continuity with Maximus by stressing that the mediation exercised by "quasi-hypostatic" *Sophia* (the "personating" dimension of the divine essence itself) nonetheless lies paradoxically on either side of the divide to be mediated and never "in the middle."[35] Thus, either wisdom is the uncreated divine essence, or it is the created principle of mysteriously vital and "personating" power that shapes the universe from within. No "formal distinction" of the divine Wisdom from the divine essence is ever clearly invoked by Bulgakov and it would, in fact, be adverse to the entire character of his theological ontology.

When it comes to the fundamental division in interpreting the distinction between the imparticipable and the participated, it is therefore clear

---

31. Cf. Milbank, "The Force of Identity," 194–216.

32. Ibid.

33. Pseudo-Dionysius, *DN* 4.13: 712A.

34. Confessor, *Amb.* 7, 41.

35. Cf. Milbank, "Sophiology and Theurgy," 45–85.

that Christianity has remained consistently wedded to the view that participation goes "all the way up"—"radical participation." However, it is also possible to argue for a certain affinity between this version and the theurgic current within Neo-Platonism. Indeed, the strange thing is that Bradshaw himself partially makes this argument, and renders it a crucial aspect of his book.

Non-theurgic Neo-Platonism in the tradition of Plotinus (although the latter is by no means entirely without theurgic elements)[36] tends to emphasize a retreat into the soul, which is also an ascent upwards into the ontological "sphere" of soul that lies above the body. This ascent continues through the sphere of the intellect up to very threshold of the One, where (aporetically) the climb cannot be completed on pain of abolition of the soul and the intellect in favor of a merging with, and mystical "non-comprehension" of, ineffable unity. *Via* Avicenna this tradition encourages a transmutation of the Platonic doctrine of recollection of transcendent forms through the operation of occasional "triggers," into a doctrine of *a priori* understanding in the depths of the soul. Ultimately, both Descartes and Kant stand within this lineage.

By comparison, theurgic Neo-Platonism after Iamblichus tends to emphasize how the soul is "fully descended" into the body and remains there in order to execute ritual acts, which attract the "descent" of the divine power. While the capacity of the divine to descend remains distinct from the question of participation, there is clearly a strong link: for the ability of the divine at any level to descend suggests that the higher realm itself condescends, rather than being but the passive subject of an ontological declension. And, since, at any level, according to Proclus, the higher rank is relatively imparticipable (for its specific dignity can never be fully communicated) this implies, as already argued, a paradox in the idea of theurgic descent: what cannot decline, nevertheless does, in a kenotic fashion. In principle this paradox can reach up "all the way to the top" and one can conceive the One itself as the origin of descent and even as in itself descending, precisely because the very highest is so by virtue of its unlimited "spatial" reach.

Such an explicit extremity of paradox is perhaps only arrived at within Pseudo-Dionysius' Christianization of the theurgic, in the course of his incorporation of the ideas of Proclus. It should, however, be noted here that there are also Christian equivalences of the theurgic prior to Pseudo-Dionysius and that, for all Augustine's opposition to what he saw as the magical, demon-invoking character of pagan theurgics, there is a certain equivalent

---

36. However, Plotinus tends to view theurgic descent as being to the intellectual life of the soul rather than to the cosmos or to external ritual.

of the theurgic moment in his *Confessiones*.[37] It is singing a psalm that "shows" (in a Wittgensteinian sense) to us the answer to the conundrum of time, while such liturgical action is only possible because God himself has descended into time at the incarnation in order to counteract its fallen tendency to "dispersal." Finally, the entire book concludes with a joining of the self with the cosmos to sing a cosmic hymn of praise.

What is more, Augustine's interest in number, and even adoption of an ontology of number, which runs through the whole course of his works, is to a large degree of Neo-Pythagorean inspiration, and an increase in the Pythagorean dimension was, as already alluded to, one characteristic of theurgic Neo-Platonism. O'Meara notes a specific parallel in Augustine's early work *De Ordine* (II xiv, 39– xvi, 44) in which he refers to the fact that Pythagoras led his disciples to the heights of contemplation through the study of mathematics and then finally applied this number-based curriculum to politics. However, O'Meara wrongly argues that Augustine's later critique of both empire and pagan magic in the *City of God* imply a complete rejection of this earlier Pythagorean approach to the political.[38] He claims this on the basis of the view that Augustine later rejects any theurgic-style integration of *theoria* (θεορια) and politics which would regard political life on earth as training for the divine life, or any earthly city as a reflection of an archetypal heavenly one. The latter notion was much more to the fore in Iamblichus and Proclus than in Plato himself: but it *does* find its echo in Augustine, who is of course here drawing out also a biblical theme. Right up to the end of his career, a participation in "Jerusalem, our mother who is above," remained an important theme for him, and the "City of God" is an eternal and eschatological as well as temporary reality. In the latter respect, it is *not* the mere aggregate of the truly saved, but a literal earthly polity that combines elevated theory and popular practice as crucially conjoined elements for the way of ascent.[39]

Most importantly of all, one can construe Augustine's reworked account of deification in terms of a greater stress upon free divine descending grace as parallel to the greater stress upon divine descent within later Neo-Platonism. This parallel only seems counter-intuitive in the light of the excessive account of divine predestination in Augustine's final anti-Pelagian writings—an excess from which the Western church mostly retreated. But

37. It is not impossible that Augustine knew something of Iamblichu's works: see O'Meara, *Cosmopolis*, 151.

38. Augustine's later retraction of the endorsement of Pythagoras in the *De Ordine* at *Retractiones* I. 3. 3, clearly alludes to its apparent endorsement of a merely pagan and philosophic ascent to the divine and approach to the political.

39. See Milbank, *Theology and Social Theory*, 382–442.

so long as divine grace remains linked to synergy of divine and human will and to sacramental mediation (as it is in the bulk of Augustine's writings), then one can see how the critique of "Pelagian ascent" in the case of inner-Christian debates is truly comparable to the critique of "Plotinian ascent" in the case of Neo-Platonic discussions.

The structural parallels between Christianity and theurgic Neo-Platonism can therefore be extended beyond the bounds of the direct influence of the latter upon the former. Specific impulses within Christianity supporting the double and co-belonging ideas of "descent all the way down" and "participation all the way up" are clearly biblical, yet one should not atavistically seek to deny the extent to which pagan attention to its own oracles could lead it to go in a convergent direction. In the case of Iamblichus one sees above all the idea (highly consonant with Christianity) that while prayer is not about changing the minds of the gods, that neither is it mere self-therapy. Instead, it is the theoretical and practical endeavor to arrive at a kind of "atunement" with the divine that will truly allow the divine influence to flow into reality. No doubt our "atuning" is also ultimately the work of the gods, but that issue of causality lies at another ontological level. On the finite level there is a genuine synergy. When it comes to the issue of how far the divine side of causal influence belongs to the divine essence itself, then it is clear that increasingly Iamblichus ascribes to the notion of a single "divine world" comprised of the One, the Good, gods, daemons, and heroes, over against the non-divine world.[40]

The drive towards "monotheism" in his writings lies here and *not* in a tendency to posit a "one beyond the one" as a counter-movement to the general efflorescence of divine beings that was part of his deliberate defense of pagan polytheism. Indeed, as with his later successor Damascius of Athens, the positing of ever-yet greater absolutes was not an attempt to define an area absolutely reserved from all communication, but rather an attempt to indicate an "Ineffable" that could comprise both the one and the many, both absolute reserve and generous out flowing.[41] Certainly in one respect this all-encompassing "One" is thereby all the more replete and withheld, yet only to the degree that no act of self-donation lies outside its sway. No doubt the arising *aporias* here (how to avoid both pantheism and acosmism) require a Trinitarian resolution that can fully articulate the idea that God is in himself an ecstasy beyond himself, which includes an ecstatic reach towards

40. See Iamblichus, *On the Mysteries* I. 9–15; Milbank, "Sophiology and Theurgy;" Bradshaw, *Aristotle East and West*, 135–42; Shaw, *Theurgy and the Soul.*

41. See Damascius, *De Principiis*, 76–77, 83; Milbank, "The Mystery of Reason," 68–117—for Damascius see 85–91. It is relevant to the argument of this essay that Damascius sees "participation" as more ineffable than "procession."

the "external" beyond of creation. All the same, pagan theurgic philosophy increasingly approached the question of participation in terms of paradox.

To sum up the argument so far: Plato, theurgic tradition, and then Christian theology (with its ideas of creation *ex nihilo* and of the Trinity) were gradually able to render mediation ultimate and pertaining to the Godhead itself, without endorsing the idea that God requires the aid of a mediating *sphere* between divine and non-divine reality. The danger with Palamas may be that he is too Plotinian and insufficiently Iamblichan (or Proclean or Dionysian). For he too much imagines a "One beyond the gift," a distinction within the divine realm, and in consequence an unacceptable ontological *Mittelmarch*—to borrow a name from the sagas of Michael Moorcock.[42]

5. Divine Action and Human Theurgy

The most impressive part of David Bradshaw's book is his treatment of the category of *energeia* (ἐνέργεια) or *actus*. He rightly points out that its importance in Christian theology stems not, in the first place, from Aristotle, but rather from St. Paul.[43] The latter understands God primarily in terms of an active exercise of energetic power—especially in his development of Pneumatology, as already alluded. This energetic power at once *is* God and is the mode of divine self-expression. Accordingly, it is also that which God communicates, in communicating his very self. This perspective, as Bradshaw argues (in the course of some exemplary exegesis), is what allows Paul to think of human action in *synergistic* terms: our acts are at once fully ours and yet entirely God's. Human beings when they are acting aright fully concur with God in terms of both operation and trajectory.

This is so far entirely in line with my own conclusions. Equally so is Bradshaw's contention that this Pauline pattern is paralleled to some degree by the thinking of pagan theurgic Neo-Platonism—which, like all Neo-Platonism, synthesized Platonic notions of origination with Aristotelian ideas of action. One could argue that Paul implicitly does just the same thing. Again one can agree with Bradshaw when he goes on to say that in effect Pseudo-Dionysius the Areopagite combined the Pauline and the theurgic traditions.[44]

---

42. Cf. Moorcock, *Von Bek*.

43. Bradshaw, *Aristotle East and West*, 120–23.

44. Ibid., 119–52.

But where I would part company with Bradshaw is in not allowing that Thomas Aquinas perpetuates and extends just this synthesis.[45] Bradshaw's denial of this is strange, because he strongly endorses (and very well explains) the highly Thomistic view that a priority of act over possibility is required by a Christian ontological understanding. He breaks this down in Aristotelian fashion in terms of an equal priority of definition, substance, and causal sequence.[46] Respectively: a specific possibility is only definable as the possibility of a specific mode of action; possibility cannot "exist" unless it is somewhat in act; nothing merely potential can move itself, and so the potential can only be activated by the already actual.

Bradshaw also understands how Christianity came to combine an Aristotelian *actus purus* of the first mover, drawing all to itself, with a Neo-Platonic idea of the first principle as originator. It is this combination, which gives the idea of act as continuous outgoing, as a realization of what Aquinas eventually called *virtus*, or "active potential." Thus, as he says, Christian theology took over from Plotinus a notion of divine action as an emanating act, a continuous subtle flowing-forth like the immediate procession of light.[47] But Christianity, as Bradshaw also realizes, was able to think-through the combination of activity with outgoing by replacing, following Boethius, the Neo-Platonic "One" with *esse*, the infinitive of being, thereby stopping-up the *hiatus* between the anexistential and the existential that could harbor the idea of "the One beyond the gift." (My diagnosis here would seem to conflict with Jean-Luc Marion's view that the gift should be aligned with the notion of the One or the Good "beyond being."[48])

When it comes to the question of pagan theurgy, Bradshaw very insightfully realizes that the same combination that we find in Paul is at work: the idea of an operation that stems from a plenitude of activity and is always operationally effective. Rightly, he points out that this "effectiveness" is especially emphasized by the *Hermetica*,[49] and that this stress becomes an element in the eventual synthesis of divergent influences regarding the Christian notion of action—the Hermetic element being crucial to the long-term emergence of experimental science.[50] Nevertheless, the Hermetic

45. Ibid., 221–62.

46. Ibid., 1–23.

47. Ibid., 45–118.

48. Cf. Marion, *God Without Being.*

49. Bradshaw, *Aristotle East and West*, 131–35.

50. Christian apologists tend to overstress the importance for the Scientific Revolution of the nominalist-voluntarist current that traces back to the Byzantine philosopher John Philoponus. While this current matters enormously, of perhaps more fundamental importance for the Western "take-off" of science was, as David Hart argues,

corpus speaks of God's non-laborious activity as a type of making, as well as a kind of doing. It regards *energeia* as an "active power" or "cosmic force." In the case of these oracular writings the theurgic often sounds like the overtly "magical," though Bradshaw rightly stresses that for the *Hermetica*, just as much as for Iamblichus and Proclus, the theurgic is an enticement of divine power and not an attempt to manipulate this power, which remains entirely free in character.[51] All that one might add here is that this may be true of most "magic" in most human societies: it is rarely a matter of sheer automatic "recipe" and perhaps only such when it turns demonic.[52]

But in accordance with his understanding that the theurgic is not mechanical in nature, Bradshaw rightly points out how important the idea of trusting in tradition was to Proclus, and how *pistis* (πίστις) for him exceeds *gnosis* (γνῶσις) at the very summit of contemplative ascent.[53] By observing that for Proclus, as less clearly so for Plotinus, the One is involved in the causation of all that lies below the One. Bradshaw proves just how aware he is of the importance of the theoretical divide between the two Neo-Platonic masters. The greater caution in the case of Plotinus concerning the reach of both descent and ascent eventually gives rise, as already mentioned, to an evolution of the Platonic notion of recollection into an *a priori* dimension of subjective knowing through the thought of Avicenna, Bonaventure, and Duns Scotus.[54] For since the divine as the psychic does not quite reach into the corporeal realm for Plotinus, conversely the way back to unity is a matter of climbing to the already given, rather than a waiting upon an ever-renewed gift through a series of "triggering" finite encounters.[55] By contrast Proclus, after Iamblichus, sustains this more sacramental approach to recollection, reinforced by his view that matter itself recaptures something of the lost simplicity of the One, to which "doubling" intellection is oblivious.[56]

---

the Christian freeing of labor, which led, in the Western Middle Ages, to the greatest period of technological innovation in human history so far. The "take-off" then had much to do with the Baconian idea of learning from the methods of artisans, and so stressing pragmatic, effective knowledge. But before Francis Bacon this was the counsel of hermeticists and alchemists. One should also note that when it comes to physics, the nominalist current was always in creative tension with a Platonic current, all the way from Grosseteste to Galileo. See Hart, *Atheist Delusions*, 56–74; Webster, *From Paracelsus to Newton*.

51. Bradshaw, *Aristotle East and West*, 131–35.

52. Cf. Mauss, *A General Theory of Magic*.

53. Bradshaw, *Aristotle East and West*, 142–52, 268–70.

54. Cf. Schumacher, *Divine Illumination*.

55. Cf. Chrétien, "The Immemorial and Recollection," 1–39.

56. Proclus, *ET* 59; see also Trouillard, *La Mystagogie de Proclos*.

By invoking the theurgic legacy, Bradshaw therefore well grasps how the idea of *energeia* as communicating action and consequently of *energeia* as synergy goes along with the idea of radical ascent and radical descent, whereby the One is itself a donative outgoing.

He is also perfectly right to think that Palamas at heart wished to sustain this combination of ideas. But then so did Aquinas. Why does Bradshaw deny the latter truth and why is he unable to see that it is not Aquinas, but after all Palamas who, like Scotus in a parallel conceptual trajectory (though Palamas is the less drastic), compromises this tradition by introducing a distinction within the Godhead itself?

6. Essence and Energies

The supposed distinction between the essence and energies of God is of course a different distinction from that between the divine persons and the divine essence. Nevertheless, a certain tendency in some supposedly "neopatristic" modern Orthodox thought to draw the latter distinction too crudely tends to encourage an embrace of the former distinction. Moreover, as Rowan Williams pointed out, Palamas himself saw the distinction between the essence and the energies as being of the same kind as that between the essence and the persons.[57]

Person is a relational term and essence is not. Moreover, one should agree with Aquinas that the divine persons can only be defined as "substantial relations" for fear of otherwise introducing a real plurality into the godhead. Yet this does not entirely collapse the persons into the relations, because "person" is here rather the point of equipoise between relation and substance. So although a person is exhaustively a donating and receiving positional perspective "within" God, it is nevertheless entirely manifestatory of Godhead, entirely at one with the divine essence.[58] In this way, the relational distinction of persons, though not of essence, by no means entails a formal (as opposed to an "intellectual")[59] distinction between essence and persons, as it does for a Scotistic outlook, which tends, like the entire Franciscan trajectory (which derives from the pre-Franciscan Richard of St. Victor) to define person in terms of both autonomy and discrete function, rather than relationality.[60]

57. Williams, "The Philosophical Structures of Palamism;" Palamas, *Theophanies* 12.

58. Aquinas, *ST* I, Q. 29, A.4 resp.

59. Meaning a distinction merely according to our *modus cognoscendi*.

60. Specifically, the intellectual generation of the Son is seen as "natural," whereas

Quite often it has been suggested by modern commentators that the Franciscan position on the Trinity is close to that of the Eastern fathers. But this claim is highly ironic—for in truth it is a reading of the Greek sources in terms of the Franciscan scholastic legacy that engenders this illusion.[61] This reading can then appear to concur with later misreading of the legacy in the East, post Photius,[62] which have been accentuated by the supposed "neo-patristic" current in modern times. Such an insight, it should be said, greatly favors ecumenism, because it shows that *some* divisions cross the Eastern/Western frontiers, and that these divisions can be just as crucial as those that coincide with these frontiers. Increasingly, we see that what we require is a kind of "revised Anglican" position (roughly that of "Radical Orthodoxy") which coincides with the legacy of the *nouvelle théologie*: for this position there is a "long patristic period" which ends around the year 1300 (even though it starts to disintegrate before then and survives vestigially or through multiple revivals and creative revisions after that date). To some extent one can trace a *parallel collapse* of this epoch in both East and West, even if its collapse is far more marked in the latter case.

Within this perspective one can then see how the Franciscan scholastic distortion of the tradition tends retrospectively to buttress a Palamite approach to the distinction of the essence from the energies. In either case one is being invited to entertain the notion both of a certain plurality and of a certain secondariness within the Godhead—even if, in the case of the Trinity, this takes the form (as with Scotus) of equating the essence with the *monarchia*. And in this double fashion a muted form of Neo-Platonic declining emanation within the divine sphere is indeed, as Williams avers, smuggled back within Christianity. Through a further irony, Thomas Aquinas' entirely patristic refusal of any such subterfuge is perversely condemned.

One crucial reason for Bradshaw being led astray at both these points is his surprising inattention to the question of tense. As already mentioned, the ancient theologians whom he cites speak of a *single* energy within God, and they choose the singular tense to indicate an *identity* between energy and essence. They only speak of *many* energies to denote the divine activity

---

the loving procession of the Spirit is seen as "voluntary." See Boulnois, *Être et representation*, 107–50. The beginning of an understanding of person in terms of "self-command" can be traced back to Bonaventure. Cf. Riches, *Christ the End of Humanism*.

61. My position here depends upon the by now well-established view that Augustine's account of the Trinitarian persons in terms of "substantive relations" (as Aquinas later described them) is simply a more rigorous continuation of the same understanding in the Cappadocian fathers. See Lewis Ayres *Augustine and the Trinity*.

62. Cf. Milbank, "The Second Difference," 171–94.

ad extra, and hence one can infer that plurality denotes (as it logically and grammatically must) a certain diversity that is consequent upon finitude.

Indeed, Bradshaw himself rightly declares that the description of *energeia* and of the divine unity are one and the same, citing John of Damascus' definition of energy in *De Fide Orthdoxa* 1.13 as "the being of the things that are, the reason of the rational, and the intellectual act of those possessing intelligence."[63] In other words, the energy of finite things is the being of finite things, and both derive from the one source, which is God. But then to say that this *energeia* is "God himself as participated by creatures" is not to imply any distinction from the essence, but rather that, at the point where essence-as-energy is participated, it is diversified to the exact measure that there are diverse creatures. For being and energy here keep exact pace with each other, as Bradshaw himself implies.

To create beings is therefore also to pluralize energy, which is otherwise "singular" (that is to say absolutely unified, not, course, "individual"). It might seem, as Bradshaw implies, that this is belied by Gregory of Nyssa's speaking of the divine *energeiai* of wisdom, goodness, and providence as "things around the divine nature," a concept echoed by Gregory Nazianzus.[64] However, what we have here are *plural* energies seen as "tokens," "reflections," and "traces" "left behind by God," which are therefore things that proceed *from* God. As Basil puts it in another passage cited by Bradshaw: "his *energeiai* come down to us, but His essence remains beyond our reach."[65] Nothing in these writings suggests that the energies in the plural are not *created* realities. So, when the two Gregory's speak of the energies as nevertheless circulating God himself, what they surely wish to indicate is the paradox that from the divine standpoint his outgoing also entirely belongs to him, to his indivisible nature.

Here it should be noted that Barlaam's position, which Palamas vehemently opposed, might well have failed fully to recognize this point—for all his adherence to an exhaustive Latin division of the divine energy between the uncreated and the created. Hence, while, as we have seen, Palamas implies a "formal distinction" between the divine essence and the divine energies, Barlaam perhaps implied an equally "formal distinction" between the divine eternal essence and the divine will to create, in a manner that could also seem akin to Scotus, since the Greek Calabrian explicitly rejected what he saw as the Latin view that all things in God are to be identified with the divine essence. Indeed, as John Meyendorff has noted, Cardinal

---

63. Bradshaw, *Aristotle East and West*, 209.

64. Ibid., 166–68.

65. Basil, *Epistle* 234.1.

Bessarion explicitly accused him of introducing anti-Thomist Scotistic perspectives within the Byzantine orbit.[66] There is little truth therefore in the idea, frequently canvassed in the past, that, by opposing Barlaam, Palamas was, in effect, opposing Aquinas.[67] To the contrary, this opposition would rather point in the converse direction, while at the same time both theologians may have shared a certain faintly traceable "Byzantine Scotism." It seems, as I have already argued, excessive to ascribe to Palamas, as John S. Romanides does, a "real distinction" of the essence and the energies, while Romanides' claim that actually Palamas is closer to Ockham than to Scotus equally seems *de trop*, since the crucial point of resemblance that he cites to make this case, namely the non-attribution of the divine ideas to the divine essence, applies already to Scotus.[68]

All the same, Romanides is astute in pointing out that just this move must imply a certain voluntarism, such that the divine energies for Palamas are not equally intellectual and forceful, as they were (though Romanides denies this) for the Cappadocians, Pseudo-Dionysius, Maximus, and Damascene, but rather most fundamentally forceful as willed. In this respect Romanides points out that Palamas sometimes describes the energies as *Aneideioi* (Ανειδειοι), which he reasonably claims has a certain anti-Platonic resonance. Here also then, one can locate a certain parallel between late medieval tendencies in both West and East.[69]

Yet in making this case for later Eastern rupture, one needs to be fair to Bradshaw with regard to Gregory of Nyssa. For it is arguable that the latter so strongly conceives of the infinite as a *positive* property of God that it is as if he envisages a kind of ultimate "substantial darkness" exceeding all positivities of light and so requiring that even the beatific vision remain an endless *epectasis*.[70] It also seems to be the case that, via the mediation of Damascene, something of this tradition encourages Scotus' definition of God as first and foremost a positive infinity, "a certain ocean of infinite

---

66. Cf. Romanides, "Notes on the Palamite Controversy and Related Topics."

67. Cf. Williams, *The Ground of Union*. This is a fine work which rightly unsettles the usual claims for East/West duality. Perhaps though it is a little too adroit in evading technicalities.

68. Romanides, "Notes on the Palamite Controversy."

69. Ibid.

70. Cf. Milbank, "Sophiology and Theurgy," 72–73; de Andia, *Henosis*. For Gregory (e.g., *Contr. Eun.* I .42) God seems to be so *ontologically* "incomprehensible" (even to himself, as it were) that "shape" in any sense is precluded. By contrast, for Pseudo-Dionysius God is (ontologically) at once unbounded and bounded in a "contradictory" fashion.

substance,"[71] in Damascene's phrase. Scotus takes this to imply that the other divine perfections (good, wise, happy, etc.) are contained merely "virtually" in the infinite, since any fully actual containment would compromise an absolute primal simplicity, which is not diversified even according to the "reasons" of transcendental qualities which remain "formally" distinct in the infinite as much as the absolute, on account of the univocity of being. In effect then, Scotus reads the Cappadocian notion of what lies "around" God as being "other" to the divine essence in a sense that has some grounding *in res*, rather than merely in our intellectual perception. And this would seem to be precisely parallel to the position of Palamas.

One should take this as a misreading of Damascene, yet it is arguably made possible by a faint lingering of the Plotinian *aporia* within Cappadocian thought, bequeathed to later writers—according to which *aporia* the more the human person "sees" the One, the more it must become identical with the One which exceeds reason, and so forfeit any comprehension of the One, along with the power of understanding as such. In this way the perspective of participating being is not just diminished as compared with the (non)perspective of imparticipable being, but radically incommensurate with it. The lingering of this *aporia* concurs with the way in which the Cappadocian idea of the journey to the ultimate vision of only the "back parts of God" is also a turning "within" the soul and "up to" the psychic, then intellectual, and then extra-intellectual mystical sphere, for all that the "psychic" is, as with Plotinus himself, a collective and not a private realm.[72]

Yet this is at most an ambivalence: in general the theoretical wound between henology and intellectualism in Plotinus is here at least well on the way to being healed within Cappadocian understanding. So if at times there appears to be a tension between a near-conception of God as a kind of hypostasized negativity (the absolutely non-circumscribable and unformed infinite) and an affirmation of the divine excellencies, precisely because this tension is left unresolved it never in the patristic era takes the proto-Palamite form of a distinction within God himself of his essence and his outward-looking attributes.

In this respect one can now read Pseudo-Dionysius not (as for Balthasar and Daniélou) as being in simple continuity with the Cappadocians, but as imbibing elements of pagan theurgic Neo-Platonism *with just the same gesture* by which he implicitly removes the faint Plotinian residues

---

71. Scotus, *Ordinatio* I, D. 8, Q. 4, 198–200, commenting on Damascene, *Expositio fidei* I.4.

72. Cf. Milbank, "The Force of Identity."

in the Cappadocians that are perturbing for a Christian logic.[73] Thus, by comparison with the Cappadocians, Pseudo-Dionysius: more emphatically declares that the mystical path negates both negation and affirmation; defines the infinite negatively (the infinite), and declares that God is also beyond the opposition of finite and infinite; and regards the beatific vision not as endless progress into dazzling darkness, but as an immediate overwhelming by superabundant light so dazzling that it is obscure. (This reversal of metaphor is arguably important.) The three new emphases run together and they also concur with a newly theurgic emphasis upon a descent of the "blinding" divine light rather than an ascent into divine obscurity.[74]

This combination of emphases all came to be eventually absorbed by the Christian West and especially by Thomas Aquinas (the *via eminentiae*; the apophatic in-finite as opposed to Scotus' positive identity of the divine essence with infinity; the plenitudinous beatific vision unmediated by any finite being; the descent of the divine into sensory understanding and liturgical experience.)[75] The West saw them as compatible with Augustine's thinking precisely because Pseudo-Dionysius' accentuated emphasis upon descending divine gift concurs well, as I have already suggested, with Augustine's emphatically anti-Pelagian account of grace.

One should also mention here the mediating role played by the reflections of Boethius, who already combined Augustinian influence with ones stemming from the pagan theurgists. Again, as with Pseudo-Dionysius, the strange thing is that Boethius' seemingly disturbing and very early "renaissance" of pagan mythology and pagan philosophy within Christian thought, in fact allows a deepening of Christian philosophy precisely by the incorporation of elements of pagan Neo-Platonism that prove sympathetic to Christianity because they have their origin partially in attempts to *rival* Christianity. What especially matters here is once again the Proclean relationship of "height" to "scope." In one sense Boethius drastically demythologizes the biblical God by stressing that he exists and understands in an "eternal present" (*nunc stans*) and therefore does not literally remember the past, nor will the future. Equivalently, philosophy "consoles" the wise man by lifting him outside the vagaries of time. However, Boethius, after Proclus, emphasizes that divine knowledge is supreme because entirely *inclusive*: God understands all perfectly after the pure mode of subjective intelligence, but to do so is to *incorporate*, at a higher intellectual level, all

---

73. Cf. de Andia, *Henosis*.

74. This means that the French Gothic architectural tribute to the patron saint of France gets it exactly right. The Cappadocian position is, in effect, more "Romanesque."

75. Cf. Milbank and Pickstock, *Truth in Aquinas*, 88–111.

the lesser understanding of the imagination and the senses. This echoes the Proclean notion that the One "pre-includes" all of being, and the equally Proclean notion that the highest intelligence is able to reach downwards with a shaping force into everything.

But in deploying this echo, Boethius is able to make it resound further by concluding roundly that the entirely "removed" knowledge of God is also a providential knowing and causing of every single specific reality in the created order.[76] In this way the narratives about God in the Bible are saved after all, and the wise man is seen not just as the contemplative, but also as one who accepts and reads the ways of providence, operating through the instruments of fate which are the ordering patterns within things, rather in the way that for Maximus the *Logos* operates through the *logoi*. For Boethius, God is good as a Neo-Platonic One (though he is also now *esse*) in a sense that allows him to be grasped in terms of the "supra-moral," or of a biblical "religious beyond the ethical." Thus, God can deal out apparent bad fortune to the good, or good fortune to the weak, because he is always matching material conditions to spiritual needs according to the often invisible exigencies of a truly *comprehensive* vision that he alone possesses. The wise man remotely participates in this vision, *both* through contemplative ascent *and* through partial discernment of times and places. (This includes, for Boethius, as later for Aquinas, a limited acceptance of the role of juridical astrology.) In this way, Boethius managed partially to synthesize an "oriental" concern with disclosure via ascent with an Augustinian concern with time and eschatology. But this "apocalyptic" unity is rendered possible simply in "oriental" terms of the notion that scope constitutes height, now extended by Boethius from spatial to temporal relevance.

For all these reasons, one should argue that the "renaissance" of the pagan in both Boethius and Pseudo-Dionysius in fact allowed a deepening reconciliation of biblical with philosophical culture. The same thing is true in the later case of Eriugena: the theurgic and Dionysian stress on the role of "inappropriate" images of God allowed him newly to comprehend the philosophical appropriateness of the "grotesque" symbolic character of so many biblical usages.[77] This helps one, indeed, to comprehend how "renaissance" as such is a specifically Christian event: a re-reading of the classical past through Christian eyes that contributes further insight into the scope of Christianity itself. Not accidentally, King Alfred of Wessex's translation of the *De Consolatione Philosophiae* lay at the heart of the very first European Renaissance (though one can see this also as the consummation of the entire

76. Boethius, *De Consolatione Philosophiae* Book V.

77. Boulnois, *Au-delà de l'image,* 154–71.

Hiberno-British insular revival of learning after the Fall of Rome) and first great flowering of European vernacular literature in Anglo-Saxon England, which soon gave stimulus to the Carolingian Renaissance, and thence to all subsequent cultural "re-births."

Yet despite all the above, Christian suspicions of these incorporations of pagan philosophy linked to pagan practice may still linger. What does Pseudo-Dionysius means when he speaks of *proödoi* (πρόοδοι), or "processions" that, as Bradshaw rightly puts it, "both *are* God and *manifest* God,"[78] and that include the processions of the Trinity itself? Does this not imply a diversity within the Godhead? But Pseudo-Dionysius frees himself from any taint of polytheism by emphasizing a dual usage of attributes of excellence such as "being itself," "life itself," "power itself," "subsistence of peace itself."[79] In one sense these are just different ways of referring to "the one transcendent cause and source beyond source of all things." But in another sense they refer to "the provident acts of power, which come forth from God in whom nothing at all participates. I am talking here of being itself, of life itself, and of divinity itself, which shapes things in a way that each creature, according to capacity, has his share of these." Clearly then, in the first case, diversity is merely according to what Aquinas will later term our *modus significandi* and this also applies to the Trinitarian instance. But real diversity arises only in the second case, when something streams forth from God as a created excellence, to be received by specific creatures.

It might nonetheless seem as if, from this passage, it is only the "streams" that are participated in by creatures and not God himself. Indeed, Pseudo-Dionysius sounds unequivocal here. So are not the *proödoi* or *dynameis* distinguished from the divine essence in just the same way as the *energeiai* later for Palamas? But the answer is no, because Pseudo-Dionysius himself invites us to read *On the Divine Names* in paradoxical terms that imply a participation in the imparticipable. For he declares that not some secondary aspect of God, but *God himself* is "ecstatic" in character:[80] "because of the excess of his yearning goodness he comes to be outside of himself."[81] Clearly Pseudo-Dionysius must think (because God is simple and imparticipable) that this statement is also *not* true, yet he is still able to make it. But much more explicitly he states this *coincidentia oppositorum* outright: "from his transcendence beyond all He is brought down to that which is in all, in

78. Bradshaw, *Aristotle East and West*, 179–86.

79. Pseudo-Dionysius, *DN* 11.6 (PG 4: 953C–956A).

80. Pseudo-Dionysius, *DN* 4.13 (PG 4: 712 A–B).

81. Pseudo-Dionysius, *DN* 4.13 (PG 4: 712A).

accordance with his ecstatic and super-substantial power of remaining."[82] Somehow, for God to go out of himself *is* his mode of remaining. Further, the One who absolutely remains is the One who remains even when he entirely leaves himself. Utter sharing is not alien to God, because he alone cannot be self-alienated.

Curiously, it is Bradshaw himself who draws attention to this passage, yet does not see just how it precludes any Palamite gloss. Such a gloss is equally precluded by the theoretical circumstance, which he also well draws attention to, that outgoing-as-remaining implies that all creatures inevitably return to God, just as they all themselves share in his power of communicative generation. Both return and theurgic co-working with God necessarily follow upon emanation precisely because this is the emanation of the One itself.[83]

It is surely for this reason that Pseudo-Dionysius can unite as one the descent of the *proödoi* as "names" *from* God, with our liturgical utterance of "names" as names *for* God. The background to this conjuncture may well be Proclus' commentary on the *Cratylus* (a rarely commented-upon text, according to the surviving records), where he endorses Plato's view that names are "naturally" suitable to the things that they name, rather than being mere conventional labels for concepts in the mind, as for Aristotle. For this means that the guarantee of the stability of language does *not* lie in mental constancy (a position that will in the long run lead, via Porphyry's *Plotinian* reading of Aristotle's categories as more logical than ontological, to transcendentalism, idealism, and empiricism),[84] but rather in its "ritual" echo of the eternal forms themselves, which relies upon the assumption that the material things that words invoke must themselves enjoy remote kinship with the ideal realm. So unless words that lie between meaning and matter can somehow "conjure up" this link, there can be, for both Plato and Proclus, no truth. In this way, Platonism is far more friendly to the materiality of words and the necessity of images for meaning than is the Aristotelian position.[85]

82. I am here using Bradshaw's own translation. See Bradshaw, *Aristotle East and West*, 181.

83. Ibid., 182–86.

84. Adrian Pabst has shown that there is also a pre-Arabic influence route in the West for the development of the Plotinian tradition in an *a prioristic* direction which also over-semanticizes, by granting Aristotle's logic a priority over his metaphysics. This lies through Gilbert Porreta's reading of Boethius' appropriation of Porphyry's logic in a fashion that elides Boethius' "Procleanization" of this logic. Pabst argues that this Proclean dimension regarding speech about being in Boethius was then restored by Aquinas. See his *Metaphysics: the Creation of Hierarchy*. See also note 2 above.

85. Cf. van den Berg, "A Remark of Genius," 155–69.

It is true that, beyond his pagan master Proclus, Pseudo-Dionysius radicalizes this theurgic mode of participation, because he far more decisively refuses plurality within the divine, while fully ascribing to that sharp disjuncture of being implied by the doctrine of creation. Yet even in the case of Proclus, it is Bradshaw himself who once more contends against any simplistic readings of his ontological divisions in the heavenly realm. If (as Bradshaw rather implausibly denies) Pseudo-Dionysius' *proödoi* are first-cousins to Proclus' *henads*, then it turns out that the latter, rather like the former, are not just the commencement of divine communication, but also belong entirely within the *single* divine sphere, along with the originary One itself—thus they are said not to "proceed" but to "derive" from the One.[86] In their aspect as abstract excellencies they are distributed to creatures, but in themselves, as Bradshaw rightly says, they "are not simply reified divine attributes, but quasi-personal agents possessing intellects, souls, and bodies."[87] "Gods" in other words (though situated, as Proclus makes clear, above the Olympian and even the pre-Olympian deities) whose diversity may still for Proclus be subordinated, along with the "One," to a yet more transcendental mode of unity. It is true, as we have already seen, that Proclus says that the henads can be participated, whereas the One cannot. However, one cannot be entirely sure that this statement rules out a paradoxical reading according to which "the henads" denote the One insofar as it is, after all, participable. Proclus does not quite arrive at the thought of ecstasy, yet his *schema* is not entirely alien to it either.

7. The Genealogy of Forms

In this connection Bradshaw is entirely right to say that Rowan Williams has no warrant for supposing that Neo-Platonists were ever so naive as to "reify merely logical distinctions," such that attributes are wrenched away from the subjects within which they should lie—whether finite or transcendent.[88] Indeed, Neo-Platonism entirely *rests* upon (a largely correct) "henological" reading of the Platonic forms whereby, as exemplars, they are not taken to be "very big things" nor even to be "universals" (as the Neo-Platonic commentaries on Plato make clear), since, for example, the universal abstraction "animal in general" can paradoxically only ever be thought of as itself

---

86. Bradshaw, *Aristotle East and West*, 144, 270. Cf. Proclus, *ET* 21.

87. Bradshaw, *Aristotle East and West*, 270.

88. Williams, "The Philosophical Structures of Palamism;" Bradshaw, *Aristotle East and West*, 268–71. However, I would doubt if Williams would any longer subscribe to this view.

another instance of "animal," just as P. J. Cohen in modern times showed that an "indiscernible" general member of a set can still belong to a set.[89]

Thus, in the *Parmenides* (132 b-c) Plato rightly suggests that the "third man" argument deployed by Aristotle against Platonic forms as "super-individuals" must *also* apply against the "Aristotelian" view that forms are abstract universals. But in point of fact Aristotle himself denies in the *Metaphysics* that substance as essence or form is properly a universal.[90] Rather, it can exist both as the form of a particular thing and in the mode of a universal in the mind that comprehends it. But *in itself* form is indifferent to either universal or particular. Hence, Lloyd Gerson is right to say that at this point Aristotle *agrees* with Platonism about one characteristic of form, even if the Stagirite wrongly (and very oddly) supposes that for Plato forms were super-individuals.[91] Moreover, when he attacks forms as separable *universals* rather than as separable super-individuals, it is possible that he is *not* criticizing Platonic forms at all, but some other philosophical construal of their character.

Relevant here is the evidence from the *Phaedrus* (249 C) that Plato did not deny the "Aristotelian" process of acquiring a "universal" knowledge of form by a process of mental abstraction: indeed, how could the Platonic question as to the nature of the existence of "the one in many" ever arise, were we not capable of this process? However, as the Neo-Platonic commentaries on this passage suggest, "abstraction" does not render "recollection" redundant, because precisely the Aristotelian refusal of the form as mere universal (which would tend to engender a nominalist reduction of universal to fiction) leaves the question of the origin of *eidos* and of the capacity for specifically *intellectual* "recognition" of *eidos* as first derived from the senses, entirely unanswered.[92] What mediates between "abstraction" and "recollection" (of knowledge once had by a pre-existent soul) for Proclus is a certain "trace" of the forms abiding in the soul: this is not a kind of *a priori* understanding, but rather a power of the mind to synthesize and unite.[93] Thus, we do not, for Proclus, know "in advance," as for Kant, an innate conceptual repertoire, but rather we only know what the mind can do after it has done it. This of course raises in a new form the "Meno problematic" concerning how we ever seek to know the unknown: in this case, how can the mind know how to process the sense data in way that will reproduce the

89. Cf. Badiou, *Being and Event*, 367–71.

90. Aristotle, *Metaphysics*, VII, xii. 11–xvii. 12 (1038B1–1041B33).

91. Gerson, *Aristotle and Other Platonists*, 209–41.

92. Cf. Helmig, "What Is the Systematic Place," 83–97.

93. Proclus, *In Alcibiades* 191.12–192.5.

logoi that inhere in created things that it is not already aware of from the outset? Here Proclus suggests that just as the innate *logoi ousiōdeis* through active exercise and not mere passive recall recollect the forms (and this is entirely true to Plato's *Meno*, as opposed to caricatured renderings), so also an imaginative capacity for *doxa* (meaning here something like "obscure manifestation") unconsciously intuits a latency of shaping thought and thereby mediates between this capacity and sense perception.[94]

The power of the innate *logoi* could, for Proclus (perhaps for the first time in the history of philosophy), extend to the creation of new artificial forms having *no* eternal exemplars (unlike Plato's bed),[95] though it was not capable of a sheer invention rather than recognition of natural forms, since these were for him rather pre-shaped by a *logos* working independently of human beings in the cosmos. (In other words, he was a proto-Romantic, not a proto-Idealist.)

One can conclude that both Plato and the Neo-Platonists really regarded the forms as the unifying causal sources of power for the existence of a range of mutually resembling finite realities. They did not consider them as isolated "essences," but rather took them to be but aspects of that single over-arching power of unifying origination which is "the Good" and which Neo-Platonism tended to take simply as "the One" itself.[96] Again,

94. Cf. once more, Helmig, "What Is the Systematic Place."

95. Cf. Boulnois, *Au-delà de l'image*, 336–51.

96. Cf. Schumacher, "Rethinking Recollection." While the henological reading of the *Eidē* is basically correct, this should not be taken to mean that the forms are *merely* abstract universals, after Aristotle, and not in any sense whatsoever heavenly realities: as Schumacher indicates at the end of her article, the forms as unifying principles remain truly transcendent and not simply transcendental. It is just because they are transcendent that Plato can only invoke access to them in irreducibly mythical terms of the recollection by the soul of a previous life, and also for this reason that truth is first intimated as a desire for truth which is a paradoxical "knowing in advance," not fully comprehensible for a merely analytic reason. It is nevertheless because the things recollected are not "Kantian" *a priori* categories lurking in the depths of the soul itself (although Plotinian Platonism presses in this direction), that, as Schumacher stresses, the soul "recollects" not by simply drawing something up from memory that was lost, but by actively exercising a capacity for universalizing reason which alone permits it to "chime" with the universalizing activity of the forms. This activity, as she also says, is always itself united under the Form of the Good: in this sense the Platonic forms were always closer to their later usage as "ideas in God" than has been commonly supposed. The same interpretative perspective which Schumacher clearly enunciates suggests that in merely criticizing a bastardized account of the forms Aristotle also lost sight of their true explicatory function: namely in accounting for the *originating* as well as the *teleo-logical* aspect of both the univocal and the analogical power of unification. His account of universals and the universalizing capacity of the mind registers only the latter aspect. As for the notion of "unity beyond being," one should perhaps take this in the sense of "hyper-ontological," rather than simply "non-ontological." Ascription of "being" to

the distance from Aristotle here is not as marked as is often imagined; for under Aristotelian influence, as well as that of the *Parmenides,* the Neo-Platonists stressed the intellectual unity of the realm of the forms. In the case of Aristotle one can see the self-comprehending unmoved mover as playing in a vestigial way the role of the separated forms as both causing and guaranteeing the stability of immanent form as substance, which is the pre-condition for the possibility of scientific truth. The Neo-Platonists however, quite rightly felt that the Stagirite left the generative rather than teleological aspect of such grounding obscure. Yet at the same time they deployed his categories to give a much fuller account of the observable stabilities of finite being—of material substance in other words—than Plato had provided.[97] Increasingly we see the necessity and coherence of this Neo-Platonic synthesis and the way in which it constitutes indeed a perennial "philosophy as such," if we take philosophy to be (as Stoicism cannot really allow) that "more than physics" which affirms transcendence and at the same time tries to link transcendence to a "transcendental" embrace of all of reality. In other words, to link "height" with "coverage" and so "generation" with "existence." And we have already seen how it was the genius of Proclus already to make these two exigencies coincide as one principle.

For all these reasons Williams was wrong to suppose that in a crude "reification of verbal terms" lies the long-term source of the Palamite error, or that this was half-encouraged by Pseudo-Dionysius. It was no confusion about language that was responsible for a specifically philosophical enquiry into the causes of both resemblance and consistency within being, and the pursuit of that enquiry on the basis of the observation that these two things are always connected: no enduring of "substance" without the persistence of "shape," of *morphe,* or of *eidos.* Hence, the reasonable supposition—which founds all philosophy *as* philosophy, rather than mere physical cosmology—that "shape" is what supremely is and causes to be. Ontology began in this way therefore as a kind of speculative phenomenology.[98]

the ultimate was avoided only because it has too many connotations of particularity; but later, at first within Neo-Platonism itself, and then much more consistently within Christian thought, it was realized that a transcendently unifying "power-to-be" could be understood as itself the being of power—as *esse* in the infinitive.

97. Gerson, *Aristotle and Other Platonists,* 275–90.

98. One could also argue that this implicitly means that what is, as necessarily unified and self-manifesting, is most of all the beautiful. Any ontology of *morphē* is surely thereby an aesthetic ontology.

8. The Twin Legacies of Neo-Platonism

As we have already seen, Williams was also wrong to suppose that the theurgic tradition of Neo-Platonism was especially to blame for the Palamite deviation, because he thought that the twin motivation of Iamblichus and his successors in multiplying hypostases and positing yet further reserved absolutes lay both in the reifying delusion and in the desire to protect ineffability from any donative contamination. To the contrary, the intention was in the first case (in keeping with Plato himself, and probably the occult Platonic tradition, rather than Plotinus)[99] to admit "the many" to the sphere of the ultimate. In the second place, as established in section 2 above, it was to posit an absolute that would *lie beyond* the contrast of the One and the many.

It follows, to recap, that the culpable pagan lineage leading eventually to Palamas would lie if anywhere through an uncorrected Plotinian trajectory—as Williams himself indeed half-allows. For Plotinus, as already discussed, was unable to resolve the *aporia* whereby the passage from the One involves a denial of the One, such that all truth and intelligence is involved in a kind of "untruth" after all. Theurgic Neo-Platonism makes an attempt at resolution, even if it is only Christian theurgy and Trinitarian theology that fully reaches it. For, as we have seen, where participation is seen as paradoxical, the One itself is allowed to "reach down," and so finite beings can "reach up" to the One without denying their finitude, nor even their embodiment. The incommensurability of the imparticipable with the participating is overcome, even if the two can never of course coincide.

Within this *schema* the original Platonic apparatus is fully preserved: an obscure erotic yearning "to return" leads spiritual creatures to seek the truth, which is specifically "recollected" by material and temporal triggers which are occasions now not just for "recall" but for divine revelation. By contrast to this liturgical scenario (which the religion of the incarnation and the collective body of the incarnate God could hyperbolically exemplify), the lack of descent of either the One or the *psyche* in Plotinus requires a compensating, and as it were "Pelagian" ascent which is not so much erotic recall as rather retreat into the recesses of one's own soul, free of cosmic and bodily contamination.

---

99. For the vexed question of the oral transmission of secret Platonic doctrines, as arguably most indicated in Plato's epistles (especially the equiprimordiality of the One and the Two and the weaving between them—which later allowed Ralph Cudworth to argue with new textual evidence Augustine's case for a Platonic anticipation of the Trinity). Cf. Krämer, *Plato and the Foundations of Metaphysics*.

It is along this trajectory that "recollection" will become transmuted in the Latin West, following the influence of the basically Plotinian Avicenna and of Porphyry's semanticization of Aristotle's ontological categories (for Plotinian reasons of the superiority of mind over matter)[100] into a kind of *a priori* understanding. Following the same trajectory, the term *transcendens* will slowly migrate from implying a scope coterminous with being only secured by transcendent height (i.e., "everything" is *ens, unum, res, quid, aliquid, bonum, verum*, etc., only because God is eminently such) to implying a new *scope secured without height*, such that the fact of existence alone entails these meta-generic properties.[101] This shift comes about from the outset because of a new "representational" emphasis upon how being is necessarily disclosed to us, within the range of our conceptual *repertoire*. Eventually, from Suarez to Kant, the logical inference is drawn that if we can only speak of being in such "transcendental" terms, then transcendentality itself belongs on the side of cognition and not of objective reality. So the final result of trying to secure a democracy of scope without a paradoxical "suspension" of the democratic from a monarchic-aristocratic height (as for the model of political theurgism) is the enthronement of a mass subjectivism, a kind of epistemological rule that binds humans within a helpless populism of "what they cannot help but collectively believe." (In effect, the modern sham of representational democracy has turned into an endless attempt to identify the practical equivalent of such belief.)

This is the long modern story whereby the Platonic forms were depersonalized and turned into mere categories, mere universal and "transcendental" containers for the reception and classification of particular information, which was their final fate with Kant. What is crucial to grasp here is that the more they became so "de-henologized," then the *more* they became hypostasized, mutated into "reified essences" (e.g., the form of a tree as a kind of super-tree) as they become for many Franciscan theologians, rather than being any longer the mysterious transcendent powers of unifying coherence.[102] But for this move to really be possible one required also the notion that emerges in Scotus that these essences are "represented" by God to himself as if they were a secondary aspect of himself and not primordially identical with his own unity: this notion is in effect a "re-Platonizing"

100. Cf. footnote 2 above.

101. Cf. Aertsen, "The Concept of 'Transcendens,'" 133–53; Honnefelder, *La métaphysique*.

102. Cf. again Schumacher, *Divine Illumination*, and "Rethinking Recollection."

in a perverse sense, since it renders the divine ideas—or Platonic forms—
"other" than the divine essence itself.[103]

It can be seen then how Palamas' position, far from representing some
supposed timeless Eastern purity, is, on the contrary, all too kindred with
the most dubious shifts within the late medieval Latin West. Never underestimate the power of the *zeitgeist* to seep along the trade routes.

For just like the Avicennian current in the West, the Palamite theology
regresses too much back towards the paganism of Plotinus and therefore is
once more captive to the emergent Plotinian *aporia*. At this point Rowan
Williams was fundamentally right to say that Palamas seemingly avoids the
Trinitarian paradoxes of a simple God who nonetheless gives, in favor of
a "perfectly simple, indivisible, imparticipable interiority."[104] He was also
right to say that this effectively displaces the Trinity with such an ineffable
essence and to point out (as already mentioned) that Palamas declares that
the *energeiai* are distinct from the *ousia* "in the same way as the *hypostases.*"
All one need add here is that, *in either case,* Palamas makes an excessive
form of distinction, which reminds one of the formal distinctions of Scotus, who similarly subordinated the divine persons to a more fundamental
divine infinity.

9. Energy and Theophany

On my account therefore, diachronic rupture is of more significance than
synchronic contrast of traditions. For all the truth of the latter, one can trace
a parallel corruption of "the great tradition" in the late medieval period,
in both East and West. However, this perspective might plausibly be chal-
lenged by arguing that Palamas is but developing the specifically Eastern
stress upon theophanic disclosure to the whole human person, as testified
by the Bible, yet so neglected in the West. For this argument, the saint was
taken in the East to be illuminated by the uncreated light, energy, or glory of
God, unmediated by created vehicles. But this latter claim I would challenge.

First, the crucial distinction of tense, which we discovered in the Cappadocians and Pseudo-Dionysius, applies also to their successors. It is true
that Maximus, like the two Gregory's, speaks of the qualities of God which
do not begin in time, such as goodness, life, immortality, simplicity, immutability, infinity, and "reality itself" as being "the things around him" (*tōn peri
autou*). It is also true that Maximus more clearly distinguishes this "around"

---

103. Cf. Boulnois, *Être et représentation,* 405–55.

104. Williams, "The Philosophical Structures of Palamism," 36.

from a mere "outflowing."[105] However, we cannot take the "around" at all literally, especially as it would make no sense whatsoever to think of "simplicity" or "reality" as apart from God himself. In that case we must conclude that all these attributes do for Maximus belong to the very essence of God, and indeed he explicitly declares, "it is in him ["the unique Word and God"] as the Creator and Maker of beings that all the principles of things both are and subsist as one in an incomprehensible simplicity."[106] Thus, because he sees the essence as being itself active power ("the principles of things") he describes the divine *henos* as also the one divine *energeia*.[107] As the citation from the *Mystagogia* shows, this energetic unity or unified energy is also for him not numerically other than the one divine *Logos* which is the Son, by virtue of that logic just described whereby the persons, though uniquely relational, are also identical with the essence.

Consequently, Maximus' talk of the divine attributes as the "works of God" which are nonetheless not in time and are uncreated since they have never not been,[108] demands to be understood in terms of the most fundamental level of his ontology, which is the relationship between the *Logos* and the *logoi*.[109] If there are eternal "works" of God, and if the Son exhaustively manifests the eternal Father, then these works must be what is eternally expressed in the filial generation, which includes the divine knowledge in the *Logos* of all *logoi* that can be created in time. The *logoi* as the inwardly-shaping reasons of created things, which yet transcend those things, are clearly equivalent to the divine energies, and yet Maximus says that "the one *Logos* is many *logoi* and the many *logoi* are One."[110] So far from allowing that the *logoi* occupy any sort of limbo between uncreated and created, Maximus rather espouses a Trinitarian resolution of the *aporia* of there being an "outside" of God, who is all in all. God, in himself, as expressive *Logos*, includes all the diversity of what he creates, while this diversity remains at its very energetic heart, one—one, that is to say, with the very simplicity of Godhead. Thus, even when Maximus speaks explicitly of "uncreated grace" (sounding very "Western" here) he sees this as "begotten" within the Trinitarian begetting, such that the apparently ancestor-less Melchizedek is a paradigm for

105. Confessor, *Cap Gnost.* I.48–50.

106. Confessor, *Myst.* 5.

107. Confessor, *Ad Thal.*, 59.

108. Confessor, *Cap Gnost.* I.48–50.

109. Confessor, *Amb.* 7 (PG 91: 1081A–B).

110 Confessor, *Amb.* 7 (PG 91: 1087 C).

the reception of abundant grace and ante-type of Christ precisely because he was "begotten by God through the Word in the Spirit by grace."[111]

Given the priority of a Trinitarian heuristic, when Maximus declares that God "infinitely transcends" both the created works that participate and the uncreated works that are participated in,[112] one must take this to be an allusion to the inexhaustible mystery of the Paternal *arche*. The latter also, however, should be understood in terms of the unparticipable which is the very precondition for its own self-sharing.

It is only when the *Logos* emanates and is pluralized, that the *energeia* is pluralized also. Even though the outgoing *logoi* are for Maximus active, shaping forces within the cosmos, they are still created forces, very like Augustine's "seminal reasons," which represents a similar vision of the immanently disseminating divine Word.[113] Thus, while for Maximus the *logoi* are the action upon creatures of the *Logos*, they are always in the material universe mediated by the *tupois* of phenomenal, sensible reality. Human vision occurs accordingly within the "turning" between *typos* and *logos*, which is how, in the *Mystagogia*, Maximus understands the gyrations of Ezekiel's chariot wheels.[114] To a remarkable extent this passage suggests that "invisible principles" and " visible figures" have to be referred to each other for mutual illumination, in a manner consonant with Maximus' view that the *Logos* is not just the repository of principles but of the eminent, unified reality of all the *logoi*. This, in turn, harmonizes with his thoroughly theurgic Neo-Platonic view (the *Mystagogy* being directly about liturgy and architecture as theurgy) of God as exceeding even the contrast between principle and consequence.

Indeed, the entire theurgic stress of the *Mystagogia* is upon the necessity of the mediation of divine grace to occur always through the works both of divine creation and of human making. Yet this does not amount straightforwardly to a "distancing" of God, because mediation is not regarded by Maximus as a kind of regrettable need to bridge a gap. To the contrary, for Maximus, as for all the great Christian thinkers, if God is love, then he is gift and participation and therefore is only touched immediately by virtue of mediation itself. Just the same paradox that renders the imparticipable and

---

111. Confessor, *Amb.* 10, 20.

112. Confessor, *Cap Gnost* I.49.

113. One cannot perhaps entirely rule out an Augustinian influence here upon Maximus, though it has not been demonstrated.

114. Confessor, *Myst.* 2.

the participated coincident, renders also the immediate and the mediated coincident.[115]

And in this light we can see a profound *convergence* between Maximus' insistence on the mediating role of *tupois,* and Augustine's insistence in the first seven books of his *De Trinitate* that all theophanic manifestations of the persons of the Trinity always occur through created mediums. This can be allowed to be true, even *though* the East can rightly claim that Augustine overplays the notion of the mind rather than the entire human person as the *imago dei,* probably because of the inadequate development of his Christology and of a Christological site for anthropological speculation. For here the Maximian insight improves rather than destroys that of Augustine: the mediation by material signs supplies something "symbolically" crucial rather than merely "allegorically" illustrative (as tends to be the danger in Augustine), yet this by no means denies the created character of this mediation upon which Augustine rightly insists. Rather, it augments the theophanic potential of the material creation itself.

Given this synthesis, we have a fine insight into the coincidence of the unmediated and the mediated with respect to the *vestigium trinitatis* in the cosmos: *just because* there is no third between the Creator and the creation, each creature, comprising both soul *and* body, is always in the direct presence of God, but equally, for the same reason, this presence is never direct, but always mediated by the participation of created structures. Augustine, with very great rigor, banished the shadow of any divine "economy" (including the "economic Trinity") *other* than the providential unfolding of created temporality itself. Maximus' attention to the *tupois* would ensure that this insight is not compromised by losing the paradox in favor of an "immediacy" of inward, mental access to God without cosmic and corporeal mediation. We have already seen how the Scotist recension of Augustine finally realized a Western and Plotinian temptation to go in this direction.

John of Damascus remained true to Maximus in most essential respects. The properties "good," "holy," "just," etc., follow from the divine nature and are not to be in any way really distinguished from it. Together with this nature they compose one *energeia* that is "beneficently divided in divisible things," while eventually God "returns them to his own simplicity."[116] This scheme is exactly that which Aquinas took over from Damascene (and from Pseudo-Dionysius), and Bradshaw accurately comments "this makes

---

115. I owe this insight to Dr. Lucy Gardner of St. Stephen's House Oxford.
116. Damascus, *De Fide Orthodoxa,* I.14.

it plain that for John the divine *energeia* is not simply the divine activity *ad extra* but God himself as he is participated by creatures."[117]

Yes—but what is glossed over here is that, when diversified, the energy becomes "energies" and the uncreated becomes created. For one can only speak of energy in the singular from the divine perspective, according to which, paradoxically, as he shares himself he yet remains undivided. Correspondingly, the fact that creatures *qua* creatures receive God's glory as divided means that this reception is what constitutes them *as* creatures. It is not something "in addition" to their creaturehood, any more than God's glory *as divine* can be in any way pluralized. The key once more is to see that participation has to be thought as paradox, on pain of positing a common plane between Creator and creature that constitutes a kind of "third sphere" of ontological reality, which the doctrine of creation *ex nihilo* must rule out of court.

It is also important for this argument that for many of the fathers the highest term for God was not "essence" (*ousia/essentia*) but rather *To Ōn*, or alternatively "he who is," after the Septuagint version of *Exodus*. This term, which Bradshaw himself wishes to highlight, defines God in his very self as active and outgoing.[118] Therefore, it tends to suggest that "acting" and even "acting on" do not in any way diversify the divine activity insofar as it remains purely divine. The fathers may often speak in this context of the contrast between the sun as the source and the light that beams forth from the sun, but their Trinitarian use of the same analogue shows that for them it generally betokens the *identity* of ray with origin, since what would the sun be "in itself" if it did not shine forth?

As soon as one separates God from his action in any way, one tends to make an equivalent separation between the recipient of divine action and the receiving itself—as if any action could really arise outside of divine donation. This follows, because once one has construed the divine action as in some sense other than God himself, it encourages the thought of a yet more radical separation of finite being from divine being, such that it can hold to its finitude as "its own" outside a restricted sharing in divine activity. And this is confirmed by the thought that if the divine energies, though distinct from the divine essence, nevertheless remain fully God, then it would be blasphemous to say that emanated creatures simply *are* (*in toto* and in various degrees of intensity) the divine energies. Yet the latter radicalism is what the positions of Pseudo-Dionysius, Maximus, and Damascene genuinely imply, and it is this radicalism alone which remains true to the idea of

117. Bradshaw, *Aristotle East and West*, 209.
118. Ibid., 109–18.

creation *ex nihilo*. As Aquinas puts it: creatures "are the representatives of God, according to the diverse processions of their perfections."[119]

However, this radicalism is often more exemplified in the East than in the West, as I have recently indicated. For whereas in Augustine divine manifestations are usually seen as mental, as visions "arriving to" mind, in the East (and in Eriugena in the West) there is more continuing stress, in continuity with the Old Testament, upon divine "theophanic" manifestation, whereby creatures are transfigured, both in soul and body. In these instances, as later exemplified by the "hesychastic" tradition of spirituality in the East, it is as if beings are created anew, or as if the veil concealing their original paradisal reality is removed.[120]

The tradition that Bradshaw is purportedly defending does not then think in terms of energies acting as a mediating third "between" the Creator and the creation. To the contrary, it thinks of divine disclosure as drastically welling-up from within the created order and in one sense *as* that very order. If one seeks to deny this, then, as we have just seen, one engenders a certain independence of the being of finite creatures from the being of God. But in that case the entire idea of synergy, which Bradshaw seeks to argue for, is entirely undone. For one is forced then to speak of a cooperative *concursus* between infinite and finite causes, as if they both contributed "a part" and lay upon the same ontological plane.[121] But synergy rather implies a causal fusion, whereby what is finite, created action at one level, at another higher, incommensurable (though compatible) and more originating level is entirely divine, creative action.

Bradshaw is right to see an intimate link between synergy, theurgy, and the later hesychastic tradition, which (in keeping with Maximus' understanding of "turning") spoke of the human body as being occasionally illuminated by "the uncreated light." However, if a distinction of the divine essence from the divine energy compromises synergy, then it equally compromises both theurgy and the hesychastic experience—which included the "magical" invocation of God through repeated recitation of the name of Jesus. As we have already seen, Palamas, against Barlaam, *half* saw this, but his resistance did not go far enough. For if the initiative lies more with

---

119. Aquinas, *ST* I, Q.13, A.2 resp. This quotation (and one could give many others) gives the lie to Bradshaw's assertion that "Aquinas . . . transforms what for Pseudo-Dionysius had been a means of ascent towards God into a semantic device for clarifying the limits of language." For all Aquinas' greater technicality, both he and Pseudo-Dionysius are *both* equally concerned with *both* the semantics of naming *and* the experiential metaphysics of ascent.

120. Cf. Boulnois, *Au-delà de l'image,* 133–85.

121. Cf. Schmutz, "La doctrine mediévale."

divine descent than with human contemplative ascent, it follows that this ascent must be towards a radical unity with the divine essence (albeit that this remains forever uncomprehended by creatures) in order to sustain the divine simplicity at the heart of the condescending divine action. So even though the divine essence cannot, as Aquinas affirmed, be communicated, this must be understood as a paradoxical reserve within the procession that is (as Aquinas equally affirms) out of the divine essence itself.[122] Similarly, the uncreated light can only reach us from the divine side if this is God himself—otherwise we might understand our experience of this light in terms of our own Pelagian efforts at unassisted assent to a heavenly, but sub-divine realm.

The doctrine of the experience of the uncreated light is therefore not, as Bradshaw alleges, incompatible with a rigorously Thomist construal of simplicity, if one takes it, in keeping with phenomenological report, as the shining from within and yet from beyond and before itself of a created body. God himself can appear here because he still appears in an entirely *mediated* form, and not as an unmediated display of his own "lesser," because communicated, aspect. For such an unmediated display still reserves God in his essence behind an eternal mode of mediation seen as an absolute ontological *impasse*. By contrast, an always mediated display does after all convey to us the simplicity of God in his immediate presence to the process of mediation itself.

Indeed, it was precisely *because* the East at times remained truer than the West to the paradox of a "communicated incommunicable" that it insisted on an always bodily-mediated, specifically theophanic mode of divine presence. This is why both Gregory of Nyssa and the highly "Eastern" Eriugena both denied that ontic and corporeal mediation disappears even in the final beatific vision. Not only did they insist that this was through a "created light of glory," they also thought that this light continued to be apprehensible by creatures only through those specific created realities, which it illumined.[123]

We have however already indicated why this *schema* might be problematic, insofar as it suggests a further (and so over "essentialized") inaccessibility of God beyond the inaccessibility that remains even within his created, mediating light. But later than Gregory, Pseudo-Dionysius established in the further East an alternative trajectory, later followed (for the most part) by the distant West: in the beatific vision we see directly the divine light by means of the divine light without further mediation. Yet even in this case

---

122. Cf. Milbank and Pickstock, *Truth in Aquinas*, 19–59.
123. Boulnois, *Au-delà de l'image*, 133–86.

the mediation by created light remains[124] and there may well be a case for saying (beyond Aquinas) that this "pure medium" can be construed as being subtly corporeal as well as intellectual. This would allow that the resurrected body is not simply incidental to the beatific vision, while placing a stronger stress upon the circumstance that mediation by a pure medium remains, nonetheless, mediation. And the irreplaceable role of mediation even for the experience of immediacy, I am arguing, goes along with a grasp of a radically paradoxical account of participation.

So the distinguishing mark of the archaic East was not "more directness of illumination, but with a greater divine reserve," but rather "more mediated immediacy of divine illumination *because* of divine reserve." There was indeed often a difference from the West here, but the difference did *not* concern a distinction of the essence from the energies. This only arose much later in the East, and it is somewhat paralleled by the rise of "the formal distinction" in the West. But aside from the Scotist and later nominalist rupture, the West did not, as Bradshaw claims, find any difficulty in thinking of the divine presence as the presence of God himself, rather than as a mere "extrinsic" arrival of grace.

10. Action and Participation: Why Aquinas Is More Byzantine Than Palamas

One could think here of Eckhart's radical sense of the paradoxical way in which we are, at the heart of ourselves, including our bodily selves, actually "not" ourselves, but rather uncreated deity.[125] Yet he is here only radicalizing Augustine's *interior intimo meo*. As to Aquinas, Bradshaw erroneously reduces his account of creative causality to mere efficiency, where Aquinas frequently insisted that it involved, in simple fusion, also formal and teleological dimensions.[126] Bradshaw's contention here is that, without the essence/energies distinction, Aquinas cannot think of the *actus purus* composing the divine essence as proceeding outwards and reaching creatures, except at the expense of chaining God to necessity and to his own creation. Yet this ignores the fact that for Aquinas the free decision of God to create was contained within the very generation of the *Logos* from the Father, such that God is, from all eternity, the God of Love who simply *is* a free outward donation.[127] Aquinas was so little concerned about a false "reserve" in God

---

124. Aquinas, *ST* I Q.12 A.5.

125. On Eckhart see Milbank, "The Double Glory," 110–233.

126. Bradshaw, *Aristotle East and West*, 242–68.

127. Aquinas, *ST* I, Q. 34, A. 3.

that he argues that it is a sign of God's power and not the reverse that he was able to give the power of causality itself to his creatures. Just for this reason Aquinas entertains (as Bradshaw fails to recognize) the most drastic possible doctrine of synergy.

From this follows a radical construal of participation. Aquinas made the middle term of participation not "the Good," but *esse*, thereby implying the paradox that what is both "shared in" and "imitated" is nothing other than the condition of freestanding itself, which is *esse*, "to be." It is therefore when we "are" and so are most "in ourselves" that we are also most radically dependent, most given to ourselves as a gift.[128] But this renders our causal dependence upon God the most intimate sort of dependence imaginable, in testified keeping with the Proclean view that it is the highest that acts most inwardly and discretely, the first cause that is more strongly at work than secondary ones, even at the bottom of the hierarchical scale.[129]

If Bradshaw were right about Aquinas, then the latter would not have affirmed that the procession of excellencies in creatures obscurely conveys to us something of eminent excellence in God himself: like Maimonides he would have taken the divine names simply as names for divine actions and not for divine attributes.[130] This would have left God radically unknown, not in the sense of being a mysterious depth, but rather in the sense of being totally un-characterizational or else able to assume and shed characters at a whim—completely counter to Thomas' whole trajectory.

Yet this appears to be Bradshaw's view of the great Dominican. He reads Aquinas as if for him the *esse commune* of creatures participates neither in the divine energies nor in the divine essence, but only in a created "likeness" of the divine, that can be given no assignable content. Thus, he cites a passage from Aquinas' *Commentary on the Divine Names* as "common being . . . participates in a similitude of him [God]."[131] But the passage in question originally reads: *esse commune habet ipsum scilicet Deum, ut participans similitudinem Eius.*[132] This should probably be translated as "common being evidently has for itself God as [being] a participated similitude of him." But what is in any case clear, because otherwise Thomas' words would make neither contextual nor semantic sense, is that the participation is not "in" the similitude but rather *is itself* the similitude. The "resemblance"

128. Rudi te Velde grasps this point exceptionally well: see his *Aquinas on God*, 139–142.

129. Pseudo-Aristotle, *In Liber de Causis* Prop 1.

130. For an exemplary account of this contrast, see Burrell, *Knowing the Unknowable God*.

131. Bradshaw, *Aristotle East and West*, 252.

132. Aquinas, *In de div. nom*, V, lec. 2, N. 660.

to God of creatures is not for Aquinas some sort of all-too-light burden that they incidentally bear: it is rather, exactly as it is for Pseudo-Dionysius, their very condition of being in existence at all.[133]

What this indicates is that for Aquinas the imitating of God and the sharing in God are one and the same thing. Imitation can never be without participation because there is no "free-standing" entity that could copy God such that we could compare original and copy according to a *tertium comparationis* of being. Instead, since God is himself *esse*, God is the third term as well as the first, while the second term, which is the imitation only, has the ontological space in which it can exercise *mimesis* because this imitation is also a partaking. On the other hand, any "pantheism" is obviated because in turn sharing only occurs as a reflection (i.e., participating as imitating), not as a literal "portioning-out" of the indivisible God.

Equally avoided is Duns Scotus' explicit construal of participation as meaning the possession of univocal being as a finite rather than an infinite share.[134] For this permits a *tertium comparationis* (i.e., being) other than God, and therefore implicitly allows that imitation of God can be independent of a sharing-in God. Scotus' approach is in one sense more rationally rigorous than Aquinas, yet at the risk of subordinating God to *esse*, by too much regarding the participation of the finite in being as a literal "segment," this risks either the notion of finitude as outside the reach of divine omnipresence, or else pantheistic immanence (as will arrive with Spinoza) if one takes the share of being to be also a share of infinitude.

Aquinas by contrast sustains divine transcendence, but at the price of a necessary metaphysical complication, which he does not fully own up to. Imitation must, it would seem, presuppose a given entity prior to *mimesis* that can be a ground for reception. Inversely, sharing-a-part need not involve any imitation of the whole. Yet in the case of the imitation of/ participation in God, Aquinas is affirming that imitation and participation

---

133. Bradshaw instead thinks that Aquinas turns resemblance into a kind of extrinsic fact about creatures, which one must speculatively assert, yet which lacks in any substantive content. This means that he denies that Aquinas's treatment of the divine names is any longer an ontological doctrine (see note 94 above). Unfortunately far too many neoscholastic and Anglo-Saxon "analytic" renderings of Aquinas on analogy abet Bradshaw at this point. For a refutation of these readings see Milbank and Pickstock "Truth in Aquinas," 46–55; Pickstock, "Duns Scotus," 543–74, esp. 567–68 and Milbank, "On 'Thomistic Kabbalah.'" Pickstock's article is especially crucial here as, following Alain de Libera, she shows how Aquinas does indeed pay a new attention to the logical dimension of analogy and yet deploys the specifically semantic model of one pivotal meaning for an analogical term as appropriate to our unilateral *metaphysical* situation vis-à-vis God.

134. Scotus, *Ordinatio* I, D. 8, P. 1, Q. 2, N. 37–38.

are preconditions of each other: that not only the copy but also the vehicle for copying derive from sharing; that not only the share but also even the very possibility of the share derives from imitation.

This amounts to the strongest possible doctrine of both creation and grace as involving the presence of God himself to creatures, while in no way compromising the divine reserve of transcendence. The crucial paradox once more is that it is this very reserve which is communicated—both as an integrity that is shared in by creatures as their own discrete self-standing (the circumstance that "they exist") and as the divine concealed integrity that remains as the further hinterland of all the merely participating integrities.

This paradoxicality is confirmed by the way in which Aquinas— following Pseudo-Dionysius, who was in turn developing Proclus— emphasizes that to exist as a creature is to return to God and that to exist as a spiritual creature is to exist as conscious return. For Aquinas, Being as such is an out-flowing beyond itself, which is oxymoronically contained within itself: thus, the God who creates is the God who utters the *Logos*. Being is also a return upon itself, such that the God who calls is also the God of self-desiring in the Holy Spirit. For spiritual creatures to be called by God to return defines in Aquinas the very activity of knowing as such. Hence, the self that knows is at the same time the self that returns to its (true and inner) self in returning to God.

But Aquinas also echoes in his own fashion the Proclean view that the ultimate "rebound" of matter is in a unique intimacy of opposition with the ultimate purely spiritual source of all reality. Hence, in Aquinas for human beings to know something is not simply a self-mirroring, but also a mirroring of matter back to itself, such that every act of understanding concludes not only with the *redditio in se ipsum* but also with the *conversio ad phantasmata,* the recreation in the imagination of the original sensed object. In this way, the human being, as the microcosmic bond of the cosmos, unites in herself (as Boethius had already indicated) the twin circles whereby not only all ceaselessly returns to the One but all ceaselessly (as Pseudo-Dionysius and then Maximus after him stress) goes out again from the one towards the nether pole of material reality: "*motus circularis animae est secundum quod ab exterioribus intrat ad seipsum et ibi uniformiter convolvitur, sicut in quodam circulo*"[135] The ultimate paradox of participation here is that the first circle of return simply *is* the omnipresence of God, but that God as God is also the "more than himself" (as Pseudo-Dionysius puts it) of the second circle. This is not to say that an energetic *aspect* of God is more than himself,

135. Aquinas, *In de div.nom.* IV, lect 7, N. 376.

but that the very divine essence, which is absolutely replete, is also in itself "energetic," also (impossibly) "more than itself."[136]

By contrast, the Palamite position, which Bradshaw upholds, suggests a literally regional reserve beyond any communication. But in that case that which is communicated is turned into too literal a part of God, and its further distinction as "uncreated energy" means that the receptacle of this energy is correspondingly seen as too literally standing outside God. Its reception of too literal a share therefore will tend to take the form of too literal an imitation, which does not fully have its ground in the sharing of the unshareable. The illuminated hesychast is in consequence seen as directly exhibiting a part of God beyond the scope of imitation, and yet equally as "reflecting" this light in his own body by mere *mimesis* of the uncreated grace of the supernatural received light, and without any real need to be himself (in soul and body) constituted *only as* a share in this light—such that one would rightly regard transfiguration as a revealing of the still-persisting paradisal human body occluded by sin.[137] Instead of paradoxical coincidence within the participatory process of transcendent source and contingent share, which involves also the coincidence of share and copy, one has instead with Palamas an implied delineation of three separate ontological realms, which allows sharing without imitation and then imitation without sharing.

It must all the same be admitted that Palamas is confusing, and that there are passages in his works that remain entirely consistent with the vision of Maximus as already described. These passages are not really dealt with by Bradshaw, as they do not advance his "Palamite reading of Palamas." Thus, at one point Gregory declares that the energies are multiplied according to the multiplicity of creatures, and that one must think of their plurality, with respect to their uncreatedness, as if they were like rays traced from the center of a circle to its circumference, yet without any pluralization of their original unity.[138]

This perspective would seem properly to insist that the energies, insofar as they are uncreated, remain one and simple, and therefore ontologically identical with the essence. If such an ascription to a rigorously paradoxical mathematical figure in Palamas is relatively rare, it can still fairly be taken as evidence that one should not ascribe to him a full-blown "real distinction" of the energies from the essence. And yet more consistently he clearly denies

136. On all this see the somewhat enigmatic yet extremely perceptive and suggestive article of Speer, "The Epistemic Circle," 119–32.

137. This "Traherne-like" note has sometimes been sounded in the Eastern tradition. Borges' late story "The Rose of Paracelsus" gets it entirely right here: the earthly paradise has never vanished; *thinking it has* constitutes our fallenness.

138. Palamas, *Triads*, III, 25.

any real identity of the two either. In these cases he manifests certain emphases, which have to be considered a deviant betrayal of the great tradition of both East and West. These can be summarized as follows:

1. The energies as uncreated are inherently plural.[139] This is not consistent with the simplicity of the uncreated godhead.

2. Even as uncreated, some energies must be considered to "have a beginning," namely those directed towards the created order, others not.[140] Rowan Williams already pointed out the oddity and dubiety of this point, which concurs strongly with the Scotist (not Thomist) view that the divine decision to create lies outside what is contained in the Trinitarian *taxis*.[141]

3. The Dionysian "names of God" are predicated of (or manifest) the energies alone and not the divine substance.[142] This would appear to commit Palamas to a Maimonides-style agnosticism about the divine character.

4. In *The One Hundred and Fifty Chapters*, Palamas is faced with the problem that if the energies are God, yet not the substance of God, then it seems that something belongs to God which is not his substance.[143] Here, as Rowan Williams points out, he appeals to the example of the Trinitarian relations, yet has to do so in such a way as to imply that the relations and the substance are not really identical. This then opens him up to the supposedly *Western* error of elevating the divine essence to an ontological dignity above that of the Trinity. Palamas indeed speaks explicitly of "three realities" in the Godhead: substance, energy, and Trinity.[144] This dangerous diversification of God puts one in mind of Scotus' introduction of a "secondariness" of the divine knowledge and willing (comparable to Palamas' uncreated and unoriginate energies) after the absolutely defining infinitude of the divine essence and a further belatedness—in the wake of the Trinitarian processions—of the divine decision to create (comparable to Palamas' created and yet originated energies).

---

139. Palamas, *Triads*, III, 7.

140. Palamas, *Triads*, III, 8.

141. For this point and all further comparisons with Scotus below, see Pickstock, "Duns Scotus."

142. Palamas, *Triads*, III, 10.

143. Palamas, *Cap.* 135.

144. Palamas, *Cap.* 75, 126.

5. Palamas, as again Rowan Williams pointed out, is at a loss to know to which ontological category to assign "uncreated energies" if they are neither substance, accident, nor relation. He toys with the possibility of "quasi-accident" and yet admits that one cannot really allow any sort of accidentality in the case of the divine.[145] This is the real difficulty here and not Williams' notion that he must be confused about Aristotle if he can invoke such seemingly oxymoronic terminology. For in fact Aristotle *did* speak of "proper accidents" (in later scholastic terminology), which always accompany an essence and yet are not themselves *of* the essence. (This category is exploited by Aquinas in a much more drastic manner in terms of his notion of *esse* as a proper accident of created essence paradoxically more essential than essence itself.) But Palamas knows that nothing can really accompany God that is not grounded in his essence without totally destroying his simplicity. Hence, Williams is right to indicate that all that this seems to leave as a possibility is that the "energies" are a lesser sphere of declining emanation within the godhead itself. This would certainly represent a Neo-Platonic deviation within a supposedly Christian theology.

6. Not only does Palamas introduce a kind of formal distinction between the energies and the essence, he also introduces the same between the energies, or the divine attributes themselves. Thus, he insists that the divine foreknowledge is distinct from the divine will, on the grounds that otherwise God would not have foreknowledge of evil, which he does not will.[146] The ineptitude of Palamas as a metaphysician is here shown by his failure to realize that evil is not something "positive" falling outside the true scope of will as will, or even of knowing as knowing. But the persistence of distinction, which our knowledge is forced to make, even in God, for the sake, supposedly, of retaining cognitive coherence, again puts one in mind of Scotus. This is equally true of his defense of the distinction of the energies from the essence in terms of the argument that the divine will is distinct from the divine nature and yet is still fully God.[147] For Aquinas, the voluntary adds nothing to the natural in the case of God, but for Duns Scotus, this distinction (as already with Richard of St. Victor and Bonaventure) is deployed to distinguish the generation of the Son ("natural") from the procession of the Spirit ("voluntary").

145. Palamas, *Cap.* 127, 135.

146. Palamas, *Cap.* 100.

147. Palamas, *Cap.* 135.

7. Finally, Palamas offers an openly crude and non-paradoxical metaphysics of participation. He baldly states that God is "inaccessible in some respects" but "everywhere present in other respects."[148] In the very next paragraph he cites John Chrysostom in support of this divisive reading of the Johannine statement that "Of his fullness we have all received" (John 1:16), blithely unaware that it tells entirely against him. For Chrysostom in comparing the divine energy to fire writes, as cited: "For if in the case of fire that which is divided is a substance and a body, and if we both do and do not divide it, how much more will this be true in the case of the energy, indeed the energy from an incorporeal substance."[149] The whole point of this simile is that energy, like fire, remains incomprehensibly undivided in division, so that Chrysostom, instead of talking about "an area" of God that is shared as demarcated against another area that is not, rather talks about a single divine reality as being at once shared out and yet not shared out at all. One should take this as saying that what is true of the divine energy (spoken of here in the singular) is true also of the divine substance, since the energy "from" this ineffable substance can only be the energy "of" this substance. Palamas compounds his error by saying in the same paragraph that when something participates it literally possesses a "part" of something else. This contrasts with Aquinas speaking of a "quasi-part," which I have already tried to spell-out in terms of the complex way in which participation and imitation "impossibly" presuppose each other in the unique case of ontological *methexis*.[150] Because he defines participation in this way, Palamas has no real way to distinguish it from the partition of a *genus,* and therefore he suggests that if we participated in the essence of God himself, we would all be *hypostases* of God, like the persons of the Trinity.[151] But to participate in, is not fully to embody an essence, and were it so, then it would seem that we are all somehow *hypostases* of the divine energy or energies! Once more then, the young Williams is essentially vindicated with respect to Palamas: he would seem to court a bizarre combination of emanationism and pantheism.

From all the above points, and especially number 7, we can conclude that the logic of Palamas' "formal distinction" of essence from energies

---

148. Palamas, *Cap.* 109.

149. Palamas, *Cap.* 110.

150. See further Milbank and Pickstock, *Truth in Aquinas,* 19–59.

151. Palamas, *Cap.* 109.

undoes the logic of radical participation, which is the only logic that can spell out the doctrine of creation *ex nihilo*.

Equally, for reasons that we have already seen, it undoes the logic of theurgic descent. Bradshaw rightly wants to argue that this logic also spells out the implications of both creation and deification, because it insists that the *actus purus* of God is one and the same with his effective, external, kenotic operation, both in bringing finite being to be and in bringing finite being back from the brink of self-imposed annihilation. This is the tremendous insight of his important book. But I have tried to show how it would be undercut by his other claim in favor of the Palamite distinction of essence from energies. To the contrary, it is Aquinas' rigorous cleaving to divine simplicity that remains consistent with a Christian theurgic vision derived from Pseudo-Dionysius and with the radical account of participation to which this vision is inseparably conjoined.[152]

11. Eschatology and the Crisis of Mediation: West, East, and Further East

In this essay I have tried to show how perennial differences between Christian East and West are of less account than the breakdown in either case of the primordial Christian adaptation of a Platonic metaphysics of participation in the late medieval era. I have also already indicated how an older

152. Bradshaw, *Aristotle East and West*, 275–77, finally draws a cultural besides an intellectual contrast between East and West. He considers that the over-rationalism of the West, resulting from an attempt to define the essence of God, led to an overly systematizing and defensive posture, manifest in religious war, persecution, and excessively zealous moral disciplining of the laity. There is some truth in this charge, and yet a much more specific story must be told about the eventual separation of the rational from the mystical within Latin Christendom. Conversely, one could argue that the relative lack of rationally developed "scholastic" theology in the East went along with a situation where law and politics remained (in a Roman legacy), relatively secularized, and there was not the same degree of Christian renewal of law regarding, for instance, marriage and poverty as took place under Canonical influence in the West. And even if the latter, as Ivan Illich and Charles Taylor have argued, over-institutionalized charity, the East lacked the same growth of charitable institutions outside immediate political control. The relative lack also of constitutional government in the East (which continues into the present) is surely connected to this first lack. And even if piety in the West was over-clericalized, this dialectically helped to stimulate lay movements of piety in response. Bradshaw fails to realize that movements that he denigrates like courtly love, chivalry, and poetry reworking vernacular legend could lie inside as well as outside the fold of such movements. He also appears to underestimate the extent of continued lay culture in Byzantium. Finally, the horror of the latter at the behavior of the Crusaders does not negate the truth that they were initially going to the defense of Eastern churches as being part of Christendom.

"paradox of participation" can also be construed as a "paradox of mediation." If the imparticipable is itself participated, then it is equally the immediate that is itself mediated.

Since, therefore, the late Middle Ages present us with a "crisis of participation" we might expect this also to have involved a "crisis of mediation."
And the evidence for this is, indeed, forthcoming. The upshot of the hesychast controversy was three councils held at Constantinople in the years
1341, 1347, and 1351, which enshrined as Orthodox dogma the Palamite
views that: creatures *never* see the divine essence, even in the beatific vision;
and, that even during this life they can glimpse the "light of Tabor," by virtue
of a reception of uncreated grace. The apposition is surely striking: on the
one hand, mediation is never surpassed, on the other hand, even in this life
we receive immediately God himself, albeit under a secondary aspect.[153]

Yet it would be a mistake to read this as too simply implying at once a
strong commitment to the necessity of mediation and, at the same time, to
optimism about what mediation can communicate. This is true to the extent
that the East rightly insisted upon the role of the body in theophany and on
the validity of devotion to icons (whereas this was only admitted gradually
in the West, following in part the lead of Aquinas).[154] But it is untrue in the
sense that the impossibility of seeing God even at the end implies, in all too
"Plotinian" a fashion, that mediation is necessarily a *barrier* to direct vision
and hence that one is always yearning to escape it ("*epectasis*"), even though
one can never finally do so. Inversely, the stronger possibility for the councils of seeing God in this life is really the consequence of the *unmediated*
presence of "the fringe of God" himself.

In this manner a disguised suspicion of mediation is present in the
verdict of the councils, which even in some manner anticipates the Refor-
mation, as the denial of the category of created grace would imply.

Meanwhile, in the West, one can trace an apparently opposite yet se-
cretly complicit development. György Geréby has pointed out how the Latin
official dispute concerning the beatific vision, which lasted from 1331 to
1346, was almost exactly contemporary with the Greek hesychast controversy. This dispute began when the Avignon Pope John XXII, to the shock

---

153. For this and much of what follows, see Geréby, "Hidden Themes" 1204–1500.
Geréby is right about the pervasive quasi-Nestorianism in the West, but fails to point
out that, while the Franciscans were especially guilty of this, Aquinas uniquely adopted
a fully Byzantine Cyrilline Christology, stressing theandric unity. This is yet another
reason why it is a massive mistake to suppose that Franciscan theology was "more
oriental" in character. It would be far truer to claim this for the Dominican trajectory—
which was more authentically Augustinian also.

154. Cf. Boulnois, *Au-delà de l'image,* 276–83.

of his Franciscan opponents, headed by William of Ockham, reinstated, after much private patristic study, the older Western and persisting Eastern view (present in Augustine and still in Bernard of Clairvaux, but rejected by both Aquinas and Dante) that individual souls went to the waiting-room of "Abraham's bosom" immediately after death and were only sent to heaven, hell, or purgatory collectively and in unity with their bodies at the Last Judgment. The debate was closed when the papal bull of John's successor, the Franciscan Benedict XII, *Benedictus Deus,* emphatically reinstated the newer opinion, for all that it seems to downgrade the Last Judgment to a clearing-up operation, besides denying that judgment is of humans collectively and in their fully personal, embodied, and in some important sense still earth-bound forms.[155] Just as the councils in the East were really enshrining a novelty, so too in the West: in neither case was the decision simply a matter of formalizing perennial synchronic divergences.

The same Bull explicitly insisted, in diametric contrast to the Eastern councils, upon the final direct vision of the divine essence, unmediated by any creature. One should align this, as Geréby does, with the increasing Western denial of any ordinary experience of God in this life and the mounting "extrinsic" conception of the operation of grace. This gives us then the opposite contrast to the case of the East: in the end, complete vision; but for now, no vision whatsoever.

And just as the case of the East might seem to imply both optimism and necessity with regard to mediation, so likewise the case of the West might seem to imply both pessimism and non-necessity. That is to say, for now signs are but extrinsic aids and not participatory symbols, while when we see as we are seen there will be no need for any intervening vehicles at all. Yet once more, this would be but partially true. It is true with respect to the rising denial of direct experience of God in this life, but this downgrading of mediation is but a *different mode of manifestation* of the same downgrading that was occurring in the East, as I have just argued.

On the other hand, the Bull's re-affirmation of the West's traditional view of the *visio beatifica* does not really imply any such downgrading—except with respect to the too-incidental role of the body and the collectivity in the enjoyment of the vision.[156] For mediation *is* involved here in two respects. First, it is the created mind that sees, albeit without a mediating *species* and in the divine light alone. So this means that mediation by mind is not a *blockage,* as it is taken to be in the East, to the immediate vision of God. Secondly, as Aquinas makes clear, the divine light of glory that we see

155. See Ratzinger, *Eschatology: Death and Eternal Life,* 136–39.

156. On this see Blond, "The Beatific Vision of St. Thomas Aquinas," 185–212.

by remains a created light, even though it no longer falls upon anything. It is in the end therefore as if we were to wake one day and see only sunlight and the sun itself in this light, but nothing besides. Far from there being an absence of medium here therefore, there is rather a seeing *of* the medium itself and only *through* this medium to its very source. So once more, as with the case of the seeing mind, mediated vision and the sight of the unmediated are made to coincide.

And it is here that we need to reflect that, in the interplay between East and West, the *further East* is the joker in the pack. For both Iamblichus and Pseudo-Dionysius, the respective founts of pagan and Christian theurgy, were Syrians. It is their tradition that sought to hold together greater remoteness with greater proximity, greater need for mediation with greater immediacy. Thus, in the case of Pseudo-Dionysius, his *Mystical Theology* is actually one important source for the later dominant *Western* view of the beatific vision, precisely because it describes a complete entering "into" God, but as the climax of a cosmic liturgical action.[157]

In Pseudo-Dionysius therefore, we have the combination both of "complete" vision in the end and strong theophany in the here and now. He promotes this "double *hyperbole*" the most emphatically of all the patristic writers, yet in a way that does the most justice to the most genuine *élan* of all their trajectories. According to this double *hyperbole,* an infinitely saturated mediation (of both mental and bodily intuition) reveals the immediate in the end, while vision in the here and now participates in this extremity in some degree. More specifically, because there is nothing "between" God and the creation, "mediation" of the divine presence always involves a heightened awareness of something other than us in the world—including the angelic sphere—or of our own personhood. Accordingly, this heightened awareness must convey a stronger sense of the *immediate* presence of God to us. So for now mediation heightens immediacy, while in the end, immediacy elevates mediating light to parity with the divine presence.

It follows that there is nothing perennially fated about the apparent pairs of contrasting opposites; *either* the Eastern "much now, but never everything" *or* the Western "nothing now, but in the end everything." It is rather, for the "Far Eastern" theurgic resolution of this dire alternative, a case of "almost everything now, if you care to see, and in the end, the almost everything become one with the everything." Eriugena is near to this resolution—but he qualifies this with final *epectasis*; Aquinas is near it also, but his sense of the theophanic is still too weak and he has too thin an account of the role of resurrected bodies. Yet the Dionysian double *hyperbole*

157. Cf. once more de Andia, *Henosis,* 303–73.

of deification—here and hereafter—lurks just beneath both the Western and the Eastern surface.

To face instead "the dire alternatives" was to forget this. It meant that the East tended increasingly to think that mediation would stand in the way of vision in the end, while for now and always *some* measure of sheer unmediated vision was possible. Equally it meant that the West tended increasingly to think that for now we receive only information and not presence, while in the end raw presence will be vouchsafed to us as a reward for obedience, the eschatological persistence of participation being gradually played down. In *either* case, the loss of the paradoxes of both participation and mediation involve also a slackening of eschatological tension: a proper sense that the end is already now as the immediate in the mediate, and at the same time that the role of mediation is to drive us forwards to ever greater reception of what is already present. Instead, either expectation is reduced (the East) or the experience of the present as an intrinsic path to finality is diminished and compromised (the West). One result of this was foolish respective declarations of *anathema* upon perfectly traditional elements of Christian teaching: the final vision of the divine essence, created grace, the final collective and embodied judgment of all persons. In the latter respect it can be seen how a gradual loss of the sense that sacramental mediation through the structures of the created order is always necessary would encourage the view that judgment is but a private affair between God and the individual soul.

These *anathemas* need to be repented of. In order to do so, we need to remember that the way back is also the way forward. The way, curiously, of *renaissance*, of vital detour through the pagan in order to recover the biblical, of the magical in order to recover the gracious, of the always further oriental sense of the unity of the many with the One (the outgoing with the remaining) in order fully to grasp the Christian vision of the personal and the interpersonal as a scene of peace and reconciliation rather than one of final idolatrous abjection of some rather than others. Idolatrous, because any sense of a persisting refusal of the divine glory would impossibly impair the divine essence, given that the God who remains replete is the very God who gives forever without stint. Double *hyperbole* has therefore to include also the bias towards mercy for now, with only mercy and the effectiveness of mercy in the end.[158]

---

158. This Origenist conclusion is a necessary climax to the entire argument and implies that we need to marry an Eastern account of Judgment (with of course notable exceptions, like Julian of Norwich), to a Western account of final vision. The extra-Christian ecumenical reconciling of the monistic with the personal is crucial also.

11

Theurgic Attunement as Eucharistic Gnosiology

Divine *Logoi* and Energies in Maximus the Confessor and Thomas Aquinas

Nikolaos Loudovikos

Forty years have passed since Le Guillou, in his foreword for A. Riou's 1973 work *Le Monde et l'Eglise selon Maxime le Confesseur*, proposed the works of Maximus the Confessor and Thomas Aquinas as the meeting point of Eastern and Western theological traditions. Although, in order to understand Le Guillou's proposal, we have to bear in mind that for him, as for so many Eastern and Western theologians before and after him, the underlying problem has rather been the impasse of any effort of evaluating Palamite theology in light of Aquinian thought. Such claims have fruitfully promoted the Maximian studies over the last four decades, though Maximus has been very rarely compared with Aquinas. It seems unthinkable for the Western theologians not to conclude any evaluation of Eastern theology with a sort of comparison, or confrontation, or, very recently, equation of Palamas with Aquinas, but this cannot legitimately happen without checking the former's tradition. Thus, Maximus the Confessor has to be read not only *per se,* but also as a possible spiritual father of Gregory Palamas, as the latter frequently refers to the former's work. Has Palamas properly understood Maximus?

The usual Western answer is, of course, no. And this happens not only for confessional or cultural reasons, but also, as I believe, for philological reasons. I know of extremely few Western theologians who are able to exhaustively read Palamas and Maximus, and so we often see caricatured positions of them without any real reference to their texts and, unfortunately, the same has happened in the East, with Augustine and Aquinas. Now it seems that our first task is to apply in our discussions a proposal coming from modern existential psychology (K. Rogers): before I respond to your position, I must correctly describe it, and go on with my response only when you agree that your position has been correctly understood.

There is at least one recent work, which really tries to substantiate the convergences between Maximus and Palamas, on the one hand, and the divergences between Maximus and Aquinas, on the other, while also trying not to separate them on the dogmatic field. This is Antoine Lévy's book, *Le Créé et l' Incréé: Maxime le Confesseur et Thomas d' Aquin. Aux Sources de la Querelle Palamienne.*[1] I mention this book not because I fully agree with it— since, as it will become obvious, I have a different proposal to make—but because it is a really honest book, with a notable knowledge of the source texts and the adjoining discussions, and, above all, with an intention to be theologically fair. In this book, Palamas is proved to be an honest disciple of Maximus, as the Orthodox tradition of the medieval and modern period alike believed him to be. Having stopped to be considered as a theological monster coming from nowhere, Palamas can be then compared, through Maximus, with Aquinas, without obsessional confrontations. Thus, according to the author, on the ontological field, what counts for Maximus (and Palamas, who follows him, as well) is the external diffusion and operation of the uncreated *logoi* (λόγοι)/energies, while what counts more for Aquinas is the original unity of those *logoi*/energies in the divine essence.[2] On the Christological field, what we have in Maximus (and also in Palamas) is rather a divinizing synergy between divine and human energies in Christ, while in Aquinas, as this divinizing energy is identified with essence, all the activity of grace is unfolded, as natural or supernatural, in the form of a created grace.[3] For Lévy, the above means there is simply a difference of perspective between Maximus and Palamas on the one side, and Aquinas on the other, and not a deep dogmatic difference. Although this is a very legitimate conclusion, which makes me think that it perhaps preludes (along with J. Lison's and others) the emergence of a modern generation of scholars

1. Lévy, *Le Créé et l' Incréé.*
2. Ibid., 298–304.
3. Ibid., 422–24.

who have already overcome the sterile confessionalism of the past, we must carry on the discussion in order to see if there is any possibility of complementarity between Maximus and Aquinas, given that they are different but not necessarily hostile to each other.

1.

Concerning Maximus, *Difficulty 7* (*Ambiguum 7*) in the *Ambigua* is, as it is well known, a good point to start our reflection on the nature of the divine *logoi* of beings.[4] My purpose here is not of course to examine in length this valuable doctrine, but only to make some claims, which are, I think, of importance, in order to initiate our discussion on what are the main points of convergence and divergence between Maximus and Aquinas.

In this text, we learn a number of things concerning the nature and function of the *logoi*.[5] We first learn that these divine *logoi* are assumed in the hypostasis of the one *Logos*/Son of God of the Father, and he carries them—since he is the one who brings forth the divine will of the Father in the Spirit *ad extra*. Thus, "He [the divine *Logos*] held the *logoi* of all things which subsisted before the ages, and by His gracious will brought the visible and invisible creation into existence out of nothing in accordance with these *logoi*; by word (*logos*) He made, and continues to make, all things at the proper time, universals as well as particulars." What is thus eminently important here is that the divine *logoi* are divine wills moving *ad extra*. Maximus explicitly writes, "as to what I have called *logoi*, St. Dionysius the Areopagite teaches us that in Scripture they are called predeterminations and divine wills. Similarly the circle of Pantaenus, who became the teacher of the great Clement of Alexandria, says that Scripture likes to call them divine wills."[6]

There are two things to stress here. First, these *logoi* of God are clearly conceived by Maximus as "acts of His own will and we add a good reason for this: if He made everything by an act of will (and there will be no contradiction of that), and it is pious and just always to say that God knows His own will, and He made each entity willingly, then it follows that God knows entities as acts/energies of His own will, because He made things willingly."[7] By so closely connecting *logoi* with divine will and divine acts *ad extra* of God the Father through the *Logos*-Son by the Spirit, Maximus

---

4. Confessor, *Amb.* 7 (PG 91: 1068D–1101C).

5. Cf. especially PG 91: 1077C–1080A.

6. Confessor, *Amb.* 7 (PG 91: 1085A).

7. Confessor, *Amb.* 7 (PG 91: 1085AB).

shows that through those *logoi*/wills/energies God creates a real relationship with beings created by him, out of nothing (i.e., outside him).

The second point is that for God this relationship cannot be identified with his essence, in any, Thomist or not, sense. Those acts/*logoi*/wills are called by Maximus:

> . . . works (ἔργα) of God without beginning in time, in which beings participate in by grace; such works are the goodness along with everything that is contained in its *logos*. And simply (such works are) every sort of life and immortality and simplicity and unchangedness and infinity, *and all that is contemplated around His essence; which are God's works without beginning in time.*[8]

This, of course, does not mean that these works can be somehow separated from God's essence, and, consequently, they cannot be separately ontologized and conceived as separate beings between God and creation as they belong to God's very being. In order to leave no "Thomist" question unanswered, he makes absolutely clear in the very next paragraph that "of all beings which are participated in or participating in, God is infinite times infinitely above. Because everything that has a divine *logos* of being behind it, is a work of God, whether it started existing in time, or it is infused as a natural power in beings, thus praising loudly God who exists in everything."[9] Because, as Maximus boldly continues, God is above all of his eternal (such as immortality, life, sanctity, virtue, being) or temporal works, "of which the temporal ones participate in the eternal and they draw their names on these."[10]

We thus see that Maximus does not hesitate to make a deep and decisive distinction without ontological separation between the essence of God and his *logoi*, which express his will, acting outside him. Maximus, as well as Palamas many centuries after him, strongly insisted that this distinction is not by any sense formal, since essence and energy co-exist without any ontological separation (ἀχωρίστως)—see for this Palamas' treatise *On Divine Energies* 28. And of course Maximus is the same author who wrote, when interpreting the Areopagite, in a "Thomist" manner, "because He (God) is intellect, then indeed He thinks of entities inasmuch as He is. And if He thinks of entities in the process of thinking of Himself, then He is those

---

8. Confessor, *Cap. Gnost.* I.48 (PG 90: 1100CD). It is not of course curious that Palamas repeats exactly the same phrases in order to characterize the uncreated energies; Cf. Antirrhet's 1981 edition, vol. 5, 248, 260, 486.

9. Confessor, *Cap. Gnost.* I.49 (PG 90: 1101A).

10. Confessor, *Cap. Gnost.* I.50 (PG 91: 1101AB).

entities."[11] For anyone who knows the Maximian way of thinking, there is no contradiction here: for Maximus, as later on for Palamas, the divine essential expression *ad extra* does not preclude a deep unfathomable ocean of divine being behind it—no uncreated (or even created) logical being can ever exhaustively express his self in an act of absolute kenosis *ad extra*, although God gives wholly and absolutely his being to the creatures. Of course, neither for Maximus nor for Palamas (as Milbank curiously insists, although without bringing any sort of textual witness[12]) does the distinction between *logoi* and essence seem to be a formal one. Furthermore, the fact that, according to Maximus, *God is beings,* does not mean either that created beings enter the divine essence, or that the divine *logoi* are both created and uncreated. As it is made absolutely clear by Maximus, created beings have their existence only through participation in the uncreated *logoi*/wills/acts "around God"—that means in a God willing, loving, and acting outside himself. We shall say more below concerning the precise meaning of this expression.

Let us now come to those Maximian texts that explicitly connect *logoi* with energies in order to reflect upon the ultimate nature of this relationship of God with creation.

> [T]hus when the mind apprehends the *logoi* in things in a natural manner, contemplating the energies of God in the infinitude of those *logoi*, it reckons that there are many—or, truth to tell, infinite—variations of the divine energies it apprehends. And it will most likely find its power feeble and its method of searching for knowledge useless before Him who indeed is true, being unable to understand how God who is in truth no one of the things that exist, and properly speaking is everything and is beyond everything, is in every *logos* of each thing separately, and in all the *logoi* of all things taken together. If therefore it is true to say that every divine energy indicates through itself God, whole and undivided, [as present] in every [creature], in accordance with the *logos* of its own particular existence—in that case, who is able to understand and express precisely how God in His entirety is undividedly and indivisibly present in all things in common, and in each entity in a way that is particular, being neither subject to a variety of distinctions in line with the infinite variations in the things in which He is present, nor compressed into the individual existence of each one; nor yet does He compress the differences between things into one unitary totality of all things,

---

11. Confessor, *Scholia* (PG 4: 324A, 325AB, 353B).

12. Cf. Milbank, "Sophiology and Theurgy," 71.

but He is truly all things in all things, never abandoning His own indivisible simplicity?[13]

I have two points to make here: first, the *logos*, as we see in this passage, creates a unique presence of God within each one of the creatures, a presence which is expressed ("indicated") through a divine energy which makes God "whole and undivided" to appear in the depth of each creature. Thus, what we "contemplate" in the depth of each *logos*/presence is a divine energy forming this presence (as a syn-energy with the created energies of beings, as we shall see below). This absolute ontological connection/identification between divine essence (*God whole and undivided*, according to the above text), *logoi*, and energies (*logos* is exclusively manifested *as energy*) primarily means here that energies, manifesting divine essence *ad extra*, are not a sort of automatic emanation from God's essence but personal, *logical* acts/wills of communication, deriving precisely from an uncreated loving hypostatic essence, who creates firm, real, and permanent relationships with an otherness created by him outside him. The second point that I wish to make is that through this *logos*/energy, God can "be everything and beyond everything" (i.e., God can create an *uncreated relationship* with every creature without losing his transcendentality). Let us not forget that one of the most important semantic nuances of the term *logos* in Greek is *relationship*, and so what we ultimately describe through this word is a *reciprocal reality of love*, unavoidably moving on through proposals and responses, or what we have already called syn-energy, something that remains true even in the deepest degree of *perichōresis* (περιχώρησις) of creation and God. Without a created *logical* response, the very reality of *logos* as proposal, invitation for reciprocity, *scheseis* (σχέσεις), would be finally annihilated. Here we come at a very crucial point concerning our comparison between Maximus and Aquinas. As we shall see below, for Aquinas any relation between God and creatures can only be *created*, while for Maximus this relationship is decisively by grace uncreated, through a *perichoresis* of human *logos*/energy, in a process of a reciprocal exchange of gifts. This is substantiated in four different texts:

Ambiguum 7 1076BC

When describing the ontology of divinization, Maximus writes that this happens when "only God acts (ἐνεργεῖ), so as there exists only one energy, that of God and of those who are worthy of God, or better, only of God, as the

---

13. Confessor, *Amb.* 22 (PG 91: 1257AB).

whole of Him, according to His goodness, has made a perichoresis of those worthy of Him in their existential wholeness."[14] This perichoresis did not happen after an abolition of the "autexousion" (the self-determination) but rather as an εκχώρησις γνωμική, a self-offering through a personal choice, since the icon wants to acent towards its archetype and does not will to move towards any other direction; it "has been engaged in the divine energy (ὡς της θείας επειλημμένης ενεργείας) and so it has become God through this divinization." It is thus clear that here we have two wills and two acts/energies, one created and the other uncreated, and the final outcome is, by grace and not by nature, only one uncreated relationship/energy, only in the sense that the created will/energy has been engaged (and of course not essentially identified with) in the uncreated divine will/energy. This results in a deeply dialogical syn-ergy/syn-energy, where the created *logos*, as will and energy, responds in the affirmative to the divine uncreated call of love and finally there happens what Maximus in his *Mystagogy* calls the "heavenly marriage" between the two.

Ambiguum 42

The term that Maximus uses in order to describe the possibility of an ontological change of nature, without losing its *logos* of being (i.e., its ontological identity) is the *tropos hyparxeos* (τρόπος ὑπάρξεως, i.e., mode of existence). This permits Maximus to explain the kind of relationship that, as he thinks, exists between God and created natures. Thus, created nature can change in God not its *logos* but its mode of existence, when, for example, it is engaged in divine energies through its own created energy and, finally, becomes innovated/deified by "acting or being acted upon above its statute."[15] We have another witness here that through changing its mode of existence a created being can not only be acted upon but also act in and through the divine energy, not of course according to its created nature, but in grace—humanity can become God not in φύσει but in θέσει, and this is why, of course, though he is in God, he is not able to understand God's nature.

Capitum quinquies centenorum centuria I, 27

For Maximus "the perfect work of love and the fulfillment of its activity is to make the attributes and the names of those who are linked by it to

---

14. Confessor, *Amb.* 22 (PG 91: 1076BC).
15. Confessor, *Amb.* 22 (PG 91: 1341D).

belong to one another. Thus it makes a human God and makes God to appear as a human, because of the one and identical agreement of will and movement of the two."[16] It is obvious that, on the Christological field now, this exchange of attitudes, this deep *"dia-logos"* of the two wills/energies in Christ, forms the one "theandric" energy of him. What interests us here is that in this Chalcedonian Christ, according to Maximus, we do not have just a passive submission of human will/energy to the divine, but a reciprocal dialogical opening out of love—we do not have a one-sided dictation but a syn-energetic *perichoresis* of the two, out of mutual love.

Ambiguum 7

In a final text, again in *Ambiguum 7*, Maximus speaks of an "exchange of disposition" between humans and God—the former becomes *philotheos* and the latter is *philanthropos*—and thus humanity is called God through grace, while God is called human through his consent to humanity.[17] Further in the same passage, the ultimate goal of divinization is for the creature to "acquire the quality of the one who includes it" (i.e., God; 1073D). This does not mean any abolition of the *autexousion* (αυτεξουσιον), the self-determination, but its "steady and unshakable resolution" (θέσις παγία καὶ αμετάθετος, 1076BC), in order to finally have "only one energy, that of God, *and of the saints of God*" (italics mine). Once again, for Maximus, any sort of passivity or *suffering* the divine energy on the part of the creatures is simply unthinkable; creatures find their real and eternal identity in their participation in God, and not simply, in a passive way, *his energy,* as Lévy's Thomist account of Maximus wants to convince us.[18]

---

16. Confessor, *De Char.* I.27 (PG 90: 1189BC). See also *Epist.* (PG 91: 573B).

17. Confessor, *Amb.* (PG 91: 1084C).

18. Lévy, *Le Créé et l' Incréé,* 179–83. The author here reads the text *Ad Thal.* 2 (PG 91: 269D–271C), but in that text Maximus clearly connects the *energeia* of the divine providence with the synergetic "movement of the particular beings towards the well-being," which he characterizes as αυθαίρετος, not in the bad sense of the *arbitrary,* as the word is translated in the modern Western dictionaries, but in the ancient not necessarily bad sense of self-choice (αυτο-αίρεσις). By reading the word in the former sense, Lévy concludes that divine energy pushes forcefully the poor created motions/energies, beyond their arbitrariness, towards itself as goal of any actuality. The distance between this "Thomist" understanding of "participation as energetic causality," according to Lévy, and the Maximian understanding of participation as dialogical synergy, is enormous, as we shall see, while Lévy avers that the two views are identical (299). The divine call does not mainly serve God's *selbstbehauptung,* but gives creatures an eschatological free, active, and creative self; it is through this reciprocity that participation is achieved.

Thus, all the above texts mean that, first, the relationship between God and creation is real and permanent, not only for creation but also for him—otherwise we could not have invitation for dialogue, proposal, energetic relationship, or, in a word, *divine logos*; and, second, that consequently, this relationship means that God indwells creation indeed, through his uncreated wills/*logoi* expressed *via* his uncreated energies, by *transforming the mode of existence of the created logoi/wills/energies into uncreated through his own graced wills/logoi/energies*, without losing their createdness. Though Maximus makes the distinction between essence and *logoi*/wills/energies, this does not mean that divine essence is flooded by the created beings, while, at the same time, it is precisely with this divine essence that creatures get in communion with God—this is why Maximus calls the *logoi* "existential ways towards God."[19]

This transformation takes place eminently in the Eucharist, thus forming a *Eucharistic ontology of dialogical reciprocity*, as I have called it in my book mentioned above. There is also a Eucharistic gnosiology, precisely in the perspective of this Eucharistic ontology. This happens because dialogue is a fundamental common presupposition, not only for ontology, but also for gnosiology, since these two are deeply interwoven. It is impossible to acquire any sort of divine knowledge unless God becomes a God-for-the-world and human beings a human-of-God, primarily in the person of Christ. In this case, humankind contemplates in Christ, by the Spirit, the deep meaning of created things as a circulation of gifts (divine *logoi*, which give existence and life, and created *logoi,* which are then given back and thus become sanctified by getting transformed in the energies expressing the divine *logoi*). Or, in other words, the human mind, in Christ, co-creates the deep divine and human meaning of beings in dialogical synergy with God, and this is perpetuated in the church, through the Eucharistically inspired act of contemplating beings as divine words and divine calls and interpreting them through human meanings and acts. In Christ (i.e., in the transforming grace of the Spirit)—who makes created knowledge into uncreated through grace (the only known possibility of having human works, words, and wills)—humans hypostatically engage with God in divine works, words, and wills.

So, for Maximus, spiritual knowledge is dialogical and that means Eucharistic; what we see is what we participate in: God's eternally dialogical mode of existence (which, in the Trinity, is called *homoousion*) transmitted

---

19. Cf. my *Eucharistic Ontology,* 84–88. Note that for Lévy, it is completely impossible for any creature to overcome its createdness, even if it enters the sphere of divine participation through its created energy, which thus becomes "supernatural," but not by grace uncreated, as this happens for Maximus (182, 194ff).

to the world in Christ. We can know God only because he really ontologically relates himself to the world in Christ, and he really transforms human created *logoi* and energies into his uncreated *logoi*/energies, by grace (i.e. in the Spirit).

2.

For Aquinas, "it is necessary to suppose ideas in the divine mind. For the Greek word 'idea' is in Latin 'forma.' Hence by ideas are understood forms of things existing apart from the things themselves." Thus, either as a type of that which is called the form, or as a principle of knowledge, and because "the world was not generated by chance, but by God acting by His intellect, . . . there must exist in the divine mind a form to the likeness of which the world was made. And in this the notion of an idea consists."[20] But this further means that "God is the similitude of all things according to His essence; therefore an idea in God is identical with His essence."[21]

Then, in what sense can we conceive of those ideas, which cannot be distinguished from divine essence? Aquinas' answer is as follows:

> Hence many ideas exist in the divine mind, as things understood by it; as can be proved thus. Inasmuch as He knows His own essence perfectly, He knows it according to every mode in which it can be known. Now it can be known not only as it is in itself, but also as it can be participated in by creatures according to some degree of likeness. But every creature has its own proper species, according to which it participates in some degree in likeness to the divine essence. So far, therefore, as God knows His essence as capable of such imitation by any creature, He knows it as the particular type and idea of that creature; and in like manner as regards other creatures. So it is clear that God understands many particular types of things and these are many ideas.[22]

If ideas are the closest Aquinian equivalent to the Maximian *logoi*, it is immediately clear that with texts like the text above, we are presented with a rather different understanding of the nature and the function of those *logoi*/ideas. The ideas here simply represent a different type of God's

20. Aquinas, *ST* I, Q. 15, A. 1, ans. For this essay, I will use *The Summa Theologica*, the Benziger Bros. 1947 edition and translated by Fathers of the English Dominican Province.

21. Aquinas, *ST* I, Q. 15, A. 1, repl. to obj. 3.

22. Aquinas, *ST* I, Q. 15, A. 2, ans.

self-understanding, regarding the possibility of an imitative participation in a likeness of the divine essence on the part of the creatures, and they do not seem to initiate any sort of real relationship of God with a real otherness outside him. For the reader of Aquinas, this is not of course a surprise, as for this author God cannot be the being of things "for if He is the being of all things, He is part of all things, but not over them"[23]—while Maximus does not hesitate to assert precisely the opposite, by calling God "sense" and "mind" and "life" and "being" of all existent things, while in himself he is absolutely above any being.[24] Thus, for Aquinas "God knows other things as seen in His essence"[25] precisely because "God's will is His essence."[26] But if the Thomist will of God is absolutely identified with God's essence, opposite to the Maximian distinction without separation between essence and will in God, then "God wills His own being and His own goodness"[27] necessarily, and "He wills Himself as the end, and other things as what is for the sake of the end."[28] As a consequence, "God's action is His essence,"[29] and thus God's act does not create any real relation outside him. As Aquinas explicitly writes, "these relations in question have no real being in God."[30] Even "beatitude is a created thing in beatified creatures; but in God, even in this way it is an uncreated thing."[31] As is further explained in the third part of the *Summa* (Q. 2, A. 7), every relation between God and the creature really exists only in the creature, as coming from the change which affects the creature, but this does not exist really in God, and it exists only in God's reason. But then, even the union between God and creation, Aquinas maintains, does not have "a real existence in God;" it is present in him only by reason. On the contrary, this relationship really exists in human being exactly because this being is created—therefore, we can say that this relation of union is something created (*quoddam creatum*). What is curious enough is that Aquinas describes this kind of created relationship of the creature with God as not a real one: "therefore there is no real relation in God to the creature, whereas in creatures there is a real relationship to God; because

---

23. Aquinas, *SCG* I, Q. 26, A. 8.

24. Confessor, *Myst.* (PG 91: 664ABC).

25. Aquinas, *SCG* I, Q. 49, A. 5.

26. Aquinas, *SCG* I, Q. 73, A. 3.

27. Aquinas, *SCG* I, Q. 80, A. 2.

28. Aquinas, *SCG* I, Q. 88, A. 4.

29. Aquinas, *SCG* I, Q. 87, A. 4.

30. Aquinas, *SCG* II, Q. 12, A. 3; I am using here the translation by James F. Anderson.

31. Aquinas, *ST* I, Q. 26, A. 3, ans.

creatures are contained under the divine order, and their very nature entails dependence on God."[32] Even if this relationship on the part of the creature

32. Aquinas, *ST* I, Q. 28, A. 1, rep. to obj. 3. It is important to reflect upon Lévy's critique of David Bradshaw's views, as they are expressed in his book *Aristotle East and West*, in Lévy's "An Introduction to Divine Relativity," 173–231. David Bradshaw in his book uses here the term *synergism*. It was not very difficult for Antoine Lévy to show that there also exists a sort of *synergism* in Aquinas' work. Far from understanding synergy as an ontological fusion of divine and human energies, Lévy concludes by asserting that "dealing with the principles of cosmic order and deifying grace, the Greek Fathers and Aquinas equally believe that participation without confusion rests on efficient causality" ("Introduction," 189). We have already seen above that, concerning Maximus, this is an inadequate interpretation of his dialogical ontology of participation. For Lévy "this means that the elect are not deprived of their own natural *energeia*. They freely use it to welcome the divine one, so that this divine *energeia* might raise their own created *energeiai* far above their natural limits, allowing limited minds to contemplate an infinite Reality. This indwelling of God in human beings is therefore described as a circular or perichoretic chain of *energeia* and pathos, perfective *actio* and perfected *passio*, generated by the causal influx of God and implying the free will of the creatures. The elect are able to see God as long as their intellectual faculty is raised to supernatural level of activity under the influx of the divine *energeia*. This circular synergy, manifesting the uninterrupted movement of God's *energeia* which pours forth from the divine essence towards the elect and comes back to its source through their contemplation, does not involve a blending between the uncreated *energeia* of God and the created *energeiai* of the creatures at any stage" (ibid., 188). It is clear that this created energy can only passively receive this "causal perfective influx" pouring forth from above. This circular synergy is determined by what L. calls the *Porphyrian Principle*, which Bradshaw attributes only to Palamas, while Lévy attributes it both to Palamas and Aquinas. This principle is described by Lévy as follows: "The fact that the intelligible substance A affects the material substance B through its own *energeia* induces relationship from B to A, but no relationship from A to B. A remains absolute, *askhetos*, at the very moment where it affects relatively, en skhesei, B. We will designate this asymmetrical system of causation, which Porphyry derives from Plotinus, as the *Porphyrian Principle*." First of all, Lévy would have to ask himself if this *Porphyrian Principle* is identical with the biblical witness of the living and conscious encounter of the righteous, the prophets, and the apostles with the living God of Abraham and Isaac, the Father of the Incarnate Son, since for Maximus and Palamas this seems to be their primary source of understanding any possible ontology of participation. I agree with Lévy that a *sort* of synergy is unquestionably present both in Palamas' and Aquinas' understanding of participation, but the question is how they understand it. In my view, Bradshaw is wrong when he unreservedly applies the *Porphyrian Principle* to Palamas, while Lévy is wrong when he applies it to both Palamas and Aquinas, since this principle can only be unreservedly applied to Aquinas. While Palamas so fervently insists throughout his work that, through his energies, God really "gets out from himself" in order to meet the created otherness outside him, Aquinas, on the contrary, insists, as we have already seen, that any relation between God and the creature really exists only in the creature, as coming from the change that affects the creature, but this does not exist really in God. This indeed reminds us of the Plotinian God/One, who "does not desire us, so as to be around us, but we desire it, so that we are around it," according to the precise translation by A. H. Armstrong of *Enn. VI, 9,8*. It is clear that for the Plotinian God, any relationship with the creatures is *not real*, while any relationship of the

is sometimes called supernatural, this does never mean uncreated.[33] It is not curious then that even concerning Christ, Aquinas thinks that his soul needs a created grace in order to get in contact with his divine nature.[34]

Western theologians have to understand sometime that all the above sounds very unusual to the Eastern theological ear. Lévy's book is valuable precisely because of its realistic understanding of this great difference between Maximus and Aquinas (as well as of the faithfulness of Gregory Palamas to Maximus), although the author tries to minimize the difference, by claiming that it is without significance when we stay on the dogmatic field. However, the question is to show how a possible reconciliation can be articulated, given that, in Aquinas, biblical inspiration often seems to be too easily adapted to the non-Christian philosophical metaphysics of participation. On the other hand, it is true that Aquinas is right both theologically and philosophically, when he so intensively stresses God's absolute unity and transcendentality. As I have claimed elsewhere,[35] there can be found even a convincing effort of overcoming metaphysics in Aquinas' work. What makes me sympathetic to modern Thomists is that they are moved by a passion for deep and real participation in God, and they read Aquinas in that way, stressing precisely the absolute unity of ideas, will, energies with divine essence, since it is exactly this unity of creatures in God that seems to them as the only safe way of participating in him, and not in beings or creatures that lie between God and creation.

Thus, it is only after this sincere appreciation of their theological aspirations that I come to propose that Aquinas has to be complemented by Maximus, precisely in order to express better what he ultimately wanted to express—for it seems to me that Aquinas, starting from a theological position (really more of philosophical than theological inspiration), finally moved to the possible existential theological consequences of participation, even suspending his initial onto-theological conviction.[36] This happens when Aquinas asserts, for example, that "God is in all things not, indeed, as part of their essence or as an accident but as an agent . . . *who acts immediately and touches it by its power. . . . The* mover and the moved must be joined together. . . . *But it belongs to the great power of God that he acts*

---

creatures with God is absolutely *real*, to use the above Thomist terms. But then how can we claim that the Thomist metaphysics of participation is primarily biblical?

33. Lévy, *Le Créé et l' Incréé*, 218.

34. Aquinas, *De Veritate* Q. 29, A. 1, Con.

35. Cf. my book *Striving for Participation*.

36. Ibid., 60–67.

immediately in all things,"[37] as "*God is in all things by his power, as all things are subject to his power.*"[38] By so clearly (much clearer than in *ScG* II, 1, 3) defining power as the principle of acting upon another, Aquinas is able to write, "without God's action all things would be reduced to nothing."[39] What is this divine essential power (since in both *ScG* and *ST* divine power is identified with divine essence), which acts immediately in all things, (i.e., *ad extra*) and touches them directly, and is it *God himself* who acts through it, thus existing in all things, and making all things subject to him through it? Gregory Palamas or Maximus the Confessor could have written the above texts, as they perfectly describe their definition of divine essential power/action/energy. Most importantly, the above texts could be perfectly matched with Aquinas' new understanding of divine will in *ST* I, 19, 1–12: "God wills both himself to be, and other things to be; but himself as the end, and other things as ordained to that end; inasmuch as it befits the divine goodness that other things should be partakers therein." Thus, "*it pertains therefore to the nature of the will to communicate as far as possible to others the good possessed*" (my italics). What will? Not the "necessary will of God (God wills his own goodness)," but his "unnecessary will" concerning things *ad extra*. It is obvious that here we have a clear distinction between essence-energies, or essence-will, identical to that of Maximus and of the Greek fathers in general, which seems unthinkable in *ScG*. The onto-theological frame has strictly remained the same, but a happy "contradiction" suspends it, in order to show both its truth and its limits. The divine power/action is now, on the one hand, identical to the essence/substance (onto-theologically), but, on the other hand, it acts outside it, without any ontological danger of a possible elimination of God's being or its simplicity. It is also clear that this divine power/action is, of course, uncreated, as it is totally identical with divine essence—but at the same time it *touches created beings* without this action being changed into created! God's will cares "unnecessarily" for created beings, without disturbing his "necessary" will, or distracting it from its devotion to the fullness of divine essence. A fully "Maximian" (if you do not dare to say "Palamite") Aquinas thus emerges. Thus, to use Lévy's terms, the Aquinian philosophico-theological "ktistocentrism" leads to an existential/theological impasse if it is not complemented with the Maximian "ktizocentrism." On the other hand, no one can seriously claim that the Maximian supposed "ktizocentrism" lacks "ktistocentrism."

37. Aquinas, *ST* I, Q. 8, A. 1.

38. Aquinas, *ST* I, Q. 8, A. 3, italics mine.

39. Aquinas, *ST* I, Q. 9, A. 2.

3.

But, it is impossible not to make a short reference to the Maximian notion of embodied participation, compared with the Thomist account of the psychosomatic (possibility of) participation. After the introduction of the human body, deeply related to the soul, to what we call the image of God in humankind, by the Cappadocians—an enterprise that stopped any Platonizing temptation and turned patristic theology back to its anthropological sources of the first century (as well as after Nemesius' correction of Origenist psychology)—Maximus' answer to this question seems groundbreaking and enigmatic: "Man is his whole."[40] Maximus explains that this not only means that the human soul is not anymore the "species" of the human body, but also that the human subject consists not in an "addition" of mind and body, or their mixture, but it is something "different from them, and around them, cohering them but not himself cohered by them (as he is not them, or something of them, or from them, or from one of them, or in them, or in some of them, as he is around them and he is so called)."[41] That means that human subjectivity is something freely achieved, built upon the given of human nature, which thus becomes, in its turn, a matter not of dictation by God, but of eschatological discussion, dialogue, between humanity and God. Furthermore, subjectivity is thus a unique and unrepeatable mode of existence of the whole world; it is this very cosmic wholeness as it is expressed as human subjectivity.

In this way Maximus inserts freedom in his theological anthropology, and divine image in humankind is from now on inconceivable without it. God's image upon humankind comprises now the latter's act of free self-creation; human nature is not just a passive given but also humanity's poetic work, plan, decision, direction of his self in God. Humans *become* what they are (i.e., *their whole*), in a dialogical way; they construct eschatologically the self, in a synergetic/dialogical way, with God, in Christ and in the Spirit, in the ecclesial communion with his fellow people: these are some of the anthropological consequences of what I have called the *Eucharistic ontology of dialogical reciprocity* in Maximus the Confessor's thought.

If the above is true, we need a specific element in humanity that exercises this creative freedom for the sake of that human whole, opening a horizon of ultimate divine meaning and highlighting the human personal course towards it. This element is mind (νοῦς), in distinction from reason (λόγος, διάνοια). In *Mystagogy* 5, where Maximus, for example, makes this

---

40. Confessor, *Amb*. (PG 91: 1101 BC).
41. Confessor, *Amb*. (PG 91: 1225 CD).

distinction, the two parts of the intellectual power of the soul are the *theoretical*, which is called mind and the *practical*, which is called reason.[42] The work of mind, which is also called wisdom, is to search for divine truth through contemplation (i.e., a direct intuition of divine *logoi* in creation, which the *logoi* can be found either in things or in the Scripture), while the work of reason is to practically act and move towards goodness through faith and virtue. What is important is that both are parts of the intellectual power of the soul, and they work together, "in the Spirit," as Maximus insists, for the union of the intellectual part with the sensible part of the soul. And they work, of course, with the body, which is closely connected to the whole process. Thus, mind provides humanity with his spiritual goal, the deep spiritual sense of his life, while reason practices the *habits* (ἕξεις), which practically realize life in Christ, and both form together the intellectual expression of the eschatological creative dialogical freedom, which brings about the fulfillment of the human subject in God. It is in this sense that Maximus considers mind and reason, in union with body, as the vehicle by which the image of God upon humankind finally reaches its archetype.[43]

When Maximus says that the human mind *contemplates* God he does not mean that it *understands* God, but that it opens human freedom to God's freedom as love. That means that the mind understands in God, by the Spirit, the deep meaning of created things as a circulation of gifts given by God and returned to him in Christ. In other words, that the mind co-creates the deep meaning of beings in dialogical synergy with God, by bringing a created universe of beings and acts to him and receiving them back as the God-like kat-holicity in Christ. Thus, mind provides us with a spiritual understanding of God's *logoi*/acts/energies in creation (i.e., of God) as God-for-the-world, or God-in-the-world.

Let us now come to Aquinas. For him, as it is widely known, the human soul is, in an Aristotelian fashion, absolutely connected with a body, but it is difficult for him to combine his perfectly holistic anthropology with his anthropology of participation: "the mind which sees the divine substance must be completely cut of from the bodily senses, either by death or by ecstasy."[44] Any possibility of a charismatic transformation of the bodily senses, so familiar in the Greek patristic tradition, is completely lacking here, as for Aquinas the main reason for the weakness of our intellect's ability to see God is its connection with the body. Thus, the intellectual contemplation seems to swallow up the bodily participation. Consequently,

---

42. Confessor, *Myst.* (PG 91: 672D–684A).

43. Confessor, *Amb.*(PG 91: 1077B).

44. Aquinas, *SCG* III, Q. 46, A. 2.

all who saw God in this life saw him "either in reference to an imaginary vision, or even a corporeal one,"[45] as the presence of the body seems to be an insurmountable obstacle for this vision. It is thus clear that the Neoplatonico-Aristotelian presuppositions of Aquinian anthropology powerfully persist: "every intellect naturally desires the vision of the divine substance, but natural desire cannot be incapable of fulfillment. Therefore, any created intellect whatever can attain to the vision of the divine substance, and the inferiority of its nature is no impediment."[46] No other presuppositions seem to be required here in order for the intellect to see God, other than its natural kinship with him. This is not of course to see him completely, as this kinship has a certain limit imposed by the intellect's createdness.[47]

Let me now switch to Aquinas' understanding of beatitude, as it is described in his *Summa Theologica*. There are two kinds of beatitude: first, the beatitude of God (i.e., "the perfect good of an intellectual nature"); and, second, the beatitude of every intellectual nature, which consists in understanding. "Now in God to be and to understand are one and the same thing; differing only in the manner of our understanding them. Beatitude must therefore be assigned to God in respect of his intellect; as also to be blessed, who are called blessed (*beati*) by reason of the assimilation to his beatitude."[48] It is, furthermore, clear that beatitude "is a created thing in beatified creatures; but in God . . . it is an uncreated thing."[49] It seems again absolutely impossible for the creatures to participate in God's being as it really is, because every created beatitude "pre-exists wholly in a more eminent degree in the divine beatitude," analogically, thus creating an onto-theological gap between what God is and what of him is participated in.[50] It is curious enough that the Thomists who complain about Palamas (i.e., that, by his doctrine of the energies, he prevents us from participating in God's essence) do not see that, for Aquinas, any such participation is much more strictly forbidden.

Contrary to Maximus and Palamas, for whom the transformation of human senses through grace in order for a psychosomatic participation in God starts in this life, Aquinas ascribes the direct vision to the next life, as "God cannot be seen in his essence by a mere human being, except he be

45. Aquinas, *SCG* III, Q. 46, A. 3.

46. Aquinas, *SCG* III, Q. 57, A. 4.

47. Aquinas, *SCG* III, Q. 55, A. 5–6.

48. Aquinas, *SCG ST* I, Q. 26, A. 3, ans.

49. Aquinas, *SCG ST* I, Q. 26, A. 3, ans.

50. Aquinas, *SCG* I, Q. 26, A. 4, Ans.

separated from this mortal life."[51] This is because "our soul, as long as we live in this life, has its being in corporeal matter; hence naturally it knows only what has a form in matter, or what can be known by such a form."

But this can be taken to mean that the created light/grace given by God is insufficient to liberate the human soul ontologically from the burden of the body in this life, in order for it to directly and intellectually unite with the divine essence. For if this is true, then the impression is given that the vision of God after death is not the result of any sort of grace but is simply a natural result of the liberation of the soul from body. Thus, any visit of the created/supernatural grace/light in this life has as its main goal our deliverance from the body. How can we conceive of Chalcedonian Christology in these terms? In addition, what is the role of the Holy Spirit here? Is his role confined to helping us to get off our bodily nature, along with the passive part of our soul? Do we need the Spirit at all to accomplish this? Thus, the remarkable Aquinian anthropology of the psychosomatic human synthesis seems to collapse when he discusses the anthropological ground of participation.

4.

I completely understand (and I am in agreement with) the effort of Aquinas' modern disciples in interpreting his thought in terms, finally, of a theology of deep participation in God, beyond any onto-theological inelasticity, and without intermediate or intervening ontologized divine or created beings (and I am sure that neither Maximus nor Palamas ever made such ontologization, as it is impossible to find such evidence in their texts). If Aquinas is read from this perspective, not only does his metaphysics of divine unity prove to be a legitimate theological assimilation of ancient Greek metaphysics, corrected through this doctrine of participation, but this metaphysics can support some modern enthusiastic pro-Maximians and pro-Palamites, who easily speak of *logoi* and energies and remember the forgotten doctrine of the unity of God behind any theology of diffusion of God's words and acts. It is thus in the perspective of the above-mentioned author's own reading that I propose *the Maximian completion of Aquinian thought*. First, we need to understand God's relationship with creation as real in both parts and reciprocal. Without this, our metaphysics of divine unity is correct but our theology of participation is incomplete. Second, we need to understand this relationship not only as created, but also as uncreated, as a change of the mode of existence of the created essences or *logoi* or energies into uncreated,

51. Aquinas, *SCG* I, Q. 12, A. 11.

through grace. Thus, God really offers his self to the world as a divine *theopoiia* in order to divinize creation out of a *theopoiesis* through grace.[52] Otherwise, nothing is really offered to the world, and we then desperately try to find our place within the firm eternal divine unity. A psychologist would perhaps even have the temptation to understand this sort of doctrine about God as the theological consonance of the psychoanalytic definition of narcissism. Speaking psychologically of narcissism, we mean an intersubjectivity, which really takes place only outside me, while inside me the other is contained in the private world of my self, and in the very definition of it. That means that the other exists only through me and for me.

Therefore, we need Maximus in order to cure any theological doctrine of divine unity from its inherent narcissism. In this case, our worshipping of God cannot be a theurgic attunement (what a fine term coined by John Milbank!) if this does not finally become a Eucharistic gnosiology. My theurgic attunement can simply be my theurgic narcissistic response reflecting God's narcissism, if this God is not really present in my world, making me God by grace; while Eucharistic gnosiology is an amazing encounter with Christ's God, full of loving and joyful kenotic humility, getting out of his self-sufficiency in favor of me, and opening for me, in Christ, the possibility of this psychosomatic participational knowledge of all things in him, *hic et nunc*.

52. These are the terms that I used in my book *Striving for Participation*, 238–41, in order to describe the dialogical reciprocity between God and his world in Christ.

12

The Metaphysics of Maximus
Becoming One with God

TORSTEIN T. TOLLEFSEN

What does St. Maximus have in mind when he talks about deification? The question could be put in more precise terms: in what way does deification affect the ontological constitution of man? This is the topic of the present paper. The doctrine of deification is central to Byzantine and Orthodox theology, and the term itself suggests that this doctrine teaches that *man shall become God*. This may sound familiar to some people but highly unfamiliar to others. With this in mind, I should like to quote a major father of the third century, St. Basil the Great:

> When a sunbeam falls on a transparent substance, the substance itself becomes brilliant, and radiates light from itself. So too Spirit-bearing souls, illumined by Him, finally become spiritual themselves, and their grace is sent forth to others. From this comes knowledge of the future, understanding of mysteries, apprehension of hidden things, distribution of wonderful gifts, heavenly citizenship, a place in the choir of angles, endless joy in the presence of God, and becoming like God, and, the highest of all desires, becoming God.[1]

---

1. Basil, *De Spiritu Sancto* 23.

Whether one is familiar or unfamiliar with such formulas, one should not avoid the tremendous ontological challenge they set before us. The term "tremendous" is well put here I think since, as Rudolf Otto pointed out early in the twentieth century, one of the basic properties in which the holy is met, is in its character as *mysterium tremendum*. Abraham's words in Genesis illustrate the "terror," the awe felt by man in the presence of God, according to Otto: "like a stored-up electricity, discharging itself upon anyone who comes too near:"[2] "Indeed now, I who am but dust and ashes have taken it upon myself to speak to the Lord" (Gen 18:27). This, I think, should definitely be remembered by the philosopher who tries to dissect conceptually such an unheard of mystery as deification, since much talk has the tendency to belittle even the most sacred topics.

Rudolf Otto, in his well-known book from 1917, *Das Heilige*, says: "A characteristic common to all types of mysticism is the *Identification*, in different degrees of completeness, of the personal self with the transcendent Reality."[3] In the German original the term is "*Verselbigung mit dem Transzendenten*."[4] I am not happy with the term. I would have preferred *unification* to identification or "*Verselbigung*." Philosophically speaking, one may think of different kinds of unity. Identity, however, is a strong form of unity, which suggests that the one entity becomes *the same* as the other, not similar to something or closely attached to it in intimate communion. Whatever one thinks deification is does not violate a certain basic principle in much patristic metaphysics—viz., *the principle of the integrity of nature*. There are texts in which Maximus clearly shows how each particular being has properties that constitute it in its own distinctive character in addition to properties that it has in common with other beings of the same species.[5] On the next level, species differs, but have common properties with other species within their class (genus). There is, in other words, differentiation and unity throughout the whole system of the created world, and beings preserve their natural identity in their *logos* (λόγος), while at the same time are made such that they (should) coexist, not only ontologically or as a taxonomic system, but in mutual harmony. In *Ambiguum* 22, Maximus says that things are different by reason of the *logoi* (λόγοι) by which they were created.[6] He defines "essential difference" thus: "a *logos* by which the es-

---

2. Otto, *The Idea of the Holy*, 18.

3. Otto, quoted from the English translation of *The Idea of the Holy* from 1978, first published in 1923, 22.

4. Ibid., 25.

5. For the whole logical system one should consult *Amb.* 41 (PG 91: 1312B–1313B).

6. Confessor, *Amb.* 22 (PG 91: 1256D).

sence, that is to say the nature, remains both undiminished and unchanged, unmixed and unconfused" (λόγος καθ᾽ ὅν ἡ οὐσία, ἤγουν φύσις, ἀμείωτός τε καὶ ἄτρεπτος, ἄφυρτος ὁμοῦ καὶ ἀσύγχυτος διαμένει).[7] One thing cannot become something quite other than itself, but is preserved essentially as itself throughout its whole history.

Beings may though suffer some kind of change and even radical transformation, but such change or transformation never consists in being transposed from one essential definition into another. In that case, the original being would have been lost, and if this transformation was thought to be deification, it would in a sense not be that, since the ontological continuity between the entity in its first and second state would have been broken: it is not preserved as itself, it has become something other, a different kind of "thing." If deification is a gift given to created beings, then the being in question still has to exist in a kind of ontological continuity with what it was before the gift was received and conceived in gratitude towards the Giver.

St. Maximus has some rather strong expressions about deification. In *Ambiguum 7*, he says: "And in such a way one becomes God, one receives to be God from God" (καθ᾽ ὅν γίνεται θεός, ἐκ τοῦ θεοῦ τὸ θεὸς εἶναι λαμβάνων).[8] A bit further on he says that man, through the *logoi* of his being, well-being, and eternal being, "places himself wholly in God alone, wholly imprinting and forming God alone in himself, so that by grace he is God and is called God" (καὶ δι᾽ αὐτῶν ἑαυτὸν μὲν τῷ θεῷ μόνῳ δι᾽ ὅλου ἐνθέμενος, τὸν δὲ θεὸν μόνον ἑαυτῷ δι᾽ ὅλου ἐντυπώσας τε καὶ μορφώσας, ὥστε καὶ αὐτὸν εἶναί τε χάριτι καὶ καλεῖσθαι θεόν).[9] In *Ambiguum 41* Maximus speaks of the human task, fulfilled in Christ, that man should mediate between all divisions of beings, and unite the uncreated nature with the created, "showing them to be one and the same through the possession of grace" (ἓν καὶ ταὐτὸν δείξειε κατὰ τὴν ἕξιν τῆς χάριτος).[10] Maximus continues: "the whole being wholly interpenetrated by God, and become completely whatever God is, save essential identity" (ὅλος ὅλῳ περιχωρήσας ὁλικῶς τῷ θεῷ, καὶ γενόμενος πᾶν εἴ τί πέρ ἐστιν ὁ θεός, χωρὶς τῆς κατ᾽ οὐσίαν ταὐτότητος). The final text I put forward is from the 10th *Ambiguum*, where Maximus speaks of possessing the

7. Confessor, *Th. Pol.* 14 (PG 91: 149D). These adjectives are equivalent in logical force with the four Chalcedonian adverbs that define the relation between divine and human nature in Christ. I shall return to this below.

8. Confessor, *Amb.* 7 (PG 91: 1084A).

9. Confessor, *Amb.* 7 (PG 91: 1084C).

10. Confessor, *Amb.* 41 (PG 91: 1308B). One should note that Maximus here speaks of being ταὐτόν, which is the term one would translate as "identical with." However, this identity or sameness does not mean that the being of man is changed into something else, cf. below.

sole divine and eternal life of the indwelling Logos; man no longer bears in himself the temporal life and its motions, but has "become without beginning and end" (γέγονε καὶ ἄναρχος καὶ ἀτελεύτητος), a saying that sounds strikingly paradoxical.[11] The term ἄναρχος definitely signifies exclusively a divine attribute. Maximus here speaks of man, a being with a temporal beginning and a temporal end (even if essentially immortal) that receives the divine attribute of being *beginningless*. How should we understand this? I shall return to that question below.

What are the ontological conditions that make deification possible? On the one hand, one has the divine benevolence. God condescends to his creatures and executes his activity in them. However, in order that man may receive such an immense divine gift, man himself must have an ontological structure or constitution that makes it possible.

Maximus makes a distinction between the *logos* and the *tropos* of something. The first define the essential being or nature, the second characterizes possible modes under which that nature might exist.[12] The mode of existence is "the scheme in which it naturally acts (ἐνεργεῖν) and is acted upon (ἐνεργεῖσθαι), which can frequently change and undergo alteration without changing at all the nature along with it." An example of acting could be a virtuous deed. An example of being acted upon would be to be exposed to external influences, like divine love or physical conditions, but especially, as we shall see, exposed to a transforming divine influence. According to Maximus, man may be subject to a certain *innovation* (καινοτομία) in his modes, but not in his *logos* of nature. When acted upon by God, the mode of human existence is changed, and man even becomes capable to act beyond his normal scope.

We should like to know more precisely what this means. To be exposed to divine influence in such a way that man becomes what Maximus in strong words has said he should become, presupposes that man becomes a *participant* in something distinctly and exclusively *divine*. This, however, cannot be the divine essence, since Maximus explicitly denies such a possibility (cf. above). What then? In *Chapters on Knowledge* (1, 47–50) Maximus introduces a rather daring terminology. He speaks of two kinds of divine "works" (ἔργα): on the one hand there are creatures ("works He began to make"), on the other hand there are "works without beginning" (ἔργα ὧν οὐκ ἤρξατο ποιῆσαι). Examples of the second kind of divine works are goodness, life, immortality, simplicity, etc. These "works" are further said to be "participated beings" (ὄντα μεθεκτά) in which creatures may participate.

---

11. Confessor, *Amb.* 10 (PG 91: 1144C).

12. Cf. Confessor, *Amb.* 42 (PG 91: 1341D).

This terminology sounds as if something manifested from God, not being his essence, is strangely reified. However, I am convinced that this is not Maximus' intention. The most problematic term is, of course, *being*. The term *work* is ambiguous in Greek, as it is in English (and in Norwegian for that matter, the word is "*verk*"): it may mean the *result* of a certain activity or the *activity* itself. It is a reasonable interpretation of Maximus, I believe, if we understand the word here as synonymous with ἐνέργεια (i.e., activity[13]). The innovation or change that occurs to man is due to participation in the divine activity, which becomes by grace the mode in which the creature lives and is transposed beyond the capacity inherent in it according to its *logos* of being. The talk of God's activity as participated *being* should, accordingly, be interpreted dynamically and not as if there existed any kind of lower beings around God. To my knowledge, there is nothing in Maximus that suggests any other reasonable interpretation.

Maximus obviously thinks that natural human activity is executed in the mode of divine activity in such a way that man even receives and may be characterized by divine predicates, such as divine goodness, life, and immortality, yes even the property of being without beginning and end, as we saw above.[14] Man becomes wholly interpenetrated by God, and becomes all that God is.

There is a lot of interesting material in Maximus' writings that is relevant to characterize the condition of deification. However, I shall only make a small comment on one thing, viz., in want of a better word, the "epistemic" contents of deification. The Maximian conception of God excludes in a radical way any identification ("*Verselbigung*") with the essence of God. One might, on the other hand, wonder if deification is a kind of elevated *contemplation* of God as an object of the mind, but that is not so. There is neither identification nor contemplation of God as an object. When Maximus characterizes the deified condition, he turns (in *Ad Thalassium* 60) to a different kind of terminology. He says that rational or conceptual knowledge comes to an end in *experience* and *sensation* (πεῖρα, αἴσθεσις).[15] The point is, probably, that this kind of terminology is suited to describe the condition in which the lover achieves *union* with his beloved. This union is somehow a differentiated condition that I shall try to investigate a bit closer.

How, exactly, should we define the relation between created and uncreated being in the condition of deification? I suggest that what Maximus says about union and distinction in the God-man is relevant to describe the

13. Cf. Confessor, *Cap. Gnost.* I.47.

14. Confessor, *Amb.* 10 (PG 91: 1144C).

15. Confessor, *Ad Thal.* 60 (CCSG 22, 75–77).

deification of man as well. The *Ambiguum* 5 is central in this connection. Maximus says that there is a *difference* (διαφορά) between the natural activities beheld *without division* (ἀδιαιρέτως) in the basic ontological constitution of the God-man, and there is a *union* (ἔνωσις) of natural activities beheld *without confusion* (ἀσυγχύτως) in the monadic mode of the hypostatic being of Christ.[16] Maximus wants to define, in accordance with the convenient tool of Chalcedonian terminology, the most intimate kind of union without the complete confusion of the two kinds of being that are involved. Division is a kind of difference and confusion is a kind of union. Created and uncreated being are different but even so not divided, they are unified but still not confused.[17] But where does this lead us? In a way we are within the domain of logical or, more precisely, of ontological description, and it is difficult to imagine exactly how the two kinds of being are related. It is as if they penetrate into one another's sphere without ever becoming genuinely unified. To use a metaphor: they function more like oil on water in relation to one another. What the terminology suggests is a kind of parallel existence or a parallel dynamic, but in what sense does this permit us to say that man is deified? What happens with the nature and activity of the human being?

What are the features of the union that Maximus has in mind? In his *Opusculum* 18 (Ὅροι ἐνώσεων) he lists twelve kinds of union, three of which are of interest in the present context: juxtaposition (παράθεσις), blending (κρᾶσις), and confusion (σύγχυσις). As an example of juxtaposition, he gives boards placed together. Blending is when fluids, like wine and water, are mixed together. Confusion means that things are dissolved into one another in such a way that a third something comes to be. Aristotle's doctrine of mixture was much discussed in Hellenistic and Late Antique philosophy.[18] One of Maximus' primary sources was, probably, the third chapter of Nemesius of Emesa's *De natura hominis*. According to Nemesius, juxtaposition is a mere parallel existence of two things placed together. He further considers blending to be a kind of juxtaposition, but the particles in the mixture of two liquids are so tiny that this avoids our perception.[19] According to

---

16. Confessor, *Amb.* 5 (CCSG 48, 25).

17. I disagree with Törönen, who, in the introduction to his book *Union and Distinction*, complains about what he calls the pan-Chalcedonism of making the Chalcedonian adverbs basic logical tools in Maximus. Cf. Tollefsen, *The Christocentric Cosmology*, 10. I agree with Törönen that union and distinction are basic logical concepts in Maximus' thinking, but the so-called Chalcedonian logic is just a special application of these concepts. In addition to *Amb.* 5, one should consult *Th. Pol.* 18 (PG 91: 213A–216A), in which Maximus lists a lot of different kinds of unions, one of which is confusion.

18. Cf. Sorabji, *The Philosophy of the Commentators*, 290–315.

19. Nemesius, *De natura hominis* 3 (PG 40: 593A).

several philosophers, a blend is demonstrated to be a kind of juxtaposition since the two liquids may be separated by artificial means.[20] The blend of oil and water that I used as a metaphor above is obviously a kind of juxtaposition. Is this the way we should think about the union of the two natures in Christ? Is this the way we should think of the unity between divine activity and human nature in the new mode of deification? As a matter of fact, it is not. In this connection, something said by St. Gregory of Nyssa is illustrating: the human nature of Christ, when mixed with the divine, no longer remained within its own measures and properties (ἐν τοῖς οἰκείοις μέτροις καὶ ἰδιώμασιν), its own limits and properties (ἐν τοῖς ἑαυτῆς ὅροις τε καὶ ἰδιώμασι).[21] I think it points in the same direction when Maximus says that in deification man imprints and forms God in himself, so that man transcends temporal life and its activities and receives divine attributes, for instance, becoming without beginning and end. If deification consists in a new mode (*tropos*) of being, then what exists in this new mode has suffered some kind of ontological transformation. Something happens with the measures, limits, and properties of man, to use the terminology of St. Gregory. According to Maximus, man is created with a capacity for actualization beyond the obvious limits we normally experience, but only God can effect this actualization. Maximus says that Christ became incarnate for our sake, so that we can transcend nature (ὑπὲρ φύσιν ἐκαίνισε).[22] The presence of divine activity in man makes him something he was not before, a new creature. Even if Maximus guards the principle of the integration and preservation of nature according to the divine *logos* for each creature, the goal of his ontology of man is to show forth the possibility of the dynamics of transformation.

How could the union be described philosophically? We know already that confusion is ruled out in principle, because even if man becomes a new creature this does not occur in the way that his original nature is destroyed and a third something (*tertium quid*) results from the union of divine activity and human nature. Maximus says that man shall transcend nature, and his mode of being is definitely thought to suffer an expansion of human nature and activity beyond the present limits and properties. Maybe one more glance at Nemesius' text could highlight this a bit further. Nemesius speaks of the union of soul and body and develops his topic further into the subject of the incarnation. However, what he says could be applied to

20. Cf. Sorabji, *Philosophy of the Commentators*, 294, 297–300. Sorabji reports that he has witnessed the success of an experiment of separating liquids that employed the device mentioned in the ancient texts (ibid., 299).

21. Nyssa, *Contra Eunomium*, GNO 2, 124, and 130.

22. Confessor, *Amb.* 5 (CCSG 48, 32).

the doctrine of deification as well. The concept we need is a concept that goes beyond the kind of external union conceived in notions of juxtaposition and blending. On the other hand, one has to avoid the extreme kind of union conceived by confusion. The solution is the concept of *unconfused union* (ἀσύγχυτος ἕνωσις). Nemesius, however, appealing to what Porphyry says about the union of soul and body, expands a bit on this concept:[23] an essence may be assumed in such a way that it completes another essence. If we apply this to deification, we may say that the divine activity completes the whole potential of human nature and even transforms it into a new mode of being beyond itself. In this way, the union is not conceived to be an external one, similar to juxtaposition, it is rather an intimate one in which man is transformed creature, transcending his own nature by living the divine life.

As long as one remains in the world of ontological categories one easily slips into the relaxed, philosophical attitude that sets its tools to dissect what in fact is something quite other than a subject for intellectual exercise. It is not at all surprising that the most powerful formulas describing the union of man and God in deification are not of the nature of philosophical concepts, but are rather metaphors. Moreover, the most striking metaphor, for all who have observed the phenomenon, is red-hot iron.[24] Of course, we are still able *conceptually* to distinguish fire and iron as two different things, but even so the iron is in a quite new condition, it is transformed until the most unrecognizable new form: is this reddish white, intensely hot, and almost frightening thing really iron? Here we should recall the words of Rudolf Otto: the divine is met with "like a stored-up electricity, discharging itself upon anyone who comes too near." The metaphor of red-hot iron is a lot more striking than the metaphor of oil on water because the substance of iron is definitely affected. Something radical has happened to it while nothing striking happens to water or to oil when they are mixed. Philosophical categories may guard the proper distinctions, but maybe fail to grasp the exact character of the unity between created and uncreated being in the condition of deification. On this background, I feel it is not out of the way to talk about the divine activity as *energy* that transforms creatures into an unimaginable glory.

---

23. Cf. Nemesius, *De natura deorum* 3 (PG 40: 601B–605A). Cf. Tollefsen, *The Christocentric Cosmology*, 203–4.

24. Cf. Confessor, *Amb.* 5 (CCSG 48, 33).

13

Maximus the Confessor's View on Participation Reconsidered

VLADIMIR CVETKOVIĆ

Participation is a concept widely used by Maximus in his works. However, modern scholars have not paid sufficient attention to Maximus' usage of this concept. This is due, on the one hand, to the fact that there is still an ongoing debate on whether Maximus developed a precise doctrine of participation or whether he merely used the language of participation occasionally. On the other hand, numerous scholars limited themselves to observe that Maximus owes his concept of participation to the previous Platonic tradition, without a real attempt to investigate whether he contributes any novel significant insights to his dealing with this notion.

The first extensive scholarly attempt to define the meaning of participation for Maximus comes from Eric Perl in his doctoral dissertation.[1] Perl argued that participation in Maximus, like in Proclus and Dionysius the Areopagite, is understood as causal activity, or God's self-impartation in creation. According to Perl, creatures do not only exist by their participation in God, but God creates them in order to participate in him.[2] He demonstrates that, in Maximus, participation needs to be understood ontologically. By emphasizing the ontological dimension of participation, Perl

1. Perl, "Methexis."
2. Ibid., 117.

rejects Garigues' view on participation as a harmony of wills between God and human beings.[3] Distinguishing between the intentional participation based on the harmony of divine and human wills and the participation in Neoplatonic and Dionysian sense, which is understood as possession of the participated by the participants, Perl situates Maximus in the Neoplatonic tradition, especially seeing him as a follower of Proclus.

Another scholar who examined the concept of participation in Maximus is Torstein Tollefsen.[4] He disagreed with Jean-Claude Larchet, who claimed that, apart from using the language of participation, Maximus did not develop a clear doctrine of participation.[5] Similarly to Perl, Tollefsen attempted to place Maximus' doctrine of participation within a long tradition of authors (from Plato, over Plotinus, to Proclus) who used this concept. The study demonstrates that Maximus had rich and consistent usage of the concept. It also reveals that Maximus' concept of participation is quite similar to that of Proclus, suggesting that Dionysius the Areopagite might be the most likely source of this concept in Maximus.[6] Tollefsen claims that, by following Proclus, Maximus divides beings into three categories: the "unparticipated," the "participated," and the "participants."[7] However, in spite of showing how the two authors differ when applying this tripartite scheme in some aspects, Tollefsen concludes that in Maximus, like in Proclus, the highest cause (*Logos* in Maximus) is not participated in by anything. Tollefsen convincingly based this conclusion on a few passages from Maximus' work, which clearly suggest that the *Logos* (Λόγος) of God is unparticipated. Applying the Proclean logic to Maximus, Tollefsen suggests that beings participate in divine activity or, as Maximus calls it, the uncreated works of God. The uncreated works of God in which created beings participate by grace are goodness, life, immortality, simplicity, immutability, infinity, and virtue.[8] It is possible for created beings to take part in this realm of the divine attributes, but the supreme realm of God himself remains totally inaccessible by participation.

---

3. Garrigues, "L'énergie divine et la grâce," 272–96.

4. Tollefsen, "Did St. Maximus the Confessor," 618–25; Tollefsen, *The Christocentric Cosmology*, 190–224.

5. Larchet, *La divinisation de l'homme*, 600–601, n. 305.

6. Tollefsen, "Did St. Maximus the Confessor," 622.

7. Ibid., 622. Repeated also in Tollefsen, *The Christocentric Cosmology*, 215.

8. Confessor, *Cap. Gnost.* I.48 (PG 90: 1100C–1101), 137. Tollefsen deals extensively with the divine activity and the uncreated works of God in *The Christocentric Cosmology*, 138–89.

In his book, *Aristotle East and West,* David Bradshaw draws a similar conclusion to that of Tollefsen, relying on the same passage from Maximus' *Ambiguum* 7:[9]

> There is the same duality here as in the pagan Neoplatonists: the *Logos* is wholly transcendent and unparticipated, yet becomes "many" by its procession into beings, and can even be said to be equivalent to the many *logoi* (λόγοι). Maximus illustrates the relation of the *Logos* to creatures by the familiar illustration of a center and its rays. Whereas the pagan Neo-Platonists typically understand this relation in terms of an impersonal necessity, however, for Maximus the plurality of the *logoi* is due to the divine will.[10]

It seems to me that Bradshaw applies the same model as Tollefsen; firstly, by stressing Maximus' similarity with the Neoplatonists, and then by dissociating Maximus from the same Neoplatonists. For Bradshaw, the similarity between Maximus and Neoplatonists is evident in the unparticipated nature of *Logos* and in the procession of *Logos* into many *logoi*. While moving within this Neoplatonic framework, Maximus adapts it to meet the purpose of Christian belief. According to Bradshaw, Maximus' corrective of Neoplatonic metaphysics is in his perception of the procession of one *Logos* into many *logoi* not as necessary deed of the impersonal One, but as willing and creative act of the Christian God. Not elaborating further the purpose of the duality he refers to, Bradshaw leaves the reader to conclude that the *Logos* as the highest reality is unparticipated, while at the same time it is shared by many *logoi*.

It is the purpose of this article to refute this view on participation, which undoubtedly leads to the conclusion that the highest reality in Maximus is unparticipated. In my opinion, this view on participation is characterized by an attempt to overemphasize Maximus' indebtedness to a Neoplatonic, particularly a Proclean metaphysical framework at the expense of the fundamental structure of Maximus' thought expressed in the triad creation–incarnation–deification. In his forthcoming book,[11] by recognizing the aforementioned fundamental Christian structure of Maximus' thought, Tollefsen opts for a more dynamic concept of participation than the one he exposed in the *Christocentric Cosmology*. His "dynamic" concept of participation stresses more the connection between participation and

9. Confessor, *Amb.* 7 (PG 91: 1081BC).

10. Bradshaw, *Aristotle East and West,* 205.

11. Tollefsen, *Activity and Participation.*

activity.[12] My view on "dynamic" participation in Maximus is different from the one adopted by Tollefsen, because it is based on the model of ontological development in three stages so often used by Maximus.[13] If the threefold scheme is applicable to many spheres of both the divine plan and human activities, why should it not be used to explain the participation as a gradually advancing notion? As the incarnation of *Logos* drastically altered the relationship between God and human being, one would expect that this event established a new model of participation. Assuming also that the deification of human beings—and through them that of the whole creation—is seen by Maximus as the purpose of both the creation and the incarnation, then the terms of fullness rather than the language of "part-taking" would better express this anticipated state. Therefore, it is difficult to suppose that Maximus employs the Neoplatonic conceptual framework without adapting it to his Christian vision, which underlines the role of Christ in the divine design.

In my view, the investigation of Maximus' language of participation enables us to distinguish three modes of participation in God, which correspond to three periods in the history of salvation: the Old Testament, the New Testament, and the age to come. The first mode of participation, mostly elaborated by Perl and Tollefsen,[14] is the participation of created beings in divine intentions or *logoi*. It is rightly pointed out that the *Logos* remains unparticipated at this stage. The second mode of participation made possible by the incarnation of *Logos* is the participation of human beings in the church as Christ's body or, to be more precise, the participation of believers in the body and blood of Christ through the Eucharist. This mode of participation was under scrutiny in Nikolaos Loudovikos' book, *A Eucharistic Ontology*.[15] The third, and final, mode of participation, which is restricted to the age to come or the kingdom of heaven, consists in the full participation or identity with Christ attained through perfect likeness with him. Maximus' analogy of the Old Testament as a shadow and the New Testament as an icon of the ultimate truth of the future age[16] may be employed in order to understand these three modes of participation. The investigation of Eucharistic participation as the icon of the eschatological mode of the perfect

---

12. See the end of Introduction to *Activity and Participation*.

13. The example of this tripartite structure is seen in Maximus' triads such as: shadow–icon–truth, becoming–movement–rest, being–well being–eternal well being, practical contemplation–natural contemplation–theological contemplation, deacon–presbyter–bishop, etc.

14. Perl, "Methexis," 147–79; Tollefsen, *The Christocentric Cosmology*, 64–137.

15. Loudovikos, *A Eucharistic Ontology*, 165–94.

16. Confessor, *Scholia* (PG 4: 137).

participation may be of particular importance for the proper understanding of the notion of participation in Maximus.

The main contention of this article is that, for Maximus, the participation in the highest principle, or God the *Logos*, is possible. In order to demonstrate this, I intend to base my argument especially on passages from *Ad Thalassium* 59 and *Mystagogia* 21–24, which did not attract the attention of scholars in regard with the concept of participation. My aim is not only to dissociate Maximus from Proclus, but also to show Maximus' originality in the treatment of this concept in a liturgical or Eucharistic and eschatological context.

Let us begin by having a quick glance at those passages from Maximus' works that speak against participation in the highest principle. In *Ambiguum 7* Maximus states the following:

> We are speechless before the sublime teaching about the *Logos*, for He cannot be expressed in the words or conceived in thought. Although he is beyond being and nothing can participate in him in any way, nor is he any of the totality of things that can be known in relationship to other things, nevertheless we affirm that the one *Logos* is many *logoi* and many *logoi* are One.[17]

It is obvious from this passage that Maximus' denial that *Logos* is participated by any being has a clear apophatic context. Maximus here suggests that, by the reading of the statement not in an apophatic, but in a cataphatic context, it is possible to understand how one *Logos*, without being divided, is shared by many *logoi*, and how many *logoi* are One by virtue of their unity with one *Logos*. The duality to which Bradshaw refers to in the above-quoted passage may be explained by the distinction between the apophatic and the cataphatic methods that Maximus combines. However, even if the cited passage is seen exclusively from an apophatic perspective without any possible cataphatic connotations, it is difficult to conclude that the *Logos* is unparticipated. The apophatic method consists not in negating some affirmative content, but in going beyond any affirmation and negation about this content. Thus, Maximus' apophatic approach in the quoted passage aims not to deny any participation of beings in *Logos*, but to negate any affirmative statement about the possibility of such participation, which remains beyond human understanding. What Maximus clearly denies is that beings participate in God's essence, not only because this claim establishes identity

---

17. Confessor, *Amb.* 7 (PG 91: 1081B), 57: Ὑπεξῃρημένης οὖν τῆς ἄκρας καὶ ἀποφατικῆς τοῦ Λόγου θεολογίας, καθ' ἥν οὔτε λέγεται, οὔτε νοεῖται, οὔτε ἔστι τό σύνολόν τι τῶν ἄλλω συνεγνωσμένων, ὡς ὑπερούσιος, οὐδέ ὑπό τινος οὐδαμῶς καθ' ὁτιοῦν μετέχεται, πολλοί λόγοι ὁ εἷς λόγος ἐστί, καί εἷς οἱ πολλοί.

with God in nature, but also because it jeopardizes the specific differences of created beings. Apart from negating the participation of beings in the divine essence, Maximus applies apophatic language to the possibility of participation in other aspects of the divine being, such as divine hypostases and divine energies.

God, in whose essence created beings do not participate, but who wills that those capable of so doing shall participate in him according to some other mode, never issues from the hiddenness of his essence; for even that mode according to which he wills to be participated in remains perpetually concealed from all men. Thus, just as God of his own will is participated in—the manner of this being known to him alone—in the surpassing power of his goodness, he freely brings into existence participating beings, according to the principle which he alone understands.[18]

While God conceals the way in which beings participate in him, he allows them by his will to do so. Moreover, God creates beings in order to participate in him.

It is worth noticing that by combining the apophatic and cataphatic methods almost always when portraying the relationship between God and creation, Maximus is careful not to identify God either with some of his attributes, or with the fullness of his attributes. The passage from *The Centuries on Love* III.46 is an excellent illustration of Maximus' intention:

> God, full beyond all fullness, brought creatures into being not because He had need of anything, but so that they might participate in Him in proportion (ἀναλόγως) to their capacity and that He Himself might rejoice in His works (cf. Ps 104:31), through seeing them ever filled overflowing with His inexhaustible gifts.[19]

Here Maximus also uses both apophatic and cataphatic language. The apophatic language is evident in the statement about God, who is "full beyond all fullness," while the cataphatic approach dominates the rest of the sentence. By using the expressions "full beyond fullness" and beyond "the

18. Confessor, *Cap. Gnost.* I.5, 7 (PG 90: 1180C–1181A), 165: Ὁ τοῖς οὖσι μή κατ᾽ οὐσίαν ὑπάρχων μεθεκτός, κατ᾽ ἄλλον δέ τρόπον μετέχεσθαι τοῖς δυναμένοις βουλόμενος, τοῦ κατ᾽ οὐσίαν κρυφίου παντελῶς οὐκ ἐξίσταται· ὁπότε καί αὐτός ὁ τρόπος, καθ᾽ ὅν θέλων μετέχεται, μένει διηνεκῶς τοῖς πᾶσιν ἀνέκφαντος. Οὐκοῦν, ὥσπερ ὁ Θεός θέλων μετέχεται, καθ᾽ ὅν αὐτός οἶδε τρόπον· οὕτω καί θέλων ὑπέστησε τά μετέχοντα, καθ᾽ ὅν αὐτός ἐπίσταται λόγον, δι᾽ ὑπερβάλλουσαν ἀγαθότητος δύναμιν.

19. Confessor, *De Char.* III.46 (PG 90: 1029CD), 90: Οὐχ ὡς προσδεόμενός τινος ὁ ὑπερπλήρης Θεός παρήγαγεν εἰς τό εἶναι τά γεγονότα, ἀλλ᾽ ἵνα αὐτά μέν αὐτοῦ ἀναλόγως μετέχοντα ἀπολαύσῃ, αὐτός δέ εὐφρανθῇ ἐπί τοῖς ἔργοις αὐτοῦ, ὁρῶν αὐτά εὐφραινόμενα καί τόν ἀκόρεστον ἀκορέστως ἀεί κορεννύμενα.

totality of things that can be known in relationship to other things," Maximus emphasizes that God cannot be apprehended as the fullness or totality of his attributes that we have opportunity to experience. By being combined with the cataphatic statements about God, these expressions suggest that by participating or sharing some or the totality of divine attributes granted to human beings through grace they do not exhaust their participation in God. Moreover, stating that "creatures participate in God" and that "one *Logos* is many *logoi* and many *logoi* are One," Maximus points out that only through the direct participation of created being in the *Logos* of God, they may participate in some or the totality of his attributes. According to Maximus, the degree of participation in *Logos* and consequently in his attributes is proportional or analogous to the capacity of created beings to be filled by the divine grace.

The second passage from *Ambiguum* 10, where Maximus gives indication that Christ the *Logos* is unparticipated, develops along the same lines:

> Hearing of the bosom of Abraham, we think of God made manifest to us in the flesh as one of the seed of Abraham, truly the provider of all to all who are worthy of his grace in proportion of the quality and the quantity of each one's virtue. For he divides himself indivisibly among different pastures through the natural undivided being of unity, and is not shared out by those who participate in any way whatever. Again through the different worth of the participants he is manifested paradoxically separately to each other who share in accordance with the ineffable unity (something understood by reason).[20]

Here again Maximus underlines the fact that by participating in Christ we do not have a part of him, but the fullness of him. For this reason, Christ is indivisible because he is still *one* in the many participants. Maximus repeats this in a more elaborate form in the *Ambiguum* 22, where, among other things, he claims that God's being is present *as a whole* in an undivided manner in each thing.[21] The paradox, Maximus refers to, is that by being fully and not partially in every participant, Christ reveals himself

20. Confessor, *Amb.* 10 (PG 91: 1172BC), 135: Κόλπους δέ Ἀβράαμ ἀκούοντας τόν ἐκ σπέρματος Ἀβράαμ τόν κατά σάρκα ἡμῖν ἐπιφανέντα νοήσομεν Θεόν, τόν ὄντως πάντων χορηγικόν καί πᾶσι τοῖς ἀξίοις τῆς χάριτος ἀναλόγως τῇ κατ᾽ ἀρετήν ἑκάστου ποιότητί τε καί ποσότητι, οἷόν τινας διαφόρως νομάς ἀμερῶς ἑαυτόν ἐπιμερίζοντα καί τοῖς μετέχουσιν οὐδ᾽ ὁπωσοῦν συνδιατεμνόμενον, διά τήν κατά φύσιν ἄτμητον ὀντότητα τῆς ἑνότητος, κἄμπαλιν διά τήν διάφορον ἀξίαν τῶν μετεχόντων ταῖς μετοχαῖς παραδόξως καθ᾽ ἕνωσιν ἄρρητον ἀφοριστικῶς ἐπιφαινόμενον (οἶδεν ὁ λόγος).

21. Confessor, *Amb.* 22 (PG 91: 1257A): . . . τόν Θεόν ἀμερῶς ὅλον δι᾽ ἑαυτῆς ἐν ἑκάστῳ . . . .

distinctly to each of them in proportion (ἀναλόγως) to their worthiness or natural receptive power.

The reasons why I was inspired to give an alternative interpretation of these passages are mainly based on other passages, which are written in a liturgical and eschatological context. The first of these passages comes from *Ad Thalassium*:

> The salvation of souls is the end of the faith (1 Pet. 1.9), and the end of the faith is the true revelation of the object of faith. The true revelation of the object of faith is coinherence (interpenetration) of the object of faith in every faithful proportional to his faith, and the interpenetration of the Object of the faith is the return of the faithful to the beginning at the end. The return of the faithful to the beginning at the end is the fulfillment of the desire, and the fulfillment of the desire is the ever-moving rest of those who desire around the desired one. The ever-moving rest is the permanent and unceasing pleasure of the desired, and the permanent and unceasing pleasure of Him is participation in supernatural Divine goods. The participation in the supernatural Divine goods is likeness of the participants to the participated, and the likeness of the participants to the participated is the actualization of the expected identity of the participants with the participated. The actualized identity of the participants with the participated is deification of those who are worthy of deification. The deification is circumscription of all times and ages and the circumference and limit of those which are in time and age.[22]

The whole eschatology of Maximus is concentrated in this quotation. Maximus uses the language of participation together with the terms

---

22. Confessor, *Ad Thal.* 59 (CCSG 7, 22): Σωτηρία δὲ τῶν ψυχῶν κυρίως ἐστὶ τὸ τέλος τῆς πίστεως· τέλος δὲ πίστεώς ἐστιν ἡ τοῦ πιστευθέντος ἀληθὴς ἀποκάλυψις· ἀληθὴς δὲ τοῦ πιστευθέντος ἐστὶν ἀποκάλυψις ἡ κατὰ ἀναλογίαν τῆς ἐν ἑκάστῳ πίστεως ἄρρητος τοῦ πεπιστευμένου περιχώρησις· περιχώρησις δὲ τοῦ πεπιστευμένου καθέστηκεν ἡ πρὸς τὴν ἀρχὴν κατὰ τὸ τέλος τῶν πεπιστευκότων ἐπάνοδος· ἡ δὲ πρὸς τὴν οἰκείαν ἀρχὴν κατὰ τὸ τέλος τῶν πεπιστευκότων ἐπάνοδός ἐστιν ἡ τῆς ἐφέσεως πλήρωσις· ἐφέσεως δὲ πλήρωσίς ἐστιν ἡ περὶ τὸ ἐφετὸν τῶν ἐφιεμένων ἀεικίνητος στάσις· ἀεικίνητος δὲ στάσις ἐστὶν ἡ τοῦ ἐφετοῦ διηνεκής τε καὶ ἀδιάστατος ἀπόλαυσις· ἀπόλαυσις δὲ διηνεκὴς καὶ ἀδιάστατος ἡ τῶν ὑπὲρ φύσιν θείων καθέστηκε μέθεξις· μέθεξις δὲ τῶν ὑπὲρ φύσιν θείων ἐστὶν ἡ πρὸς τὸ μετεχόμενον τῶν μετεχόντων ὁμοίωσις· ἡ δὲ πρὸς τὸ μετεχόμενον τῶν μετεχόντων ὁμοίωσίς ἐστιν ἡ κατ' ἐνέργειαν πρὸς αὐτὸ τὸ μετεχόμενον τῶν μετεχόντων δι' ὁμοιότητος ἐνδεχομένη ταυτότης· ἡ δὲ τῶν μετεχόντων ἐνδεχομένη κατ' ἐνέργειαν δι' ὁμοιότητος πρὸς τὸ μετεχόμενον ταυτότης ἐστὶν ἡ θέωσις τῶν ἀξιουμένων θεώσεως· ἡ δὲ θέωσίς ἐστι καθ' ὑπογραφῆς λόγον πάντων τῶν χρόνων καὶ τῶν αἰώνων καὶ τῶν ἐν χρόνῳ καὶ αἰῶνι περιοχὴ καὶ πέρας· The English translation is mine.

of likeness and identity. By participating in the supernatural divine goods, participants acquire the likeness not of the supernatural goods themselves, but of the one who possesses these goods as his attributes, that is the *Logos* of God, Christ himself. Therefore, the participation in the divine goods is the participation in the likeness of God. By attaining identity with God, the human beings also attain identity with his attributes or supernatural divine goods and not the other way around. The divine attributes such as goodness, life, immortality, simplicity, immutability, infinity cannot be attained by the human being's natural disposition or fitness. Quite the opposite, the human beings acquire them only in relationship with Christ, and by God's grace. This aspect is confirmed by a quotation from Maximus' *Mystagogia* 24.

> By the "One is holy" and what follows, we have a grace and fa-
> miliarity, which unites us to God himself. By Holy Communion
> of the spotless and life-giving mysteries we are given fellowship
> and identity with him by participation in likeness, by which
> man is deemed worthy from man to become God.[23]

The liturgical context of this quotation corresponds to the eschatological context of the previous. Before turning to the more in-depth analysis of this passage, let us make its context clearer. First, it is important to notice that the *Mystagogia* is the work of Maximus, where he interprets symbolically the liturgical moments from an eschatological perspective. Thus, from the point when the bishop descends from the throne and the dismissal of the catechumens that signifies the second coming of Christ, everything happens in the kingdom of God. The climax of the liturgy is the Eucharist, which signifies a complete identity with Christ. Now, what does "One is holy" mean for Maximus? "One is Holy, one is Lord Jesus Christ, to the glory of God the Father." "Amen" is chanted by the liturgical community immediately after the bishop or the priest comes out from the altar with the consecrated gifts (bread and wine as the body and the blood of Christ), and it is a reply to his words "The Holy Gifts to the Holy People." This statement is a kind of denial that the holy people and the holy gifts are holy by virtue of, for example, moral and virtuous life or by virtue of a ritual. But, at the same time it is an affirmation of the holiness of both the people and the gifts

---

23. Ibid., *Myst.* 24 (PG 91: 704D), 207: Διὰ δὲ τοῦ «Εἶς ἅγιος» καὶ τῶν ἑξῆς τὴν πρὸς αὐτὸν τὸν Θεὸν ἑνοποιὸν χάριν καὶ οἰκειότητα. Διὰ δὲ τῆς ἁγίας μεταλήψεως τῶν ἀχράντων καὶ ζωοποιῶν μυστηρίων τὴν πρὸς αὐτὸν κατὰ μέθεξιν ἐνδεχομένην δι᾽ ὁμοιότητος κοινωνίαν τε καὶ ταυτότητα, δι᾽ ἧς γενέσθαι θεὸς ἐξ ἀνθρώπου καταξιοῦται ὁ ἄνθρωπος.

by virtue of their relationship with Christ. Therefore, the statement "One is holy" refers to the sole source of holiness, which is Christ.

A few chapters earlier, in *Mystagogia* 21, Maximus offers a more elaborate interpretation of the profession "One is Holy:"

> The profession "One is Holy" and what follows, which is voiced by the people at the end of the mystical service, represents the gathering and union beyond reason and understanding which will take place between those who have been mystically and wisely initiated by God and the mysterious oneness of the divine simplicity in the incorruptible age of the spiritual world.[24]

Maximus once more repeats that "the mode of participation" remains concealed to the human rational and intellectual powers since the gathering and union attained between God and his people is beyond reason and understanding. By referring to the "mysterious oneness of the divine simplicity" Maximus clarifies that the union of human beings is not only with the manifold of supernatural divine goods, but primarily with the one God in his simplicity. Only by virtue of participation in the likeness of God, we participate in the supernatural divine goods such as goodness, eternity, or infinity. Therefore, Maximus explains that the chant "One is Holy" signifies the grace that unites us with God. Holiness, goodness, eternity, and other gifts of divine grace make us participants of the divine likeness.

Maximus' definition of the Holy Communion from *Mystagogia* 24 corresponds with the definition from *Mystagogia* 21, where he describes the whole process in the following words:

> . . . as the climax of everything, comes the distribution of the sacrament, which transforms into itself and renders similar to the causal good by grace and participation those who worthily share in it.[25]

Thus, those who are worthy of receiving Holy Communion transform into and become similar to Christ by attaining fellowship and identity with

---

24. Confessor, *Myst.* 21 (PG 91: 696D–697A), 203: Ἡ δὲ κατὰ τὸ τέλος τῆς μυστικῆς ἱερουργίας παρὰ παντὸς τοῦ λαοῦ γινομένη τοῦ «Εἷς ἅγιος» καὶ τῶν ἑξῆς ὁμολογία τὴν ὑπὲρ λόγον καὶ νοῦν πρὸς τὸ ἓν τῆς θείας ἁπλότητος κρύφιον γενησομένην τῶν μυστικῶς τε καὶ σοφῶς κατὰ Θεὸν τετελεσμένων συναγωγήν τε καὶ ἕνωσιν δηλοῖ, ἐν τῷ ἀφθάρτῳ τῶν νοητῶν αἰῶνι καθ' ὃν τῆς ἀφανοῦς καὶ ὑπεραρρήτου δόξης τὸ φῶς ἐνοπτεύοντες τῆς μακαρίας μετὰ τῶν ἄνω δυνάμεων, καὶ αὐτοὶ δεκτικοὶ γίγνονται καθαρότητος·

25. Confessor, *Myst.* 21 (PG 91: 697A), 203: μεθ' ἥν, ὡς τέλος πάντων, ἡ τοῦ μυστηρίου μετάδοσις γίνεται μεταποιοῦσα πρὸς ἑαυτὴν καὶ ὁμοίους τῷ κατ' αἰτίαν ἀγαθῷ κατὰ χάριν καὶ μέθεξιν ἀποφαίνουσα τοὺς ἀξίως μεταλαμβάνοντας. English translation in Berthold, *Selected Writings*, 203.

him by participation in likeness. The whole logic of Maximus' reasoning is as follows: by participating in divine attributes we participate in the likeness of God. At this moment Maximus still uses the language of participation, because this is the complete identity with God, which has not been achieved. The complete identity with God is something that ought to happen in the future kingdom, and it is symbolically revealed at every Eucharistic liturgy by receiving the Holy Mysteries. While participating in the likeness of God in this life we cannot achieve full identity with the divine. The reason for this is that we are limited by our natural capacities or by our natural *logos*, which determines our fitness and receptivity to receive grace to a certain extent. Therefore, the limitations imposed to the *oros* of being by its *logos* causes the limitation in power and potency to receive God fully or to participate in him perfectly. The participation of the rational being in God in this life is ended when the rational being reaches its natural consummation. Maximus describes this process as a kind of departure from oneself. The rational being reaches the rest (στάσις) of his natural movement, when he is fully embraced by God.

> It [i.e., the rational being] no longer wants anything from itself, for it knows itself to be wholly embraced, and intentionally and by choice it wholly receives the life-giving delimitation. When it is wholly embraced it no longer wishes to be embraced at all by itself but is sufficed by that which embraces it. In the same way air is illuminated by light and iron is wholly inflamed by fire, as is the case with other things of this sort.[26]

The new state of the rational beings is characterized by two features. Firstly, the rational beings, being surrounded by the divine, experience a certain transformation of their natural limit. By being circumscribed by God, the limits of rational being are terminated. In this sense, the rational being is not any more limited to receive the divine grace according to its natural power. Maximus claims this once more in another passage from the same *Ambiguum*:

> It is absolutely necessary that everything will cease its wilful movement toward something else when the ultimate beauty that satisfies our desire appears. In so far as we are able we will

---

26. Confessor, *Amb.* 7 (PG 91: 1073D–76A), 51: . . . ἑκουσίως ὅλον κατὰ προαίρεσιν τὴν σωτήριον περιγραφὴν δεχόμενον, ἵν᾿ ὅλον ὅλῳ ποιωθῇ τῷ περιγράφοντι, ὡς μηδ᾿ ὅλως λοιπόν βούλεσθαι ἐξ ἑαυτοῦ αὐτό ἐκεῖνο ὅλον γνωρίζεσθαι δύνασθαι τό περιγραφόμενον, ἀλλ᾿ ἐκ τοῦ περιγράφοντος· ὡς ἀὴρ δι᾿ ὅλου πεφωτισμένος φωτί, καί πυρί σίδηρος, ὅλος ὅλῳ πεπυρακτωμένος, ἤ εἴ τι ἄλλο τῶν τοιούτων ἐστίν.

participate without being restricted, as it were, being uncontainably contained.[27]

The power of created beings to participate in divinity will be extended to the degree necessary to accommodate the infinite God fully in themselves, by containing the grace of God infinitely. Paradoxically, God who, by his nature is infinite and uncontained, is contained by us because of our infinity.

The second feature of the transformed being is passivity in receiving divine grace to infinite extent. Maximus describes the new state by the metaphors of the light-air and fire-iron, frequently used in Christology. Just as the light and fire play an active role in illuminating the air and heating the iron, the role of God in deification is active and the rational beings receive divine grace passively in the same way in which the air and the fire receive the light and the heat passively. Maximus affirms the passivity of the rational beings in other works. He clearly states this in *Ad Thalassium* 22:

> Existing here and now, we arrive at the end of the ages as active agents and reach the end of the exertion of our power and activity. But in the ages to come we shall undergo by grace the transformation unto deification and no longer be active but passive.[28]

The same example of fire and light offers more conclusions about the future state. Firstly, the rational beings gain the divine attributes just as the air emits light and iron radiates heat. Therefore, it is established a full identity of the human being with God, because all the divine attributes are fully adopted, without any remains. At this stage, it is no longer possible to use the language of participation, because participation refers to a certain share in something, while here the human being does not have a share of God, rather the human being receives God fully, becoming god himself. The only distinction is that the beings are divine only by grace and not by nature or essence.

Secondly, while the identification of the human being with the divine is something achieved, the beings of the human and the divine are not

27. Confessor, *Amb.* 7 (PG 91: 1076D), 51: Ἀνάγκη γάρ πᾶσα τῆς κατ' ἔφεσιν τά πάντα περί τι ἄλλο παύσασθαι ἐξουσιαστικῆς κινήσεως, τοῦ ἐσχάτου φανέντος ὀρεκτοῦ καί μετεχομένου, καί ἀναλόγως τῇ τῶν μετεχόντων δυνάμει ἀχωρήτως, ἵν' οὕτως εἴπω, χωρουμένου· English translation in Blowers and Wilken, *On the Cosmic Mystery*, 53.

28. Confessor, *Ad Thal.* 22, 141: Ἐνταῦθα τοίνυν ὄντες, ὡς ποιοῦντες εἰς αἰώνων τέλη καταντῶμεν, πέρας λαμβανούσης ἡμῶν κατά τό ποιεῖν τῆς δυνάμεώς τε καί τῆς ἐνεργείας. Ἐν δὲ τοῖς αἰῶσι τοῖς ἐπερχομένοις, πάσχοντες τὴν πρὸς τὸ θεοῦσθαι χάριτι μεταποίησιν, οὐ ποιοῦμεν ἀλλὰ πάσχομεν, καί διά τοῦτο οὐ λήγομεν θεουργούμενοι.

confused because the distinctiveness of the natures is preserved. Thus, the illuminated air is still air, just as the red-hot iron is still iron. It is important to emphasize this aspect, since the perfect likeness of air with light and iron with fire does not mean that the differences are abolished. As Perl remarked, the participation in likeness of created beings with God needs to be understood not simply as resemblance, but as "the combination of ontological identity and difference."[29] In Maximus' examples, while the identity of air and iron with light and fire is demonstrated in the ability of air to emanate light and iron to radiate fire, both air and iron remain different in nature from light and fire.

It is important to stress here one more aspect of this union-in-difference, which deals with the preserved differences of the manifold of the created order in the union with the One. It seems to me that one of the reasons for Tollefsen's earlier denial of the participation in God as the highest principle is due to Perl's identification of the *Logos* of God with the highest universal, in whom all the *logoi* are contained.[30] I completely agree with Tollefsen's critique of Perl's claim that the *Logos* cannot serve as the highest universal. Perl's claims that Christ unites all creatures by being common to all like the species of horse unites the individual horses by being common to all of them neglects a very important aspect of Christ's identity with each of the creatures. If Christ is identical with the creatures as the highest universal, then in order to attain likeness with him all the creatures have to restrain from their particular differences. However, this is hardly Maximus' point. In my view, his point here is that the beings participate in Christ by perfecting their gifts like being, well-being or goodness, eternal-well being or life and wisdom by which they resemble the image and likeness of God. All of these gifts are implemented differently in each particular creature depending on its *logos* and on its natural fitness. As Maximus observes in *Ambiguum* 22, the mystery of participation, which is beyond reason, lies in the power of *Logos* to be in each *logos* of each thing in itself and in all the *logoi* together.[31]

To sum up, the passages where Maximus claims that the highest principle or the *Logos* of God is unparticipated should be read in a strictly apophatic context. They also illustrate Maximus' intention to preserve the transcendent nature of the *Logos* of God in spite of both the incarnation of his wills as the *logoi* in the created beings and his incarnation in the God-man Jesus Christ. I have argued in favor of three different modes of participation in God, which enable us to understand better the dynamism

---

29. Perl, "Methexis," 140.

30. Tollefsen, *The Christocentric Cosmology*, 90; Perl, "Methexis," 140.

31. Confessor, *Amb.* 22 (PG 91: 1257B).

of participation. The first mode of participation in God is mainly restricted to the participation in his *logoi* or wills about the created universe and each particular being within. The second mode of participation made possible by the incarnation of God is participation in his church as his body. Since the liturgy, for Maximus, has iconic character and it represents both the anticipation and the proclamation of the future splendor, the participation in God through the Eucharist is just a foretaste of the way of participating in God in the heavenly kingdom. The participation in God or, better said, the identity with God in likeness, represents the third and the last mode of participation. Thus, the concept of gradual participation in Maximus differs from that of Proclus, in several aspects. First, in Maximus the created beings are able to participate in the highest reality. Second, the participation of created beings in the *Logos* of God is by activities of both God and human beings. Finally, in the ultimate union with God in the heavenly kingdom, the created beings are not reduced to the "manifestations" of the impersonal One like in Proclus, but they fully preserve their natural identity and at the same time attain divine identity.

14

Christ and the Contemplation of Nature in Maximus the Confessor's *Ambigua to John*

Joshua Lollar

Maximus the Confessor gave what would become the decisive articulation of Byzantine Christology through the course of the controversies over the activities and wills in Christ in the seventh century. The technicalities of this Christology, which were defined later in Maximus' life, derive ultimately from his profound philosophy of nature, a philosophy that was a central aspect of Maximus' thinking throughout all his works. As such, I would like to make a few remarks here about Maximus' vision of Christ and the contemplation of nature—θεωρία φυσική—as he expresses it in his *Ambigua to John*, his collection of speculative chapters of commentary on various difficult passages from Gregory the Theologian.[1] These chapters, I argue, have as their overarching concern the articulation of the meaning of philosophy and, more precisely, the demonstration of the scope of the contemplation of nature within the philosophical life as Maximus understood it. As he says in the tenth *Ambiguum*, "creation, by virtue of its own *logos*, teaches ethical, natural, and theological philosophy from its composition of

---

1. Cf. Lollar, "'To See into the Life of Things,'" for a thorough treatment of the contemplation of nature in Maximus and his predecessors.

heaven, earth, and the things in the midst of them," so that the "thorough inspection of creation" itself yields insight into philosophy as a whole.[2] It is within this framework that I would like to show some of the main features of how Maximus thinks about nature and its contemplation with reference to Christ and the economy of salvation.

I.

The term θεωρία, "contemplation," as Maximus uses it, refers to a number of different but related phenomena. Ears accustomed to the Aristotelian understanding of philosophy will hear in θεωρία that mode of philosophical endeavor that is other than πρᾶξις, the life of study and reflection as opposed to moral and political action. This understanding is present in Maximus though he goes to great lengths to articulate the inseparability of theoretical and practical philosophy. With respect to θεωρία itself, and not as considered in relation to πρᾶξις, Maximus uses the term to refer to the speculative and somewhat open-ended interpretation of Scripture, the natural world, or the writings of the fathers, in short, to the activity of a philosopher or scholar. It may also take on a narrower meaning still and refer to the intellect's encounter with true being as the prelude to the ultimate encounter with the God beyond intellect and being. The term φύσις, usually translated as "nature," likewise has a polyvalent meaning for Maximus. It may mean what we might call the "essence" of a thing and in this case is roughly equivalent to οὐσία. It may also be taken in its more etymological sense (φύω meaning to cause to spring forth or grow, as in a plant—φυτόν) and refer to a thing precisely as something that has "come into being." Third, and related to this second meaning, φύσις as "nature" may be taken to refer to the cosmos as a whole, as the whole of what has come into being. Taken together, the phrase "θεωρία φυσική"—"natural contemplation"—refers to the systematic study, but also to the more devotional apprehension, of the things of the world and of the world as a whole. It is directed to the world as characterized by generation, growth, change, and movement, and seeks to discern and account for the coherence underlying the instability of natural phenomena.

For Maximus, the "world" as κόσμος refers, as it does for ancient Greeks generally, to the universe as an ordered whole (κοσμεῖν: "to arrange, set in order, adorn"), but this order, which is the manifestation of the principles and purposes (λόγοι) of the divine mind, has come to manifestation as creation (κτίσις) and so is nearly always thought of by Maximus in terms of its finitude and dependence upon divine reality. Moreover, Maximus'

---

2. Confessor, *Amb.*10 (PG 91: 1136C4–9).

analysis of the "world" or "creation" will often take one aspect of the world—principally the human being—as a synecdoche for the whole, for Maximus' understanding of the doctrine of creation is bound to his vision of the incarnation of Christ. As he says in his interpretation of the Israelite tabernacle (Exod 25:8–9), "the tent of testimony is the mysterious economy of the incarnation of the Word of God," but it is also "the image of the whole creation, both intellectual and sensual, . . . the image of sensual nature alone, . . . of human nature alone, . . . and also of soul alone,"[3] and more famously, "the Word of God who is God wishes for the mystery of His embodiment to be actualized always and in everything."[4] World, humanity, and incarnate Christ are inseparably linked in Maximus' thought and are at the heart of his reflections on the contemplation of nature.

This panel has been devoted to "philosophy and metaphysics" and this inevitably raises the question for us of how Maximus the philosopher relates to Maximus the theologian and I am indeed broaching this question directly by including the particularity of Christ and the general concept of nature in the title of this paper. But we should be aware, from the beginning, of the fact that, for Maximus, φιλοσοφία as "devotion to wisdom" is nothing other than φιλοθεΐα; the love of wisdom is the love of the divine, the love of God.[5] Thus, on the one hand, the delimitation of a theological from a strictly philosophical methodology is not straightforwardly applicable to Maximus. For example, a typical way of distinguishing between philosophy and theology would be to assert that theology is founded upon the church's tradition of the study of the revelation of Scripture, whereas philosophy is founded upon the exercise of human reason as it reflects upon itself and the world. In Maximus' *Ambigua to John*, however, Scripture and the world are two manifestations of the *same* reality, of the wise providence of God that governs the world according to the law of his goodness.[6]

This is not to say that theology is not related to meditation upon Scripture for Maximus; far from it. It is to say, however, that theology is also related to meditation upon the world. Likewise, philosophy as the practice of asceticism, the knowledge of beings, and union with the divine is mediated through both the cosmic order and the revelation of Scripture. On the other hand, it is clear in the *Ambigua to John* that the categories of human thought that obtain in the world do not obtain with respect to God, at least when

---

3. Confessor, *Amb.* 61 (PG 91: 1385C13–1388A6).

4. Confessor, *Amb.* 7 (PG 91: 1084C14–D2).

5. Confessor, *Amb.* 37 (PG 91: 1296B11–12): φιλοσοφία, ταὐτὸν δέ ἐστιν εἰπεῖν φιλοθεΐα.

6. Cf. Confessor, *Amb.* 10 (PG 91: 1129B3–6); *Amb.* 37 (PG 91: 1293B1–8).

Maximus is speaking, within apophatic theology, of the divinity "beyond being." However, he will also say that the essence of the world itself is ineffable and unknowable.[7] Thus, the relationship of kataphatic and apophatic theology in the *Ambiga to John* is a complicated one.

Maximus' three well-known stages of spiritual development—the practical or ascetical life, the contemplation of nature, and mystical theology—are mentioned throughout the *Ambigua to John* as governing specific, if not perfectly discrete, domains of human life so that, while a typically modern division between philosophy and theology is irrelevant to Maximus, there yet remains a distinction between ethics, the contemplation of nature, and mystical theology. But these three are so thoroughly implicated in one another that any attempt to define what Maximus is doing when he distinguishes them is inevitably frustrated from the start. While there is a clear hierarchy that leads from the ethical through the natural to the theological in Maximus, he tends to give a "mixed transmission (τὴν μικτὴν παράδοσιν)" of the various aspects of philosophy in a way reminiscent of some of the Stoics.[8]

Sherwood dates the composition of the *Ambigua to John* to the years 628–30 CE, when Maximus was residing in North Africa.[9] Maximus writes in the prefatory letter to the *Ambigua* that the text is based upon discussions he had at the monastery of Cyzicus with an Archbishop John and his monks: "when I received your honorable epistle ordering me to send you a report set down in writing of our discussion concerning each of the chapters of the orations of St. Gregory the Theologian that were perplexing to us, over which we labored when we were together . . . ."[10] Generally speaking, the *Ambigua to John* belong, like Maximus' *Questions to Thalassius* and *Questions and Doubts*, to the genre of *erotapokriseis*, or "Questions and Responses." A difficulty (ἀπορία) from a traditional text—or simply a traditional difficulty—is posed, and then an answer resolving, or at least clarifying, the question is given. This genre of intellectual discourse, which followed in the mode of the Alexandrian commentators on Aristotle of the fifth and sixth centuries, was well established in Maximus' day, both in the philosophical schools and amongst Christian theologians, though it appears to have been more popular amongst the Christians.[11]

---

7. Cf. Confessor, *Amb.* 17 (PG 91: 1229B8–12).

8. Cf. Diogenes Laertes VII.39–41 (Long and Sedley, *The Hellenistic Philosophers*, 26B).

9. Sherwood, *An Annotated Date-List*, 31.

10. Confessor, *Amb.* (PG 91: 1064B6–10).

11 Some of this discussion comes from my *Ambigua to Thomas, Second Letter to Thomas* (Turnhout: Brepols, 2010), 17–20. For a thorough discussion of the genre, see

In general, collections of *erotapokriseis* were arranged in no particular order, and the collections themselves tend to present an artificial sense of unity, since in many cases, particular questions and answers were conceived and written independently of each other, though there would often be a certain coherence with respect to subject matter. Amongst Christian authors, where the genre was especially common in exercises of scriptural interpretation, a certain order and coherence of collections of *erotapokriseis* can be discerned and was due to the dependence of the order of questions on the structure of the scriptural narrative, but even here we find examples of apparently random collections of questions and answers.[12]

While Maximus' collection of *erotapokriseis* that have come to be called the *Ambigua* (Ἄπορα) *to John* do generally fit the description of the genre just given, I argue that Maximus' *Ambigua to John* are more purposeful in their collection than would have been typical of collections of *erotapokriseis*; Maximus, I claim, is using the difficulties in Gregory as an occasion to articulate his own vision of Christian spiritual philosophy and of the role of the contemplation of nature within that philosophy. The *Ambigua* are a sprawling, repetitive, complicated collection of short and long speculative essays—some of which read like notes for a handbook—that raise nearly as many questions as they answer, but despite the unsystematic presentation of the *Ambigua* as a whole, there is, I think, a general, if vague, sense of coherence within the overall architecture of its collection of chapters.

I divide the *Ambigua* into five major sections and a conclusion:

1. *Ambigua* 6–8[13] give an initial account of the relationship between soul and body and a foundational analysis of the passibility of human nature. These three *Ambigua* comment on a series of three quotations from Gregory's oration *On the Love of the Poor* (*Or.* 14), and through the course of Maximus' exposition, which is conceptually continuous through these first three chapters, Maximus establishes the nature of human being as a mixture of matter and spirit, which means, initially, that the human being finds himself in perplexity. As an explication of the fundamental experience of human affectivity or πάθος, it provides a foundational analysis of human being in the world for which pas-

---

Dörrie and Dörries, "Erotapokriseis," 342–70 (Maximus at 359–61). Cf. also Daley, "Boethius' Theological Tracts," 158–91, especially 163–76; and Öhler, "Aristotle in Byzantium," 133–46. Earlier pagan examples of the genre would be Porphyry's *Homeric Questions* (Ὁμηρικὰ ζητήματα); Aristotle's own fragmentary Ἀπορήματα Ὁμηρικά; or Plutarch's *Platonic Questions* (Πλατωνικὰ ζητήματα).

12. See Bardy, "La littérature patristique," 210–36, 341–69, 515–37; and also (42), 328–52.

13. Confessor, *Amb.* 1–5 constitute an independent work, the *Ambigua to Thomas*.

sibility and the distress of living between time and eternity and matter and spirit are the basic experiences of human life. The human being is estranged from the world and the body and yet finds himself engulfed by what surrounds him (περὶ αὐτόν) so that he is in danger of forgetting his divine source and final end.[14]

2. *Ambigua* 9–22 deal with theoretical issues concerning the nature of philosophy and expound Maximus' vision for the philosophic life as a response to the passibility he analyzes in *Ambigua* 6–8. He studies the nature of language in *Amb.* 9, 16, 17, 18, 20, and 22; the relationship between praxis and contemplation in *Amb.* 10; and the nature of the soul in *Amb.* 10, 15, and 19.

3. *Ambigua* 23–30 are concerned with questions pertaining to the use of language with respect to the relationship between God and the world (*Amb.* 23), that of the Father and Son (*Amb.* 24–28), and the titles, or divine names, that are given to the Son (*Amb.* 30).

4. *Ambigua* 31–44 speak of the various aspects of the economy of salvation as the renewal of nature and the contemplation of nature in Christ.

5. *Ambigua* 45–68 give scriptural examples of responses to the coming of the Word and the renewal of nature in Christ.

6. Conclusion: *Ambiguum* 71[15] serves as a sort of epilogue to the collection of *Ambigua* and, commenting on a line from Gregory's poetry in which the Word "plays in all kinds of forms," places all of Maximus' speculation about the cosmos within the domain of this "play." It thus returns to a central theme of the first section (*Amb.* 6–8), where the world is considered as pedagogy for the soul, and in this way completes the cycle of Maximus' reflections.

I emphasize that this scheme is very general and is intended simply to mark certain basic divisions in the collection of chapters. Maximus circles around many of the same themes through the course of the *Ambigua*, speaking of human passibility, the nature of praxis and contemplation, the interpretation of Scripture, and the economy of salvation across the divisions of the broad sections I have identified and there are most definitely a number of chapters that have no significant relationship to the ones around

---

14. Cf. *Amb.* 8 (PG 91: 1104A2–8).

15. *Amb.* 69 makes a pedestrian point about the difference between a complete and incomplete sentence, and *Amb.* 70 makes a general remark about Gregory's use of rhetoric in his exhortation to virtue. *Amb.* 70 is not entirely unrelated to *Amb.* 71 with its emphasis on the Word's adaptation to the diverse members of his "audience" for their instruction.

them (or are simply insignificant) and could have more naturally been placed elsewhere; they have been placed where they are simply because the quotation they are explaining comes next in the sequence of the oration Maximus happens to be interpreting. Nevertheless, this organization of the chapters into a few large groups does emerge from the study of the *Ambigua* as a whole and it indicates the basic scope of Maximus' concerns in the text.

II.

So much for the scope and architecture of the *Ambigua to John*. I would like now to devote the remainder of this essay to a brief analysis of how Maximus understands Christ and the contemplation of nature in a series of later chapters in the *Ambigua*, for it is here that Maximus speaks of the center of his theology, the *Theos-Logos* himself, in terms of his central philosophical concern, nature and its contemplation.

In *Ambiguum* 45, Maximus gives a contemplation of human nature in its original state and through the course of the text Maximus articulates the place of the contemplation of nature within his vision of philosophy. He begins with a quotation from Gregory's *Second Oration on Pascha* (*Or.* 45) in which Gregory says that the first human being was "naked in simplicity and in artless life, having no veil or defense (πρόβλημα) . . . ."[16] In his interpretation of Gregory's text, Maximus takes the first human being's experience of the world as the paradigmatic example of the contemplation of nature. The "nakedness" of the first human being is an indication that his contemplation of nature was not characterized by multiplicity (τῆς περὶ φύσιν ποικίλης θεωρίας καὶ γνώσεως) in that he did not need first to think in terms of the phenomena that appear to the senses in order to come to an understanding of divine things (τῆς ἐπ' αἰσθήσεσι τῶν φαινομένων διανοίας πρὸς κατανόησιν τῶν θείων), for he had as his simple covering (προβολή) only the uniform, simple, and constitutive virtue and knowledge that pertain to the things after God.[17]

It is the complex form of contemplation that was originally excluded from the human experience of the world. The first human being, in both virtue and contemplation, existed in a state of simplicity and immediate apprehension of reality. In addition, he was "outside of the variegated method of asceticism and virtue (τῆς περὶ πρᾶξιν καὶ ἀρετὴν πολυτρόπου μεθοδείας ὑπάρχων ἐκτός), but rather possessed the undefiled *logoi* of the virtues as a

---

16. Nazianzen, *Oration* 45.8.

17. Confessor, *Amb.* 45 (PG 91: 1356A11–B1).

habit (κατὰ τὴν ἕξιν)."[18] This sort of immediacy of knowledge and virtue is reminiscent of the way in which the saints achieve the highest levels of philosophy "without a struggle (ἀμαχῶς)" as Maximus describes it in *Ambiguum* 10.

Indeed, the focus of this *Ambiguum* is not primarily on a hypothetical state of Adam before the fall; as Maximus says in *Ambiguum* 42, the first created human being was moved towards evil and emptied out the power of his nature "together with coming into being (ἅμα τῷ γενέσθαι)."[19] The "original" state of humanity is conceived by Maximus first of all as a potentiality. The original work of mediation that was placed before the first human being, which Maximus discusses in *Ambiguum* 41, is all placed in the subjunctive or the optative in that text: "that he may acquire (λάβῃ) God;" "he would have made (ποιήσειεν) one earth;" "he would have made (ποιήσειεν) one sensuous creation;" "he would have made (ποιήσῃ) one creation;" "he would have shown (δείξειε) [the uncreated and the created] to be one."[20] The first human being of course did not fulfill this potentiality; it is in the Word-made-human that we see the fulfillment of the original intention for creation.

Maximus interprets the "loss" of this "original state" in Adam's transgression as his failure to contemplate the world according to its true nature as sustained by divine reality. Adam "fashioned a living death for himself," because, as Maximus speculates, he thought life depended upon food and the flux of material bodies so that he took and ate the fruit of the tree of the knowledge of good and evil rather than relying upon "the bread that comes down from heaven" (John 6:33–35). In this way, Adam became the forefather of those who fall into the contemplation of "fantasies that have not been created (οὐ ποιητέων), are unnatural (ἀφυσίκων), and non-intellectual (ἀνοήτων)."[21]

In contrast to the fall of Adam's understanding, in which he mistakenly invested the flux of material existence with an autonomous life-sustaining force, a true contemplation of nature reveals that the mixture and flow of bodies into each other actually demonstrates the finitude and corruptibility of the world:

For, by thoroughly inspecting the present world in a systematic way (ἐπιστημόνως), as much as is possible, and having wisely unfurled the conceptually enfolded *logos* (τὸν συνεπτυγμένον κατ᾽ ἔννοιαν σοφῶς

---

18. Confessor, *Amb.* 45 (PG 91: 1356A7–9).

19. Confessor, *Amb.* 42 (PG 91: 1321B1–3).

20. Confessor, *Amb.* 41 (PG 91: 1305C6, 1305D6, 1305D12, 1308A12, 1308B7).

21. Confessor, *Amb.* 37 (PG 91: 1296B8–11).

ἐξαπλώσαντες λόγον) of the bodies that are variously joined to one another in the world, the saints have discovered the bodies' sensual, apprehensible, and general qualities, all of which are encompassed by and folded in on each other by the interlocking of the particular existence around each reality.[22]

This understanding of the qualities of created things leads to the recognition that the generation and continuity of individual things are supported by the process of combination and decomposition. Thus, on the one hand, the world is composed through corruption and mutation, and this observation leads to the recognition that the world is unstable and does not "persist of necessity in an unbroken sequence." Adam, however, looked to this process of combination and decomposition for his source of life, and so took corruption into him.

In contrast, Maximus says that the saints see the world as a harmonious, consistent, ordered whole that maintains its cyclical rhythms by the providence of God and requires no addition or difference to exist "more beautifully" than it does now.

> The saints have observed the endurance, the arrangement, and the placement of the things that have come to be, as well as their way of being, according to which everything is established in accordance with each one's own species, unmixed and free from disorder: the revolution of the stars that progresses in a consistent way, never exchanging one course for another; the cycle of the year that progresses in an orderly manner wherein the stars are restored to the place from which they started; that each year has an equal number of nights and days, each increasing and decreasing along with its portion, with their increase and decrease progressing neither by a greater nor lesser measure. From all of these, they know the one who oversees beings to be the one whom they understand is God and Fashioner of all things.[23]

When the world partakes of God and does not feed on itself, it is able to persist and maintain its unity along with its distinctions. God "distributes Himself without division as diverse portions to all those who are worthy of grace in proportion to the quality and quantity of each one's virtue," and this distribution is not a decomposition or division even though "He appears individually when each person partakes of Him."[24] This is not, however, the world Adam strove to acquire through his partaking of the fruit; he grasped at a world independent of divine reality and dependent on its own corrup-

22. Confessor, *Amb.* 10 (PG 91: 1169B6–12).

23. Confessor, *Amb.* 10 (PG 91: 1176B12–C14).

24. Confessor, *Amb.* 10 (PG 91: 1172C1–7).

tion and alteration for the continuity of its existence. The world as it really is maintains its order and rational progression, exhibiting the cyclic continuity that, for Maximus, leads directly to an awareness of "the Fashioner of all things:"

> Who, seeing the beauty and grandeur of the creations of God does not immediately understand (οὐκ εὐθὺς ἐννοήσει) that he is the Originator of their existence as Source, Cause, and Maker of being, and does not run in thought toward Him alone?[25]

The immediacy of this understanding is important. While Maximus does make arguments about causality, which construct a chain of reasoning from observable effects to necessary causes, such arguments are analyses after the fact of the fundamental experience of the beauty of creation itself.

So, we have the world as "ungovernable (ἀκράτητον)" and in "constant flux,"[26] a world that feeds on itself to its own corruption, a world from which the ascetic is voluntarily estranged; but we also have the world of beauty and grandeur, a universe that revolves with perfectly measured motion, where time unfolds rationally with no fluctuation. These two orientations arise from philosophy's two-fold structure of praxis and contemplation. The notion of the world as "ungovernable" comes from Maximus' interpretation of the Parable of the Rich Man and Lazarus (Luke 16:19–31) in which he argues that the rich man had possession neither of this life, because of its constant change, nor of the life to come, since his desire was only for this world.[27] Lazarus, however, endured estrangement from the world and even his own body for the sake of the world to come. This interpretation comes within a consideration of the need for purification of soul and body and the exercise of virtue. In this context, the world, when taken on its own, becomes the material of ascetical endeavor and thus is regarded as a mass of unstable and corruptible beings that devour one another in order to sustain the process of generation. It is *this* world, as opposed to the age *to come*. When the saint recognizes the world as unstable and accepts alienation from it, the saint does not attempt to possess the world and the world therefore gives of itself freely and prolifically. The saint does not attempt to grasp the world and keep it from passing away; the world therefore reveals its inner coherence and endurance, its harmonious cycle of procession and return. The saint has not been ravished by the initial beauty of the world; he "runs" through it, we might even say "into" it, to its inner meaning, which is divine reality itself;

---

25. Confessor, *Amb.* 10 (PG 91: 1176D3–7).
26. Confessor, *Amb.* 10 (PG 91: 1172B6–7).
27. Confessor, *Amb.* 10 (PG 91: 1169D13–1172D8).

the true, final necessity of the world's beauty is therefore made manifest. Maximus thus gives an example, within the context of the transgression of Adam, of his understanding of the relationship between the practical/ethical life, which has the acquisition of ἀπάθεια as its end, and θεωρία φυσική, whose path traces a way *through* the world and beyond it (διάβασις ὑπὲρ κόσμον). It is withdrawal and the acquisition of ἀπάθεια that allow the saint to see the world as it is in its harmonious functioning, in contrast to Adam who grasped for a corruptibility he thought would sustain him.

Maximus sees the renewal of nature and the renewal of the contemplation of nature in which the world is contemplated together with its cause in Christ as the economy that overcomes and heals the original transgression of Adam. Because this transgression of contemplating the world in a false way is presented by Scripture as an act of eating, Maximus very fittingly considers the economy of salvation in the same terms, terms that are subtly but definitely Eucharistic. We might say conversely that Maximus understands partaking of Christ in this section in terms of the contemplation of nature. The disciple comes to partake of Christ as the means of partaking of the renewed knowledge of the world, and the renewed knowledge of the world is none other than the transfigured cosmos that appears together with the divinity of Christ.[28] In this sequence of thought, Maximus shows how the Word of God plants himself in the world and as the "sun of righteousness" causes himself to grow in the world until he becomes "the substance in the entirety of things (τὸν ἐν τοῖς ὅλοις λόγον τοῖς πράγμασιν οὐσίαν γίνεσθαι)." The disciples then partake of the world as body of Christ and the body of Christ as world.

In *Ambiguum* 46, Maximus employs the Dionysian concept of divine names and gives a concrete example of a "natural contemplation" of a name of the Lord. He begins from a passage in Gregory's *Second Oration on Pascha* in which the Theologian refers to Christ as "the Sun of righteousness" (quoting Mal 4:2): "[He is] one year old as the Sun of righteousness, beginning from there [ἐκεῖθεν, referring to the Father on Maximus' interpretation], circumscribed by being seen."[29] Maximus begins:

> Our savior has many titles and the way of understanding how they refer can lead in many different ways when we contemplate the purpose of each one, for it is possible for the many thoughts that come through natural contemplation when something is

28. Cf. *Amb.* 10 (PG 91: 1160B13–1165D1).

29. Nazianzen, *Oration* 45.13.

taken as a title of the Lord—in the sense that the Lord is the paradigm for that which the title names—to be applied to Him.[30]

What follows, then, is an example of natural contemplation in which Maximus shows how the Lord may receive the name of "Sun."

He begins the contemplation with a description of the "uninterrupted motion of time." Starting from Gregory's notion that the Lord is "one year old," Maximus defines one year as "the restoration of the sun to the place in the heavens from which it began (ἡ τοῦ ἡλίου ἀπὸ τοῦ αὐτοῦ σημείου εἰς τὸ αὐτὸ σημεῖον ἀποκατάστασις)."[31] The motion of the duration of a year—as divided into hours, days, weeks, months, and seasons—proceeds in a consistent and continuous manner. Maximus then applies this cyclical notion of the duration of a year to the Lord, writing that

> The "acceptable year of the Lord" (Isa 62:2), as it is written, is—to take the passage allegorically—the whole duration of the ages. At the beginning of this duration, God thought it good to bring beings into being, and to give existence to what did not exist, and through His providence, like an intellectual Sun whose power holds the universe together in stability and which rises up to send forth a ray of light downward, He thought it fitting that He should diversify the ways [He is present in the world] (ποικῖλαι τοὺς τρόπους ἀξιώσας) until the completion of all the ages in order to bring those in whom He had sown his own goodness to full maturation. Then he will gather the fruits of his own seed unmixed with weeds and pure of all chaff-like residue and anything else that might be mixed in and the whole purpose (ὁ σύμπας λόγος) of the motion of moveable things will be completed, for those who are worthy will have received the final blessedness of deification that has been promised.[32]

The creation of all things is here compared to the sowing of seeds and bringing them to fruition. The concept of the σπερματικὸς λόγος, the rational principle that is sown like a seed, is a common theme in both the ancient patristic tradition and amongst the pagan philosophers, especially the Stoics. For Maximus, God the Word has sown the seeds of his own goodness in beings and he "shines" upon them like the sun to make them grow. He has

---

30. Confessor, *Amb.* 46 (PG 91: 1356C5–11): Πολλαὶ τοῦ Σωτῆρος ἡμῶν εἰσιν αἱ προσηγορίαι, καὶ, πολύτροπος ὁ ἐφ᾽ ἑκάστῃ κατὰ τὴν αὐτῆς ἐπίνοιαν τῆς κατὰ θεωρίαν ἀναγωγῆς καθέστηκε τρόπος, διὰ τὸ πολλὰς κατὰ τὴν φυσικὴν θεωρίαν τοῦ παραδειγματικῶς εἰς προσηγορίαν τοῦ κυρίου λαμβανομένου πράγματος ἐπιδέχεσθαι δύνασθαι θεωρημάτων ἐπιβολάς.

31. Confessor, *Amb.* 46 (PG 91: 1356D7–8).

32. Confessor, *Amb.* 46 (PG 91: 1357A9–B9).

"diversified the ways [he is present in the world]" by sending down his rays upon the seeds of his own goodness, which he has placed within created things.

The passage from Gregory goes on to speak of the "return" of the Sun of "righteousness to Himself," and though Maximus does not quote this phrase, he concludes this line of interpretation with the same idea:

> And so, the Lord is called "the Sun of righteousness" as the Maker and the one who perfects the ages, as the beginning and end of all things, as the Fashioner of the wise five-fold order[33] of those things foreknown in His providence, and as the one who fills all things with everlasting light by ever bestowing His goodness upon them. It is He who ripens and prepares for the God and Father those who widen their own intellectual pathways for the reception of His blessed ray of light.[34]

Maximus follows Gregory's notion of the Word as the Sun of righteousness "being born of the Father, light from light, true God from true God,"[35] inseminating his goodness in created things so that he is "circumscribed by being seen," shining upon them to cause them to grow, which in a sense, is to cause himself to grow in them, and then to bring the fruit of that growth, which again is the fruit of his own goodness, to the Father, thus completing the "cycle of the year," "the acceptable year of the Lord." Maximus considers this fulfillment of the year of the Lord in terms of the gathering of "spiritual knowledge of intellectual realities through the rigorous natural contemplation of the *logoi* of phenomena."[36] Thus, the contemplation of nature is precisely the way in which beings come to fulfillment for thought and this fulfillment is the blooming of the very Word himself in created things.

Because Maximus is drawing quotations from Gregory's *Second Oration on Pascha*, it is quite to be expected that the imagery of partaking of the sacrifice should come to the fore. In *Ambiguum 47*, Maximus transposes the canonical philosophical problem of the one and the many to the question of how each person encounters the one, unified Christ in many, individual ways, in accordance with each person's faith and level of spiritual life. He begins from a quotation of Gregory in which the Theologian says, "It is no surprise that a sheep is required for each and every house."[37] Maximus poses a question in response:

33. Probably a reference to the five-fold division of created things in *Amb.* 41.

34. Confessor, *Amb.* 46 (PG 91: 1357B9–C4).

35. Confessor, *Amb.* 46 (PG 91: 1357C12–14).

36. Confessor, *Amb.* 46 (PG 91: 1357C8–10).

37. Nazianzen, *Oration* 45.14.

> Since there is one Christ who is proclaimed mystically through
> the law, the prophets, and the magnificence of creation to those
> who are able to hear and see spiritually, how does the law, which
> presents a complete type of Christ, order that many sheep be
> sacrificed at the houses of the patriarchs?[38]

In response, Maximus shows how different people partake of Christ
in different ways and to different degrees in proportion to the measure of
grace and power each person has. Specifically, Maximus applies the stages
of philosophy to the different levels of Christ's being. The one engaged in the
practical life partakes of Christ's body; one involved in natural contemplation partakes of his soul; the theologian passes beyond the soul of Christ
and the "symbolic contemplation of beings" that characterizes natural contemplation and comes to the intellect of Christ; and the one who passes
beyond the discourse of theology comes to the divinity of Christ "through
an all-encompassing apophasis (δι' ἀποφάσεως παντελοῦς)."[39] Maximus follows the sacrificial imagery of Gregory's oration and places the crucifixion
of Christ as the starting point for this journey from the body of Christ all
the way to his divinity. Each person "sacrifices the lamb and partakes of
its flesh, taking his fill of Jesus"[40] in his own way so that the Word who has
diversified the manner of his presence in the world maintains his unity even
as he "becomes all things for all" (1 Cor 9:22; 15:28; Col 3:11).[41]

Ambiguum 48 continues with the imagery of partaking of Christ and
gives a more detailed account of what Gregory has called the "spiritual di-
gestion" of the Word.[42] Each part of the Passover lamb, which is a type of
Christ, signifies a particular aspect of the spiritual life. The one who possesses the principles of theology in faith eats the head of the Christ; the one
who receives these principles with knowledge eats the ears; the one who
"considers creation spiritually" and brings the *logoi* of both sensual and
intellectual reality into unity partakes of the eyes. The breast is for the one
who proclaims his theological knowledge, the hands for the one who keeps
the commandments.[43]

The Word, by being "eaten" intellectually, nourishes those who partake
of him and indeed "becomes the substance in the entirety of things (τὸν
ἐν τοῖς ὅλοις λόγον τοῖς πράγμασιν οὐσίαν γίνεσθαι)," even as he is "beyond

38. Confessor, *Amb.* 47 (PG 91: 1357D7–1360A4).
39. Confessor, *Amb.* 47 (PG 91: 1360C6–D2).
40. Confessor, *Amb.* 47 (PG 91: 1360D9–11).
41. Confessor, *Amb.* 47 (PG 91: 1361A4).
42. Nazianzen, *Oration* 45.16.
43. Confessor, *Amb.* 48 (PG 91: 1364C1–1365B3).

nature and *logos* (ὑπὲρ φύσιν καὶ λόγον)."[44] Maximus thus takes the metaphysical doctrine of the presence of the Λόγος in all things and transposes
it into the Eucharistic imagery of feeding on the Word. This completes the
sequence of this series of *Ambigua*, which speak of the contemplation of
nature in terms of insemination, growth, fruition, and finally offering and
partaking. Even though the metaphors shift from the planting and growth
of grain (bread for the Eucharist) to the partaking of the Passover lamb this
sequence of thought in the *Ambigua* clearly holds together as a reflection
upon partaking of the presence of Christ in all things. In this Christological understanding of natural contemplation, which is the culmination of
Maximus' presentation of philosophy in the *Ambigua to John*, to partake of
the world in natural contemplation is to partake of Christ, and to partake of
Christ is to partake of the substance of all things.

---

44. Confessor, *Amb.* 47 (PG 91: 1365C4–5).

Bibliography

Aertsen, Jan A. "The Concept of 'Transcendens' in the Middle Ages: What Is Beyond and What Is Common." In *Platonic Ideas and Concept Formation in Ancient and Medieval Thought*, edited by Gerd van Riel and Gabriel Macé, 133–53. Leuven: Leuven University Press, 2004.

Alfeyev, Hilarion. *The Spiritual World of Isaac the Syrian*. Cistercian Studies. Kalamazoo, MI: Cistercian, 2000.

Allchin, A. M. "Foreword" to Lars Thunberg, *Man and the Cosmos: The Vision of St Maximus the Confessor*. Crestwood, NY: St. Vladimyr's Seminary Press, 1985.

Allen, Pauline, and Bronwen Neil, eds. *Maximus the Confessor and His Companions: Documents from Exile*. Oxford: Oxford University Press, 2002.

Allnatt, Chalres. *Cathedra Petri: A Brief Summary of the Chief Titles and Prerogatives Ascribed to St. Peter and to His See and Successors, by the Early Fathers and Councils of the Church*. London: Burns and Oates, 1875.

Andia, Ysabel de. *Henosis: L'Union À Dieu Chez Denys L'Areopagite*. Leiden: Brill, 1996.

Aquinas, Thomas. "Contra Errores Graecorum." In *Ending the Byzantine Greek Schism: Containing: The 14th C. Apologia of Demetrios Kydones for Unity with Rome & the "Contra Errores Graecorum" of St. Thomas Aquinas*, edited by James Likoudis. Steubenville: Catholics United for the Faith, 1992.

Athanasius. "Contra Gentes and De Incarnatione." Edited by Robert Thomson. Oxford Early Christian Texts. Oxford: Oxford University Press, 1971.

Ayres, Lewis. *Augustine and the Trinity*. Cambridge: Cambridge University Press, 2010.

Badiou, Alain. *Being and Event*. Edited by Oliver Feltham. London: Continuum, 2005.

Balthasar, Hans Urs von. *Cosmic Liturgy: The Universe according to Maximus the Confessor*. San Francisco: Ignatius, 2003.

Bardy, Gustave. "La Littérature Patristique Des Quaestiones et Responsiones Sur l'Écriture Sainte." *Revue Biblique* 41 (1932) 210–36.

Basil of Caesarea. *Saint Basil: The Letters*. The Loeb Classical Library. Edited by Roy J. Deferrari. Vol 3. London: W. Heinemann, 1930.

——. *Saint Basile, Lettres I, 3 Vols*. Edited by Y. Courtonne. Paris, n.d.

Bathrellos, Demetrios. *The Byzantine Christ: Person, Nature, and Will in the Christology of St Maximus the Confessor*. Oxford: Oxford University Press, 2004.

Berg, Robert van den. "A Remark of Genius and Well-Worthy of Platonic Principles: Proclus' Criticism of Porphyry's Semantic Theory." In *Platonic Ideas and Concept-Formation in Ancient and Medieval Thought*, edited by Gerd van Riel and Gabriel Macé, 155–69. Leuven: Leuven University Press, 2004.

Berthold, G. C. "The Cappadocian Roots of Maximus the Confessor." In *Maximus Confessor: Actes Du Symposium Sur Maxime Le Confesseur*, edited by Felix Heinzer and Christoph Schönborn, 51–60. Fribourg: Éditions Universitaires Fribourg Suisse, 1982.

Bessarion of Nicea. *Oratio Dogmatica de Unione*. Edited by Emmanuel Candal. CF 7. Rome: Pontificium Institutum Orientalium Studiorum, 1958.

———. "Refutatio Capitum Syllogisticorum Marci Ephesii." Edited by J. P. Migne. PG 161. Paris: Migne, 1865.

Blond, Phillip. "The Beatific Vision of St Thomas Aquinas." In *Encounter between Eastern Orthodoxy and Radical Orthodoxy*, edited by Adrian Pabst and Christoph Schneider, 185–212. Farnham, UK: Ashgate, 2009.

Blowers, Paul. *Exegesis and Spiritual Pedagogy in Maximus the Confessor: An Investigation of the Quaestiones Ad Thalassium*. South Bend, IN: : University of Notre Dame Press, 1991.

———. "The Passion of Jesus Christ in Maximus the Confessor: A Reconsideration." *Studia Patristica* 37 (2001) 361–77.

———. "Unfinished Creative Business: Maximus the Confessor, Evolutionary Theodicy, and Human Stewardship in Creation." In *On Earth as It Is in Heaven: Cultivating a Christian Theology of Creation*, edited by David Meconi, S.J., 174–90. Grand Rapids: Eerdmans, 2016.

———. "The World in the Mirror of Holy Scripture: Maximus the Confessor's Short Hermeneutical Treatise in Ambiguum Ad Joannem 41." In *In Dominico Eloquio: Essays on Patristic Exegesis in Honor of Robert Louis Wilken*, edited by Paul Blowers et al., 408–26. Grand Rapids: Eerdmans, 2002.

Boulnois, Olivier. *Au-Delà de L'image: Une Archéologie Du Visuel Au Moyen Âge, Ve-XVIe Siècle*. Paris: Seuil, 2008.

———. *Être et Representation*. Paris: Presses Universitaires de France, 1999.

Bradshaw, David. *Aristotle East and West: Metaphysics and the Division of Christendom*. Cambridge: Cambridge University Press, 2004.

———. "Maximus the Confessor." In *The Cambridge History of Philosophy in Late Antiquity*, edited by Lloyd Gerson, Vol. 2, 813–28. Cambridge: Cambridge University Press, 2010.

Burrell, David B. *Knowing the Unknowable God: Ibn-Sina, Maimonides, Aquinas*. South Bend, IN: : Notre Dame University Press, 1987.

Busse, A. *Porphyrii Isagoge Et in Aristotelis Categorias Commentarium, Vol. IV I*. Berlin: de Gruyter, 1887.

Calabasilas, Nilus. "Five Discourses against the Conclusions of the Latins on the Matter of the Holy Spirit." In *Sur Le Saint-Esprit*, edited by Théophile Kislas, 379–81. Paris: Cerf, 2001.

Chiaradonna, R. "What Is Porphyry's Isagoge?" *Documenti E Studi Sulla Tradizione Filosofica Medievale* 19 (2008) 1–30.

Chrétien, Jean-Louis. "The Immemorial and Recollection." In *The Unforgettable and the Unhoped For*, 1–39. New York: Fordham University Press, 2002.

Clément, Oliver. *Essor Du Christianisme Oriental*. Paris: Presses Universitaires de France, 1964.

———. *You Are Peter: An Orthodox Theologian's Reflections on the Exercise of Papal Primacy*. Edited by M. S. Laird. New York: New City, 2003.

Colish, Marcia. "John the Scot's Christology in Relation to His Greek Sources." *Downside Review* 102 (1982) 138–45.

Congar, Yves. *I Believe in the Holy Spirit*. Edited by David Smith. New York: Crossroad, 1997.

Cooper, Adam. *The Body in St. Maximus the Confessor: Holy Flesh, Wholly Deified*. Oxford: Oxford University Press, 2005.

Cross, R. "Gregory of Nyssa on Universals." *Vigiliae Christianae* 56 (2002) 372–410.

Daley, Brian. "Boethius' Theological Tracts and Early Byzantine Scholasticism." *Medieval Studies* 46 (1984) 158–91.

Dalmais, I. H. "La Théorie Des 'logoi' Des Créatures Chez S. Maxime Le Confesseur." *Revue Des Sciences Philosophiques et Théologiques* 36 (1952) 244–49.

Dalrymple, William. *From the Holy Mountain: A Journey among the Christians of the Middle East*. New York: Holt, 1998.

Davidson, Ivor J. "Not My Will But Yours Be Done: The Ontological Dynamics of Incarnational Intention." *International Journal of Systematic Theology* 7.2 (2005) 178–204.

DeVille, Adam. *Orthodoxy and the Roman Papacy: Ut Unum Sint and the Prospects of East-West Unity*. South Bend, IN: University of Notre Dame Press, 2011.

Dihle, Albrecht. *The Theory of Will in Classical Antiquity*. Berkeley: University of California Press, 1982.

Dinan, Stephen A. "The Particularity of Moral Knowledge." *The Thomist* 50 (1986) 66–84.

Doucet, Marcel. "La Volonté Humaine Du Christ, Spécialement En Son Agonie. Maxime Le Confessuer, Interpréte de l'Écriture." *Science et Esprit* 37.2 (1985) 123–59.

Due, William La. *The Chair of St. Peter: A History of the Papacy*. New York: Orbis, 1999.

Dvornik, Francis. *Byzantium and the Roman Primacy*. New York: Fordham University Press, 1966.

Eno, Robert. *The Rise of the Papacy*. Wilmington, DE: Michael Glazier, 1990.

Erismann, C. *L'Homme Commun: La Genèse Du Réalisme Ontologique Durant Le Haut Moyen Âge Latin*. Paris: Vrin, 2011.

———. "A World of Hypostases: John of Damascus' Rethinking of Aristotle's Categorical Ontology." *Studia Patristica* 50 (2011) 251–69.

Eriugena, John Scotus. "De Divisione Naturae." Edited by J. P. Migne. PL 122. Paris, 1855.

———. *Periphyseon*. Edited by Édouard Jeauneau. CCCM 161–65. Turnhout: Brepols, 1996.

———. *Periphyseon: The Division of Nature*. Edited by I. P. Sheldon-Williams and J. O'Meara. Montreal: Bellarmin, 1987.

Evagrius. *Peri Logismon*. Edited by Paul Gehin, Claire Guillaumont, and Antoine Guillaumont. SC 438. Paris: Cerf, 1998.

Florovsky, Georges. "Cur Deus Homo? The Motive of the Incarnation." In *Creation and Redemption, The Collected Works*, Vol. 3, 163–70. Belmont, MA: Nordland, 1976.

Frede, M. "Les Catégories d'Aristote et Les Pères de l'Eglise Grecs." In *Les Catégories et Leur Histoire*, edited by L. Bruun, O., Corti, 135–73. Paris: Vrin, 2005.

Frede, Michael. *A Free Will: Origins of the Notion in Ancient Thought*. Berkeley: University of California Press, 2011.

Garrigues, Juan Miguel. "L'énergie Divine et La Grâce Chez Maxime Le Confesseur." *Istina* 19 (1974) 272–96.

———. "Le Sens Primaute Romaine Chez Le Maxime Le Confesseur." *Istina* 21 (1976) 6–24.

Gauthier, R.-A. "Saint Maxime Le Confesseur et La Psychologie de L-Acte Humain." *Recherches de Théologie Ancienne et Médiévale* 21 (1954) 51–100.

Gauthier, R.-A., and Jean Yves Jolif. *Aristote: l'Éthique À Nicomaque, Vol. 1, Pt. 1.* 2nd ed. Leuven: Leuven University Press, 1970.

Geréby, György. "Hidden Themes in Fourteenth-Century Byzantine and Latin Theological Debates: Monarchianism and Crypto-Dyophysitism." In *Greeks, Latins, and Intellectual History 1204–1500*, edited by Martin Hinterberger and Chris Schabel, 200–203. Leuven: Leuven University Press, 2011.

Gersh, Stephen. "The Structure of the Return in Eriugena's Periphyseon." In *Begriff Und Metapher. Sprachform Des Denkens Bei Eriugena*, edited by Werner Beierwaltes, 108–25. Heidelberg: Winter, 1990.

Gerson, Lloyd P. *Aristotle and Other Platonists.* Ithaca, NY: Cornell University Press, 2005.

Ghellinck, J. de. "Quelques Appréciations de La Dialectique et d'Aristote Durant Les Conflits Trinitaires Du IVe S." *Revue D'histoire Ecclésiastique* 26 (1930) 5–42.

Gill, Joseph, ed. *Acta Graeca Acta Greca Concilii Florentini Cum Versione Latina, Concilium Florentinum, Documenta et Scriptores, Vol 1–2.* Rome: Pontificium Institutum Orientalium Studiorum, n.d.

———. "John Beccus, Patriarch of Constantinople." In *Church Union: Rome and Byzantium 1204–1453*, 251–66. London: Variorum Reprints, 1979.

———. *Quae Supersunt Actorum Graecorum Concilii Florentini: Res Florentinae Gestae.* Synodo Florentina Gestis, Concilium Florentinum V. Rome: Pontificium Institutum Orientalium Studiorum, 1953.

Gleede, B. *The Development of the Term Ἐνυπόστατος from Origen to John of Damascus.* Leiden: Brill, 2012.

Gockel, M. "A Dubious Christological Formula? Leontius of Byzantium and the Anhypostasis-Enhypostasis Theory." *The Journal of Theological Studies* 51 (2000) 515–32.

Gondreau, Paul. "St. Thomas Aquinas, the Communication of Idioms, and the Suffering of Christ in the Garden of Gethsemane." In *Divine Impassibility and the Mystery of Human Suffering*, edited by James F. Keating and Thomas Joseph White, 214–45. Grand Rapids: Eerdmans, 2009.

Gregory of Cyrpus. *Apologia pro Tomo Suo.* Edited by J. P. Migne. PG 142. Paris: Migne, 1865.

Gregory of Nyssa. *De Oratione Dominica, Hom. 5.* Edited by J. H. Callahan. Gregorii Nysseni Opera VII, 2. Leiden: Brill, 1992.

Guiu, Adrian. "Christology and Philosophical Culture in Maximus the Confessor's Ambiguum 41." *Studia Patristica* 48 (2010) 111–16.

Harrison, Peter. *The Bible, Protestantism, and the Rise of Natural Science.* Cambridge: Cambridge University Press, 1998.

Hausherr, Irénée. "L'imitation de Jésus Christ Dans La Spiritualité Byzantine." In *Mélanges Offerts Au R.P.F. Cavallera*, 231–59. Toulouse: Institut Catholique, 1948.

———. *Philautie: De La Tendresse Pour Soi À La Charité Selon Saint Maxime Le Confesseur.* Orientalia Christiana Analecta. Vol. 137. Rome: Pontifical Institutum Orientalium Studiorum, 1952.

————. "Un Précurseur de La Théorie Scotiste Sur La Fin de l'Incarnation. Isaac de Ninive (VIIe Siècle)." *Recherches de Sciences Religieuses* 22 (1932) 316–20.

Heinzer, Felix. "L'explication Trinitaire Chez L'économie Chez Maxime Le Confesseur." In *Maximus Confessor: Actes Du Symposium Sur Maxime Le Confesseur*, edited by Felix Heinzer and Christoph Schönborn, 159–72. Fribourg: Éditions Universitaires Fribourg Suisse, 1982.

Heinzer, Felix, and Christoph Schönborn, eds. *Maximus Confessor: Actes Du Symposium Sur Maxime Le Confesseur, Fribourg, 2–5 Septembre 1980*. Fribourg: Éditions Universitaires Fribourg Suisse, 1982.

Helmig, Christopher. "What Is the Systematic Place of Abstraction and Concept Formation in Plato's Philosophy? Ancient and Modern Readings of Phaedrus 249 B–c." In *Platonic Ideas and Concept Formation in Ancient and Medieval Thought*, edited by Gerd van Riel and Gabriel Macé, 83–97. Leuven: Leuven University Press, 2004.

Honnefelder, Ludger. *La Métaphysique Comme Science Transcedentale*. Edited by I. Mandrella. Paris: Presses Universitaires de France, 2002.

Hopkins, Gerard Manley. *Poems of Gerard Manley Hopkins*. Edited by Robert Bridges. London: Oxford University Press, 1965.

Irenaeus. *Contre Les Hérésies. Livre V. Édition Critique D'après Les Versions Arménienne et Latine Par Adelin Rousseau [and Others]*. Sources Chrétiennes 153. Edited by Adelin Rousseau. Paris: Cerf, 1969.

Jeauneau, É. "Jean l'Erigène et Les Ambigua Ad Iohannem de Maxime Le Confesseur." In *Maximus Confessor. Actes Du Symposium Sur Maxime Le Confesseur*, edited by Felix Heinzer and Christoph Schönborn, 343–64. Fribourg: Éditions Universitaires Fribourg Suisse, 1982.

————. "Jean Scot Traducteur de Maxime Le Confesseur." In *The Sacred Nectar of the Greeks: The Study of Greeks in the West in the Early Middle Ages*, edited by M. W. Herren, 257–76. London: University of London King's College, 1988.

Kahn, Charles H. "Discovering the Will: From Aristotle to Augustine." In *The Question of Eclecticism: Studies in Later Greek Philosophy*, edited by John M. Dillon and A. A. Long, 234–59. Berkeley: University of California Press, 1988.

Karayiannis, Vasilios. *Maxime Le Confesseur: Essence et Energies de Dieu, Théologie Historique 93*. Paris: Beauchesne, 1993.

————. "O AGIOS MAXIMOS O OMOLOGHTHS KAI H EKKLHSIA THS KUPROU." *Apostolos Varnavas* 53 (1992) 379–98.

Kattan, A. E. *Verleiblichung Und Synergie. Grundzüge Der Bibelhermeneutik Bei Maximus Confessor*. Leiden: Brill, 1993.

Kavanagh, C. "The Influence of Maximus the Confessor on Eriugena's Treatment of Aristotle's Categories." *American Catholic Philosophical Quarterly* 79 (2005) 567–96.

Keats, John. *The Letters of John Keats*. Edited by M. B. Forman. 2nd ed. Oxford: Oxford University Press, 1935.

Kerr, Fergus. *After Aquinas: Versions of Thomism*. Oxford: Blackwell, 2002.

Krämer, Hans Joachim. *Plato and the Foundations of Metaphysics*. Edited by John R. Catan. New York: SUNY Press, 1990.

Krausmüller, D. "Making Sense of the Formula of Chalcedon: The Cappadocians and Aristotle in Leontius of Byzantium's Contra Nestorianos et Eutychianos." *Vigiliae Christianae* 65 (2011) 484–513.

Lackner, W. "Studien Zur Philosophischen Schultradition Und Zu Den Nemesioszitaten Bei Maximos Dem Bekenner." Graz, Austria: University of Graz Press, 1962.

Lang, U. M. "Anhypostatos-Enhypostatos: Church Fathers, Protestant Orthodoxy and Karl Barth." *The Journal of Theological Studies, New Series* 49 (1998) 630–57.

Larchet, Jean-Claude. *La Divinisation de L'homme Selon Saint Maxime Le Confesseur.* Paris: Cerf, 1996.

————. *Maxime Le Confesseur, Mediateur Entre l'Orient et l'Occident.* Paris: Cerf, 1998.

————. "À Propos de La Récente Clarification Du Conseil Pontifical Pour La Promotion de L'Unité Des Chrétiens." *Le Messager Orthodoxe* 129 (1997) 3–58.

————. "The Question of the Roman Primacy in the Thought of Saint Maximus the Confessor." In *The Petrine Ministry*, edited by Cardinal Walter Kaspar, 188–209. New York: Newman, 2006.

Lethel, F.-M. *Théologie de L'agonie Du Christ: La Liberté Humaine Du Fils de Dieu et Son Importance Sotériologique Mises En Lumière Par Saint Maxime Confesseur, Théologie Historique 52.* Paris: Beauchesne, 1979.

Lévy, Antoine. *Le Créé et L' Incréé: Maxime Le Confesseur et Thomas D' Aquin. Aux Sources de La Querelle Palamienne, Librairie Philosophique.* Paris: Vrin, 2006.

Lollar, Joshua. "'To See into the Life of Things:' The Contemplation of Nature in Maximus the Confessor's Ambigua to John." South Bend, IN: University of Notre Dame, 2011.

Long, A. A., and D. N. Sedley. *The Hellenistic Philosophers.* Cambridge: Cambridge University Press, 1987.

Loosen, J. *Logos und Pneuma im Begnadeten Menschen Bei Maximus Confessor.* Münster: Aschendorffsche Verlagsbuchhandulng, 1941.

Lossky, Vladimir. "The Procession of the Holy Spirit in Orthodox Trinitarian Doctrine." In *In the Image and Likeness of God*, 79–96. Crestwood, NY: St. Vladimir's Seminary Press, 1985.

Loudovikos, Nikolaos. *A Eucharistic Ontology: Maximus the Confessor's Eschatological Ontology of Being as Dialogical Reciprocity.* Brookline, MA: Holy Cross Orthodox Press, 2010.

————. *Striving for Participation: Being and Methexis in Gregory Palamas and Thomas Aquinas.* Athens: Armos, 2010.

Louth, Andrew. "The Ecclesiology of Saint Maximos the Confessor." *International Journal for the Study of the Christian Church* 4 (2004) 109–20.

————. "St Maximus the Confessor between East and West." *Studia Patristica* 32 (1997) 33–45

Lubac, Henri de. *Medieval Exegesis. The Four Senses of Scripture.* Edited by M. Sebanc. Grand Rapids: Eerdmans, 1998.

Madden, John D. "The Authenticity of Early Definitions of Will (Θελησις)." In *Maximus Confessor: Actes Du Symposium Sur Maxime Le Confesseur*, edited by Felix Heinzer and Christoph Schönborn, 61–79. Fribourg: Éditions Universitaires Fribourg Suisse, 1982.

Mansi, G. D., ed. *Sacrorum conciliorum nova et amplissima collectio.* 31 vols. Edited by Giovanni Domenico Mansi. Florence and Venice, 1759–98. Rev. ed. by Jean P. Martin and Louis Petit. 53 vols. 1901–27. Reprint. Paris: Arnheim, and Leipzig, 1960–62.

Marenbon, John. *The Philosophy of Peter Abelard.* Cambridge: Cambridge University Press, 1997.

Marion, Jean-Luc. *God Without Being.* Chicago: Chicago University Press, 1991.

Mark of Ephesus. "Laetentur Caeli." In *Decrees of the Ecumenical Councils,* Vol. 1, edited by Norman Tanner and Alberigo Giuseppe, 65. Washington, DC: Georgetown University Press, 1990.

———. "Relatio de Rebus a Se." In *Marci Eugenici, Metropolitae Ephesi, Opera Antiunionistica,* edited by Ludivico Petit. Synodo Florentina Gestis, Concilium Florentinum X, 140. Rome: Pontificium Institutum Orientalium Studiorum, 1977.

Marrou, Henri Irénée. *Histoire De l'Éducation Dans l'Antiquité.* Univers Hi. Paris: Seuil, 1948.

Marx, Hans-Jürgen. *Filioque Und Verbot Eines Anderen Glaubens Auf Dem Florentinum: Zum Pluralismus in Dogmatischen Formeln.* Sankt Augustin, Germany: Steyler Verlag, 1977.

Maudlin, Tim. "Distilling Metaphysics from Quantum Physics." In *The Oxford Handbook of Metaphysics,* edited by M. J. Loux and D. W. Zimmerman, 461–87. Oxford: Oxford University Press, 2003.

Mauss, Marcel. *A General Theory of Magic.* Edited by Robert Brain. London: Routledge, 2001.

Maximus the Confessor. *Ambigua.* Translated by Dumitru Staniloae. Bucuresti: Editura Institului Biblic, 2006.

———. "Diversa Capita Ad Theologiam et Oeconomiam Spectantia Deque Virtute Ac Vitio 4." In *The Philokalia,* edited by G. E. H. Palmer, Philip Sherrard, and Kallistos Ware, Vol. 2. London: Faber and Faber, 1981.

———. *Ex Epistola Sancti Maximi Scripta Ad Abbatem Thalassium.* Edited by J. P. Migne. PL 129. Paris: Migne, 1865.

———. "Letter of Maximus to Anastasius, His Disciple." In *Maximus the Confessor and His Companions: Documents from Exile,* edited by Pauline Allen, 120–23. Oxford: Oxford University Press, 2002.

———. *Maximus the Confessor and His Companions: Documents from Exile.* Edited by Pauline Allen and Bronwen Neil. Oxford: Oxford University Press, 2002.

———. *Mystagogia.* Edited by C. Boudignon. CCSG 69. Turnhout: Brepols, 2011.

———. *On the Cosmic Mystery of Jesus Christ: Selected Writings from St. Maximus the Confessor.* Edited by R. L. Blowers, P. M., Wilken. Crestwood, NY: St. Vladimir's Seminary Press, 2003.

———. *Opuscula Theologica et Polemica.* in *Prp. Maxim Ispovednik: Bogoslovsko-polemicheskia sochineniya (Opuscula theologia et polemica).* Translated by D. Chernoglazov and A. Choufrine; edited by G. Benevich. St. Petersburg: RHGA, 2014.

———. *Opuscula Theologica et Polemica.* Edited by J. P. Migne. PG 91. Paris: Migne, 1865.

———. "Quaestiones et Dubia." In *St. Maximus the Confessor: Questions and Doubts,* edited by Despina Prassas. Dekalb: University of Northern Illinois Press, 2010.

———. *Quastiones et Dubia.* Edited by José Declerk. CCSG 10. Turnhout: Brepols, 2010.

———. *Quastiones Ad Thalassium.* Edited by Carl Laga and Carlos Steel. *Maximi Confessoris Quaestiones Ad Thalassium.* CCSG 22. Turnhout: Brepols, 1990.

———. *St. Maximus the Confessor: The Ascetic Life, The Four Centuries on Charity.* Edited by Polycarp Sherwood. Ancient Christian Writers 21. Ramsey, NJ: Paulist, 1955.

Maximus the Confessor and John Scottus Erigena. "Maximi Confessoris Ambigua Ad Iohannem: Iuxta Iohannis Scotti Eriugenae Latinam Interpretationem." Edited by Édouard Jeauneau. CCSG 18. Turnhout: Brepols, 1988.

Maximus the Confessor and A. Louth. *Maximus the Confessor*. Edited by Andrew Louth. The Early Church Fathers. London: Routledge, 1996.

McFarland, Ian A. "'Naturally and by Grace:' Maximus the Confessor on the Operation of the Will." *Scottish Journal of Theology* 58 (2005) 410–33.

———. "Willing Is Not Choosing: Some Anthropological Implications of Dyothelite Christology." *International Journal of Systematic Theology* 9.1 (2007) 3–23.

McGinn, Bernard. *The Growth of Mysticism*. New York: Crossroad Herder, 2007.

Melina, Livio. *The Epiphany of Love: Toward a Theological Understanding of Christian Action*. Grand Rapids: Eerdmans, 2010.

Meyendorff, John. "Free Will (Γνώμη) in Saint Maximus the Confessor." In *The Ecumenical World of Orthodox Civilization*, edited by Andrew Blane, 71–75. Paris: Mouton, 1974.

———, ed. *The Primacy of Peter*. Crestwood, NY: St. Vladimir's Seminary Press, 1992.

Milbank, John. "The Double Glory, or Paradox versus Dialectic." In *The Monstrosity of Christ: Paradox versus Dialectic*, 110–233. Boston: MIT Press, 2009.

———. "The Mystery of Reason." In *The Grandeur of Reason: Religion, Tradition and Universalism*, edited by P. Candler and C. Cunningham, 68–117. London: SCM, 2010.

———. "Sophiology and Theurgy: The New Theological Horizon." In *Encounter Between Eastern Orthodoxy and Radical Orthodoxy: Transfiguring the World through the Word*, edited by Adrian Pabst and Christoph Schneider, 45–85. Farnham, UK: Ashgate, 2009.

———. *Theology and Social Theory: Beyond Secular Reason*. Oxford: Blackwell, 2006.

———. *The Word Made Strange: Theology, Language, Culture*. Oxford: Blackwell, 1997.

Milbank, John, and Catherine Pickstock. *Truth in Aquinas*. London: Routledge, 2001.

Moore, Edward. "Origen of Alexandria and St. Maximus the Confessor: An Analysis and Critical Evaluation of Their Eschatological Doctrines." PhD, St. Elias School of Orthodox Theology Seward, 2004. http://dissertation.com/book.php?book=15 81122616&method=ISBN.

Moule, C. F. D. "The Manhood of Jesus in the New Testament." In *Christ Father and History: Cambridge Studies in Christology*, edited by S. W. Sykes and J. P. Clayton. Cambridge: Cambridge University Press, 1972.

Moutafakis, N. J. "Christology and Its Philosophical Complexities in the Thought of Leontius of Byzantium." *History of Philosophy Quarterly* 10 (1993) 99–119.

Mueller-Jourdan, P. *Typologie Spatio-Temporelle de L'ecclesia Byzantine: La Mystagogie de Maxime Le Confesseur Dans La Culture Philosophique de L'antiquité Tardive*. Leiden: Brill, 2005.

O'Meara, Dominic J. *Platonopolis: Platonic Political Philosophy in Late Antiquity*. Oxford: Oxford University Press, 2003.

Oehler, K. "Die Dialektik Des Johannes Damaskenos." In *Antike Philosophie Und Byzantinisches Mittelalter*, edited by C. H. Beck, 287–99. Munich: Beck, 1969.

Öhler, Klaus. "Aristotle in Byzantium." *Greek, Roman, and Byzantine Studies* 5.2 (1964) 133–46.

Otten, Willemien. "The Dialectic of Return in Eriugena's 'Periphyseon.'" *Harvard Theological Review* 84.4 (1991) 399–421.

————. "Nature and Scripture: Demise of a Medieval Analogy." *Harvard Theological Review* 88.2 (1995) 257–84.

Otto, Rudolf. *The Idea of the Holy: An Inquiry into the Non-Rational Factor in the Idea of the Divine and Its Relation to the Rational.* Edited by John W. Harvey. 2nd ed. New York: Oxford University Press, 1958.

Pabst, Adrian. *Metaphysics: The Creation of Hierarchy.* Grand Rapids: Eerdmans, 2011.

Palamas, Gregory. *Logos Apodeiktikos.* In *Grhgorivou Tou' Palama' Suggravmmata,* edited by Boris Bobrinsky. Thessalonica: n.p., 1962.

Palmer, G. E. H., Philip Sherrard, and Kallistos Ware, eds. *The Philokalia. The Complete Text.* Vol. 2. London: Faber & Faber, 1981.

Perl, Eric. "Metaphysics and Christology in Maximus Confessor and Eriugena." In *Eriugena: East and West,* edited by B. McGinn and W. Otten, 253–70. South Bend, IN: , and London: University of Notre Dame Press, 1994.

————. "Methexis: Creation, Incarnation, Deification in St Maximus." PhD, Yale University, 1991.

Pickstock, Catherine. "Duns Scotus: His Historical and Contemporary Significance." *Modern Theology* 21.4 (2005) 543–74.

Piret, P. "Christologie et Théologie Trinitaire Chez Maxime Le Confesseur, D'après Sa Formule Des Natures Desquelles, En Lesquelles et Lesquelles Est Le Christ." In *Maximus Confessor: Actes Du Symposium Sur Maxime Le Confesseur,* edited by Felix Heinzer and Christoph Schönborn, 215–22. Fribourg: Éditions Universitaires Fribourg Suisse, 1982.

————. *Le Christ et La Trinité Selon Maxime Le Confesseur, Théologie Historique 69.* Paris: Beauchesne, 1983.

Proclus. *The Elements of Theology.* Edited by E.R. Dodds. Oxford: Oxford University Press, 1963.

————. *In Primum Euclidis Elementorum Librum Commentarii 50:16–51.* Edited by G. Friedlein. Leipzig: Teubneri, 1873.

Reindl, H. "Der Aristotelismus Bei Leontius von Byzanz." PhD diss., University of Munich, 1953.

Renczes, P.-G. "La Gloria Del Padre E Pianezza Dell'umano: L'apporto Di Massimo Il Confessore a Una Precisazione Dell'antropologia Teologica Dei Padre." In *Il Bene E La Persona Nell' Agire,* edited by L. Melina and J.-J. Pérez-Soba, 147–57. Rome: Lateran University Press, 2002.

Renczes, Philipp Gabriel. *Agir de Dieu et Liberté de L'homme: Recherches Sur L'anthropologie Théologique de Saint Maxime Le Confesseur.* Paris: Cerf, 2003.

Riches, Aaron. *Christ the End of Humanism.* Grand Rapids: Eerdmans, 2011.

Richter, G. *Die Dialektik Des Johannes von Damaskos: Eine Untersuchung Des Textes Nach Seinen Quellen Und Seiner Bedeutung.* Passau, Germany: Buch-Kunstverl, 1964.

Riedinger, R., ed. *Acta Conciliorum Oecumenicorum Series 2, Vol. 1: Concilium Lateranense A. 649 Celebratum.* Berlin: de Gruyter, 1984.

Riou, A. *Le Monde et l'Église Selon Maxime Le Confesseur.* Paris: Beauchesne, 1973.

Rogers, Katherin. "Augsutine's Compatibilism." *Religious Studies* 40 (2004) 415–35.

Romanides, John S. "Notes on the Palamite Controversy and Related Topics," n.d. http://www.romanity.org/htm/rom.15.en.notes_on_the_palamite_controversy.01.htm.

Rome, Anastasius of. "Anastasius Ad Ioannem Diaconum." Edited by J. P. Migne. PL 129. Paris: Migne, 1855.

Roosen, B. "Epifanovich Revisited. (Pseudo) Maximi Confessoris Opuscula Varia: A Critical Edition with Extensive Notes on Manuscript Tradition and Authenticity." PhD diss., Katholieke Universiteit Leuven, 2001.

Rossum, Joost van. "The Λόγοι of Creation and the Divine 'Energies' in Maximus the Confessor and Gregory Palamas." *Studia Patristica* 27 (1993) 212–17.

Rouéché, Mossmann. "A Middle Byzantine Handbook of Logic Terminology." *Jahrbuch Der Österreichischen Byzantinistik* 29 (1980) 71–98.

———. "Stephanus the Philosopher and Ps. Elias: A Case of Mistaken Identity." *Byzantine and Modern Greek Studies* 36 (2012) 120–38.

Russell, Norman. *The Doctrine of Deification in the Greek Patristic Tradition.* Oxford: Oxford University Press, 2004.

Schatz, Klaus. *Papal Primacy: From Its Origins to the Present.* Collegeville, MN: Liturgical, 1996.

Schimmelpfennig, Bernhard. *The Papacy.* New York: Columbia University Press, 1992.

Schmutz, Jacob. "La Doctrine Mediévale Des Causes et La Théologie de La Nature Pure (XIIIe–XVII E Siècles)." *Revue Thomiste* 101.1–2 (2001) 217–64.

Schneider, Christoph. "The Transformation of Eros: Reflections on Desire in Jacques Lacan." In *Encounter between Eastern Orthodoxy and Radical Orthodoxy: Transfiguring the World through the Word*, edited by Adrian Pabst and Christoph Schneider, 271–89. Farnham, UK: Ashgate, 2009.

Schumacher, Lydia. *Divine Illumination: The History and Future of Augustine's Theory of Knowledge.* Oxford: Blackwell, 2011.

———. "Rethinking Recollection and Plato's Doctrine of Forms." *Lyceum* 11.2 (2010) 1–19. http://lyceumphilosophy.com/?q=node/131.

Scott, T. Kermit. *Augustine: His Thought in Context.* New York: Paulist, 1995.

Shaw, Gregory. *Theurgy and the Soul: The Neo-Platonism of Iamblichus.* University Park, PA: Pennsylvania State University Press, 1995.

Sheldon-Williams, I. P. "The Greek Christian Platonist tradition from the Cappadocians to Maximus and Eriugena." In *The Cambridge History of Later Greek and Early Medieval Philosophy*, edited by Armstrong Arthur Hilary, 425–536. Cambridge: Cambridge University Press, 1967.

———. "Eriugena's Greek Sources." In *The Mind of Eriugena*, edited by L. Bieler J. J. O'Meara, 1–15. Dublin: Irish University Press, 1973.

Sherwood, Polycarp. *An Annotated Date List of the Works of St. Maximus the Confessor.* Rome: Herder, 1952.

———. *The Earlier Ambigua of Saint Maximus the Confessor and His Refutation of Origenism.* Rome: "Orbis Catholicus," Herder, 1955.

Siclari, A. *Giovanni Di Damasco: La Funzione Della "Dialectica.* Perugia, Italy: Benucci, 1978.

Siecienski, Edward. "The Authenticity of Maximus the Confessor's Letter to Marinus: The Argument from Theological Consistency." *Vigiliae Christianae* 61 (2007) 189–227.

———. *The Filioque: History of a Doctrinal Controversy.* Oxford: Oxford University Press, 2010.

Sophronius of Jerusalem. *Sophronius of Jerusalem and Seventh Century Heresy: The Synodical Letter and Other Documents.* Edited by Pauline Allen. Oxford: Oxford University Press, 2009.

Sophrony, Archimandrite. *His Life Is Mine*. Crestwood, NY: St Vladimirs Seminary Press, 1977.

Sorabji, Richard. *Emotion and Peace of Mind: From Stoic Agitation to Christian Temptation*. Oxford: Oxford University Press, 2000.

———. *The Philosophy of the Commentators, Vol. 2: Physics*. London: Duckworth, 2004.

Speer, Andreas. "The Epistemic Circle: Thomas Aquinas on the Foundation of Knowledge." In *Platonic Ideas and Concept Formation in Ancient and Medieval Thought*, edited by Gerd van Riel and Gabriel Macé, 119–32. Leuven: Leuven University Press, 2004.

Staniloae, Dumitru. "The Procession of the Holy Spirit from the Father and His Relation to the Son as the Basis of Our Deification and Adoption." In *Spirit of God, Spirit of Christ: Ecumenical Reflections on the Filioque Controversy*, edited by Lukas Vischer, 174–86. London: SPCK, 1981.

———. *Theology and the Church*. Edited by Robert Barringer. Crestwood, NY: St. Vladimir's Seminary Press, n.d.

Stock, Brian. "The Philosophical Anthropology of Johannes Scottus Eriugena." *Studi Medievali*, 3a series VIII (1967) 1–57.

Syropoulos, Sylvester. "Memoirs." In *Les "Mémoires" Du Grand Ecclésiarque de l'Église de Constantinople Sylvestre Syropoulos Sur Le Concile de Florence (1438–1439)*, CF 9, edited by V. Laurent. Rome: Pontificium Institutum Orientalium Studiorum, 1971. http://www.syropoulos.co.uk/translation.htm.

Tanner, Norman P., ed. *Decrees of the Ecumenical Councils Vol. 1*. London: Sheed and Ward, 1990.

Thunberg, Lars. *Man and the Cosmos: The Vision of St Maximus the Confessor*. Crestwood, NY: St Vladimirs Seminary Press, 1985.

———. *Microcosm and Mediator: The Theological Anthropology of Maximus Confessor*. Lund: Gleerup, 1965.

Tierny, Brian. *The Origins of Papal Infallibility*. Leiden: Brill, 1972.

Tollefsen, Torstein. *The Christocentric Cosmology of St. Maximus the Confessor*. Oxford: Oxford University Press, 2008.

———. "Did St. Maximus the Confessor Have a Concept of Participation." *Studia Patristica* 37 (2001) 618–25.

———. "The Problem of Omnipresence in Plotinus Ennead IV, 4–5: A Reply." *Dionysius* 4 (1980) 194–200.

———. "Unity in Plurality, according to St. Maximus the Confessor." *Diotima* 28 (2002) 115–22.

Törönen, M. *Union and Distinction in the Thought of St Maximus the Confessor*. Oxford: Oxford University Press, 2006.

Torrance, Alexis. "Personhood and Patristics in Orthodox Theology: Reassessing the Debate." *Heythrop Journal of Philosophy and Religion* 52 (2011) 700–707.

Trouillard, Jean. *La Mystagogie de Proclos*. Paris: Broché, 1982.

———. "La Virtus Gnostica Selon Jean Scot Érigène." *Revue de Theologie et de Philosophie* 115 (1983) 331–54.

Velde, Rudi te. *Aquinas on God*. Aldershot, UK: Ashgate, 2006.

Ware, Kallistos. "'Forgive Us . . . as We Forgive:' Forgiveness in the Psalms and the Lord's Prayer." In *Meditations of the Heart: The Psalms in Early Christian Thought and Practice: Essays in Honour of Andrew Louth*, edited by Andreas Andreopoulos, Augustine Casiday, and Carol Harrison, 53–76. Turnhout: Brepols, 2011.

———. "The Meaning of 'Pathos' in Abba Isaias and Theodoret of Cyrus." *Studia Patristica* 20 (1989) 315–22.

Weinandy, Thomas G. *Does God Suffer?* Edinburgh: T. & T. Clark, 2000.

Wendebourg, D. *Geist Oder Energie. Zur Frage Der Innergöttlichen Verankerung Des Christlichen Lebens in Der Byzantinischen Theologie.* München: Kaiser, 1980.

Wildberg, C. "Three Neoplatonic Introductions to Philosophy: Ammonius, David, and Elias." *Hermathena* 149 (1991) 33–51.

Williams, A. N. *The Ground of Union: Deification in Aquinas and Palamas.* Oxford: Oxford University Press, 1999.

Williams, Rowan. *Arius.* London: SCM, 2001.

———. "The Philosophical Structures of Palamism." *Eastern Churches Review* 9 (1977) 27–44.

———. *Sergii Bulgakov. Towards a Russian Political Theology.* Edinburgh: Bloomsbury T. & T. Clark, 1999.

Yeago, D. "Jesus of Nazareth and Cosmic Redemption: The Relevance of St. Maximus the Confessor." *Modern Theology* 12 (1996) 163–93.

Zizioulas, John. "One Single Source: An Orthodox Response to the Clarification on the Filioque," n.d. http://agrino.org/cyberdesert/zizioulas.htm.

Index

Abraham, 76, 124

Action, human, 100–101

Adam, 120–21, 252–55

Aeropagite, Pseudo-Dionysius, the ("Denys"), xvi, xxi, 9, 82, 91, 94, 138, 149, 152, 157, 162, 163, 166, 172, 173, 174, 175, 176, 177–79, 181, 184, 187, 188, 190, 193, 194, 196, 199, 202, 206, 231, 232, 255

Age of Ascent, 116

Alexandria, Athanasius of, 78–79, 107

Alexandria, Clement, 82

Alexandria, Cyril of, 74

Alexandria, School of, 52, 53

Allchin, Canon A. M., 70

Ammonius, 54

Anastasius (the Librarian of Rome), xix, 34–35

Aneideioi (Ἀνειδειοι), 172

Antichrist, 32

Anthropology, 3, 4, 5–17, 30, 71–80, 82–83, 86ff, 102–14, 120–22, 187, 218–21

Aphrodisias, Alexander of, 54

Apokatastasis, 139

Apophaticism, xxv, 173, 174, 235, 236, 243, 248, 258

Ἀπορία (aporia). See under Confessor, Maximus

Aquinas, Thomas, xiv, xx, xxv, 4, 35, 42, 86, 113, 158–61, 167, 169, 170, 172, 174, 175, 176, 187, 189, 190–99, 200, 201, 202–6, 209, 213, 214, 216, 217, 219–21

Aristotle, xiii, xiv, xxii, 51, 52, 53, 54, 56, 57, 59, 60, 62, 63, 64, 72, 102, 103, 108, 111, 112, 140, 166, 177, 179, 181, 183, 197, 228, 233, 248
  categories, xiv, 51, 52, 53, 54, 56, 60, 63, 64, 140, 177, 181, 183
  character, 108
  δύναμις (power), 112
  ἐνέργειἄ (activity or energy)(see also Energia (ἐνέργειἄ)), 112
  logic, 51–52, 53, 54, 56, 60, 140
  προαίρεσις (choice), 111
  substances (primary and secondary), 56, 57, 59

Augustine of Hippo, 4, 9, 14, 102, 108, 159, 163, 164, 165, 174, 175, 186, 187, 189, 191, 201, 205

Autexousion (αυτεξούσιον), 210, 211

Avicenna, 159, 160, 163, 168, 183, 184

Balthasar, Hans Urs von, xix, 90, 96–98, 130, 173

Balthrellos, Demetrios, 90, 96

Basil of Caesarea. See Caesarea, Basil of

Beccas, Patriarch John, 35

Bessarion, Basilios, 38, 39, 172

Blowers, Paul, ix, 93–94

Body, the, xiii, 18, 28, 82–83, 92, 107, 108, 128, 129, 131–33, 139, 140, 154, 163, 187, 189, 190, 191, 195, 198, 200, 201, 218, 219, 220, 221, 229, 230, 249, 250, 254

Boethius, 9, 52, 157, 174, 175, 194

Bonaventure, 168, 197

Bonn Conferences, 40
Bradshaw, David, xiii, 152–53, 158,
    159, 163, 166–69, 170–72,
    176–78, 187–91, 192–93, 195,
    199, 233, 235,
Bulgakov, Sergei, 147
    Sophia, 147, 162
Byzantium, Leontius of, 50, 52, 53, 61

Cabasilus, Nilas, 36, 37
Caesarea, Basil of, 32, 56, 107, 116,
    171, 223
Calabria, Barlaam of, 159, 172, 173,
    189
Cappadocians, xvi, xxi, xxii, 9, 53, 56,
    58, 116, 117, 158, 172, 173, 174,
    218
Carolingians, 35
Cataphaticism (or kataphaticism),
    174, 235–37, 248
Chalcedon, Council of, 52, 53
Christology, 27, 81, 85, 89ff, 98, 115ff,
    133, 140, 187, 221, 242, 245
  chalcedonian, 221
  dyothelitism, 85–86, 98
  monenergism, 103, 112
  monothelitism, xxiv, 34, 40, 41, 42,
    43, 46–47, 49, 74, 80, 91, 92, 103,
    104, 106, 112, 115, 126, 133
Chrysostom, John, 69, 198
Cvetković, Vladimir, xiii, xxi
Confessor, Maximus
  ἀπορία (difficulty), xxii, 248–49
  ἄσκησις (asceticism), xxiii–xxiv, 254
  beauty, 75, 77, 241, 254, 255
  being–well-being–eternal being,
    xxiii, 110, 131
  contemplation (θεωρία) 245–59
  deification (or divinization, or
    theosis), 77–80, 95, 109, 110, 114,
    116, 126, 131, 137, 138, 139, 140,
    150, 155, 209, 210, 211, 223, 225,
    226, 227, 228, 229, 230, 233, 234,
    238, 242, 256 (*see* also Deifica-
    tion (or divinization, or *theosis*))
  division of being, 3, 5–7, 71,
    227–28

δύναμις (faculty or power), 110,
    112, 113, 120
education, xx–xxi
ἐνέργειἄ (activity or energy), 113,
    143, 186
enhypostaton, 61–64
erotapokriseis (questions and re-
    sponse), 248–49
eschatology, xv, 128, 137, 139, 140,
    143, 147, 218, 219, 234, 235,
    238–39 (*see* also deification
    under Confessor, Maximus)
essence–energies distinction,
    184–87
filiation, 118, 129, 132
Filioque, 31–40, 49, 116
ἐκπορεύεσθαι and προϊέναι (proces-
    sion and flowing forth), 43–45
hypostasis, 36, 58, 59, 60–64, 86, 91,
    206, 236
imitation of Christ (*imitatio
    Christi*), 71–79, 83–84
image and likeness, 79, 120–22, 129
immanence (of universals), 61–63
imparticipable (or unparticipable),
    185–86, 207–8, 234–37, 243–44
Incarnation, 69–70
inherence, 63
kenosis, 72–76, 119–20
knowledge (and epistemology),
    7–11, 18, 218–19, 227
liturgy, xxi, 148, 186, 235, 238, 239,
    241, 244 (*see* also Theurgy)
λόγοι (*logoi*), ix, xxiv, 16, 23, 54, 56,
    83, 109, 110, 114, 119, 137, 138,
    140, 144, 145, 147, 162, 175, 180,
    185–86, 204, 205–9, 212–13,
    219, 221, 224, 225, 233–37, 243,
    244, 251, 257, 258
λόγος (*logos*), ix, xxii, xxiv–xxv, 17,
    20, 21, 56, 59, 60, 76, 88, 98, 117,
    127, 143, 145, 146, 148, 158, 180,
    186, 206, 207, 208, 209, 210, 212,
    224, 226, 227, 229, 241, 243, 245,
    252, 259
Λόγος (*Logos*), xxiv, xxv, 7, 9, 10,
    11, 13, 15, 16, 17, 20, 23, 25, 29,
    30, 33, 34, 73, 77, 78, 83, 86, 90,

91, 92, 96, 97, 107, 116, 117, 118,
119–22, 123, 125, 126, 128, 129,
130, 131, 132, 133, 138, 140, 142,
144, 145, 146, 147, 148, 162, 175,
185, 186, 191, 194, 206, 226, 232,
233, 234, 235, 237, 239, 243, 244,
251

mediator, cosmic (humankind),
5–7, 30, 194, 252–53

μέθεξις (participation), 77 (*see* also
participation under Confessor,
Maximus)

μίμησις (imitation), 75, 193–94,
195 (*see* also imitation of Christ
under Confessor, Maximus)

motion, 109, 226, 254, 256–57

ousia, 57–60

nature, 246–47

nous, 33, 72, 104, 125, 142, 218

nous-logos-pneuma, xxiv

participation, xxi, 33, 76–78, 79, 80,
83, 122, 137, 138, 139, 142, 144,
149, 152, 186, 208, 211, 214, 218,
221, 227, 231–44

Papacy, 31–32, 40–43

tantum–quantum, 75–78, 211,
237–38

temptation, 73–74

theoplastia (θεοπλαστία), 122

theosis (θέωσις)(*see* Deification)

three laws, 120

time, 22, 23, 116, 117, 119, 125,
127, 131, 137, 138, 139, 145, 148,
184, 206, 207, 238, 250, 254, 256

Trinity, the, 32–34, 59, 116, 117,
122, 123, 140, 143, 185, 186, 188

triple generation, 127–31

tropos, xxii, 117, 142, 148, 226 (*see*
also under Will)

two books and two garments of
Christ, 19–23

unity and distinction, 10, 140,
228–30

unconfused union (ἀσύγχυτος
ἕνωσις), 230

unity, 15–17, 30 (*see* also mediator,
cosmic (humankind) under
Confessor, Maximus)

stages of return (πρακτική, θεωρία
φύσική, θεολογία), 17–19

universals, 50, 51, 53, 56–64

virtues, xxii–xxiii

will (θέλημα), 80–81, 87, 91–93,
95–96, 103, 104, 105, 110, 111,
113 (*see* also Will)

βούλησις (wish), 87, 105, 110, 111
(*see* also under Will)

freewill, 94ff, 109–10, 218, 219 (*see*
also under Will)

γνώμη (gnomic), 80, 86, 90, 99,
105–10, 142 (*see* also under Will)

instinct and intention, 95–98 (*see*
also under Will)

natural will, 103, 104, 106, 110–11
(*see* also under Will)

προαίρεσις (choice), 105ff, 111 (*see*
also under Will)

rational, 104ff (*see* also under Will)

Congar, Yves Cardinal, 44

Constantinople, Stephen of, 50

Constantinople, Third Council of, 115

Contemplation (θεωρία), xxi, 17, 18,
20, 22, 29, 83, 140, 155, 164, 219,
227, 245–59

Cooper, Adam, xiii, 47

Creation, x, xxii, xxiii, xxiv, 3, 5, 6, 7,
9–17, 19–23, 24, 25, 26, 28, 29,
30, 55, 56, 69, 70, 79, 83, 107,
116–18, 119, 120, 121, 122, 131,
133, 137, 138, 139, 140, 142, 146,
158, 159, 162, 166, 168, 178, 180,
186, 187, 188, 189, 191, 194, 199,
202, 206, 207, 208, 209, 212, 214,
216, 219, 221, 222, 231, 234, 236,
245, 246, 247, 252, 254, 256, 258

Cubicularius, John, 80

Culture, 143, 145

Cusa, Nicholas, 153

Cyprus, Gregory of, 35

Cyril, of Alexandria, 32, 33, 91

Damascus/Damascene, John, xv, xvi,
53, 64, 110, 172, 173, 187, 188

Daniélou, Jean, 173

Davidson, Ivor, 85–86

Descent, Age of, 116

Deification (or divinization, or *theosis*), xiii, 77–80, 95, 109, 110, 114, 116, 126, 131, 137, 138, 139, 140, 150, 155, 158, 164, 199, 203, 209, 210, 211, 223, 224, 225, 226, 227, 228, 229, 230, 233, 234, 238, 242, 256. *See* also under Confessor, Maximus
Demiurge, 54
Dialogical, xv, 210, 211, 212, 218, 219
Divine Names, 176, 192, 250, 255–56 *See* also under Metaphysics spck (processions)
Donation. *See* Gift
Donne, John, 143
Doucet, Marcel, 90, 96
Dyothelitism. *See* under Christology

Eckhart, Meister, 191
Ekstatic, 142
Ekthesis, 42, 89
Ellampsesi (ελλάμψεσι), 159
Elijah, 75
Emanation, 138, 153, 155, 160, 170, 177, 197, 198, 209
Emesa, Nemesius of, 105, 113, 218, 228, 229, 230
Energia (ἐνέργειά), 103, 112, 113, 125, 143, 158, 159, 166–78, 184, 185, 186, 187, 188, 209, 210, 226, 227. *See* also Metaphysics, essence-energies distinction
Epektasis (or *epectasis*), 83, 172, 200, 202, 241–42
Ephesus, Council of, 91
Epictetus, 102
Epiphanius, of Salamis, 32
Erismann, Christophe, xiv
Eriugena, John Scottus, 3–30, 35, 65
  exitus and *reditus* (from God and return to God), 6–7, 11, 13, 15, 24–29
  Fall, the, 12–17, 19, 26, 27, 29
  knowledge (and epistemology), 8–11, 13–14, 18–19
  liberal arts, 18–19
  mediator, cosmic, 12–13

officina omnium (total workshop of creation), 3, 6
sapientia create (creating wisdom), 11, 13, 15, 26
sapientia creatix (creative wisdom), 11, 26
unity, 15–17, 24–27
Eros. *See* Love
Erotapokriseis (questions and response), 248–49. *See* also Confessor, Maximus
Eschatology, xv, 128, 137, 139, 140, 143, 147, 164, 175, 199, 203, 218, 219, 234, 235, 238–39. *See* also under Confessor, Maximus
Essence–energies distinction. *See* under Metaphysics
Eucharist, xvi, 143, 145, 146, 212, 234, 235–39, 240, 241, 244, 255, 259
Εὐδοχία (benevolent plan), 122–27
Eunomius, 117
Evagrius, 82, 144
Exitus and *reditus* (from God and return to God). *See* Eriugena, John Scottus

Faith (πίστις), 168
Fall, the, 3, 12–17, 19, 26, 27, 29, 69, 70, 78, 82, 86, 90, 99, 164, 251–53, 255. *See* also under Eriugena, John Scottus
Father, 122–27
Filioque, xix, 31–40. *See* under Confessor, Maximus
Florovsky, Georges, 70
Formal distinction (in God), 157–61, 169, 171, 197, 198, 207ff
Franciscan, 161, 169, 170, 183, 201
Freedom, 113, 218, 219
Freewill. *See* under Confessor, Maximus, *See* under Will

Galen, 113
Gariggues, Jean–Miguel, 232
Gauthier, R. A., 102, 110–11
Geréby, György, 200, 201
Gerson, Lloyd, 179

Gethsemane, garden of, 74, 85, 88ff, 101, 104

Gift, xxiii, 35, 94, 117, 118, 120, 139, 144, 145, 146, 153–54, 156, 157, 158, 165, 166, 167, 168, 174, 186, 188, 191, 192, 209, 212, 219, 223, 225, 226, 236, 239, 240, 243

Girard, René, 72

Gnosis (γνῶσις), 168

Grace, ix, 28, 75, 76, 77, 78, 79, 80, 118, 120, 128, 129, 131, 139, 150, 158, 164, 165, 174, 185, 186, 191, 194, 195, 200, 201, 203, 205, 207, 209, 210, 211, 212, 213, 216, 220, 221, 222, 223, 225, 227, 232, 237, 239, 240, 241, 242, 253, 258
  created grace, 200, 203, 205, 209, 216
  uncreated grace, 185, 195, 200

Granados Garcia, Luis, xiv

Great, Basil the, 32, 107, 116

Guillou, M. J. Le, xx, 204

Guiu, Adrian, xiv

Habit (ἕξη), 218

Halleaux, Andres, 44

Henology. *See* under Metaphysics

Heraclitus, 77

Hermeticism, 167–68

Hesychism, xix, 189, 195, 200

Hippo, Augustine of. *See* Augustine of Hippo

Homoousios (ὁμοούσιος), 59, 115, 126, 212

Honorius I, Pope, 43

Hopkins, Gerard Manley, 79

Hypostasis. See under Metaphysics

Hypostatic Union, 91

Iamblichus, 113, 149, 154, 155, 156, 163, 164, 165, 166, 168, 182, 202

Incarnation, 15, 16, 27, 28, 29, 69, 70, 77, 78, 79, 80, 98, 116, 124–30, 131, 148, 164, 182, 229, 233, 234, 243, 244, 247

Infinity, 159, 160, 172, 174, 184, 207, 232, 239, 240, 242

Inherence, 52, 63. *See* also under Confessor, Maximus

Instinct, 95–98

Intention, 95–98

Jeauneau, E., 4

Job, 124, 125

Kant, Immanuel, 96, 163, 179, 183

Kataphaticism. *See* Cataphaticism

Kenosis. See under Confessor, Maximus

Knowledge (and epistemology). *See* under Confessor, Maximus. *See* under Eriugena, John Scotus

Lacan, Jacques, 143, 147

Larchet, Jean–Claude, xx, 46, 47, 126, 232

Lazarus, 254

Leibniz, Gottfried, 108

Léthel, F. –M., xx

Lévy, Antoine, xx, xxv, 205, 211, 216, 217

Light, uncreated, 184, 189, 190, 201–2, 256–57

Liturgy, xiii, xiv, xx, xxi, 148, 164, 174, 177, 182, 186, 202, 235, 238, 239, 241, 244

Λόγοι (*logoi*). *See* under Confessor, Maximus

Logic, Aristotelian, 51

Λόγος (*Logos*). *See* under Confessor, Maximus

Λόγος (*logos*). *See* under Confessor, Maximus

Lollar, Joshua, xiv

Loosen, Josef, 116

Love, 83–84, 144, 157
  agape, 83, 144, 157
  dispassionate, 144–45, 147
  eros, 82–83, 142ff
  self–love (φιλαυτία), 82

Loudovikos, Nikolaos, xiv, 142, 143, 145, 234

Louth, Andrew, xv, xix–xxv, 46

Lyons, Council of, 35

Lyons, Irenaeus of, 78, 122

Madden, Thomas, 111
Marinus, 34
Mary, 125
Martyrdom, 75
McFarland, Ian A., 86
Mediator, cosmic (humankind). *See* under Confessor, Maximus
Melchizedek, 75, 76, 185
Melina, Livio, 86, 98
Mentalité, xx
Metaphysics ix, x, xiii, xvi, 23, 52, 137, 138, 139, 140, 141, 142, 143–46, 153, 178–82, 198, 199, 216, 221–22, 224, 233, 247
  accidents, 197
  pure act (God as), 199
  divine ideas, 213
  eidos, 179
  emanation, 138, 153, 155, 160, 170, 177, 197, 198, 209
  esse, 167, 175, 192, 193, 197
  essence–energies distinction, 79–80, 117, 140, 152ff, 157–61, 169, 171, 184–87, 189, 190, 194–98, 201–2, 207ff, 226–27, 232, 256–57
  formal distinction (*see* Formal distinction)
  identity and difference, 7, 10, 11, 15, 58, 117, 140, 143, 160, 191, 208, 224, 228, 236, 243, 253
  Good, the, 180
  henology, 173, 178
  monotheism, 155, 157, 165
  nature, 144ff, 224, 246–47
  ontology (*see* Ontology)
  pantheism, 165, 193, 198
  paradox (*see* Paradox)
  participation (*see* Participation)
  perichōresis (περιχώρησις), 126, 209, 210, 211, 225, 238
  play, 139, 140
  Porphryian Tree, 138, 139, 140
  processions (πρόοδοι), 176–78, 189, 196
  pure act (God as), 199
  real distinction (*see* Real distinction)

recollection, 163, 168, 179, 183
reification, 178, 181, 183, 227
similitude (likeness), 192–93
transcendentals, 173, 177, 183
transcendentalism, 183
union and distinction (*see* also under Confessor, Maximus)
Meyendorff, John, 171
Miaphysites, 52. *See* also Christology
Milan, Ambrose, 4
Milbank, John, xv, xxv, 208, 222
Monenergism. *See* under Christology
Monopatrism, 44
Monotheism. *See* under Metaphysics
Monothelitism. *See* under Christology
Moses, 75, 124–25
Motion, 28, 109, 162, 226, 254, 256–57
Mutuality, 145–47

Nazianzen (or Nazianzus), Gregory, 15, 116, 122, 128, 132, 141, 171, 249, 250, 251
Neoplatonism (or Neoplatonic, or Neoplatonist), xxi, 9, 24, 50, 51, 52, 53, 54, 55, 56, 138, 140, 149, 152, 153, 154, 156, 157, 160, 163, 164, 165, 166, 167, 168, 170, 173, 174, 175, 178, 179, 180, 181, 182–84, 186, 197, 220, 232, 233, 234
  identity and difference, 140, 143
  emanations, 153
  One (αρχή), the, 24, 27, 138, 153, 154, 155, 156, 163, 165, 166, 167, 168, 169, 173, 175, 176, 177, 178, 180, 182, 194, 203, 233, 243, 244
  synthesis, 180–81
Nestorianism, 115, 126
Ninevah, Isaac of (Isaac the Syrian), 70
Nominalism, 62
Nous. *See* under Confessor, Maximus
Nyssa, Gregory of, xiii, 9–11, 50, 56, 70, 75, 82, 83, 107, 162, 171, 172, 190, 229

Ockham, William of, 172, 201

Oikonomia, Divine, xxiv
O'Meara, John J., 164
One (αρχή), the. *See* under
  Neoplatonism
Ontology, 14–15, 142, 145, 146,
  154–56, 224–25, 226, 230
  being, 227
  eucharistic, xv, 143, 145, 204, 212,
    218, 222, 234
  hypostasis, 9, 36, 52, 56–57, 58, 59,
    60–64, 86, 91, 105, 173, 182, 183,
    184, 198, 206, 236
  other, the, 147
  ousia (οὐσία), 52, 53, 56–63, 113,
    117, 158, 162, 184, 188, 225, 246,
    255, 258
  theology, onto-, 217
  theurgic, 154–56, 161–66
  remaining-procession-return, 156
Origen, xxi, xxv, 70
Otto, Rudolf von, 224, 230
Ousia (οὐσία). *See* under Ontology
Οὐσια-δύναμις-ἐνέργεια, 113

Palamas, Gregory, xiv, xx, 36, 79,
    149ff, 152, 153, 157, 158, 159,
    160–61, 166, 169, 170, 171, 172,
    173, 176, 177, 181, 182, 184, 189,
    191, 195, 196–98, 199, 200, 204,
    205, 207, 208, 216, 217, 220, 221
Pantaenus, 206
Pantheism. *See* under Metaphysics
Papacy, 31–32, 40–43
Paradox, 143, 145, 153, 156, 157, 158,
    162, 163, 166, 171, 176, 178, 182,
    183, 184, 186, 187, 188, 190, 191,
    192, 194, 195, 197, 198, 200, 203,
    226, 237, 242
Participation, xiv, xxi, 75, 76, 77, 78,
    79, 80, 83, 122, 137, 138, 139,
    142, 144, 149, 152, 153–61,
    161–66, 176, 178, 182, 186, 187,
    188, 191, 191–99, 200, 203, 208,
    211, 214, 216, 217, 218, 219, 220,
    221, 222, 227, 231–44
  dynamic, 233, 234, 243–44
  imparticible (or unparticible),
    152, 153, 154, 155, 156, 157,

    162, 185–86, 207–8, 232, 233,
    234–37, 243–44
  methexis (μέθεξις), xiv, 77, 104, 153,
    157, 198, 226
  paradox, 166, 191–92, 200, 203,
    237–38, 242
  participated, 152, 153, 155, 156,
    162, 171, 176, 178, 186, 187, 188,
    192, 198, 200, 207, 213, 220, 226,
    227, 232, 235, 236, 238
  radical, 157,158, 163, 173, 178, 188,
    191, 192, 199
  unparticipated-participated-par-
    ticipating, 152, 156, 157, 232
Passion (or desire), 82, 142–48. *See*
  also Love
Passiology, 93–94
Pastor Aeternus, 43, 45
Paul, St., 78
Perl, Eric, 231, 232, 234, 243
Pelagianism, 76, 79, 164, 165, 174,
    182, 190
Perichōresis (περιχώρησις). *See* under
  Metaphysics
Personalism, Christian, 87
Philoponus, John, 52
Photius, 35, 37, 170
Physis, 52, 53
Piret, P., xx
Plato, 54, 55, 62, 63, 102, 143, 149,
    152, 153, 155, 161, 163, 164, 166,
    167, 168, 172, 177, 178–81, 182,
    183, 184, 199, 218, 231, 232
Plotinus, 138, 152, 154, 155, 156, 160,
    163, 165, 166, 167, 168, 173, 177,
    182, 183, 184, 187, 200, 232
Pneumatology, 115ff
Porphyry, 51, 53–56, 138, 139, 140,
    154
  genera and species, 54
  logic, 53–56
  λόγοι (*logoi*), 54 (*see also* Λόγοι)
  universals, 50, 54–55
  Porphryian Tree (*see* under
    Metaphysics)
  virtues, 154

Prayer, 18, 75, 78, 85, 88, 89, 90, 91,
  92, 93, 95, 97, 100, 103, 104, 107,
  119, 130, 165
Primacy, Papal, xix
Processionem (of the Holy Spirit), 35
Proclus, 138, 149, 152, 155–57, 163,
  164, 166, 168, 174, 175, 177, 178,
  179–81, 192, 194, 231, 232, 233,
  235, 244
Pyrrhus, 48, 113
Pythagorsa, 155, 164

Raithu, Theodore of, 52
Real distinction (in God), 157
Riou, A., xx, 204
Romanides, John S., 172

Salvation, 78
Scala naturae, 138
Scheseis (σχέσεις), 209
Schism, Great, 31, 32, 48, 49
Schism, Photian, 34
Schneider, Christoph, 142, 143, 147
Scholasticism, 110, 111, 113
Scotus, John Duns, xiv, 35, 70, 157,
  159–61, 168, 169, 170, 171, 172,
  173, 174, 183, 184, 193, 196, 197
Sherwood, Dom Polycarp, 72
Siecienski, Edward, xv
Simplicity, divine, 149, 152, 157, 159,
  162, 168, 173, 184, 185, 187, 190,
  196, 197, 199, 207, 209, 214–17,
  226, 232, 239, 240
Sophrony, Fr., 76
Sorabji, Richard, 102, 111–12
Soteriology, 79, 80
Spirit, Holy, 21–40, 43, 45–47, 71, 81,
  100, 107, 115ff, 122–27, 130, 132,
  133, 146, 158, 186, 194, 197, 206,
  212, 213, 218, 219, 221, 223
Stephanos, the Philosopher, xxi
Stoicism, 54, 112, 24
Suárez, Francisco, 183
Subordinationism, 117
Συνεργία (synergy), 122–27, 132, 133

Tarasius, Patriarch, 35

Theandric activity, 91, 94, 98–99, 103,
  211
Theodore, Pope, 34
Theologian, Gregory the, xxiv, 119
Theophany, 169, 184, 187, 189, 190,
  200, 202, 256. *See also* Light,
  uncreated
Theurgos, 129
Theurgy, 149, 152–53, 154–57,
  163–69, 173, 174, 175, 177, 178,
  182, 183, 186, 189, 199, 202, 204,
  222
Thunberg, Lars, 57, 77, 121, 128
Time, xiii, 15, 22, 23, 116, 117, 119,
  125, 127, 131, 137, 138, 139, 145,
  147, 164, 174, 175, 184, 206, 207,
  238, 250, 254, 256
Tollefsen, Torstein, xv, xxi, 56, 232,
  233, 234, 243
Törönen, Melchisedec, xvi
Tremendum, mysterium, 224
Trinity, the, xv, xxii, 32, 34, 44, 45, 59,
  76, 107, 116, 117, 122, 123, 124,
  130, 143, 147, 153, 158, 159, 160,
  162, 165, 166, 170, 176, 182, 184,
  185, 186, 187, 188, 196, 198, 212
Typos, 89

Uncreated works (or energies),
  184–87, 196, 205, 208, 212, 226,
  232
Unity and distinction. *See* under
  Confessor, Maximus. *See* under
  Eriugena, John Scottus
Unity, 15–17. *See also* under Confes-
  sor, Maximus. *See also* under
  Eriugena, John Scottus
Universals, 50–64, 178, 179, 206

Victor, Richard of St., 169, 197
Vision, beatific, 172, 174, 190, 191,
  200, 201, 202, 219–21
Voluntarism, 114, 172, 197
Voluntas. See Will

Will
  action (*see* Action, human)
  freewill, 94ff, 102ff, 114, 218, 219

instinct and intention, 95–98
θέλημα (will), 103
voluntas, 111
Ware, Kallistos (Timothy), xvi

Williams, Rowan, xvi, xxi, xxii, 149,
152–55, 169, 170, 178, 181, 182,
184, 196, 197, 198
Williams, I–P. Sheldon, 4

Made in the USA
Columbia, SC
08 May 2021

37505350R10186